Mass Media
and
American Politics

Politics and Public Policy Series

Advisory Editor
Robert L. Peabody
Johns Hopkins University

Interest Groups, Lobbying
and Policymaking
Norman J. Ornstein
Shirley Elder

Financing Politics:
Money, Elections and Political
Reform, Second Edition
Herbert E. Alexander

Congressional Procedures and
the Policy Process
Walter J. Oleszek

Invitation to Struggle:
Congress, the President and
Foreign Policy
Cecil V. Crabb, Jr.
Pat M. Holt

Mass Media
and
American Politics

Doris A. Graber
University of Illinois, Chicago Circle

Congressional Quarterly Press
a division of
CONGRESSIONAL QUARTERLY INC.
1414 22nd Street N.W., Washington, D.C. 20037

Cover Design: Richard Pottern

Printed in the United States of America

Library of Congress Cataloging in Publication Data

Graber, Doris Appel, 1923-
    Mass media and American politics.

    Bibliography: p.
    Includes index.
    1. Mass media — Social aspects — United
States.   2. Mass media — Political aspects —
United States.   I. Title.

HN90.M3G7   302.2′3   80-10836
ISBN 0-87187-181-5

To

Jack, Jim, Lee, Susan, and Tom —
my very special students

Foreword

The twentieth century has been characterized by, among other things, automobiles, airplanes, space travel, computers, and nuclear power. Among the technological changes of the century, the expansion of the mass media, particularly television, has surpassed anyone's imagination. When people can watch, and to some degree share in, events occurring halfway around the world, our universe shrinks. At the same time, as we take our first steps into outer space, our horizons expand. Somehow this seems appropriate — McLuhan's global village and Buck Rogers, too.

The relationship between the mass media and contemporary politics in America is now fundamental. The two most cataclysmic events in recent political history — the Vietnam War and Watergate — owe much of their shape and effect to their coverage by the media. Some aspects of the connection between politics and media have been investigated, but in *Mass Media and American Politics,* Doris Graber brings together the many heretofore scattered research findings about these relationships and presents them in a comprehensive narrative. She then analyzes and comments on these findings and their meaning for the American political system.

We often forget that the era of truly "mass" media is comparatively recent. From the first use of movable metal type in 1436 to the penny press of the mid-nineteenth century, the reading public was comparatively small and the appetite for news limited to people whose circumstances allowed them the time and money for reading. Gradually, as the mass market grew, anyone who could read could afford a newspaper.

In contrast to print media, radio and television came much later but spread more rapidly. By 1928, only 32 years after Marconi demonstrated the electromagnetic wave principle, cheap radios were in such supply that Herbert Hoover, the Republican presidential candidate, could launch a successful campaign by making seven major radio addresses across the country. Perhaps the most efficient user of radio was President Franklin D. Roosevelt; listening to his "fireside chats" became a form of reassurance to a public trying to struggle out of the depression.

Although demonstrated as early as 1926, television was not successfully marketed until after World War II. Television's impact on politics has been almost beyond measure. Beginning with the first one-minute spots used in Dwight D. Eisenhower's 1952 campaign, through the "making" of such presidential candidates as John F. Kennedy in 1960 and Jimmy Carter in 1976, television news and advertising has come to dominate national electoral politics.

Doris Graber, however, goes far beyond elections in her survey of media and politics, to look at the role of media in a democratic society, the ownership and control of media organizations, media and the First Amendment, the impact of media on individual political beliefs, media and government institutions, coverage of crises and foreign affairs, and communications policy.

Professor Graber brings a wide and varied training and experience to this book. She received her Ph.D. from Columbia University in the fields of international law and international relations. She currently teaches at the University of Illinois, Chicago Circle, and has held other research and editorial positions. She has written several books and numerous articles in the areas of public opinion and the media. Professor Graber has also been engaged in a major research project on the impact of mass media on political socialization and voting — the "Three Sites Project" — and some of the findings of that study appear in this book.

Eighty percent of Americans are reached each day by newspapers or television or both. It would be surprising if this massive exposure did not have political effects. *Mass Media and American Politics* will make readers more alert to what these effects are and, perhaps, to what they should be.

Robert L. Peabody

Preface

Three major concerns prompted me to write this book. First among them is my strong conviction that the mass media play a tremendously important role in contemporary politics, a role that needs to be fully and continuously explored. Just imagine what would happen if all mass media ceased to function tomorrow and remained inactive for an entire year! No news about events at home and abroad. No explanations about shortages or failures of public services. No announcements of new programs and facilities. Presidents, governors, and mayors, and legislators at all levels would be slowed or immobilized by lack of information and interpretation. And you — how would you fare, relying solely on your own daily experiences and word-of-mouth? Indeed, media are vital for public and private life; the image of a modern world without them is eerie and frightening.

My second major reason for writing this book is dissatisfaction with the way in which the story of the impact of the mass media on politics is commonly treated. Most social science accounts tell merely part of the story, concentrating on the effects of the media in election campaigns. Even within this narrow compass, they usually explore only the impact of the media on attitudes and voting behavior of individual citizens. They do not often acknowledge that the media have become a central part of the campaign, determining who may or may not run, what issues will be stressed, and the political shape of future elections. More significantly, such a narrow focus on elections ignores the much larger area of politics that does not concern elections, and that, too, is crucially affected by media performance.

Finally, this book was written to fill a gap in social science teaching. Students in the social sciences, by and large, are not exposed enough to the role the media play in the political system and the lives of politicians. Politicians themselves have long known of the importance of publicity or lack of publicity and the use of media images as bases for political action, but teachers and students have largely neglected these matters. The time has therefore come to provide a book written from a political perspective that will both stimulate and facilitate study of the mass media in their political context.

The plan of the book is simple. The first three chapters deal with the mass media as institutions in the American political system. These chapters show how the media are both molded by and reflect that system and how they affect its performance and the interplay among public and private institutions. Media organizational structures and operations, and the impact which structure and personnel have on media offerings are explained and assessed.

The next two chapters focus on the effects of news on individuals. Chapter 4 deals with the rights that newspeople and the general public enjoy to make their views heard and to be protected from harmful publicity. Chapter 5 examines the effects of media on individual perceptions and political behavior. Much of this material on political learning is based on hitherto unpublished data from my own research combining content analysis and interview techniques. The text therefore contains numerous references to the Three Sites Project in which I collaborated with Maxwell E. McCombs, John Ben Snow Professor of Newspaper Research at Syracuse University, and David H. Weaver, Associate Professor and Director of the Bureau of Media Research, Indiana University. In 1976-77, we undertook a massive year-long study of mass media impact on political learning and perceptions of four panels of voters in three American cities.

The impact of the media in a variety of political situations is the subject of Chapters 6 through 9 of the book. The focus is on the functions media perform in elections, in presidential, congressional, and judicial politics, during manmade and natural crises and disasters, and the steadily growing part they play in the conduct of foreign policy. Chapter 10 looks at emerging policy trends and the major forces shaping them.

Although the book deals with all of the mass media, primary emphasis is on news produced by television and newspapers. I chose this emphasis so that I could explore the various topics in reasonable depth while still keeping the book modest in size. The choice is justifiable because television and newspapers are the chief information sources for people in public and private life. Late in 1979, a Roper poll showed television as a prime source of news for 67 percent of the public and newspapers as a prime source for 49 percent. Only 20 percent of the public named radio as a prime source of news and only 5 percent named either magazines or personal conversations.

The choice of topics for the book and the manner of presentation have been strongly influenced by my students at the University of Illinois, Chicago Circle. I am grateful for their keen interest and probing questions about the political impact of the mass media which encouraged me to develop a series of courses — and now this book — to answer these questions.

So many people have helped in the creation of *Mass Media and American Politics* that I cannot mention them all. Their contributions are deeply appreciated. Special thanks are due to Jean L. Woy, political science editor at Congressional Quarterly, who worked with the manuscript beyond the call of duty to keep the presentation orderly and the length moderate. Edie N. Goldenberg and William C. Adams, the two colleagues who read the manuscript, did so with exceptional care, and I am grateful to them for a number of very constructive suggestions. I hope that they have saved me from most of the errors that manage to creep into every book. If errors remain, I assume responsibility for the gremlins who put them there. I am also indebted to Anne Spray, my research assistant, who did yeoman work in gathering data for several chapters, checking the accuracy of facts and the smoothness of form, and compiling the index. Finally, Mary Lou Jackowicz performed various editorial tasks with zest and efficiency, and Angie Garcia presided at the typewriter, thanks to the generosity of the Political Science Department at the University of Illinois, Chicago Circle.

Doris A. Graber

Contents

1

Media Power and Government Control

"It was wonderful finding out that Nixon," who complained throughout much of his career that the press was determined to destroy him, "was in fact a creation of the press." So wrote David Halberstam, Pulitzer prize-winning newspaper reporter, in a book that chronicles the relationship between the high and the mighty in the world of government and the high and the mighty in the world of the media. According to Halberstam's story, Kyle Palmer, chief political writer for the *Los Angeles Times* in the years after World War II, took Nixon under his wing and put the paper at his service. Palmer created the image of "White Knight Nixon. Young. Clean-cut. War veteran. Quaker background but not afraid to fight. Family man. Straight shooter. Not afraid to duck the issue of Americanism."[1]

Nixon's congressional opponent, Jerry Voorhis, was destroyed by the paper's portrayal of him as a left-wing, procommunist radical. The paper denied him coverage to rebut its charges. Thanks to his media friends, Nixon won a seat in Congress. Four years later, Palmer encouraged Nixon to run for the Senate, again offering him the paper's support. The key campaign issue, he suggested, should be communism. Nixon's opponent, Helen Gahagan Douglas, was dubbed the pink lady. As with Voorhis, her rebuttals to charges of communist affiliation were denied coverage. Nixon won the senatorial race and was launched on a career which, despite some reverses, climaxed in the White House.

It is ironic that the power of the press, which had done so much to propel Richard Nixon into the highest office of the land, ultimately launched his downfall as well. Without the persistent probing by *Washington Post* reporters into the misdeeds of the Nixon administration, the Watergate scandal would very likely have remained a minor story. A steady stream of news and commentary turned it into a major political crisis which forced the president to resign and led to criminal convictions for his top aides. Thanks to the influence of the press, constitutional curbs on presidential power were reasserted and major abuses halted.

POLITICAL IMPORTANCE OF MASS MEDIA

The Nixon story is but one example of how mass media can influence American politics. News stories shape the perceptions of reality of millions of people in all walks of life.[2] They take Americans to the battlefields of the world in Vietnam or the Middle East. They give them ringside seats for walks on the moon or oil explorations beneath the sea. They provide the nation with shared political experiences, like watching presidential election debates or Senate deliberations about new treaties, which then form a common basis for mass political action.

Attention to the mass media is all pervasive among twentieth-century Americans. Seventy-three percent of American adults claim to be regular newspaper readers, and almost every American household has a television set which is in use for an average of nearly seven hours per day. On a typical evening, 98 million people — half the country's population — is watching television between 8 and 9 P.M. If a spectacular program is broadcast, as many as 75 to 80 million people may watch it simultaneously.[3]

The average recent American high school graduate has spent more time in front of a television set than in school, much of it during preschool and elementary school days. Even in school much learning of current events is based on information provided by the media. As adults, Americans spend nearly half of their leisure time watching television,

"Dad, if a tree falls in the forest, and the media aren't there to cover it, has the tree really fallen?"

Drawing by Robert Mankoff; reprinted from the *Saturday Review* listening to the radio, or reading newspapers and magazines. Averaged out over an entire week, this amounts to seven hours of exposure per day to some form of mass media news or entertainment. Television occupies three-fourths of this time. It is the primary source of news and entertainment for the average American and the most trusted.[4]

Media images are especially potent when they involve aspects of life that people experience only through the media, rather than directly in their own neighborhoods. Popular images of politicians and their work habits, criminals and crime, big business activities, moon walks and space flights — and their impact on ordinary people — are not generally experienced firsthand. Rather, they are shaped largely by the images portrayed in news and fictional stories in print and electronic media. For example, television exaggerates the dangers of becoming a victim of crime. Heavy viewers, we find, fear crime more and take more protective measures than do light viewers.

The media are also behavior models. In the process of image creation, the media indicate which attitudes and behaviors are acceptable and even praiseworthy in a given society, and which are unacceptable or outside the mainstream. Audiences can learn how to behave in ordinary social and work situations, how to cope with major personal crises, and how to evaluate major social institutions like the medical profession or the police. By providing common symbols, stereotypes, and behavior models, the media help to integrate and homogenize American society.[5]

Media stories also indicate what is deemed important or unimportant by America's dominant groups, what conforms to prevailing standards of justice and morality, and how various events are related to each other.[6] In the process the media present a set of cultural values that their audiences are likely to accept in whole or in part as typical for American society.

Much politically relevant information is conveyed through programs that are not explicitly concerned with politics. Many entertainment shows on television, for example, depict social institutions, such as the police or the schools, in ways which convey esteem or heap scorn on them. They also express social judgments about various types of people. For instance, television has long depicted blacks and women as socially inferior and limited in abilities. This type of coverage conveys a message that may be accepted at face value by the audience. Unsophisticated audience members may believe that this is the way it is, ought to be, and will continue to be.

Not only are the media the chief source of most people's views of the world, but they are also the fastest way known to disperse information throughout an entire society. News of the assassination of President John F. Kennedy spread with incredible speed; better than 90 percent of the American people heard the news within 90 minutes of the murder either directly from radio or television, or secondhand from other people who had received mass media messages.

FUNCTIONS OF THE MASS MEDIA

What major functions do the mass media perform? A three-fold typology developed by Harold Lasswell is useful to outline them. The three major functions which the media fulfill in modern society are:

- Surveillance of the world to report ongoing events
- Interpretation of the meaning of events
- Socialization of individuals into their cultural settings.[7]

The manner in which these functions are performed affects the lives of individuals, groups, and social organizations, as well as the course of domestic and international politics.

Surveillance

Surveillance serves two major purposes. For the political community at large, "public" surveillance throws the spotlight of publicity on selected people, organizations, and events. This may make them matters of general public concern and political action. For individual citizens, in their private capacities, "private" surveillance informs them about current events. While it may lead to political activities, its primary functions are gratification of personal needs and quieting of anxieties. The media, as Marshall McLuhan has observed, are "sense extensions" for individuals who cannot directly experience most of the events of interest to them and their communities.[8]

Public Surveillance. Public surveillance is politically significant because it sets the agenda for civic concern and action. Newspeople determine what is "news" — what will be covered and what ignored — and thereby affect who and what will have a good chance to become matters for political discussion and action.[9] Without media coverage, these people and events might have no influence, or reduced influence, on decisionmakers.[10] Undesirable conditions that may be tolerated while they remain obscure may quickly become intolerable in the glare of publicity.

An example will illustrate the power of publicity. In the late 1970s, national television news carried a story about a family poisoned by arsenic after repairing their leaky dishwasher with a readily available chemical sealer. The label on the sealer did not mention that it contained arsenic. The only indication that the product might be dangerous was a warning that it should not be used on fishtanks. There was no mention of danger to humans.

The arsenic poisoning story was publicized throughout the country and stimulated demands by the public and officials to prohibit distribution of arsenic-compound sealers. At that time many other poisonous products were in common use. Had the media publicized them prominently, action might have been taken to bar their distribution, too. In some instances, media stories about potentially harmful substances have created scares that have harmed entire industries or stopped research.[11] These consequences, good or bad, are common products of media surveillance.

Fear of publicity can be as powerful a force in shaping action as actual exposure. Politicians and business leaders are always aware of the damage an unfavorable story can do, and act accordingly. Public surveillance can also have a strong impact on economic conditions. If media stories dwell on crime and corruption, individuals may move their homes and businesses to the suburbs, leaving the central city deserted and even less safe and depriving it of tax revenues. Speculation that international conflicts or oil embargoes are in the offing may scare investors, producing fluctuations in domestic and international stock markets and commodity exchanges. This may have serious economic, and hence, political, consequences.

The media not only bring matters to public attention; they also can doom people and events to obscurity by inattention. The media ignore matters that do not seem newsworthy or that fail to catch their attention. Lack of coverage may spring from the necessity to limit publication because the information supply exceeds the media's capacity to transmit it. It also may spring from conscious attempts to suppress information for ideological or political reasons.

Left-liberal social critics have charged for many years that the selection power has been used to strengthen white middle-class values and to suppress socialist viewpoints. They claim that these choices are made to please the ideological preferences of media owners. Critics also claim that the media have deliberately suppressed the facts about dangerous products, such as alcohol and tobacco, and about the socially harmful activities of large corporations.[12] Right-wing critics complain that the media give undue attention to the views of the enemies of the established social and political order.

Media people deny these charges from both ends of the political spectrum. They defend their choices on the basis of the general criteria of newsworthiness (treated more fully in Chapter 3), shaped by an appraisal of the public's concerns and interests. Like the social critics, they can muster a broad array of evidence to support their claims. The truth probably lies somewhere between the battling forces.

Besides calling attention to matters of potential public concern, the media also provide cues to the public about the degree of importance of an issue. Matters covered prominently by the media — on the front page, with big headlines and pictures, or as a major television or radio feature — are likely to be considered most important by media audiences. Matters buried in the back pages are far less likely to be perceived as important.[13] Coverage, even though it is brief and comparatively inconspicuous, lends an aura of significance to most publicized subjects.

Through the sheer fact of coverage, the media are also able to confer status on individuals and organizations. Television made black civil rights leaders household names around the nation. Martin Luther King, Jr. and Stokely Carmichael became national figures. A political candidate whose efforts to win an election are widely publicized, a social crusader or movement whose goals become front-page news, a convicted murderer or terrorist who wins a hearing on radio or television, often become instant celebrities. Their unpublicized counterparts remain obscure and bereft of political influence.

Because the attention of the media is crucial for political success, actors on the political scene deliberately engage in behavior or manufacture situations likely to receive media coverage. Daniel Boorstin has labelled events arranged primarily to stimulate media coverage "pseudo-events."[14] They may range from news conferences called by public figures when there is really no news to announce, to physical assaults on people and property designed to dramatize grievances.

Decisions about what to publish and thereby put on the civic agenda, and what to omit are not completely up to the discretion of media personnel. Audience size must be maintained, and well-known persons and major domestic or international events must be covered. Journalists' sense of civic responsibility, or the need to meet the pressures of competition, may leave no choice.[15] However, after all the mandatory events are reported, there remains an extremely wide range of persons and events for which coverage is optional.

The power of the media over setting the civic agenda is a matter of concern because it is not controlled by a system of formal checks and balances like power at the governmental level. It is not subject to periodic review through the electoral process. If media emphases or claims are incorrect, there are few remedies. Citizens can be protected from false advertising through "truth in advertising" laws. But there is no way in which they can be protected from false political claims or improper news selection by media personnel without impairing the crucial rights to free speech and a free press.

Private Surveillance. Average citizens may not think much about the broader political impact of the stories they read and the news they watch. Rather, they are interested in using the media to keep in touch with what they see as personally important. The media are their eyes and ears to the world, their means of surveillance, which tell them about economic conditions, weather and sports, jobs, fashions, social and cultural events, health and science, and the public and private lives of famous people.

Being able to stay informed gives people a comforting reassurance, whether or not they remember what they read or hear or see. Even though the news may be bad, at least there will be no unsettling surprises. It is reassuring to know that the political system continues to operate in the face of constant crises and frequent mistakes. This feeling is very important for people's peace of mind. It tends to keep them politically quiescent because there is no need to act if political leaders are doing their job. This, in turn, has important consequences for the stability of the political system and the ability of government to function.[16]

Another significant private function that the mass media fulfill for many folks is entertainment, companionship, tension relief, and a way to pass the time without physical or mental exertion. These are major personal needs that the mass media can satisfy more conveniently than other institutions in modern America. Through the media, people who might otherwise be frustrated and dissatisfied can participate vicariously in current political events, in sports and musical events, in the lives of famous people, and in the lives of television families and communities.[17]

Interpretation

Media not only survey the events of the day and make them the focus of public and private attention, they also interpret their meaning, put them into context, and speculate about their consequences. Most incidents lend themselves to a variety of interpretations, depending on the values and experiences of the interpreter. The kind of interpretation that is chosen then affects the political consequences of the report. For example, in 1977, a series of fires occurred in a dilapidated Hispanic neighborhood in Chicago. Several lives were lost and there was substantial property damage. Investigations of the most damaging blazes showed that they had been caused by careless use of barbecue pits by apartment dwellers.

But the news stories about these fires emphasized an ethnic prejudice theme. Stories charged that the neighborhood in question had been allowed to deteriorate because city authorities were not sufficiently concerned with the welfare of Hispanics. Deaths were blamed on the city's failure to hire Spanish-speaking firemen and to teach Spanish to members of the force. Consequently, neighborhood people could not be instructed to escape safely in case of fire.

This type of coverage, which was widely quoted during public meetings in the neighborhood, increased tensions between the city's Spanish-speaking and English-speaking populations. Hispanics used harsh words about ethnic prejudice. Those whom they accused denied the charges vehemently and hurled countercharges. The thrust of the news also led to passage of a city ordinance which required that firemen in Hispanic neighborhoods must learn Spanish.

The media might have covered this story quite differently with different results and less ethnic polarization. They could have treated the fires as run-of-the-mill disasters, caused by human negligence. They could have quoted the views of fire fighters who placed the blame on the

Spanish-speaking community for careless practices and failure to learn English and to make plans for fire safety. This might have put the burden of learning a new language on Hispanics, rather than English-speaking fire fighters.

The type of play the story received depended on a number of circumstances. But the primary factor was the reporter's or editor's decision — made independently or at the behest of interest groups — to play up a particular angle and to choose informants and facts accordingly. The way the situation was depicted thus determined who became interested in it, how much support it received from various public officials, and the manner of resolution.

By suggesting the causes and relationships of various events, the media may shape opinions even without advising their audiences what to think or think about. The media usually do not tell voters how to vote, but if they picture candidates as promise breakers or shady dealers, they can encourage opinions that may affect voting choices.

The items that media personnel select to illustrate a point or characterize a political actor need not be intrinsically important to be influential in shaping opinions and evaluations. During the 1968 presidential election campaign, for example, the media reported that Senator Edmund Muskie had cried during a confrontation with a newspaper publisher about an alleged slur of his wife. This incident, which could easily have been ignored, was interpreted as a sign that Muskie was emotionally unstable and therefore unfit to be president. [18]

Socialization

The third major mass media function mentioned by Lasswell is political socialization. This is the process that involves the learning of basic values and orientations that prepares individuals to fit into their cultural milieu. It will be discussed more fully in Chapter 5. Originally, mass media studies did not put much stress on the socialization function because it was thought that it was primarily performed by parents of young children and by the schools. [19] Studies conducted in the 1970s finally put the spotlight on the media as primary factors in political socialization. [20] They showed that the bulk of information that young people acquire about the nature of their political world comes from the mass media. It reaches them either directly through exposure to the electronic and print media, or indirectly through mass media exposure of their families, teachers, acquaintances, and peers. This information presents specific facts as well as general values. It indicates the elements which make for power, success, and dominance in society and provides models for behavior. [21] Young people make heavy use of such information because they lack established attitude and behavior patterns.

Public opinion polls show that most of the new orientations and opinions that adults acquire during their lifetime also are based on information supplied by the mass media. People do not necessarily adopt the precise attitudes and opinions that may be suggested by the media. Rather, mass media information provides the ingredients that people use to adjust their existing attitudes and opinions to keep pace with a changing world. One must therefore credit the mass media with a sizeable share of continuing adult political socialization and resocialization. Examples of resocialization — the restructuring of established basic attitudes — are the shifts in sexual morality and racial attitudes that the American public has undergone since mid-century and the changing views on relations with communist countries.[22]

STUDYING MASS MEDIA EFFECTS

The public believes that the media have an important impact on the conduct of politics and on public thinking, and politicians behave on the basis of the same assumption. But many social scientists think otherwise. Who is right? Why is there such a discrepancy between traditional social science appraisals of mass media effects and the general feeling, reflected by public policies, that the mass media are extremely influential?

Three major reasons account primarily for the discrepancies. To begin with, social scientists have generally taken a narrow approach to the study of media effects. Second, theories about the ways in which people use newspapers, television, radio, and other mass media have enhanced the belief in "minimal effects" because these theories suggest that people are disinclined to learn from the media. Finally, social scientists have encountered great difficulties in measuring effects because media stimuli make their impact as part of a complex combination of social stimuli.

Early Studies and Results

Focus on Vote Choices. Eager for neat, readily quantifiable research designs, social scientists began to study the effects of the mass media primarily in one narrow area: vote change as a result of media coverage of presidential elections. Among these early studies, several are considered classics. The first was *The People's Choice* by Paul Lazarsfeld, Bernard Berelson, and Hazel Gaudet of Columbia University.[23] It reported how people made their voting choices in Erie County, Pennsylvania, in the 1940 presidential election. Sequels followed in short order. The best known are *Voting: A Study of Opinion Formation in a Presidential Campaign* by the Columbia group of researchers, Bernard Berelson, Paul Lazarsfeld and William McPhee;[24] *The Voter Decides*, by a group of researchers from the University of Michigan, Angus Campbell, Gerald Gurin, and Warren E. Miller;[25] and the Michigan group's

The American Voter, by Angus Campbell, Philip E. Converse, Warren
E. Miller, and Donald Stokes.[26]

The basic assumption behind the early voting studies was that media influence during a well-publicized campaign would bring about
changes in voting intentions. If vote intent remained unchanged, this
meant that the media lacked impact.

Studies of voting trends over a period of several elections have
shown that this assumption is incorrect. Instead, we have learned that
there may be measurable media influence even when vote intent remains stable. Moreover, media effects vary, depending on the office at
stake and the historical period. At the time of the early voting studies,
change of vote intent was quite uncommon in presidential elections because people's choices then hinged heavily on their allegiance to one of
the two major parties. Predictably, only a few people changed their voting intentions as a result of media coverage.

Had the investigators concentrated on other settings, such as judicial or nonpartisan elections, for which few voting cues outside the media were available, they might have discovered greater media-induced
attitude change. Substantial media influence might have been discovered even in presidential elections if changes in people's trust and affec-
tion or knowledge about the candidates and the election had been explored. The early studies largely ignored these other types of media influences because they did not result in easily measurable behavior and
attitude changes. Yet such changes constitute important media influences which are crucial components of a variety of political behaviors,
quite aside from voting decisions.

The early voting studies focused almost exclusively on the individual citizen and failed to trace the linkages between effects on individuals
and effects on the social groups to which they belong and through which
they influence political events. Farm workers in California, after reading
stories about illegal Mexican immigrants taking jobs from American
workers and depressing wage scales, might not change their votes. But
they might well use their union to testify against legislation permitting
illegal immigrants to remain in the United States. They might even
participate in violence against farmers who hire large numbers of alien
workers. In turn, these activities might well affect U.S.-Mexican relations and harm the worldwide image of the United States. Yet the early
studies of media effects totally ignored such impacts on the total political system and its component parts.

The findings that media effects were minimal were so pervasive in
early research that after an initial flurry in the 1940s and 1950s, social
science research into mass media effects fell to a low ebb. In study after
study dealing with political socialization and learning, the mass media
were hardly mentioned as an important factor.

Learning Theories. The early negative findings were all the more
believable because they tied in well with theories of persuasion. Mass

media messages presumably missed their mark because they are impersonal, directed to no one in particular. They are not tailored to the needs of specific individuals, as are the messages of parents, teachers, and friends. They do not permit immediate feedback which then could lead to the adjustment of the message to make it more suitable for the receiver. Furthermore, there is no compulsion to listen and no need to answer. Hence it is easy to ignore the message.

Further support for the "minimal effects" theories came from a series of so-called cognitive consistency theories. They are based on the notion that it is painful for average individuals to be presented with information which is incompatible with cherished beliefs. To avoid this painful experience, people expose themselves very selectively to the media. Social scientists do have evidence that people are indeed selective in their use of the media and search for information that reinforces what they already believe and know. But, as we shall discuss more fully in Chapter 5, the evidence is anything but clear-cut.

Recent Research

More recent research has demonstrated that the impact of the mass media is much greater than once thought, if one defines "effects" more broadly to include factual learning and attitude change and if one looks beyond the individual to effects on political systems and subsystems. Still, research into mass media effects remains hampered by serious measurement problems.

Measuring Complex Effects. Mass media effects are difficult to measure, both at the level of the individual and at the societal level, because they are highly complex and elusive. The most common measuring device at the individual level — self-assessment of impact elicited during a poll — is notoriously unreliable. We do not know, at the present time, how to measure thoughts. Even if these thoughts lead to overt behavior, we cannot readily trace the connection between cognitive stimuli and action. Actions spring from a variety of motivations among which media impact may be only a small part. Moreover, people who are exposed to the mass media already possess a fund of knowledge and attitudes which they bring to bear on new information. Since we do not know precisely what this information is, nor the rules by which it is combined with incoming information, we cannot pinpoint the exact contribution which mass media make to the individual's cognitions, feelings, and actions.

To complicate matters further, the impact of the mass media varies, depending on the subject matter. For instance, media impact apparently was greater on civil rights and the conduct of the Vietnam war than on energy policy.[27] Assessment of television's role in spurring opposition to the Vietnam war illustrates the problems faced in proving media impact. A number of analysts ascribe the public's growing dissatisfaction with United States involvement in Vietnam to media treatment of the war.[28] Television for the first time brought an ongoing war into American living rooms. In vivid colors, it showed dead and wounded people, blazing villages, and the faces of horrified children. Starting with the Tet offensive, which called optimistic reports about the impending victorious conclusion of the Vietnam war into question, there was a constant barrage of antiwar stories.[29] Demands to get out of the war were featured while little attention was paid to requests to fight the war more vigorously. It is easy to demonstrate the thrust of coverage and to document the growth of the antiwar sentiment. It is well-nigh impossible to establish the precise contribution that media coverage made to changing the public's views by picturing the war as an unnecessary, rather than a necessary, evil.

Similarly, it is difficult to prove that sharp curtailment of media coverage of Vietnam, after United States forces had been withdrawn, prevented a turnaround in policy and public sentiment. Americans in and out of government learned very little about what happened in Vietnam and the adjacent countries in the wake of the communist takeover. Atrocity stories coming from Cambodia, for instance, which the French press published because of that country's earlier ties to Cambodia, were given very little play in the American press. But one cannot be sure that ample coverage of the atrocities in the American press would have made Americans regret the withdrawal of American military might from Southeast Asia.

Unanticipated Effects. Measurement of media effects has also suffered because unanticipated effects are frequently ignored. If the anticipated effects fail to materialize, the researcher may claim there are no effects. For example, there have been frequent mass media campaigns by public service organizations and private groups to foster concern about environmental pollution. These campaigns have shown the ill effects of pollution and the steps needed to clean up the environment. After some of these publicity campaigns, researchers have tested how much people learned about pollution and ways to reduce it. The investigations generally showed that most people learned very few facts from the campaigns.

But when the attitudes of individuals towards big business were measured, social scientists found a sizeable change between pre- and post-campaign attitudes. Although most people had not learned the specific messages that the sponsors had tried to convey, they had learned that big business was responsible for much pollution. Therefore they blamed big business and voiced resentment against it. So the antipollution campaigns had a distinct effect, but not the effect which had been expected and would normally be measured in post-campaign tests. [30]

A Case Study: Britain and Appeasement. A historical incident, Britain's decision to appease Adolf Hitler rather than fighting him prior to Germany's conquest of Czechoslovakia, illustrates the difficulty of measuring the contribution which mass media publicity makes to a particular political situation. In 1936, Hitler marched into the Rhineland in violation of German treaty obligations. In 1938 he annexed Austria. Annexation of Czechoslovakia followed in 1939. Major European powers, including Britain, had pursued a policy of appeasement during the earlier conquests. In the wake of the fall of Czechoslovakia, appeasement ended and Britain belatedly pledged to fight against further German aggression.

During and after the second World War, the question was frequently raised in Britain and elsewhere why the British had not opposed Hitler earlier, before he had gained strength through his early conquests. A British scholar, Colin Seymour-Ure, has placed the brunt of the blame for the appeasement policy on *The Times* of London.[31] His views find support in the writings of such British notables as Prime Minister Anthony Eden and Lord Vansittart of the British Foreign Office, as well as such well-known historians as Martin Gilbert[32] and A. J. P. Taylor.[33]

The Times did not have to persuade governmental leaders to adopt the appeasement position, although *Times* top brass were in a good position to do so because of close friendship ties with Britain's political leaders. Most of these leaders were already convinced. Rather, *The Times*, through its advocacy of appeasement, gave a strong boost to their cause and made it extremely difficult for the opposition to organize. It also reinforced the general consensus in the country and among the leadership that appeasement was the proper policy for a nation which was still war-weary from the First World War which had ended only 20 years earlier.

In this period, *The Times* was considered a national institution in Britain which watched wisely and well over the interests of the nation. It was ranked as the best and most influential of all British daily papers, read by nearly all prominent people in public and private life. When *The Times* supported a policy, Britain's leaders and people took note.

The Times was also widely regarded abroad as the official voice of the British government, which gave its editorials extraordinary political weight. This is why British historians claim that "no single factor contributed so much" to the German annexation of Czechoslovakia as a pro-appeasement *Times* editorial in 1938 "suggesting that Czecho-Slovakia might be wise in her own interests to let the Sudeten-German areas go." The editorial may have assured Hitler that he could safely proceed with the conquest without British military opposition.[34] Protests against the editorial and warnings about its dangerous consequences came immediately from members of the British cabinet, the British Foreign Office, British diplomats abroad, Czech leaders, the Russian ambassador in London, and the French government. There were even rumors that the editorial had been planted by the German Embassy in London as a clever ploy to aid the cause of Germany. The warnings about the Fuehrer's next move turned out to be correct. Hitler took Czechoslovakia.

However, the role of *The Times* is not as clear as it may seem. Other analysts of the events which preceded World War II believe that *The Times* played only a minor role. They note that even without prodding from *The Times,* appeasement was extremely popular before 1939 with Britain's political leaders, particularly Prime Minister Neville Chamberlain, and with the British public. They point to the fact that in a special election in 1933, a pro-rearmament Conservative candidate running in a district which normally elected Conservatives, was soundly beaten by a pacifist Labour Party candidate. Furthermore, in 1935, an antimilitary lobby group, the Peace Pledge Union, was able to collect 11,500,000 votes in Britain for its Peace Ballot straw poll. Natural hatred of war was reinforced by bitter memories of the losses suffered by Britain in World War I and fears that World War II, with the rapid development of air warfare capabilities, would be infinitely more horrible for soldiers and civilians alike. Moreover, Britain was militarily unprepared for war and assistance from France, the United States, and the Soviet Union was uncertain.

It is nearly impossible to prove conclusively how crucial the position of *The Times* was to Britain's maintenance of an appeasement policy and to Hitler's decision to invade Czechoslovakia. It is equally impossible to prove that *The Times* played no role because British policy makers already favored appeasement. Neither will we ever know for sure whether Hitler would have ventured his attack on Czechoslovakia had he lacked the intimation that Britain would not interfere.

This type of uncertainty has made social scientists shy away from assessing the influence of the mass media on political events. In fact, social scientists often deny that effects exist when these effects defy measurement. This is unfortunate since many effects which cannot be measured precisely can be observed in the field and studied in the laboratory.

Statistical versus Political Significance. Not only has it been difficult to measure the impact of mass media precisely when they are but one influence among many, but social scientists have also been rather rigid in interpreting the significance of media influence when it has been found. They have falsely equated statistical significance with political significance. But a small amount of impact may carry a vast amount of clout. Nonetheless, social scientists tend to report their measurements without projecting the effects that these measurements imply.

An example is the failure to acknowledge that even small opinion changes, attributable to the media, can have major political effects. During an election, only one or two percent of the voters may change their voting decision because of media stories. That is a very small, statistically negligible effect. Politically, however, it may be a major effect because many important elections, including several presidential elections, have been decided by a margin of two percent of the votes. In the 1976 presidential race, if two percent of the vote had gone to the losing candidate, Gerald Ford would have stayed in the White House, Jimmy Carter would have remained a peanut farmer. Two percent of the voters sounds like a small number, but it runs into thousands, and even hundreds of thousands when translated into actual numbers.

Influencing Elites. Another major problem with social science research on mass media effects has been the concentration on measuring effects of the media on ordinary individuals, rather than on political elites. This ignores the fact that the average individual, despite our fictions to the contrary, is politically fairly unimportant. Mass media impact on a handful of political decisionmakers usually is vastly more significant than similar impact on thousands of ordinary individuals. In addition, the impact on decisionmakers is likely to be far more profound because mass media information relates more closely to their immediate concerns. They may pay close attention to stories in which the public is not interested and which it often fails to understand.

If a major newspaper, for instance, carries a series of articles on corrupt use of money in elections, and these stories are read by influential people who can press for corrective legislation, the impact can be momentous. If convinced of the need for change, a handful of legislators may be in a position to bring it about. In such a case, the media have not merely influenced a handful of people; they have spawned political action which may affect millions.

At times, media impact on small groups can have less positive effects. For example, if a broadcast of details of a race riot attracts even a small portion of the audience to the riot site and stimulates some to participate, the situation may escalate beyond control. This type of effect, too, has generally been ignored by social scientists.

In light of what we have said thus far, it seems totally unrealistic to claim that the media are not important in setting the stage for ongoing political developments, in shaping the views and behaviors of political elites and other selected groups, and in influencing the general public's perception of political life. As Theodore White has put it, with great fervor:

> The power of the press in America is a primordial one. It sets the agenda of public discussion; and this sweeping political power is unrestrained by any law. It determines what people will talk and think about — an authority that in other nations is reserved for tyrants, priests, parties and mandarins.
> No major act of the American Congress, no foreign adventure, no act of diplomacy, no great social reform can succeed in the United States unless the press prepares the public mind.[35]

Even if one takes a totally negative position, arguing that the media are nothing but a conduit of information over which they have no control, one cannot deny that people throughout the world of politics consider the media important and behave accordingly. This importance — which is an effect of media coverage — is reflected in the fact that governments throughout the world, in totalitarian as well as nontotalitarian regimes, seek to control the flow of information produced by the media, lest it subvert the prevailing political system.

GOVERNMENT CONTROL OF MASS MEDIA: ASSUMPTIONS AND METHODS

Governmental attempts to control and manipulate the media are universal because governments throughout the world believe media effects are important political forces. This belief is based on the assumption that institutions which control public information shape public knowledge and behavior and thereby determine the support or opposition of citizens and officials to the government and its policies. Through control over mass information institutions, governments everywhere seek to preserve the political system as a whole as well as to regulate the media and other social institutions which depend on them for publicity. While control occurs in all societies, its nature and purposes vary. Authoritarian countries control more extensively and more rigidly than nonauthoritarian ones. But all systems merely represent specific points on a continuum of control. We shall outline common types of control systems in a general manner under four headings, following a scheme developed by Fred Siebert, Theodore Peterson, and Wilbur Schramm in their book *Four Theories of the Press*.[36]

According to Siebert, Peterson, and Schramm, authoritarian control systems are of two types: those which are nonideological and simply represent a desire by the ruling classes to keep tight control over media output so that it does not interfere with the conduct of government, and those which are based on the ideology of communism. The latter actively use and control the media to support ideological goals. Examples of nonideological control can be found in states ruled by military governments, such as Argentina or Ethiopia. Examples of control based on communism are found in the Soviet Union and the People's Republic of China.

Nonauthoritarian systems are also of two types. But these types are not linked to differences in political ideology. Rather, they are linked to differences in philosophies about the role which the media ought to carve out for themselves in countries where they enjoy a great deal of freedom. The two types of nonauthoritarian control systems have been labeled "libertarian" and "social responsibility." Libertarian systems give the press a very free range to report whatever seems to please audiences the most. Social responsibility systems demand that the press operate for the betterment of society so that media audiences are spurred to behave in socially responsible ways. The United States and Western Europe have provided examples of each of these philosophies at various times in their histories.[37]

In today's world, authoritarian systems of media control are clearly dominant in the majority of countries. Authoritarian countries are even trying to impose such systems universally by controlling international aspects of news reporting in all countries. In sessions of the United Nations Economic and Social Council (UNESCO), they have opposed freedom of reporting by newspeople stationed outside their own countries. They have argued that only news that supports the established regime should be permitted and that newspeople should be subject to supervision by officials of the host country.

Role of Media in Authoritarian Regimes

What are the basic assumptions which underlie authoritarian and nonauthoritarian philosophies of media operation, and what types of governmental structures and practices have been invented to implement the philosophies?

In communist and other authoritarian systems, it is assumed that the government is basically good and operates for the benefit of its people. Since the government is well-intentioned, and its policies are carefully determined, it follows that the mass media must not interfere with the operations of the government. It is not a proper function of the press to criticize the basic system or its rulers, beyond pointing out minor deficiencies in policy and suggesting adjustments in line with prevailing policies. Basically, the press is a supporter of the government and its policies, rather than its adversary and critic. However, criticism about inefficiencies or corruption of minor officials may be allowed. For instance, in 1977 and 1978, *Pravda,* the official Russian newspaper, published a series of articles on shoddy housing construction and industrial pollution on the Dnieper River. Criticism may even extend to top leaders after they have been ousted from leadership.

In most authoritarian polities, the mass media must take positions which further the goals of the government. News must accord with the prevailing ideology and confirm its accuracy. But the media may be free to provide information or entertainment of their choice, as long as the offerings do not hurt the state or interfere with public policies.

In communist societies, the role of the media is more stringently defined. The likely political and social effects of a story, rather than its newsworthiness, determine what will be published and what will be buried in silence. For instance, there are comparatively few stories about accidents, disasters, and crime because these matters are believed to be devoid of value in teaching people proper conduct.

Instead, newspeople are encouraged to publish socially useful propaganda that will persuade people to adhere to the system. According to Lenin, the press must be a propagandist, agitator, and organizer for the revolutionary aims of communist societies. It must be closely integrated with other instruments of state power, serving the public by publishing stories that will unify people around the right ideas of life and politics.

Even entertainment programs must serve political purposes. Thus music and drama performances must carry appropriate social messages or have historical significance. Rock music, modernistic art, and sexually explicit theater are generally banned from public performances, particularly if they are to be broadcast to a wide audience. For performances which are deemed to have social merit, funding is available, even if the audience is small. The government supports such works financially because they serve the important public purpose of shaping people's minds in support of the system.

Role of Media in Nonauthoritarian Regimes

The basic assumptions underlying control systems in democratic countries contrast sharply with those of authoritarian societies. Here the media serve the public rather than the government. Governments are viewed as fallible servants of the people, potentially corrupt, stupid, or abusive of citizens. Because of their inherent weaknesses and because individuals' rights to judge their government is highly prized, governments must be criticized if they misbehave.

The media are viewed as impartial reporters of good and evil who scrutinize the passing scene on behalf of the public and report whatever journalists consider newsworthy. Journalists serve as the watchdog fourth branch of government which monitors excesses and misbehavior of the executive, legislative, and judicial branches. Through playing an adversary role, they provide the feedback which democratic systems need to remain on course. If, as the result of this scrutiny, governments fall and public officials are ousted, this is as it should be.

This, broadly stated, is the theory behind the role of media in democratic societies. The practice is less clear-cut. Neither newspeople nor governments are fully comfortable with the watchdog role, so each tries to blunt it. The media generally support the political system, limiting their criticism to what are seen as perversions of fundamental social and political values. They may share information with government agencies such as the FBI and CIA. At times, reporters may even withhold important news at government request to spare the government or particular officials from embarrassment or interference. This happened, for instance, when the *New York Times* withheld news about the forthcoming Bay of Pigs invasion of Cuba in 1961.[38] Government officials, in an effort to keep their images untarnished by media attacks, may use reward and punishment tactics to keep the media watchdog in line. These tactics are described more fully in Chapter 7.

The chief role of the mass media in free societies is to provide information and entertainment to the general public. According to the libertarian philosophy, anything that happens which is interesting or involves important people or events is news. Following appropriate verification, news should be reported quickly, accurately, and objectively, without any attempt to convey a particular point of view. Those matters which have the widest audience appeal should be stressed, even if that means sex and violence stories and entertainment rather than information.

Although audiences may learn important things from the media, teaching is not the chief media role. Nor is it their role to question the truth or accuracy or merits of the information supplied to them by their sources. Rather, it is left to the news audience to decide what to believe and what to question.

In contrast to libertarians, adherents to social responsibility tenets believe that news and entertainment presented by the mass media should reflect a social conscience. Media personnel should be participants in the political process, not merely reporters of the passing scene. As guardians of the public welfare, they should spur political action when necessary. If reporters think, for instance, that pollution or racial segregation are prevalent social evils, they should cover these stories in depth and make them news, even when nothing new has happened. Likewise, undesirable viewpoints and questionable accusations should be denied exposure, however sensational they may be. If reporters believe that government is hiding information under the cloak of national security, they should expose the facts.

Comparison of the type of journalism advocated by social responsibility journalists with the type of journalism advocated by communist journalists reveals some surprising philosophical resemblances. Both approaches involve using the media to support the basic ideals of their societies and to shape people into more perfect social beings. Both are convinced their goals are good and would not be achieved in a media system dominated by the whims of owners or audiences.

The similarities should not, of course, be exaggerated. Social advocacy in nonauthoritarian systems certainly lacks the clout it has in systems where media control is monopolized by the government. Nevertheless, it frightens and antagonizes many news professionals and other people. If one admits that the media should be used to influence social thought and behavior for "good" purposes, it becomes difficult to prevent their use for a variety of purposes that may seem good to some but bad to others. Critics of social responsibility journalism point out that journalists do not have a public mandate to act as arbiters of social values and policies. They lack the legitimacy that in a democracy comes only from being elected by the public or appointed by elected officials.

Whatever the merits or faults of these arguments may be, at the present time, social responsibility journalism is popular with a sizable proportion of the profession.[39] Pulitzer prizes and other honors go to journalists who have successfully exposed questionable practices in the interest of social improvement. The most prominent "villains" are usually big government and big business.[40]

Control Methods: Authoritarian Systems

The methods by which governments control the media vary, depending on the type of political system. So do the major objectives for control. In authoritarian societies, the major objective is to place control into the hands of friends of the regime and to make sure that their output remains supportive of most government policies. In nonauthoritarian regimes, the major objective is to avoid publicity that endangers national defense capabilities or violates widely held social norms. There is little attempt to keep foes of the regime out of the media business.

In many authoritarian societies, control over media content is accomplished by limiting access to the media business. For example, the government may grant newspaper franchises only to carefully selected people who support the government fully in all its endeavors. Often such franchises bestow monopoly control, and people who lack them cannot enter the newspaper business. Control through franchising media entrepreneurs is quite common for electronic media, even in democratic countries, because of the limited availability of television and radio channels. But in democratic countries it is not generally used to shut out political opponents. Nor is it applied to newspapers. In the United States, for instance, anyone with enough financial resources may start a newspaper or magazine or newsletter. No permits are required.

Other methods used primarily by authoritarian countries to control publications are subsidies to favorite publishers or favoritism in the allocation of tightly controlled paper stocks for printing newspapers and magazines. Newspaper publishers whose activities displease the government may find themselves out of business because they lack paper. These types of economic controls may be imposed quite openly through formal rationing and subsidy schemes, or they may be imposed informally — the government may merely inform a disliked publisher that paper stocks are insufficient to supply that particular enterprise.

Media may also be controlled through manipulating access to news. For instance, the government may release information only to favored publications, putting less favored ones effectively out of business. While such practices are common in authoritarian societies, they occasionally happen on a smaller scale in more open societies as well. For instance, President Nixon barred *Washington Post* reporters from his press plane because he was angry with their stories about his presidency.[41]

In addition to controlling entry into the news business through franchises and access to news, authoritarian governments often limit *what* may be published. Several methods are used. In some countries, nothing may be printed or broadcast until it has first passed the government censor. The censor may delete any story which the government deems objectionable. Elsewhere, these deletions are made after the papers or magazines have already been printed. This leaves tantalizing white spots or missing pages. Television and radio scripts are often prepared directly by government officials and must be broadcast without editorial changes.

Authoritarian societies frequently use treason and sedition laws to control media output. Treason and sedition are usually broadly defined in these countries so that anything that is critical of the government is deemed treasonable or seditious. People judged guilty of these crimes may be severely punished. The punishment may be removal from the media business, prison sentences, or even death. These are extremely strong deterrents to keep people from publishing stories which attack the government.

Most publishers in totalitarian societies avoid difficulties with the official censor and with treason and sedition laws by refraining from using material which is likely to be objectionable. Government censorship then becomes replaced largely by self-censorship, making the job of the official censor much easier.

When authoritarian regimes are communist, media control is simplified because the government owns and operates all mass media and has full control over their programs. Additionally, communist countries frequently block out all unapproved communications from abroad. This includes jamming of foreign broadcasts and prohibition on the importation of foreign printed materials. The strictness with which these controls are applied waxes and wanes, depending on the communist country's relations with various noncommunist powers. But even during friendly interludes, communist countries rigidly control any information from abroad that might undermine their political system.

Control Methods: Nonauthoritarian Regimes

In democratic societies, official control of the mass media is deemed largely unnecessary. Anyone who wants to enter the media business may do so. In the United States, the First Amendment to the Constitution, which provides that "Congress shall make no law . . . abridging the freedom of speech, or of the press," has given the media an exceptionally strong basis for resisting government controls. But the courts have ruled that the protection is not absolute and must give way on occasion to social rights which the courts deem superior.

Competition among papers, magazines, and television and radio stations will presumably produce a variety of opinions. If some media attack the government, other media will support it. Positive and negative, as well as right and wrong information will somehow balance out. The underlying, very intriguing, assumption is that the audience will be able to extract the truth from these conflicting reports. Unfortunately this attractive theory does not match the plain facts. Average citizens generally do not have time to expose themselves to a wide array of media opinions. When they are confronted with clashing opinions they find it difficult to judge their merits. Anyone who has listened to the promises and claims made by contending politicians knows how difficult it is to evaluate them. Confusion and resigned disinterest, rather than enlightenment, are the likely outcomes.

Even in societies with basically open communications systems, there are some controls to guard against excesses by the media. They are exercised formally by legislators and courts, and informally through social pressures. In the United States, the courts have generally ruled that these controls may be enforced only after they have been violated. Courts have been very loathe to impose "prior restraint" by granting injunctions which would stop publication of information on the grounds that it would cause irreparable harm. But informal social and political pressures and the fear of indictments after publication have restrained presentation of potentially forbidden materials.

Basically, controls in nonauthoritarian societies fall into four categories: (1) treason and sedition laws; (2) shielding sensitive governmental proceedings; (3) protecting individual reputations and privacy; and (4) protecting the prevailing moral standards of the community. All societies have treason and sedition laws that prohibit publication of information which must be kept secret to protect the country against foreign and domestic enemies who endanger its national survival. The big problem is to determine the point at which secrecy is essential so that freedom to publish must give way. In democratic societies, media and the government are in a constant struggle to determine this exact point. Governments lean towards protection; the media lean towards disclosure.

There is little argument that treason and sedition are beyond the boundaries of unrestricted publication, even in an open society. Curbs on publication of government secrets — so-called classified information — are more controversial. Governments try to establish controls over the publication of material that may be harmful to themselves or to individuals. For instance, confidential reports about the performance of government agencies, records of bidding on public jobs, and conversations during closed meetings are generally shielded from publicity. Finally, most governments also have laws against obscenity and laws protecting the reputations of individuals or groups. All of these controls on publication are discussed more fully in Chapter 4.

Defining the limits of government restraint on information raises difficult questions for democratic societies. Does any degree of official censorship open the way for the destruction of free expression? What guidelines are available to determine how far censorship should go?

What types of material, if any, can harm children? Or adults? Should expressed prejudice be prohibited on the ground that it damages the self-image of minorities? The answers are controversial and problematic.

In addition to formal control of potentially "dangerous" news in authoritarian and nonauthoritarian societies, there are many informal restraints as well. All governmental units, and often many of their subdivisions have their own information control systems by which they determine what news to release, how to present it, and what news to cover up. These informal control systems are discussed in Chapter 7.

The limitations on the freedom of publication which we encounter even in nonauthoritarian societies raise questions about the actual freedom enjoyed by the media, compared to their counterparts in authoritarian societies. In fact, the degree of restraint varies so sharply that the systems are fundamentally different. In authoritarian societies, the media are essentially an arm of government whose purpose is to support the regime in power. In nonauthoritarian societies, the media are free to oppose the regime, to weaken it, and even topple it. While they rarely carry their power to the latter extreme, the potential exists. It is this potential that makes the media in nonauthoritarian societies a genuine restraint on governmental abuses of power and a potent shaper of governmental action.

SUMMARY

In this chapter we have argued that the mass media are an important influence on politics because they regularly and rapidly present politically crucial information to huge audiences. These audiences include political elites and decisionmakers, as well as large numbers of average citizens whose political activities, however sporadic, are shaped by information from the mass media.

The mass media are more than passive transmission agents for available information. Decisions made by media personnel determine what information becomes available to media audiences and what remains unavailable. By putting stories into perspective and interpreting them, media personnel assign meaning to the information and indicate the values by which it ought to be judged. News shaping is unavoidable because space is limited and because facts do not speak for themselves. Hence the media have the power to control much of the raw material needed by political elites and the general public for thinking about the political world and planning political action. At times, newspeople even *generate* political action directly through their own investigations or indirectly through their capacity to stimulate pseudo-events.

Although social scientists have remained somewhat skeptical about claims of large-scale media impact on politics, governments everywhere profess to be keenly aware of the political importance of the media. Governments therefore have developed philosophies about the political role to be played by the media in their societies and about the proper ways to control media impact on government activities. These philosophies have been implemented by constitutional and legal rules as well as a host of informal arrangements. In this chapter, we have briefly described how the basic philosophies, constitutional arrangements, and legal provisions differ in authoritarian and nonauthoritarian regimes.

NOTES

1. David Halberstam, *The Powers That Be* (New York: Knopf, 1979), p. 256.
2. For a compact overview of the literature on mass media effects, particularly television, see George Comstock, "The Impact of Television on American Institutions," *Journal of Communication* 28 (Spring 1978): 12-28.
3. A good source for media statistics is Christopher H. Sterling and Timothy R. Haight, eds., *The Mass Media: Aspen Institute Guide to Communication Industry Trends* (New York: Praeger, 1978).
4. These figures are averages based on Roper Organization Surveys. People's media exposure patterns differ, depending on age, social background, education, ethnic origins, and similar characteristics. These variations are discussed in Chapter 5. For politicians, close attention to the media is a professional requirement.
5. John M. Phelan, *Mediaworld: Programming the Public* (New York: Seabury Press, 1977).
6. The clues which mass media stories supply to the culture of their societies are discussed by George Gerbner in "Toward 'Cultural Indicators': the Analysis of Mass Mediated Public Message Systems," in George Gerbner, Ole R. Holsti, Klaus Krippendorff, William J. Paisley, Philip J. Stone, eds., *The Analysis of Communication Content* (New York: John Wiley, 1969), pp. 123-32.
7. Lasswell discusses the three functions in Harold D. Lasswell, "The Structure and Function of Communication in Society" in Wilbur Schramm, ed., *Mass Communications* (Urbana: University of Illinois Press, 1949), p. 103.
8. Marshall McLuhan, *Understanding Media: The Extensions of Man* (New York: McGraw-Hill, 1966).
9. Chapter 3 gives a more detailed definition of "news."
10. Evidence that the media set the agenda for national issues is presented in Donald L. Shaw and Maxwell McCombs, *The Emergence of American Political Issues: The Agenda-Setting Function of the Press* (St. Paul: West Publishing, 1977) and sources cited there. Wenmouth Williams, Jr. and David C. Larsen, "Agenda-Setting in an Off-Election Year," *Journalism Quarterly* 54 (Winter 1977): 744-749 reviews agenda-setting for local issues, as well as the differential role played by various types of media in setting civic and personal agendas.
11. Colin Seymour-Ure, *The Political Impact of Mass Media* (London: Constable, 1974), p. 21 outlines the various types of media influences.
12. Examples of such criticisms can be found in Herbert Schiller, *Mass Communication and American Empire* (New York: Augustus, Kelley, 1969) and Robert Cirino, *Power to Persuade: Mass Media and the News* (New York: Bantam, 1974).
13. Maxwell E. McCombs and John B. Mauro, "Predicting Newspaper Readership from Content Characteristics," *Journalism Quarterly* 54 (Spring 1977): 3-7.

14. Daniel Boorstin, *The Image: A Guide to Pseudo-Events,* (New York: Atheneum, 1961).
15. Criteria of what constitutes "news" are discussed fully by Bernard Roshco, *Newsmaking* (Chicago: University of Chicago Press, 1975), Chapter 3.
16. The results of reassuring publicity are discussed by Murray Edelman, *The Symbolic Uses of Politics* (Urbana: University of Illinois Press, 1964), pp. 38-43.
17. George Comstock, Steven Chaffee, Natan Katzman, Maxwell McCombs, and Donald Roberts, *Television and Human Behavior* (New York: Columbia University Press, 1978), pp. 423-451.
18. The story is told more fully in Theodore White, *The Making of the President, 1972* (New York: Bantam, 1973).
19. Earlier writings include David Easton and Jack Dennis, *Children in the Political System: Origins of Political Legitimacy* (New York: McGraw-Hill, 1969); Fred I. Greenstein, *Children and Politics* (New Haven: Yale University Press, 1965); Richard Dawson and Kenneth Prewitt, *Political Socialization* (Boston: Little, Brown, 1969) and Robert D. Hess and Judith Torney, *The Development of Political Attitudes in Children* (Chicago: Aldine, 1967).
20. Examples include Sidney Kraus and Dennis Davis, *The Effects of Mass Communication on Political Behavior* (University Park, Pa.: Pennsylvania State University Press, 1976); Gary O. Coldevin, "Internationalism and Mass Communications," *Journalism Quarterly* 49 (Summer 1972): 365-368; Neil Hollander, "Adolescents and the War: The Sources of Socialization," *Journalism Quarterly* 48 (Autumn 1971): 472-479; and Steven H. Chaffee, H.L. Scott Ward and Leonard Tipton, "Mass Communication and Political Socialization," *Journalism Quarterly* 47 (Winter 1970): 647-659.
21. Phelan, in *Mediaworld: Programming the Public,* contends that the mass media have replaced more traditional social groups as the source of behavior models and demonstrator of the ideals of society.
22. Evidence for the public's evaluation of the impact of the mass media comes from successive Roper polls and the author's Three Sites Project.
23. Paul Lazarsfeld, Bernard Berelson, and Hazel Gaudet, *The People's Choice* (New York: Columbia University Press, 1944).
24. Bernard Berelson, Paul Lazarsfeld, and William McPhee, *Voting: A Study of Opinion Formation in a Presidential Campaign* (Chicago: University of Chicago Press, 1954).
25. Angus Campbell, Gerald Gurin, and Warren E. Miller, *The Voter Decides* (Evanston, Illinois: Row, Peterson, 1954).
26. Angus Campbell, Philip E. Converse, Warren E. Miller, and Donald Stokes, *The American Voter* (New York: Wiley, 1960).
27. Edmund B. Lambeth, "Perceived Influence of the Press on Energy Policy Making," *Journalism Quarterly* 55 (Spring 1978): 11-18.
28. Halberstam, *The Powers That Be,* pp. 483-515. Also see Michael Arlen, *Living-Room War* (New York: Viking, 1969).
29. Peter Braestrup, *Big Story* (New York: Doubleday Anchor, 1978).
30. Unpublished research reported at roundtable on "Public Opinion and Public Policy: Reciprocal Influences," Chicago: Midwest Political Science Association meeting, 1979.
31. The analysis that follows is based on his account in Seymour-Ure, *The Political Impact of Mass Media,* pp. 67-98.
32. Martin Gilbert, *The Roots of Appeasement* (London: Weidenfeld & Nicholson, 1966).
33. A. J. P. Taylor, *The Origins of the Second World War* (London: Hamish Hamilton, 1961).
34. Seymour-Ure, *The Political Impact of Mass Media,* p. 79.

35. Theodore White, *The Making of the President, 1972,* p. 327.
36. Fred Siebert, Theodore Peterson, and Wilbur Schramm, *Four Theories of the Press* (Urbana: University of Illinois Press, 1963).
37. For a brief account of media history in the United States, see Bernard Roshco, *Newsmaking* (Chicago: University of Chicago Press, 1975), 23-57.
38. James Aronson, *The Press and the Cold War* (Indianapolis: Bobbs-Merrill, 1970), pp. 165-169.
39. Johnstone *et al.* in a study of North American journalists in the early 1970s report that only 35 percent believe in neutral reporting. John Johnstone, Edward Slawski, and William Bowman, *The Newspeople* (Urbana: University of Illinois Press, 1976), pp. 117-123.
40. See, for example, Bernard Rubin, *Media, Politics, Democracy* (New York: Oxford University Press, 1977) and Erik Barnouw, *The Sponsor: Notes on a Modern Potentate* (New York: Oxford University Press, 1978).
41. This and many similar incidents are reported in William E. Porter, *Assault on the Media: The Nixon Years* (Ann Arbor: University of Michigan Press, 1976).

READINGS

Arlen, Michael. *Living-Room War.* New York: Viking, 1969.

Aronson, James. *The Press and the Cold War.* Indianapolis: Bobbs-Merrill, 1970.

Braestrup, Peter. *Big Story.* New York: Doubleday Anchor, 1978.

Halberstam, David. *The Powers That Be.* New York: Knopf, 1979.

Phelan, John M. *Mediaworld: Programming the Public.* New York: Seabury Press, 1977.

Seymour-Ure, Colin. *The Political Impact of Mass Media.* London: Constable, 1974.

Siebert, Fred; Peterson, Theodore; and Schramm, Wilbur. *Four Theories of the Press.* Urbana: University of Illinois Press, 1963.

2

Ownership, Regulation, and Guidance of Media

On November 15, 1971, Clay T. Whitehead, director of President Nixon's White House Office of Telecommunications Policy, responded to a White House request for plans to reorganize public broadcasting. "We stand to gain substantially from an increase in the relative power of local stations," wrote Whitehead. "They are generally less liberal and more concerned with education than with controversial national affairs. Further, a decentralized system would have far less influence and be far less attractive to social activists."[1] Why was President Nixon eager to reorganize public broadcasting? Why did Whitehead propose to move control from a national corporation to local stations?

Why did Representative Morris K. Udall tell delegates to a conference on media concentration on December 14, 1978 that, "I firmly believe we have seen the emergence of media giants with such potential for economic abuse and without redeeming social benefit that the time has come to say, 'Enough. There has to be a limit to gigantism' "?[2]

And why did media critic William Small state flatly, "The control of the news product . . . is spread across many people. . . . The multiplicity of this responsibility is the greatest protection for the public."?[3]

At the root of all these questions lies the concern about the immense power available to those who can control the information that reaches the general public and political elites. President Nixon knew that the Corporation for Public Broadcasting, which controlled public television, was opposed to his political philosophy and the aims of his administration. This is why he resented its members, why he wanted to remove them and put control into more docile hands. Representative Udall fears that "monopolization of our mass media" will put control of the public information supply into the hands of a few giant business enterprises which could wield it to their own advantage. William Small repeats the traditional American remedy for large and menacing concentrations of power — checks and balances and diversification of control.

Concern about control of the media has been a central issue in American politics since colonial days, but has become particularly important in the twentieth century, because new technological developments and forms of business concentration have raised major public policy issues. In this chapter, we shall explore some of these issues and the evidence put forth to support different points of view. We shall weigh the pros and cons of public and private control, along with arguments for and against big business influence in the media business. We shall also assess the impact of internal and external pressures on the industry, including those arising from the nature of its personnel and from citizen lobby groups. The public policy issues involved in media control are so complex, so intertwined with political predispositions and preferences, that no approach stands out as clearly "best." It therefore is no wonder that attempts to legislate have produced clashes of views, litigation, and little agreement on what the laws should be.

PUBLIC, SEMIPUBLIC, AND PRIVATE CONTROL

Control of the media takes a number of forms. Each affects the nature of media output. We have already discussed the authoritarian pattern of total government control and its effects. We have also mentioned that some government control and operation of media, particularly radio and television, is common in nonauthoritarian countries as well, but that control over content is much looser.

Public Control

In the United States the outright control by government over media is comparatively limited. However, the federal government does control broadcasts to American military posts abroad. It also has various types of foreign propaganda outlets and a host of domestic programs supplied by various federal agencies. Together, these services equal the volume of commercial broadcasts produced in the United States. Nearly half of the total available radio frequency space belongs to the federal government, which uses it for radio services supplied by the executive branch. These broadcast activities are outside the control of ordinary regulatory agencies. Those which involve broadcasts to foreign countries normally receive little attention within the United States. In fact, some of the programs put out by propaganda agencies like the Voice of America are barred from the domestic airwaves.[4]

Semipublic Control

Another control pattern involves media operation by semipublic institutions. The American public broadcasting system is an example. It represents a mixture of public financing and programming and private operation of radio and television stations. The public broadcasting system was created through the Public Broadcasting Act of 1967 to support educational or public service television stations whose programs do not generally attract large audiences. These stations usually cannot find enough commercial sponsors to pay for their shows.

Roughly one-fourth of American television stations are involved. In 1979, the system encompassed 280 noncommercial television stations. It also included 200 noncommercial FM radio stations linked together as National Public Radio. The administrative arrangements for the public broadcast system, now regulated under the Public Telecommunications Act of 1978, have been complex. A Corporation for Public Broadcasting, staffed by political appointees, has run the general administration. Rather than telling public television stations what specific programs they should feature, it has guided programming by paying for some types of programs and refusing to pay for others. This has constituted effective pursestring control by government. A separate Public Broadcast Service has produced television programs. Because this division of labor has not worked out well, the Carter administration and a special Carnegie Commission Report on the Future of Public Broadcasting have proposed major organizational changes. These involve splitting the Corporation for Public Broadcasting into separate management and program development units and transforming the Public Broadcast Service into a triple network, offering three simultaneous program options. These changes are intended to eliminate barriers to innovative programming, particularly for news and public affairs, and to increase barriers to political meddling with public broadcasting by the government.

Private foundations, which are usually backed by big business enterprises, have also put money into the public broadcasting system. Like government, this has given them influence over programming. Nearly 43 percent of all prime time programs distributed in 1977 by public broadcasting involved corporate financing. In addition, the general public has had an impact on the system through donations and through community advisory boards attached to public television.

In practice, public television has been used primarily for experimental programs, cultural offerings like classical music and ballet, academic lectures and documentaries, certain sports broadcasts, and minority-oriented programs. While it has provided a sophisticated alternative to commercial programs, its appeal to the general public has been small. On an average day or evening, only 3 percent of the television audience tunes in to public television.[5] Even minority groups, for whom a number of public broadcast programs are presumably tailored, prefer the entertainment provided by commercial stations. Because of its limited appeal and high cost to the public, there have been demands to disband the system completely and reallocate its frequencies to commercial channels. Some of its programs might then be shown on commercial stations with federal subsidies.[6]

Although the Corporation for Public Broadcasting was structured to minimize governmental control over its programs, the public broadcast system has been subject to considerable political pressures. President Nixon, as mentioned, tried to pressure the Public Broadcasting Service to alter its programming. To make the system more responsive to government pressure, some control over local programming was shifted from Washington personnel to the more pliable local managers. As expected, this change led to more traditional programming. Such attempts are evidence that dependence on public funds may mean subservience to government control, despite barriers to direct government influence.

Private Control

Finally, there are a vast variety of control systems in which control is essentially in private hands, even though it is exercised subject to the laws and regulations of various governmental agencies. Private control systems, discussed in detail below, range from individual ownership, where one person owns a newspaper or radio or television station, through ownership by huge corporate conglomerates.

Concern About Media Control

One reason for concern about media control and ownership is expressed in the old adage that "He who pays the piper calls the tune." If the "wrong" social forces assume control of media output, they acquire power to shape politics and public opinion. Someone who fears government and its policies would disapprove of direct operation of the media by government and be leery about government control of privately operated media. Someone else who is afraid of the business ethics of private individuals would not want media control in private hands or subject to the direct influence of large corporate enterprises.

Public policy issues raised by the debate over the merits of public or private ownership of television illustrate the pros and cons. Control by government is apt to be single-minded and political, judging from most government-controlled systems throughout the world. France, Israel, and Sweden furnish examples. However, Britain's experiences with operating radio and television through the British Broadcasting Corporation (BBC) show that governments can, if they wish, set up systems where programming is reasonably free from direct political interference.

Big business control over television, if divided among various large corporations, is likely to bring more conflicting interests into play than is true for government control. For instance, a conglomerate heavily involved in export industries will not share the views on tariffs of a conglomerate interested primarily in domestic manufacturing. Even within conglomerates, the interests of various components may clash, thus moderating the stands of the general management and lessening the chances that business interests will dominate programming.

While there is more chance for countervailing pressures in the business setting than in government, when it comes to support for controversial policies, the pressures springing from profit considerations are well-nigh irresistible under business control. Governments are free from such pressure because they can use tax money to finance whatever programs they deem in the public interest. Although they must consider internal power struggles, they do not need to concern themselves with the size of their audiences. Private owners do, because their income depends on small fees from audiences or on large fees from advertisers and other sponsors. The latter want to attract large numbers of viewers, particularly those in the 18-to-49-year age group who hold the bulk of purchasing power. Mass appeal, rather than any social or cultural concerns, becomes the primary consideration.

Given the pros and cons of government and business control, which is the better system? The answer depends on one's assessment of the motivations of the public and private sector, and one's beliefs about the proper role of the media. In today's America, when distrust of government is high, and people view "Big Media" as a counterfoil to "Big Government," private control is the option preferred by most people. In terms of programming, the choice of this option means that the bulk of television fare will be geared to simple, emotion-laden programming that attracts large, diverse audiences. It also means shying away from controversial or troublesome issues that may arouse opposition, reduce media audiences, diminish advertising revenues, and possibly be rejected for broadcast by network-affiliated stations.

While such programming draws the wrath of many people, particularly among intellectual elites, one can argue that their disdain constitutes intellectual snobbery. Who is to say that the mass public's tastes are inferior to those of elites? The argument that people would choose educational programs over fluffy entertainment, if they had the chance, can also be refuted easily. Proof is plentiful that the mass public does indeed choose light entertainment over more serious information. In the print news field, for example, magazines specializing in sex or violence far outsell journals that treat political and social issues seriously. Movies featuring sex or violence attract huge crowds willing to pay heavily in time and money to be exposed to heinous crimes and explicit sex.

Related to the concerns about domination of the media by government or private business interests is the fear of undue concentration of power. Diversity of ownership presumably encourages the expression of a wide variety of views, which, to many Americans, is the essence of democracy. There must be a wide open marketplace into which ideas and opinions flow freely. But there is no agreement on how great diversity of ownership must be to assure this adequate flow of information and the opportunity for freedom of expression. The American public appears to be more concerned about concentration of media ownership in comparatively few hands than about control of media by private enterprise. Social reformers, on the other hand, are more concerned about business control, claiming that it leads to catering to cheap mass tastes.

PATTERNS OF PRIVATE OWNERSHIP

The facts about media control patterns are relatively simple to explain. But there is much disagreement about their consequences. The overarching feature in the United States is that media control is predominantly in private hands. This may mean small or big business interests, labor groups, religious or ethnic organizations, or any other type of interest represented in American society.

Business Configurations

The general trend in America toward business combinations is strongly evident in the media business. There are *independents,* of course, individuals or corporations that run a single media enterprise and nothing else. The small-town publisher who owns one newspaper or radio or television station is an example. However, their numbers are on the decline.

Multiple owners have become increasingly common. These are individuals or corporations who own several media of the same type — several radio stations, several newspapers, or several television stations. Since there are fewer than 2,000 daily newspapers in the entire United States and fewer than 5,000 AM and 4,000 FM radio stations and fewer than 600 commercial VHF television stations, one may question whether a chain of 20 or 30 of these media ought to be controlled by one owner.[7] However, this has been the trend.

Even more common than the trend toward multiple owners has been the trend toward *cross-media ownership.* This involves ownership by an individual or corporation of a combination of several media, such as newspapers and television stations, or newspapers and radio stations. This ownership pattern is of most concern when one owner controls a variety of media in the same location. For instance, the same person might own a town's newspaper, television, and radio station. This would mean that one owner controlled all information sources.

A fourth pattern encompasses *conglomerates.* Conglomerates are individuals or corporations who own media enterprises along with other types of businesses. Radio Corporation of America (RCA) is an example. Figure 2-1 illustrates how diverse RCA's interests are. Those who are wary about the public-mindedness of large corporations fear that their business interests may color their news policies. If, for instance, there is a soundly based demand to reduce the defense establishment, or to oppose construction of a missile system, the management of a conglomerate like RCA, which holds many defense contracts, may not examine these questions open-mindedly.

In major urban centers, most media are owned by individuals or corporations who fall into the multiple-owner, cross-media, and conglomerate classifications. In Chicago, for instance, this holds true of

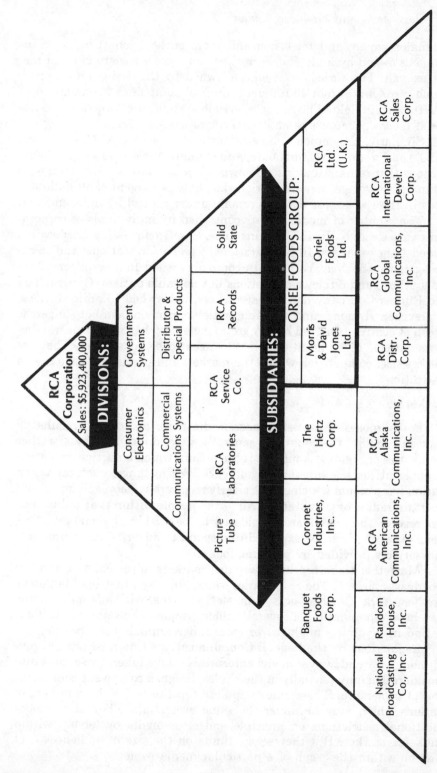

Figure 2-1. The Diverse Holdings of RCA

all major papers and television and radio outlets. The *Chicago Sun-Times* is owned by Field Enterprises, which owns a variety of other media as well. The *Chicago Tribune* is owned by the Tribune Company, which owns more than 40 different kinds of companies inside and outside the media field. The major television stations are owned by the national television networks and the *Tribune* conglomerate.

Similarly, the major radio stations are owned by ABC, CBS, and NBC, the *Tribune*, Westinghouse, and similar conglomerates. The radio stations that remain under single ownership are mostly very small with comparatively weak signals. Nationwide, only 24 percent of all radio stations in the 100 largest markets remain under control by independents.

The number of media outlets controlled by individuals or corporations varies widely. In 1977, for instance, Cox Broadcasting Corporation owned 17 newspapers, 10 radio stations, 5 television stations, and 36 cable systems; the *New York Times* company owned 15 newspapers, 2 radio stations, and 6 television stations but no cable outlets. General Tire and Rubber Company had no newspapers, but owned 13 radio stations, 4 television stations, and 42 cable outlets.[8] But one cannot judge the sweep of control exercised by any group merely by looking at the number of its outlets. Three additional factors need to be considered. They are market size, competition within the market, and prestige of each media institution.

Market Size

For purposes of assessing mass media performance and regulating electronic media, the country is generally divided into "markets" rather than states or regions. A market is the area in which a particular station or paper attracts a substantial audience. For instance, each television station has a signal which can be clearly received by people living within a certain radius of that station. All of the people within that radius who can receive the signal are considered to be within the market. This means that they can be expected to respond to advertising for products and services provided by program sponsors.

Altogether there are 400 newspaper markets in the country and 230 broadcast markets. Their size varies widely. In major metropolitan areas like New York, Chicago, or Los Angeles, a market with a 50-mile radius may have a population of several million people. The same radius for a station in Wyoming might cover more range animals than people.

Regulations by the Federal Communications Commission, the government's watchdog over media enterprises,[9] have taken these facts into consideration only partially in their rules designed to prevent concentration of ownership. These rules stipulate top limits for the numbers of stations which may be under the same ownership. They also impose additional restrictions on multiple and cross-media ownership within the same market. But they set no limits on the size of audiences that may be within the reach of a particular media owner.

In the mid-1970s the FCC limited owners to seven AM radio stations, seven FM radio stations, and seven television stations, of which no more than five could be regular wave length (VHF).[10] This meant that in the electronic field, it was possible for an owner to be in 21 different markets, each reaching the homes of millions of people. At present, three out of every four television stations in the 100 most densely populated markets, which serve 87 percent of the nation's households, belong to multiple owner groups.

For newspapers, there are no limits to the numbers of markets that may be entered. More than 60 percent of America's daily papers, boasting 72 percent of total circulation, are controlled by national and regional chains. There are more than 150 such chains, but the majority control fewer than 10 papers. In the mid-1970s, Gannett was the leader with 73 dailies, followed by Thompson (57), Knight-Ridder (34), Walls (32), and Newhouse (30). In circulation figures, Knight-Ridder was tops at 3,725,000 papers per day, each reaching several readers. It was followed by Newhouse (3,530,000), the Chicago Tribune Company (2,995,000), and Gannett (2,940,000).[11] The ten largest chains accounted for approximately one-third of the total daily newspaper circulation in the United States. This means that one-third of the papers read in the United States on any given day transmit news screened by personnel from only ten large business enterprises. Projections of present consolidation trends could make this two-thirds well before the end of the century. While individual papers within chains generally enjoy editorial page autonomy, they do tend to be more uniform in political endorsements than independently owned papers.[12]

Influence is even more concentrated for television. Three huge conglomerate-owned networks, NBC, CBS, and ABC, each own five television stations with a combined audience of roughly 100 million people. The parent companies, RCA, the Columbia Broadcasting System, and the American Broadcasting System, owned other media enterprises such as recording companies, publishing houses, movie theaters, and radio and television equipment and supply companies, as well as such unrelated ventures as real estate firms, car-rental companies, food supply houses, and home furnishing manufacturers.

The networks specialize in the production of television and radio programs. Unlike other owners of large numbers of radio and television stations, they are not directly under FCC control because production of programs is not deemed part of the regulated broadcasting business.[13] However, the broadcast stations which each network owns are within the regulatory reach of the FCC, as are the "affiliates" — stations that regularly subscribe to the programs produced by a network.

The 15 network-owned television stations are in the largest media markets. This means New York, Chicago, and Los Angeles for all three networks, supplemented variously by Philadelphia, Washington, D.C., St. Louis, Detroit, and San Francisco. In addition to controlling programming for its five wholly owned stations, each network also supplies the bulk of programming for its affiliates. Since the vast majority of commercial stations are network affiliated (roughly 550 affiliates to 90 independents), most televised information reaching 85 percent of the country's households is subject to choices and decisions made by network personnel. In addition, networks also control radio outlets domestically as well as radio and television stations abroad. To keep these figures in proper perspective, one must keep in mind that the three networks compete vigorously with each other for public favor.

The capstone to the picture of tightly held control over information is supplied by the wire service companies. A huge share of the news stories appearing in nearly every paper in the country, and featured on television or radio news, comes from the wires of the Associated Press and United Press International. The roots of these two organizations go back to 1848 when six New York newspapers formed a cooperative association to share the cost of collecting foreign news. Out of this initial effort grew huge organizations that employ reporters scattered throughout the world to collect and report news. News stories and bulletins are then transmitted electronically to subscriber papers, radio, and television stations. Practically every news source (99 percent) in the United States that disseminates news daily is served by either AP or UPI, or both. In addition, there are a handful of other wire services, such as those operated by the *New York Times,* the *Los Angeles Times,* and the *Chicago Tribune,* which have a more limited clientele of subscribers.

News stories and bulletins supplied by the wire services are used either verbatim by their clients or rewritten. Depending on the resources available to a particular news organization for gathering and writing its own news, the proportion of wire service stories used directly, or in rewritten form, may vary from less than 10 percent to 80 percent or more of all stories. For many newspapers, a look at the mix of stories carried by wire services on any particular day will accurately foretell the mix of stories carried by the paper.[14] Wire service stories tend to predominate for foreign news and even for national news for smaller papers and stations that cannot afford their own correspondents. This means that a large share of news production in the United States is dominated by two giant news producing companies. However, it is worth emphasizing that none of the situations of limited competition which we have discussed involves monopoly controls. Even in one-newspaper towns, there is usually some intermedia competition in the news supply.

Intramarket Competition

To preserve competition within each market, FCC rules now prohibit cross-media ownership within the same market. However, this rule does not affect most radio and television combinations existing prior to 1970 or newspaper and broadcast media combinations existing before

1975. To reduce dominance by the networks, the FCC also mandates that in markets with more than three television or radio broadcast stations, at least one of each three must be reserved for owners who are not affiliated with any network.

Despite efforts to increase intramarket competition, near-monopoly (oligopoly) conditions prevail in the majority of markets. Electronic media are generally owned in pairs, limiting the total number of media owners in the community. Intramarket newspaper competition has also become rare. In 97 percent of all American cities, there is only one daily newspaper. Newspaper competition continues in the largest cities, but their populations constitute less than a third of the total United States population. The birth of a number of suburban dailies in a few major cities has not substantially altered the situation. In addition to a monopoly over local print news, paper owners frequently own a local television or radio station as well. However, the FCC has forced newspapers to relinquish broadcast properties whenever the combination enjoyed a total monopoly within the market.

Prestige Leadership

A further reason for homogeneity in news supply is the fact that there is wide agreement among journalists about the nature of "news" and the elements of good reporting. Just as there are widely accepted standards of professionalism in law or medicine or engineering, so there are norms in journalism that members of the profession learn to accept. As part of this system of norms, certain members and products are widely accepted as models, whose influence reaches far beyond their own organization. Critics call this the "jackal syndrome" or "pack journalism."[15] In the political news field, the *New York Times* is the "lion" whom the jackals follow. In television, Walter Cronkite or David Brinkley are models for the profession. Other news professionals watch what information these sources present, how they present it, and what interpretations they give to it, and often adjust their presentations accordingly.[16]

Small Business versus Big Business Control

In the private sector, there has been a steady trend towards consolidation, placing control of information into an increasingly limited number of organizations. As we shall point out in Chapter 3, economic factors are largely responsible. Worldwide news gathering and production of television programs are very expensive. Only large, well-financed organizations, which can spread the costs over many customers, can provide the type of lavish programming to which the American public has become accustomed.[17]

Is it sound public policy to allow the rapid pace of consolidation of media enterprises to continue? Aside from the issue of concentration of control in too few hands, policymakers have expressed fears that central-ized control may mean neglect of local needs.[18] The evidence, however, does not support this fear. The same holds true for evidence that the me-dia giants suppress anti-business news and stress anti-labor, pro-Repub-lican, and pro-war stories. It is true that many important stories are not published and some of them would be poor publicity for big business. But there is no hard evidence that the choices that must be made to cope with an oversupply of news are dictated by narrow self-interest.[19] In fact, many recent broadcasts, movies, magazines, and newspaper fea-tures have carried stories critical of business.

Similarly, the charge that business interests are responsible for the general support by media personnel of the existing political system is not borne out. It seems much more likely that American journalists in large organizations, like their colleagues in small, independently owned enterprises, are interested in appealing to their audiences and so reflect the values of mainstream American society. All of this does not prove that pro-business bias is nonexistent, but it raises some doubts about its nature and extent.[20]

What about the argument that small, individually owned enter-prises would produce better programming, more suited to local needs? One way to test this assertion is to compare the amount of news and other public service programs offered by various types of television sta-tions. Such a comparison shows that, by and large, such programming has been more plentiful on stations owned by big business and by conglomerates than on privately owned stations.[21] Network stations do best of all. The story is quite similar in the newspaper field. Here the pa-pers selected as best in public service coverage by professional journal-ists generally are papers controlled by large business enterprises.

The contention that individually owned stations provide poorer public service than their conglomerate cousins is subject to some res-ervations. The measures of public service programming used by the FCC and most media studies are primarily quantitative. They gauge how much broadcasting time is spent on certain kinds of programs, but do not analyze the quality of programming. However, it is quite plausible that big business control actually means qualitatively superior pro-grams. Larger enterprises are able to absorb the losses which are often incurred in the production of documentaries and public service pro-grams. They have more talent and money available to spend on re-search, investigations, and costly entertainment shows.

In 1975, it cost $800,000 to produce a two-hour movie for television. Half-hour broadcasts of the *Mary Tyler Moore Show* or *All in the Fam-ily,* shown twice, came to roughly $150,000. Peter Falk, the star of *Columbo,* received $100,000 for each episode. The right to broadcast NFL games came to $60 million yearly. Price tags for most documentaries were comparable. Production costs since 1975 have continued to rise by 8 percent annually.

The evidence presented thus far indicates that some of the arguments made against big business control of media are exaggerated. So are some of the arguments made in favor of control by small enterprises. When FCC rules have forced smaller stations to spend some of their time on non-network programs, the results generally have been poor. Unable to afford costly original programs produced locally, these stations have filled their non-network hours with cheap canned movies or syndicated quiz or talent shows. The arguments cannot be settled definitively until more thorough comparisons of the quality of programs have been made. In the meantime, it is important to recognize that present policies designed to reduce media concentration and encourage local programming rest on questionable assumptions.

CURBS ON PRIVATE CONTROL OF THE MEDIA

FCC Regulations

Even though control over media offerings is largely in private hands in the United States, the federal government regulates some aspects of media management. The chief control agency is the Federal Communications Commission (FCC), a seven-member bipartisan body appointed by the president with Senate approval. In theory, the commission is an independent regulatory body. In practice, congressional pursestrings, industry pressures, and presidential control over appointment of new members, including naming the chairman, have gravely curtailed its independence. The commission's authority is also weakened because its rulings can be appealed to the courts and have been overturned on a number of occasions.

The FCC's primary area of responsibility is control over the electronic media. The print media are essentially uncontrolled, except for antitrust and monopoly laws which have been used by the Justice Department to curtail print media monopolies. However, economically weak newspapers are permitted to combine their business and production facilities, free from these restraints, as long as their news and editorial processes remain separate.

FCC control takes four forms: (1) rules limiting the number of stations subject to control by a single organization; (2) examination of goals and performance of stations as part of triannual licensing; (3) rules mandating public service and local interest programs; and (4) rules to guarantee fair treatment to individuals and protect their rights. The FCC's record of enforcing these rules, which represent major public policies, has earned it the reputation of being a benign and ineffective watchdog at best, and an industry-kept lap dog at worst.

Rules Limiting Station Ownership. As indicated earlier, to prevent high concentrations of media ownership and assure diversity of information sources, the FCC limits the number of stations which television and radio owners may control. It does not limit the number of households which may be within the range of any one group of owners. Consequently, while most media chains reach only a small percentage of the nation's homes, the ten largest groups each command an audience of more than 5 million households, each with three to six people. This gives each owner a chance to dominate the radio or TV information supply of up to 30 million people, nearly a sixth of the nation.

Since 1970, the FCC has also had a one-to-a-customer rule that prohibits any party from acquiring more than one AM and FM radio station or more than one television station in the same market. The rule has led to greater dispersion of station ownership, but has not required the break-up of existing groups which violate the one-to-a-customer rule. Similar rules restrict newspaper-television or newspaper-radio combinations. About one-third of all groups with television interests still have newspaper properties. Many of these were bought at the urging of the FCC, who thought at one time that this type of combination would lead to better news services. Late in 1977, in anticipation of rules forcing the divestiture of properties in the same market, several owners arranged swaps of properties. For instance, the *Washington Post* and *Detroit News* arranged to exchange television stations so that the *Post* would own a Detroit station and the *News* a Washington station.

Station owners are very eager to retain their licenses. Station ownership is usually enormously profitable. Moreover, no investment is required to get a license originally. Stations in top markets yield millions of dollars in advertising revenues and profits. For instance, *TV Digest* reports that ABC's pretax profits in 1976 from its five stations amounted to $72 million. CBS earned $45 million from its five stations and NBC earned $41 million. These figures do not include profits earned from programs provided to affiliates. Licenses of profitable stations can be sold for a high price since the demand exceeds supply. Many buyers represent chains which are eager to enlarge their reach so that they can guarantee an audience of many million households to their advertisers.

The FCC rarely uses its major power — refusal of license renewal at the end of three years — to lessen ownership concentration. It did so in 1969 in a case that involved a Boston television station, WHDH-TV, which was owned by a local newspaper company which also operated two local radio stations and held a controlling interest in a cable television company. The FCC decided to award the license to a competitor, Boston Broadcasting Inc., controlled by a citizens' group. It was the first time that a license had been awarded to a competing applicant in a case involving the media concentration issue. The decision shocked the media industry because it threatened loss of lucrative licenses even when a station had done its job well. Senator John O. Pastore, then chairman of the Senate Communications Subcommittee, expressed fear that license withdrawal might henceforth be used capriciously for political reasons.

His efforts finally led to new FCC rules which nearly guarantee license renewal to stations if they perform their job satisfactorily.

Licensing as Performance Control. What does satisfactory performance entail? The Communications Act of 1934 stipulates that television and radio must "serve the public interest, convenience, and necessity." But beyond requiring that broadcasters must ascertain the needs and interests of a community by talking with its leaders, there are no prescriptions for interpreting these guidelines. This leaves a great deal of leeway to the media and the FCC to determine what types of programs serve these goals. In applying the rules, the FCC has looked at the mix of various types of programs, the proportion of public service offerings, and the inclusion of programs geared to the needs and interests of selected community groups. It has not scrutinized the subject matter of broadcasts in detail.

This hands-off attitude has applied both to ordering broadcasting of certain information and to curtailing its dissemination. For instance, the FCC declined a viewer's request to order stations to provide information about Russian and Chinese political and military activities in North Korea. The viewer had argued that the American public needed this information to put reports about U.S. military activities in Southeast Asia into perspective. Similarly, despite concerted public lobbying, the FCC would not order the networks to delay programming unsuitable for children until late evening and reserve the early evening broadcast hours for "family" programs. However, the FCC let it be known that it would not prevent the industry from instituting such a plan on its own.

Through its licensing of new outlets, the FCC has tried to ensure that a new licensee will meet the needs of a different socioeconomic group of people than those already served by existing stations in the area. But once a license has been granted, the owners hold it for good, and may even sell it with little government intervention. If a station fulfills the requirements of public service broadcasting, does not engage in discriminatory or fraudulent practices, and there are few or no complaints about poor programming, renewal has been automatic.

Since the 1970s, numerous civic groups have entered renewal hearings to protest the type of programming which a particular station has offered or omitted. As a result of such pressures, the FCC has reluctantly withdrawn licenses from a few stations over the years. These withdrawals have made broadcasters more careful than in the past to avoid practices that might arouse public opposition.

Compared to regulatory agencies in other countries, even Western Europe, Canada, and Australia, the FCC controls with a very light ahnd. It could, if it wished, define what constitutes "programming in the public interest." It would be more rigorous about enforcing its rulings and verifying station performance records at license renewal time. The threat of license withdrawal for rule violations could be used as a much more powerful deterrent to misbehavior and lever to control programming than is true now. Part of the problem is that the FCC staff is much too small to cope with all the duties assigned to the agency. In fact, it is chronically behind schedule even for routine matters, such as its annual reports.

Public Service and Local Programming. The FCC has stipulated the minimum amount of time which ought to be devoted to public service programs. Under the 5-5-10 rule, 5 percent of programming should be for local affairs, 5 percent for news and public affairs, and 10 percent for nonentertainment programs. Beyond checking a station's log to ascertain that it records the minimum amount of public service programming, the FCC does not examine the nature of programs which the station labels as "public service." Most stations' logs exceed the stipulated amount.

To assure that stations leave some time for programs of interest to local communities, the FCC also requires that one prime time hour between 7 and 11 P.M. be set aside for non-network programs. However, under the "Prime Time Access Rule," stations may fill all or part of the local programming slot with network news or public affairs programs, documentaries, or children's shows. The Prime Time Access Rule has not worked out very well in practice because, as discussed earlier, most stations find it too costly to produce original programs.

Fair Treatment Rules. The FCC has also made rules about access to the airways for candidates for political office and for people who have been the subject of media attacks. These types of controls are discussed in Chapter 4.

The Decontrol Debate. The fact that the restrictions which the FCC has imposed on broadcast media do not apply to the print media has raised a good deal of controversy in recent years. The argument that such restrictions are justified because access to the airwaves is limited has been contested.[22] In light of new technical developments, such as cable television and communications satellites, the number of broadcasts that can reach the average American has been vastly expanded. Whereas competition among broadcasters has been rising, it has been falling among daily newspapers. The average American is generally limited to one local newspaper. The high cost of starting a newspaper (and a finite advertising pool) discourages would-be competitors. Some contend, therefore, that television and radio are far more competitive than the unregulated newspaper business, and so, the argument goes, should be freed of all controls.

This type of argument has been quite prominent in the debates surrounding efforts to revise the Communications Act of 1934. It led the House of Representatives Communications Subcommittee under the chairmanship of Representative Lionel Van Deerlin of California to come up with a plan to remove nearly all the controls under which radio and television stations now operate. Under this 1979 plan, the fair treatment provisions would be totally eliminated, except in local elections, on the theory that sufficient electronic media outlets exist to cancel out unfairness by any single outlet. Stations would still be expected to treat controversial public issues equitably and to provide news, public affairs programs, and locally produced programs throughout the broadcast day. But competition of the marketplace, rather than government rules, would be the regulatory mechanism.

The potential use of licensing as a tool to force broadcasters to conform to government policies would also be restricted under the new legislation. Cable television would be completely free from federal licensing controls at the federal level. Radio licenses would be granted indefinitely, subject to revocation only for violation of law. Television licenses would vest indefinitely after 10 years, after two initial five-year licensing terms. New licenses would be awarded by lottery with a top limit of five radio and five television stations for any group or individual owner.

Under this plan, licensees would pay fees based on the value of advertising accounts in the station's market. This income would support public television, subsidize minority ownership of stations, provide rural telecommunications development, and defray the costs of telecommunications regulations. Public broadcast stations, whose programs would be federally financed, would be prohibited from accepting any private funding, thus freeing them from all commercial pressures.

Opponents to extensive deregulation consolidated their forces behind another bill, introduced by Democratic Senator Ernest Hollings of South Carolina. Under this bill, radio would be deregulated, but most of the restrictions presently imposed on television would remain in force. Like the Van Deerlin proposal, the Hollings bill would impose a fee on radio and television licensees for use of the broadcast spectrum.

The future of such legislative proposals is cloudy. They are opposed in whole or in part by industry lobbies, public interest groups, and representatives of public television. But even though such bills have rough legislative sailing, the trends towards deregulation that they represent are strong enough to find expression in the rules and regulations issued by the FCC, if it remains in control. For instance, Charles Ferris, appointed as chairman of the FCC in 1977, has said that he prefers the rule of market forces over government regulation. He favors "zero-based" regulations under which the slate of existing regulations would periodically be wiped clean and their merits reconsidered. Diversity, he believes, should be attained through increasing the number of stations rather than by government fiat. Likewise, fairness and sound programming should be achieved through audience pressure against stations, networks and advertisers, rather than through government regulations. Other FCC commissioners have also voiced support for such views.

Control by Industry Associations

Several other forms of mass media control need to be considered briefly. Among these are *industry lobbies*. Radio and television interests, especially the networks and their affiliated stations, are active lobbyists. Most belong to the National Association of Broadcasters (NAB), a powerful Washington lobby. It has a membership of nearly 5,000 radio and television stations and a staff of more than 100 people. The networks have additional lobbying agents in Washington. They are in continuous contact with the FCC and are particularly concerned about any efforts made to curb the freedom networks now enjoy in programming.

Besides the NAB, there are a number of other trade associations that also engage in lobbying, often at cross-purposes to each other. For newspapers, the American Newspaper Publishers Association (ANPA) is one of the most prominent. These associations try to influence appointments to the FCC and to establish industry control over new technology that threatens to alter established practices. The networks, for instance, through their lobbying efforts, have tried to stifle cable television and to acquire control over domestic satellites.

To forestall regulation by outside bodies, the industry has also developed mechanisms for self-control. The NAB has had a radio code since 1929 and a television code since 1952 which set forth rules on program content and form. Both codes have been modernized periodically.

The impact of the codes has been limited. They apply only to NAB member stations that choose to subscribe to them. In 1977, for instance, 25 percent of all TV stations were not NAB members and nearly half of the members did not subscribe to the codes.[23] Penalties for code violations are minimal. The worst penalty is withdrawal of a station's right to list itself as a subscriber to the code. Therefore, the code exerts only a limited amount of moral pressure on the industry. It also serves to blunt demands by pressure groups for government intervention to set and enforce standards.

Somewhat stronger pressures on program content arose in the 1970s from advertisers who actually withdrew their commercials from programs they considered obscene or excessively violent. Sears Roebuck was one of the earliest and largest to do so. Others, like Procter and Gamble, the top television advertiser in the nation, retained consultants to seek out acceptable programs and avoid unacceptable ones. In the wake of such pressures, there was a temporary drop in the number of programs featuring violence, particularly during prime time hours. There is deep concern, however, that advertisers, spurred by pressure groups, could become unofficial censors like the anticommunist black lists of the 1950s which led to dismissals of performers suspected of having left-wing orientations. Examples of what might be in store were cancellation by General Motors of sponsorship of an Eastertime program on the life of Jesus, because of objections from evangelist groups, and crippling withdrawals of advertising from a CBS documentary on gun control and from a series of interviews featuring ex-president Nixon. The gun control lobby and Nixon foes originated these pressures.

Citizen Control

Various citizen lobbies have also tried to gain some control over broadcasting. One of the most influential is the National Citizens' Committee for Broadcasting, headed by former FCC Commissioner Nicholas Johnson. He has been one of the most articulate and influential critics of the shallowness of broadcasting and the weakness of government control. The FCC, Johnson has said, is a sleeping lapdog rather than a working watchdog.

Citizen efforts to influence the quality of broadcasting began in earnest in 1966 when the Office of Communication of the United Church of Christ, a public interest lobby, was allowed by the FCC to challenge the renewal of a TV license for a Jackson, Mississippi station, WLBT-TV, on the grounds that the station had discriminated against black viewers.[24] Blacks then constituted 45 percent of the Jackson population. The challenge failed, but it was the beginning of efforts by many other citizen groups to challenge license renewals.

" ... AND IF ANY STATION SHOWS PROGRAMS NOT APPROVED OF BY THE PTA, THIS SET WILL AUTOMATICALLY SELF-DESTRUCT ! "

Reprinted, courtesy of the *Chicago Tribune*

Success finally came in 1975 when the FCC refused to renew licenses of eight educational TV stations in Alabama and failed to grant a construction permit for a ninth station because citizen groups had charged racial discrimination in employment at these stations and in access by blacks to programs.[25] Since then, numerous stations have yielded to citizen pressure for increased minority employment and programming.

In addition to the more than 60 organizations concerned exclusively with media reform, other organizations, such as the Parent Teacher Association, National Organization for Women, and the American Medical Association have lobbied on a variety of media issues. These include concern about coverage, stereotyping, access to the media and to media employment and ownership, advertising on children's programs, and enforcement of existing program regulations. The groups' tactics include monitoring of media content, publicizing the findings, and direct pressure on broadcasters, advertisers, media audiences, and government control agencies. For instance, protest by PTA members led to advertiser pressures, which helped to reduce the number of violent programs shown in the early evening hours. Legal activities range from challenges to license renewals to damage suits for the harmful effects of media content.[26]

It is difficult to assess the precise influence of these organizations, either individually or collectively, because many of their goals overlap with each other and with other forces that affect media policy. It seems defensible to argue, nonetheless, that the causes for which they have worked have prospered over the years, and that part of the credit belongs to them. It also seems fair to say that these groups have a long road to travel before they can match the clout and resources enjoyed by the broadcast lobby and by public officials involved in media control.[27]

CONTROL BY MEDIA PERSONNEL

Thus far we have discussed the influence of government, media owners, associations, and audiences over media output. We now turn to the influence of the people who actually produce the news and entertainment programs: reporters, writers, editors, producers, and the like. They control the specific stories that become "news." As William Small puts it: "This is the rubbing point, the actual confrontation with what is happening. It is also the point of greatest influence."[28] What determines their choices and shapes the flow of news and entertainment?

We will employ three approaches to answer this question. First, there is personality theory, which explains newspeople's professional behavior in terms of personality and social background factors. A second approach is organization theory. Since newspeople operate within news production organizations, this approach seeks to explain their behavior by examining organizational pressures and goals. Lastly, one can seek clues to the influence that media personnel exercise in role theory. Depending on the professional role conceptions which media personnel adopt, the products will vary. For instance, journalists who take a libertarian approach to the news will behave differently from those who take a social responsibility approach.

Background and Personality Factors. Factors known to influence occupational performance include social background qualities (which may be shared by large groups of people of similar backgrounds) and traits that are idiosyncratic to particular individuals. Examples of background factors are level of education, race, and sex. Their impact on professional orientations is often a matter of heated scientific and political controversy. Idiosyncratic factors include artistic tastes, emotional outlook, and intellectual interests. Idiosyncratic factors explain why different newspeople will choose one story over another or will give a different emphasis to the same news story or entertainment plot. Personality factors and organizational logic intertwine, with the latter setting the broad boundaries of what is acceptable news.

What are some of the personality and background factors that influence the substance and shape of news? To answer this question, we shall present data collected by John Johnstone, Edward Slawski, and William Bowman for their study *The Newspeople*.[29] Other studies support these findings, which are based on telephone interviews with roughly 1,300 newspeople randomly selected in Canada and the United States.[30] The sample was divided into two groups — one comprised of journalists working in "prominent" news organizations such as the major networks, big city newspapers, and wire service organizations; the other included newspeople from small towns and relatively little-known news enterprises. The sample was further divided into supervisory (42 percent) and nonsupervisory (58 percent) personnel.

As shown in Table 2-1, Johnstone, Slawski, and Bowman found that the social profile of newspeople closely resembled the profile of self-employed male professionals in the U.S. The majority of newspeople everywhere were upper-middle class in training and background, with the political and social views prevalent among intellectuals who are part of that class. Generally speaking, this held true to a greater degree among newspeople in larger, more prestigious organizations, which often set the standards for what is considered high-quality news and entertainment. In the group working for prominent organizations, 66 percent of the executives had fathers who were professionals, managers, or business executives; 59 percent of the staffers likewise came from middle- and upper-middle class homes. In the less prominent organizations 46 percent of the executives and 48 percent of the staffers came from middle class homes. Comparable figures for the general population were 18 percent.

In 1971, the year of the survey, none of the executives in the prominent media were black. At the staff level, blacks constituted 4 percent.

Table 2-1 Selected Characteristics of Journalists

Characteristic	Prominent Organizations		Nonprominent Organizations	
	Executives (N=404)*	Staffers (N=828)	Executives (N=1,816)	Staffers (N=2,247)
Father with professional/ managerial job	66%	59%	46%	48%
Black race	0	4	6	3
Female sex	9	22	14	27
College graduate	75	80	55	50
Democrats	44	43	31	35
Republicans	9	16	32	28
Independents	45	34	31	32
Other	3	7	7	5
Left-leaning	73	53	29	41
Middle roaders	27	30	47	41
Right-leaning	10	17	5	3

* Bases are weighted.
SOURCE: John Johnstone, Edward Slawski and William Bowman, *The Newspeople* (Urbana, Ill.: University of Illinois Press, 1976), pp. 225-226.

In the less prominent organizations, 6 percent of the executives and 3 percent of the staffers were black. Most of them worked for organizations serving the black community. Seven years later, little had changed. Only 1 percent of the personnel in the print media were black. In broadcasting, the figure was 7 percent.

Blacks, Hispanics, and Asian-Americans, who constituted 14 percent of the population in 1978, owned less than 1 percent of radio and television stations (69 of 8,169 radio stations and 1 of 965 TV stations). This was true despite federal efforts to bring ownership more in line with the demographic composition of the country on the assumption that a heterogeneous country is best served by a diversity of media owners and staff. If minorities are uniquely qualified to assess the needs of their own groups, racial and ethnic underrepresentation is undesirable.

Likewise, if balanced presentation of information requires that media organizations have women staffers in proportion to their numbers, the media do not measure up. In the prominent organizations, women made up 9 percent of the executives and 22 percent of the staff. In the nonprominent media, 14 percent of the executives and 27 percent of the staffers were women. Newspeople are also generally younger, more urbanized, and have greater job mobility than the general population.

What effect do these characteristics have on the news product? The evidence does not allow us to make definite claims. It may be debatable, as well, whether media organizations need to be a microcosm of the larger society. Nevertheless, there appear to be certain connections between the product and the demographic characteristics of the personnel. There is, for example, emphasis on established white middle class groups and values, to the neglect of minority and poor people. There is also stress on urban, rather than rural, affairs, and a heavy dose of primarily male-dominated sports. These patterns do suggest that news output reflects reporters' backgrounds.[31]

Like other professionals, newspeople have far more formal education than the general population. In the group working for prominent organizations, 75 percent of the executives and 80 percent of the staffers were college graduates, as were 35 percent of the executives and 50 percent of the staffers in the less prominent organizations. Newspeople without college degrees usually had received no professional training as journalists and so were less likely to have been exposed to social responsibility attitudes so prevalent on American college campuses. When asked about their professional goals, they were more likely to stress neutral reporting of facts, rather than interpretation and social advocacy. In fact, Johnstone and his associates found that education was the single most important factor among background characteristics which affect newspeople's general philosophy of reporting. People with more schooling were more liberal and more social-responsibility oriented.

Only a very small percentage of the working press in prominent news organizations were Republicans. Among executives, 44 percent were Democrats, 45 percent were Independents, and 8.5 percent were Republicans. Among the staffers, 43 percent were Democrats, 34 percent were Independents, and 16 percent were Republicans. The rest had other affiliations. Comparable figures for the general population were 40 percent Democrats, 34 percent Independents and 23 percent Republicans. Surprisingly, executives showed fewer Republican leanings than staffers. The large numbers who called themselves "Independents" were more likely to lean in a Democratic than a Republican direction.

These data on party affiliation show that media owners, although they themselves usually share the Republican leanings of the big business community, hire Democrats and liberal Independents to operate their media properties. The political orientations of the personnel frequently are reflected in the overall tone of the media. Economic and social liberalism prevails, as does a preference for an internationalist foreign policy, caution about military intervention, and some suspicion about the ethics of established large institutions, particularly the government. However, in deference to the greater conservatism of media audiences, reporters claim that they restrain their liberalism somewhat.[32] Media personnel do take meticulous care to treat the major parties evenly and fairly in election campaign coverage. Such evenhandedness may spring from anticipation of scrutiny and criticism in this area. Bias has rarely been investigated in less sensitive subject areas, so we do not fully know in which topic areas biased coverage is a problem.[33]

Among the nonprominent media, the patterns of party affiliation and political leanings were different. The executives' affiliations were split in nearly even thirds; 31 percent were Democrats, 32 percent were Republicans, and 31 percent were Independents. Among the staffers, 35 percent were Democrats, 32 percent were Independents, and 28 percent were Republicans. The rest were otherwise affiliated. This distribution, with its substantially larger share of Republicans, mirrors rural, small-town politics in many sections of the country. A circular effect seems to be at work: people in small towns perpetuate their more conservative outlook because their media, taking their cues from the audience, are comparatively conservative. However, the strength of Republican influence is less than appears on the surface because the majority of Independents lean towards the Democrats.

When newspeople were asked about their general political orientations, 63 percent of the executives in prominent organizations said they leaned toward the left as did 53 percent of their staff. In contrast to this strong left-ward orientation, only 28 percent of the executives in nonprominent organizations leaned left. Among staffers, the figure was 41 percent. While these political orientations are muted by organizational and audience pressures, they leave a distinct impact nonetheless. Hence it is not surprising that news in major metropolitan areas, which harbor the more prominent news organizations, is substantially more liberal than news in the rest of the country, judging from comparisons of editorials throughout the nation.[34]

On the idiosyncratic level, compared to personnel in other business enterprises, a person who enters the journalism profession generally is more idealistic, more humanistic, likes a great deal of independence, and prefers nonroutine work.[35] Social psychologists have discovered that such people tend to be on the left end of the political spectrum, interested in reforming society, opposed to regimentation, and fiercely protective of their personal and professional independence.

Reporters' unique life experiences are also important in shaping their views of the world. It matters what personal contacts they are able to make. Washington-based reporters, for instance, may be able to use friendships with well-connected government officials to get important scoops. But, as a result of close personal ties with these officials, they may become captives of their sources' perspective on the world.

Organizational Factors. Many scholars have found that the influence of one's colleagues and one's setting are important elements for the news fraternity. Every news organization has its own internal power structure. The orientation of this power structure develops from the interaction of owners, producers, publishers, managing editors, editors, advertisers, news sources, reporters, audiences, and government authorities. In most news organizations today, it tends to be liberal but supportive of the existing political and social system.

When newspeople have been asked how much their editors tried to influence their reports and how frequently they were prevented from reporting stories they wanted to report, three out of four answers have been that "nobody tells us what to do and what not to do." This is true in most cases, but when top executives exercise control, it usually involves politically crucial matters. More than half of the reporters concede, moreover, that higher-ups select story assignments for them, and two-thirds are required to submit their stories to editorial scrutiny.[36] Thus the crucial phases of initiation of stories and final acceptance are subject to organizational controls. Though editorial censorship is rare, the possibility exists and serves to tether reporters to organizational norms.

Organizational pressures begin to operate even before the first day of a job. Most people join news organizations and remain with them only if they share the organization's basic philosophy. To win approval, professional recognition, and advancement, reporters learn very fast what types of stories are acceptable, and which are likely to be squelched. They behave accordingly. This is particularly true if morale is high within the organization and if, as is generally the case, newspeople feel that their organization is producing a good product (85 percent do).

Relationships with colleagues in the organization are particularly important within the larger, more prominent news enterprises. There, newspeople receive their main social and professional support from their peers, rather than from the community at large. The opposite holds true in smaller towns, where newspeople often interact quite freely with the local power structure and receive its support.

Which news media do people within the profession consider to be leaders in their field? Johnstone, Slawski, and Bowman asked newspeople to name the fairest and most reliable news organizations as well as those on which *they* relied most. Answers to these questions were quite parallel, with high scorers holding nearly identical ranks in each answer column. Combining the answers, as Table 2-2 shows, the *New York Times* ranked highest. Among the top ten, it captured 28 percent of the votes. The *New York Times* was followed by the Associated Press with 19 percent of the votes, the United Press with 13 percent, the *Washington Post* with 10 percent, the *Wall Street Journal* with 9 percent, and the *Los Angeles Times* with 5 percent. *Newsweek* also scored 5 percent and the *Christian Science Monitor* and *Time* magazine tied at 4 percent. Only one television system, CBS News, appeared among the top ten with 3 percent of the votes. Given the brevity and sketchiness of televised news, it is not surprising that most news professionals prize print sources more.

All of these highly rated news organizations give ample coverage to news and usually shy away from sensational treatment. Most of them are organizations whose main offices are located along the northeastern seaboard. This distribution supports the frequently heard claim that American journalism is intellectually dominated by the eastern press, staffed by roughly 8 percent of the news profession. These are the "generative" media which produce the news that "derivative" media distrib-

Table 2-2 Percentage of Newsmen Voting News Organization "Fairest," "Most Reliable," "Most Relied On"*

Organization	Rank	% of Vote
New York Times	1	28
Associated Press	2	19
United Press International	3	13
Washington Post	4	10
Wall Street Journal	5	9
Los Angeles Times	6	5
Newsweek	7	5
Christian Science Monitor	8	4
Time	9	4
CBS News	10	3

* Based on votes of 1,349 newspeople.
SOURCE: Johnstone, *The Newspeople*, p. 224.

ute.[37] The heavy reliance throughout the country on the same news sources is one reason why patterns of American news coverage are broadly similar. Regardless of regional and local social and political differences, Americans share most of their news. While this provides a basis for national solidarity, it does mean that these pacesetter media have considerable power over national public opinion.

Role Models. Editors and reporters may take their cues about story importance and interpretation from the pacesetting media, but they shape their overall news policies according to their own views about the role that media should play in society. We have already considered the effects of the social responsibility role compared with more detached stances. Obviously, role choices shape news and so are politically significant.

The importance of role models for news production was graphically demonstrated in 1978 when the Australian publisher Rupert Murdoch bought several American publications, including the *New York Post,* the *Village Voice, New West* magazine, and *New York* magazine. The staffs of these organizations brought suit to stop the sale because they were unhappy about the role model Murdoch had adopted for his other publications, one designed primarily to entertain and shock the public. The courts declined to interfere on the grounds that the choice of a role model is an editorial function.[38]

Readers who live in the large cities or subscribe to out-of-town papers often can select the types of papers they want. They may choose role models presented by, for example, the *Wall Street Journal* (for business news) or *The New York Times* for broad general coverage. Most people, however, cannot pick and choose so easily. They are limited to a single print source and a few radio and television stations and therefore to the role models of these sources.

SUMMARY

In this chapter we have examined the most common types of control over the media. The national government holds full control over a vast overseas radio and television operation. It exercises partial control over a farflung system of public television and radio broadcasting that provides an alternative to commercial programming.

For the average American, these government-controlled systems are peripheral, compared to privately owned print and electronic media enterprises. The major political problem in the private sector is concentration of ownership of media and concentrated control over news and entertainment programs. With much of the media output produced and controlled by large business conglomerates, and with limited newspaper competition in most cities, there has been much concern that the American public is ill-served. Comparatively few, potentially biased, minds control the news and entertainment supply that shapes public perceptions of political issues.

We have looked into the structure of the media business and into government controls designed to avert the potential dangers of concentration. We have also tried to evaluate the impact of the existing system on the form and slant of news and entertainment. The limited available evidence suggests that many prevailing views are wrong. Further research is needed to provide a sound basis for public policies intended to control the media in the public interest.

Going beyond ownership patterns, we have traced other major influences which shape media operations and products. These include the activities of industry lobby groups and citizens' lobbies. They also include the roles played by members of the media establishment. Since media output is influenced by the people who collect information and produce stories, by the organizations which shape their approaches to their tasks, and by the conceptions of media roles which prevail among them, we have examined these facets of the control picture. They show some clearly discernible patterns and trends. Media products do tend to correspond to the expectations which flow from these trends. Still, given the diversity of influences which are brought into play when news and entertainment are produced, we as yet lack the techniques to assess the precise impact which each of these influences has on media content in general, or even on a particular story. In the next chapter we shall focus more closely on the actual news production process for additional clues to the mystery of the mix of influences which shape the news.

NOTES

1. *New York Times,* February 24, 1979.
2. *New York Times,* December 15, 1978.
3. William Small, *To Kill a Messenger* (New York: Hastings House, 1970) p. 280.
4. Erwin G. Krasnow and Lawrence D. Longley, *The Politics of Broadcast Regulation,* 2nd ed. (New York: St. Martin's Press, 1978), pp. 20-26.
5. The composition of this audience is analyzed in George Comstock, Steven Chaffee, Natan Katzman, Maxwell McCombs, and Donald Roberts, *Television and Human Behavior* (New York: Columbia University Press, 1978) pp. 116-121.
6. For example, see Bruce M. Owen, *Economics and Freedom of Expression: Media Structure and the First Amendment* (Cambridge, Mass.: Ballinger, 1975).
7. The figures are from Christopher H. Sterling and Timothy R. Haight, *The Mass Media: Aspen Institute Guide to Communication Industry Trends* (New York: Praeger, 1978), pp. 43-44.
8. Ibid., pp. 65-70.
9. The structure and operations of the FCC are discussed more fully on pp. 39-43 below.
10. AM (Amplitude Modulation) stations and VHF (Very High Frequency) stations reach the largest audiences. The newer FM (Frequency Modulation) and UHF (Ultra High Frequency) stations use different parts of the airwaves and reach fewer people. Their signals cannot be received by radio and television sets designed only for AM and VHF reception.
11. Sterling and Haight, *The Mass Media,* p. 83.
12. Daniel B. Wackman, Donald M. Gillmor, Cecilie Gaziano, and Everette E. Dennis, "Chain Newspaper Autonomy as Reflected in Presidential Campaign Endorsements," *Journalism Quarterly* 52 (Fall 1975): 411-420.
13. They are subject to operational regulations, however. For instance, one network may not operate a second network covering the same market.
14. Maxwell E. McCombs and Donald L. Shaw, "Structuring the 'Unseen Environment'," *Journal of Communication* (Spring 1976): 18-22.
15. J. Herbert Altschull, "The Journalist and Instant History: An Example of the Jackal Syndrome," *Journalism Quarterly* (Autumn 1973): 389-96.
16. For example, see J. Herbert Altschull, "Khrushchev and the Berlin 'Ultimatum': The Jackal Syndrome and the Cold War," *Journalism Quarterly* 54 (Fall 1977): 545-51.
17. A brief comparison of media systems throughout the world is presented in Jeremy Tunstall, *The Media Are American: Anglo-American Media in the World* (New York: Columbia University Press, 1977).
18. These issues are discussed at length in Richard Bunce, *Television in the Corporate Interest* (New York: Praeger, 1976); Martin H. Seiden, *Who Controls the Mass Media? Popular Myths and Economic Realities* (New York: Basic Books, 1975); and Walter S. Baer, et al. *Concentration of Mass Media Ownership: Assessing the State of Current Knowledge* (Santa Monica, Calif.: Rand Corp., 1974).
19. For a contrary view see Erik Barnouw, *The Sponsor: Notes on a Modern Potentate* (New York: Oxford University Press, 1978).
20. A scientific appraisal of the effects of owners on media output is presented in Frank Wolf, *Television Programming for News and Public Affairs: A Quantitative Analysis of Networks and Stations* (New York: Praeger, 1972).
21. Michael O. Wirth and James A. Wollert, "Public Interest Program Perfor-

mance of Multimedia-Owned TV Stations," *Journalism Quarterly* 53 (Summer 1976): 223-230.

22. See Owen, *Economics and Freedom of Expression.*
23. Joel Persky, "Self Regulation of Broadcasting — Does it Exist?" *Journal of Communication* 27 (Spring 1977): 200-210.
24. *Office of Communication of United Church of Christ v. FCC,* 359 F. 2d, 994, D.C. Cir., 1966.
25. Krasnow and Longley, *The Politics of Broadcast Regulation,* p. 44.
26. These activities are summarized in Anne W. Branscomb and Maria Savage, "The Broadcast Reform Movement at the Crossroads," *Journal of Communication* 28 (Autumn 1978): 25-34.
27. Forrest P. Chisman, "Public Interest and FCC Policy Making," *Journal of Communication* 27 (Winter 1977): 77-84.
28. William Small, *To Kill a Messenger,* p. 280.
29. John Johnstone, Edward Slawski, and William Bowman, *The Newspeople* (Urbana, Ill.: University of Illinois Press, 1976).
30. See e.g. the results of *The Washington Post* — Harvard University Study, *Washington Post,* September 29, 1976.
31. Herbert J. Gans, *Deciding What's News: A Study of CBS Evening News, NBC Nightly News, Newsweek and Time.* (New York: Pantheon Books, 1979), pp. 39-69, 116-145, 182-213.
32. Ibid., pp. 39-69, 182-213.
33. C. Richard Hofstetter, *Bias in the News: Network Television Coverage of the 1972 Election Campaign.* (Columbus: Ohio State University Press, 1976), pp. 187-207.
34. For a collection of editorials on various subjects, see Lauren R. Sass, ed., *Television: The American Medium in Crisis* (New York: Facts on File, 1979.)
35. John Hohenberg, *The Professional Journalist,* 4th ed. (New York: Holt, Rinehart & Winston, 1978), and Idowu Sobowale, "The Social-Psychological Predictors of Commitment to Journalism," Chicago: Midwest Association for Public Opinion Research paper, 1978.
36. Johnstone, et al., *The Newspeople,* p. 86.
37. Thomas E. Patterson and Ronald P. Abeles, "Mass Communications Research and the 1976 Presidential Election," *Items* 2 (June 1975): 13-18.
38. Charles Whelton, "Getting Bought: Notes from the Overground," *Village Voice,* May 2, 1977, p. 51.

READINGS

Baer, Walter S. et al. *Concentration of Mass Media Ownership: Assessing the State of Current Knowledge.* Santa Monica, Cal.: Rand Corp., 1974.

Barnouw, Erik. *The Sponsor: Notes on a Modern Potentate.* New York: Basic Books, 1975.

Hohenberg, John. *The Professional Journalist,* 4th. ed. New York: Holt, Rinehart and Winston, 1978.

Johnstone, John; Slawski, Edward; and Bowman, William. *The Newspeople.* Urbana, Ill.: University of Illinois Press, 1976.

Owen, Bruce M. *Economics and Freedom of Expression: Media Structure and the First Amendment.* Cambridge, Mass.: Ballinger, 1975.

Seiden, Martin H. *Who Controls the Mass Media? Popular Myths and Economic Realities.* New York: Basic Books, 1975.

Small, William. *To Kill a Messenger.* New York: Hastings House, 1970.

Tunstall, Jeremy. *The Media Are American: Anglo-American Media in the World.* New York: Columbia University Press, 1977.

3

Newsmaking and News Reporting

"The biggest heist of the 1970s never made it on the five o'clock news. The biggest heist of the 1970s *was* the five o'clock news. The salesmen took it. . . . By the 1970s, an extravagant proportion of television news . . . answered less to the description of 'journalism' than to that of 'show business.' " The accuser is Ron Powers, Pulitzer-prize-winning television critic. The consequences of this show business approach to news, Powers believes, are ominous.[1] When "news" programs are dominated by trivial chatter to gratify "the audience's surface whims, not supplying its deeper informational needs . . . an insidious hoax is being perpetrated on American viewers. . . . The hoax is made more insidious by the fact that very few TV news-watchers are aware of what information is *left out* of a newscast in order to make room for the audience-building gimmicks."[2]

What *should be news?* What *is news?* How do newspeople decide what to publicize? Of all the new developments each day that may be relevant to the lives and interests of audiences, which are *the news* that is likely to be published? Which are likely to be ignored? In the previous chapters, we have discussed some of the important factors which have a bearing on these questions. In this chapter, we will describe the process in detail and suggest the effects it has on the product brought forth by the mass media and the consequences it spells for politics.

MODELS OF THE NEWSMAKING PROCESS

Four models of the newsmaking process have been proposed and debated among scholars. Each represents a judgment of what the major forces behind newsmaking are or ought to be. Each of these varied conceptions of newsmaking has profound consequences for the nature of news and its political impact.

Proponents of the *mirror* model contend that news is and should be a reflection of reality. Newspeople observe the world around them and report what they see as accurately and objectively as possible. As proponents of this view say, "we don't make the news, we merely report it." The implication is that newspeople are merely a conduit for information which is produced by others. They reflect whatever comes to their attention; they do not shape it in any way.

Critics of the mirror model charge that it is unrealistic. In a vast world in which millions of significant events take place every day, it is impossible for the media merely to reflect events. Choices must be made about the general categories and specific stories to be included. Stories that are chosen inevitably loom larger than life, distorting the picture which the real world presents. Stories that are omitted drop out of the picture, leaving unrealistic gaps. Even films and photographs distort re- ality. A small group of demonstrators looks like an invading army when cameras zoom in on them.

In the *professional* model, newsmaking is viewed as an endeavor of highly skilled professionals who put together an interesting collage of events selected for importance, attractiveness to media audiences, and balance among the various elements of the news offering. For economic reasons, audience appeal is the most important consideration. This, in a sense, makes the audience the ultimate judge of what stories may pass through the gates of editorial scrutiny to publication and what will be refused passage. In a word, people are "gatekeepers." What they accept, thrives. What they reject, languishes or dies.[3]

The *organizational* model is based on organization theory. Its proponents contend that news selection emerges from the pressures inherent in organizational processes and goals. Pressures springing from interpersonal relations and professional norms within the news organiza- tion are important, as are constraints arising from technical news production processes, cost-benefit considerations, and legal regulations, such as the FCC's fairness rules.

Finally, the *political* model rests on the assumption that news everywhere is a product of the ideological biases of individual newspeople, as well as the pressures of the political environment in which the news organization operates. When the prevailing political environment is capitalist democracy, with a moderately strong social welfare orientation, as is true in the United States, this orientation sets the tone for the world view implicit in most fact and fiction programs. Supporters of the prevailing system are pictured as good guys, oppo- nents as bad guys. High-status people and institutions are covered; those who are outside the system or in low-visibility positions are gen- erally ignored.

None of these models, by itself, can explain the newsmaking pro- cess. Rather, that process is a combination of all of them. The precise mix of factors which explains newsmaking in any particular instance de- pends on the orientations of news personnel as well as on the demands of a particular medium.

THE GATEKEEPERS

Relatively few people are usually involved in the news selection, or "gatekeeping," operation. They include wire service and other reporters who make initial story choices, editors who make story assignments and accept or reject submitted stories, disc jockeys at radio stations who present 5-minute news breaks, and television program executives. For the average newspaper or news weekly, fewer than 25 people are involved. On the three major networks, the combined editorial personnel responsible for the news number fewer than 50 people.

As Malcolm Warner has described it for a single network, "*three* men constitute the 'power elite' of the television news policy." A vice president in charge of news lays down the ground rules for general news policy. An executive producer selects news and determines the sequence and length of stories and the amount of film and word coverage to be given to them. The number three person is an associate executive producer who shares the executive producer's workload. Besides these three, news decisions usually involve a Washington bureau chief, a news editor who keeps up with the progress of various stories and edits films and reports, an assignment editor who apportions staff and camera crews to various locations, and one or more writers who provide copy which they or another newscaster will present on the air. Usually, there is also a copy editor who funnels wire service copy and stories from leading papers and newscasts to the newsroom personnel, reporters who collect the stories initially, and one or more newscasters/commentators. The latter may simply read or write and rewrite their own copy and decide which stories need verbal commentary or merely a raised or lowered eyebrow.[4] Most of these people are totally unknown to the public, though not to publicity seekers who vie for their attention.[5]

These few people, particularly those who make news choices for nationwide audiences, have a tremendous amount of political power at their disposal. In fact, 500 leading citizens polled by *U.S. News & World Report* in April 1974 rated television as the greatest influence on decisions and actions affecting the nation as a whole. The White House and Supreme Court were tied in second place. Newspapers were third.[6] As we saw in Chapter 1, recent studies have amply demonstrated that news stories influence what ordinary people as well as political elites will think and think about. True enough, media gatekeepers are not entirely free in their story choices. Coverage of certain stories, such as wars, assassinations, and airline hijackings, cannot be avoided. But others could be omitted. Probing into the operations of the FBI or CIA, or discussing women's role in the labor market are examples.

A few highly respected national newscasters may become extraordinarily influential individuals by singling out news events for positive or negative commentary. When Walter Cronkite or Eric Sevareid or

John Chancellor declares that voluntary price controls will not work or that Mideast peace is unattainable, popular support for these policies may plunge. A sixty-second verbal barrage on the evening news may destroy programs, politicians, and the reputations of major organizations. This power may be used wisely or unwisely.

Peter Braestrup, chief of the *Washington Post*'s Saigon Bureau during the Vietnam War, claims that it was used unwisely with regard to the conduct of that war. After an exhaustive study of news reports and commentary about the 1968 Tet offensive of the North Vietnamese, he concluded that mistaken media reports led to policies that changed the course of the war. What Walter Cronkite and other commentators had called a defeat for the South Vietnamese and American forces was really a defeat for the North Vietnamese. Yet, in the wake of these erroneous interpretations which heightened existing antiwar pressures, support for the war collapsed, American withdrawal began in earnest, and President Johnson abandoned a second-term race.[7] People may differ about the wisdom of the end result, but we do need to concern ourselves with the great weight given to such media interpretations.

GENERAL FACTORS IN NEWS SELECTION

What becomes news depends, in part, on the background, training, personal makeup, and professional socialization of news personnel. As indicated in Chapter 2, in the United States this means, by and large, upwardly mobile, well-educated white males whose political views are liberal and who subscribe in ever larger proportions to the tenets of social responsibility journalism. It does not generally mean women and minorities, although their numbers have been rising in the wake of affirmative action policies.

News personnel operate within the general political context of their societies. Most of them have internalized this context so that it becomes their frame of reference. As George Gerbner, Dean of the Annenberg School of Communication, noted, after comparing newspaper versions of the same story in different papers, there is "no fundamentally non-ideological, apolitical, non-partisan news gathering and reporting system."[8] If a reporter's political context demands favorable images of racial minorities, news and entertainment will reflect this outlook. If adverse criticism of minorities is officially mandated, the same stories which will be used elsewhere to praise minorities will be used to defame them.[9]

As discussed more fully in Chapter 2, news selection also hinges on the intraorganizational norms and professional role conceptions to which newspeople are subjected. Pressures of internal and external competition are influential as well. Within each news organization, reporters and editors compete for time and space and prominence of position for their stories. News organizations likewise compete with each other for audience attention, for advertisers and, in the case of the networks, for affiliates. If one station or network has a very popular program, others will copy the format and often will try to place an equally attractive program into a competing time slot to capture its competitor's audiences and advertisers. Likewise, papers may feel compelled to carry stories which they might otherwise ignore, simply because another medium available in the same market has carried the story. Stories in the *Washington Post, New York Times* or *Christian Science Monitor* become models to be followed.

Political pressures also leave their mark. Media personnel depend for much of their information on political leaders and are therefore subject to the manipulation by these sources which springs from intensive contact and the desire to keep relationships cordial. For instance, when journalists were asked about their relationship with Governor Nelson Rockefeller, they agreed that he "co-opted the press in varying degrees and thus avoided ... critical detachment or impassionate analysis." Newspeople admittedly were under his spell because "Rockefeller made himself and state political news interesting to reporters and their editors and then to the public. Not only did he skillfully work to make news ... but he orchestrated it superbly and, whenever he could, tried to accommodate the professional necessities of newswriters."[10] The ability to use the media to political advantage without antagonizing newspeople is the mark of the astute politician. Reporters can rarely resist such pressures without alienating powerful and important news sources.

Economic pressures are even more potent than political pressures in molding the news and entertainment which media produce. Newspapers and magazines need sufficient income to cover their production costs. Except for publications which are subsidized by individual or group sponsors, they must raise this income from subscription rates, from advertisers, or from a combination of these sources. For television and radio programming most costs are covered solely by advertising income. Media offerings must therefore appeal to large numbers of potential customers for the products that advertisers sell. This means that programs and stories must be directed either to general audiences in the prime consumption middle years, or to selected special audiences who are key targets for particular advertiser appeals. For instance, while toothpaste, laundry detergent, and breakfast cereals are best marketed to the huge nationwide audiences who watch the regular nighttime situation comedies or detective stories, personal home computers, fancy foreign sports cars, or raft trips down the Amazon are most likely to find customers among a select few. Advertisers for these products are attracted to limited circulation journals like *National Geographic* or *Psychology Today* or to specialized television documentaries.

Since the bulk of programming must be directed to the general public, television and radio must maintain a smooth flow of appealing programs throughout the prime evening hours. Paul Klein, an audience research executive at NBC, contends that people watch television as such, rather than specific programs. As long as they are satisfied through "Least-Objectionable Programming" (L.O.P.), they will remain with the station.[11] But if boring or controversial programs come on, a sizable part of the audience will defect to another station and remain tuned to it for the rest of the evening. Such considerations deter producers from mixing serious programs with light entertainment in prime time.

This need to keep audiences watching a particular station even affects the format of news and public service programs. News presentation in a bantering, joke-filled form — Happy Talk — was adopted to keep the audience tuned in for later shows. Fairly rapid public disenchantment with happy talk news, along with high popularity of a few documentaries such as the chronicles of the Adams family, show that media people occasionally underestimate the tastes of the public for serious presentations. But these are the exceptions rather than the rule. H. L. Mencken was probably right when he said that "nobody ever went broke by underestimating the public's taste." As one station manager reminded his staff somewhat condescendingly:

> Remember, the vast majority of our viewers hold blue-collar jobs. The vast majority of our viewers never went to college. The vast majority of our viewers have never been on an airplane. The vast majority of our viewers have never seen a copy of *The New York Times.* The vast majority of our viewers do not read the same books and magazines that you read, . . . in fact, many of them never read anything. . . .[12]

When we say that what is publishable news is a decision that hinges on shared attitudes of newspeople and their audiences and on the nature of their social and political settings, we are saying that there is no magical quality that makes something "news." What is publishable in one setting for one medium is not necessarily appropriate for another. Newsworthiness of individual stories will vary from country to country, audience to audience, and time to time. Thus in 1903, when the Wright brothers invited the press to Kitty Hawk to cover their attempts to fly, not a single reporter came. After the flight, only seven American newspapers considered the event newsworthy enough to print stories about the flight, and only two papers gave it front-page play. Seventy-six years later, when a pilot crossed the English Channel in the *Gossamer Albatross*, a plane using human pedal power, large crowds of reporters came and the story received nationwide press and television coverage.

CRITERIA FOR CHOOSING SPECIFIC NEWS STORIES

Beyond deciding what, in general, is publishable news, gatekeepers must choose particular news items to include in their mix of offerings. *The New York Times'* motto, "All the News That's Fit to Print," is an impossible myth. There is far more publishable news available to the paper than it can possibly use. Gatekeepers must also decide how they want to cover each item. For instance, at the height of the Vietnam War, ABC cameramen were ordered to concentrate on bloody battle scenes. This led to a story emphasis on the military. Later on, the focus was placed on internal corruption, black-marketeering, political opposition, and the treatment of ex-Viet Cong, to prepare the home front for withdrawal of American troops from Vietnam.[13]

What determines the choice of particular stories? There are five important criteria that most newspeople use. All relate to audience appeal rather than the political significance of the story, its educational value, its broad social purposes, or newspeople's political views. This emphasis, and the economic necessities which mandate it, needs to be kept in mind when media output is evaluated. It explains why the amount and kind of coverage of important issues is not commensurate with their significance in the real world at the time of publication. For instance, a single heinous crime may turn the focus on crime stories and lead to an upswing in the number and prominence of such stories. This may give the appearance of a crime wave at a time when crime rates are actually going down. A crystallizing event like the Surgeon General's Report on Smoking and Health may call attention to a long-standing problem which has not changed in newsworthiness. By the same token, an important continuing event that has already received a lot of coverage may be dropped from peak attention because its news value is declining, even though its real world significance may be increasing.[14]

Table 3-1 presents graphic evidence that news coverage and significance do not go hand in hand. A 10-year comparison of media stories with corresponding statistics on escalation of the Vietnam War, crime rates, and urban riots revealed that stories often peak ahead of events. For instance, the peak year for riots was 1968; the peak year for riot stories was 1967. In 1967, the ratio of riots to riot stories was 4 to 1; in 1968 it was 12 to 1. With riots no longer anything "special," the ratio went to 16 to 1 in 1969 and 65 to 1 in 1970.

What are the five criteria for choosing news stories? First of all, stories must have a *high impact* on readers or listeners. Ten thousand Indians starving in Calcutta would not get the amount of coverage that two children starving in Minneapolis would get. The midwestern story would have a high impact on American readers. The Calcutta story would not. People presumably want to read about things relevant to their own lives. Smoke pouring from a window next door, the death of a local mayor, or a sick youngster's lost dog make more of an impact on people than things happening far away to strangers.

The second element of newsworthiness is natural or manmade *violence, conflict, disaster,* or *scandal.* Wars, murders, strikes, earthquakes, accidents, or sex scandals involving prominent people — these are the kinds of things that excite audiences. In fact, inexpensive mass newspapers became viable business ventures in the United States only after

Table 3-1 Comparison of Media Coverage and Related Statistics for Selected Issues*

	1960	1961	1962	1963	1964	1965	1966	1967	1968	1969	1970
Number of articles on war in Vietnam	7	5	7	28	49	160	206	160	123	99	44
Number of American troops in Vietnam (in 1,000's)	—	—	—	—	23	184	385	486	536	474	334
Number of articles on crime	3	5	5	11	18	35	21	25	35	25	22
Crimes per 100,000 people	1123	—	—	1292	1440	1512	1667	1922	2235	2471	2741
Number of articles on urban riots	0	1	0	0	6	6	17	41	36	15	3
Number of civil disturbances	—	—	—	—	—	—	—	172	435	245	195

SOURCE: G. Ray Funkhouser, "Trends in Media Coverage of the Issues of the '60s," *Journalism Quarterly* 50 (Fall 1973): 536.
*Media data come from content analysis of *Time, Newsweek,* and *U.S. News & World Report.* Related statistics come from *Statistical Abstracts of the United States.*
Reprinted by permission of *Journalism Quarterly.*

1833 when the publishers of the *New York Sun* discovered that papers filled with breezy crime and sex stories far outsold their more staid competitors. Mass sales permitted sharp price reductions. Thus the "penny-press" was born.

People remember violent behavior better than nonviolent fare. For instance, in 1978, the most widely followed and remembered news event was the murder-suicide of 900 members of an American religious sect in Guyana. Ninety-eight percent of the respondents to a Gallup poll knew of the event — a number matched only by those who remembered the attack on Pearl Harbor in 1941 and those who recalled the dropping of atomic bombs on Hiroshima and Nagasaki in 1945.

A third element in newsworthiness is *familiarity*. News is attractive if it involves familiar situations about which many people are concerned or pertains to well-known people.

The public's keen interest in celebrities is demonstrated by the amazing amount of detail that people absorb and retain about the powerful and famous. More than ten years after the assassination of President John F. Kennedy, most Americans still remembered details of the funeral ceremony, as well as where they themselves were when they heard the news. The sense of personal grief and loss lingered, bridging the gap between the average person's private and public worlds. People value the feeling of personal intimacy that comes from knowing details of a famous person's life.[15]

The fourth element in newsworthiness, which is particularly important for newspapers and local television, is that an event must be *close to home*. This heavy preference for local news rests on the assumption that people are most interested in what happens near them. Local media continue to exist because local events are their exclusive province, free from competition by national television and national print media. In fact, roughly 75 percent of their space is used for local stories.[16] Since national television news must concentrate on matters of interest to viewers throughout the entire country, it cannot depict events close to everyone's home. But because the public receives so much news from Washington and a few major metropolitan areas, these cities and their newsmakers have become familiar to the nation. This, in a sense, makes them "local" events in what Marshall McLuhan has called the "global village" created by television.

Lastly, news should be *timely* and *novel*. It must be something that has just occurred and is out of the ordinary either in the sense that it does not happen all the time, like the regular departure of airplanes or the daily opening of grocery stores, or in the sense that it is not part of the lives of ordinary persons.

Among these five basic criteria, conflict, proximity, and timeliness are most important, judging from a survey of television and newspaper editors.[17] These editors were given 64 fictitious stories by a team of researchers and were asked which they would use and their reasons for

Table 3-2 Frequency of Mention of Various topics in the *Chicago Tribune, Sun Times, Daily News, CBS* and NBC Local News, ABC, CBS, NBC National News. (N=33,200 for the *Tribune*, 581 for the *Sun Times*, 506 for the *Daily News*, 7,597 for CBS local, 12,274 for NBC local, 7,962 for ABC, 8,193 for CBS, and 7,667 for NBC news. Figures in percentages.)*

	Chicago Tribune	Sun Times	Daily News	CBS local	NBC local	ABC national	CBS national	NBC national
Crime & Justice								
Police/Security	4.7	7.2	7.7	3.3	3.1	1.5	1.6	1.5
Judiciary	5.7	5.0	4.0	4.6	4.7	3.6	3.4	3.7
Corruption/terrorism	4.0	5.7	5.5	4.0	3.3	3.1	3.3	3.1
Individual crime	7.5	10.2	9.5	7.8	8.5	4.1	4.0	4.6
	21.9	28.1	26.7	19.7	19.6	12.3	12.3	12.9
Government/Politics								
Presidency	2.7	0.9	1.8	2.3	1.9	4.5	4.2	4.2
Congress	2.5	4.1	3.0	1.7	1.2	3.7	4.4	4.1
Bureaucracy	1.9	1.9	1.6	1.9	2.0	4.9	4.5	4.4
Foreign affairs	9.8	9.8	10.3	4.6	5.2	16.5	17.1	15.0
Domestic policy	12.6	13.1	13.8	5.6	4.5	6.6	7.6	7.4
Elections	7.6	10.0	11.5	6.8	6.2	15.7	15.2	15.2
State government	1.8	1.4	0.8	2.7	2.2	0.6	0.9	0.8
City government	1.9	0.3	1.2	4.3	3.2	0.7	0.5	0.5
Miscellaneous	0.6	0.7	0.0	0.9	1.0	0.7	0.6	0.4
	41.4	42.2	44.0	30.9	27.4	53.9	55.0	52.0

Economic/Social Issues								
State of economy	2.4	2.1	2.4	1.1	1.0	1.7	1.7	1.9
Business/labor	5.9	6.4	4.9	6.6	10.2	7.8	6.8	6.8
Minorities/women	2.7	2.9	3.8	2.1	2.0	2.7	2.9	2.4
Environment/ transportation	3.2	4.1	1.8	9.1	9.1	3.5	4.0	4.0
Disaster/accident	2.2	1.9	2.4	3.8	5.0	3.2	2.8	3.3
Health/medicine	2.5	2.4	1.6	3.3	4.6	2.1	2.8	3.2
Education/media/religion	4.4	2.2	2.8	4.0	4.0	2.8	3.0	2.5
Leadership style	1.2	1.5	1.4	0.2	0.2	0.8	0.7	0.6
Miscellaneous	1.7	0.7	0.6	1.3	1.2	1.8	1.4	1.5
	26.2	24.2	21.7	31.5	37.3	26.4	25.1	26.2
Human Interest/Hobbies**								
General human interest	2.9	1.9	3.4	6.0	6.8	1.8	1.8	2.3
Celebrities	3.6	1.4	2.0	2.2	2.1	1.4	1.5	1.7
Political gossip	1.6	0.5	1.2	1.4	1.4	1.4	1.1	1.4
Sports/entertainment	2.6	1.7	1.4	8.3	5.3	2.9	2.1	3.4
	10.7	5.5	8.0	17.9	15.6	7.5	6.5	8.8

Sun Times and *Daily News* data are based on sample coding of one constructed week for each paper. NBC local news is based on full hour broadcast, others on half hour. National news data are based on nine months of coding, April-December, 1976.

**When stories of this type appeared in special sections (e.g. People, Leisure, Food, etc.) they were not coded individually. Rather, the entire section was counted as one story. This depresses the Human Interest/Hobbies story count.

using them. Conspicuously absent from their choice criteria was the story's overall significance. Significance does play a part, however, when a very major event is involved, such as the outcome of a national election, the death of a well-known leader, or a major natural disaster. Still, most stories are selected primarily to satisfy the five criteria mentioned earlier.

GATHERING THE NEWS

Once newspeople agree on what is publishable news, they know where this news is most likely to happen and where to place reporters to gather it. This has led to the "beat" system. News organizations establish regular listening posts, or beats, in those places where events of interest to the public are most likely to occur. In the United States the public presumably wants to know about the affairs of political and social leaders and institutions. It wants to know about deviations in natural phenomena, scientific developments, and social occurrences, such as international wars, domestic strife, or interpersonal crime.

To report such events, news organizations establish beats at the centers of government, where they cover major political executives, legislative bodies, court systems, and international organizations. Places where deviations are most likely to be reported, such as police stations and hospitals, stock and commodity markets, and institutions recording economic trends, are monitored. Some beats are functionally defined, such as a "health" or "education" beat. Reporters assigned to them generally cover a wider array of institutions on a less regular schedule than is true of the more usual beats. Stories emanating from the traditional beats have an excellent chance of publication, either because of their intrinsic significance or because they come from a regularly covered beat. In the *New York Times* and *Washington Post,* for instance, stories from regular beats outnumber other stories two to one and capture the bulk of front-page headlines.[18]

All the major media tend to monitor the same places, so that the news patterns are stable and uniform throughout the country. As Table 3-2 documents, the media are "rivals in conformity."[19] The table is based on daily content analyses of three Chicago newspapers and five nightly news telecasts, two of them local to Chicago. It shows the proportionate frequency of mention of various news topics. It presents striking evidence that the same kinds of stories and story types — though not necessarily identical stories — are reported by newspapers, local, and national television. The same holds true for other media appealing to similar clienteles in other cities throughout the country.[20]

Each day, stories report what is new and current, of course, but the subjects and topics are familiar. News, as media scholar Leon Sigal has put it, is always "the standardized exceptional."[21] Each day's or week's news is like a familiar play with slight changes in the scenes and dialogue, and with frequent replacements in the cast of minor actors, though not major ones. News is exceptional in the sense that it does not portray ordinary events, like eating breakfast or washing clothes or taking the bus to work. It is standardized in the sense that it deals with the same types of topics in familiar ways and produces standardized patterns of news and entertainment throughout the country. Coverage of the same familiar scenes over and over again conveys to the public the feeling that all is going according to expectations and that, even if the news is bad, there is little to worry about. It has all happened before.

Even large news organizations cannot afford to have full teams of reporters and camera crews all over the country. Therefore they generally station teams in half a dozen cities. Locations are chosen for the availability of good resources in terms of equipment, support staff, and news personnel. They are not selected with an eye to covering all parts of the nation equally well or to providing diverse settings.

Table 3-3 shows the percentage of network news time, exclusive of Washington, D.C., coverage, which was devoted to various regions of the United States in broadcasts monitored from 1973 to 1975. The table also contains the percentage of the population which lived in these states (1970 Census) and an "Attention Index" which shows the discrepancy

Table 3-3 Network News Time Devoted to Regions of the U.S.*

Region	Percentage of news time	Percentage of population	Attention index**
Midwest	18.5	25	−6.5
Northeast	24.5	21	+3.5
South	12.2	12	+0.2
Southwest	5.8	10	−4.2
Pacific	21.4	13	+8.4
Middle Atlantic	4.8	7	−2.2
New England	6.5	6	+0.5
Mountain	3.1	4	−0.9
Plains	3.2	2	+1.2
Total	100	100	
Total news time (in minutes)	2,301		

*Excludes Washington, D.C., news and stories not limited to a particular location.
**This index shows the discrepancy between percentage of total population and percentage of total news devoted to the region.
SOURCE: Joseph R. Dominick, "Geographic Bias in National TV News," *Journal of Communication* 27 (Fall 1977): 96.

between percentage of total population and percentage of total news in the region. One or two states in each region received the bulk of coverage while the rest were ignored. For instance, 72 percent of northeast news time went to New York. Ninety percent of Pacific region time went to California. For the deprived states, only one or two state stories, often trivial ones, were reported. For some, there was no coverage at all, denying their news and their problems a national audience.

Ninety percent of picture coverage comes from the cities in which camera crews are regularly stationed. Besides Washington, where fully 50 percent of all news originates, these generally include New York, Cleveland, Boston, Chicago, and Los Angeles.[22] Of course, special events will be covered anywhere in the country. Every network reported the 1976 Republican convention in Kansas City and followed President Carter's visits to Camp David in the Maryland mountains, or his journeys to his home town of Plains, Georgia. A sensational murder trial in a small community like Aspen, Colorado attracted teams of reporters, as did the crash of a meteorite in Alaska. But these are exceptional events. Moreover, some of these events in remote sites are scheduled in advance so that plans can be made to have crews available.

Because of the problem of moving camera crews around, and the time needed to process and edit pictures, many stories require prior planning. This leads to an emphasis on predictable events such as formal visits by dignitaries, legislative hearings, or executive press conferences. The development of portable camera equipment producing videotapes that can be broadcast with little further processing has eased this problem somewhat. "Spot news" can be filmed and broadcast rapidly. This is only one example of the profound impact of technological developments on the content of the news.

NEWS PRODUCTION CONSTRAINTS

Many of the factors that affect news story selection spring from the requirement that news must be processed rapidly and published as quickly as possible. Time pressures explain why the press reports so many pseudo-events — events created for easy reporting by the media or for the media. In television news, these constitute almost 70 percent of all stories.[23] For example, politicians frequently plan pictorially attractive events, like dedicating a dam or visiting a fair, at just the right time and place to accommodate newspaper or broadcast deadlines. When newspeople need a quick story about a revolution in Iran or ways to cope with gas pump waiting lines, they arrange interviews with familiar leaders, whose remarks, knowledgeable or not, then instantly become *the* Iran or *the* gas shortage story.

Once stories reach print and electronic media news offices, selections have to be made extremely rapidly. Ben Bagdikian, a former *Washington Post* editor who studied gatekeeping at eight newspapers, found that stories usually are sifted and chosen on the spot. They are not assembled and carefully examined for their overall policy effect. Here is how Bagdikian described the scene in a typical newspaper office:

> The news editor arrives at 6 A.M. to find an overnight accumulation of fifty thousand words, most of it regional and national news from the wire services, some of it from the paper's reporters in outlying bureaus, who transmitted it by teletype the night before.
>
> In addition to making decisions on incoming wire stories, this particular news editor makes decisions on local stories handed him by the city editor and the state editor. He also is handed the output of two wire-photo machines that during the day produce ninety-six photographs from which he selects sixteen.[24]

In the course of the day, the news editor chooses additional items for publication by scanning the news from three wire-service machines as well as locally originated news. The editor examines roughly 110,000 words of wire news during the day, equivalent to the size of an average book. During the day, this editor must also judge and edit 5,000 words of news from the local staff. Other tasks are selection of photographs, which must be processed hours before press time, consultation with city editors about story assignments, and decisions about what to place on page one in light of the changing news scene.

Bagdikian reports that the typical newspaper gatekeeper was able to scan and discard stories in one to two seconds. When reasons for rejecting stories were investigated, only 2.5 percent were rejected because the editor did not care for the substance of the story or objected to its ideological slant. Twenty-six percent were rejected because of lack of space. The remaining 71.5 percent were rejected because they were judged to lack some or all of the elements of newsworthiness discussed earlier.

Rejection rates varied for different types of stories. Overall 89 percent of all wire service news was rejected. So were 93 percent of all human interest stories, 92 percent of crime news, 74 percent of farm news and 69 percent of science news. Even though much of the human interest information was rejected, it still constituted the largest single news category — 23 percent of total news. By contrast, science news took 5 percent of total space and farm stories 6 percent.[25]

For stories that were accepted, it took fast gatekeepers four seconds to skim through the entire story and even make minor changes. The average reading time was six seconds. Stories of 225 words were disposed of in 2 to 10 seconds. At such speeds, judgments are almost instantaneous with no time for reflection or weighing of alternatives among the total batch of news available for the day. Stories are judged more by how they balance previously selected stories than by their intrinsic importance. If the gatekeeper has ideological preferences, these are served instinctively, if at all, rather than deliberately.

Because the flood tide of information continues throughout the day, the gatekeeper accepts very few stories in the early hours of each shift.

Closer to the deadline, when news has to go to press, the pace of story selection quickens. When the deadline arrives, a new story must be extraordinarily important to replace stories that have already been accepted or are already in press. Stories left over at the tail end of the day will not ordinarily be used on the next day because by then they will be old, and newer stories will have replaced them. This means that a story which breaks late in the publishing day, unless it is very unusual or significant, has little chance for publication. What becomes news thus depends heavily on *when* it happens. West Coast afternoon stories are frequent casualties because they are generally too late to be incorporated into the network evening news, which is run on an East Coast schedule.

Public relations managers know the deadlines of important publications like the *New York Times, Wall Street Journal, Time, Newsweek,* and the network television news. They time events and news releases so that stories arrive in gatekeepers' offices precisely when needed. Thus the news production process, though it has its own irresistible momentum, is not immune to conscious control. News for which a minimum of publicity is desired is announced just past deadlines, preferably on weekends, when few newscasts are scheduled. For instance, the Nixon administration fired the special Watergate prosecutor on the weekend in what became known as the "Saturday night massacre." The hope that the timing would minimize publicity was only partially fulfilled in that case.

Publications with less frequent deadlines, such as weekly news magazines, have a lot more time to decide what to publish. News magazine staffs also have more resources than most daily papers to dig out background information and present stories in a context which helps readers to evaluate them. These magazines are therefore ideal for people who want quick, interpretive news that concentrates on a limited number of events.

Television news staffs have even less time for investigative reporting than newspapers, and far less time to provide background and interpretation for the news they present. When investigative stories do appear on television, they usually originated in the print media. A few highly popular investigative programs, such as CBS's "Sixty Minutes," are a much appreciated exception. Besides inadequate time for preparing stories, radio and television news also have the problem of insufficient time to present a story. When the average news story takes up little more than a minute, it is not surprising that it conveys primarily headlines. Complex stories must be omitted entirely if they cannot be condensed into such a brief format.

Print media have space problems as well, but they are less severe. The average newspaper must reserve 55 percent of its space for advertising. Out of its 45 percent "newshole," generally 27 percent goes for straight news stories, the remainder for features of various types. Some papers reserve a standardized amount of space for news; others expand or contract the newshole depending on the flow of news and advertising. But there is rarely enough space to cover stories as fully as reporters and editors would like. This holds true whether the paper is a slim eight-page version or five to ten times that size.[26]

Besides the need to condense a news story into a brief capsule, television reporters also need stories with visual appeal. Unfortunately, what is visually appealing may not be important. For instance, during political campaigns, motorcades, rallies, hecklers, and cheering crowds make good pictures. Candidates delivering speeches are visually dull by comparison. Television cameras therefore concentrate on the colorful scenes, rather than the speechmaker. If such scenes are flashed on the screen in competition with the speech, the pictures distract from what the candidate is saying. Events that make dull pictures may have to be omitted.

Since picture production is expensive for television as well as print, picture stories selected early are likely to be kept even if more important stories break later. Likewise, almost all information originated by the staff is used, for financial and personnel reasons. News organizations prefer stories from people already on their payroll to wire service stories by unknown reporters or stories from outside sources for which additional fees must be paid. News executives also have personal relationships with their own staffs and do not want to disappoint them by killing their stories.

EFFECTS OF GATEKEEPING

The gatekeeping influences which we have been discussing give a distinctive character to the American news product, considered as a whole. There are many exceptions, of course, when one looks at individual news outlets or at individual programs or specific news and feature stories. But, in general, several characteristics stand out. We shall discuss these under four headings, the first two adapted from Herbert Gans' study of news magazine and network television news.[27]

People in the News

The gatekeeping process winnows the group of newsworthy people down to a very small array of familiar and unfamiliar figures. Familiar people appear in three out of every four spots in the news. Most are political figures. Fewer than 50 are in the news regularly. The list is headed by the incumbent president. Other people receive coverage primarily for unusual or important activities, but incumbent presidents are covered regardless of what they do. News about presidential candidates ranks next. In presidential election years, it often outnumbers stories about the president.

A third well-covered group consists of major federal officials, such as political leaders in the House and Senate, the heads of major congressional committees, and cabinet members in active departments. In the post-Watergate period, major White House staff members have joined the circle. The Supreme Court is in the news only intermittently, generally when important decisions are announced. Agency heads rarely make the news, except when they announce new policies or feud with the president. Finally, there are some people who are regularly in the news regardless of what their current political status may be, merely because their names are household words. Members of the Kennedy clan are the prime example.

Below the federal level, the activities of governors and mayors from the larger states and cities are newsworthy if they involve major public policy issues, or if the incumbent is unusual because of race, sex, or prior newsworthy activities. Notorious individuals also receive frequent news attention if their deeds have involved well-known people. Presidential assassins, mass murderers, or members of extremist political groups like the Symbionese Liberation Army fall into this category. Ample coverage also goes to targets of congressional investigations and defendants in political trials, such as the Watergate defendants or key figures in the Pentagon Papers case.

Many powerful people are rarely covered in the news. Among the excluded are economic leaders, such as the heads of large corporations, financiers, and leaders of organized business, such as the National Association of Manufacturers or the U.S. Chamber of Commerce. A few colorful labor leaders, like George Meany and James Hoffa, have been news figures, but this was probably due more to their colorful personalities than to their jobs. Important military leaders also remain obscure except on rare occasions when they are involved in major military operations. Political party leaders surface during elections but remain in the shadows at other times. Political protest leaders, like civil rights figures or the heads of minority parties, or consumer activists like Ralph Nader, come and go from the news scene, depending on the amount of visible conflict they are able to produce. The same holds true for the heads of voluntary associations, such as antiabortion groups or church leaders.

The names of most ordinary people never make the news because their activities must be very unusual to come to the attention of newspeople. Ordinary people have their best chance for publicity if they participate in protests or riots or strikes, particularly if these are directed against the government. The next best chance goes to victims of disasters, personal tragedy, and crime, and to the actors who brought about their plight. The grisly nature of crimes, disasters, or other human tragedies, rather than the identity of the people involved, determines their newsworthiness. Ordinary people also make the news if they become involved in highly unusual life styles or social activities, or if their behavior diverges greatly from what one would normally expect of persons of their age, sex, and status. Finally, ordinary people make the news in large numbers as nameless members of groups whose statistical profile is reported or whose opinions have been tapped through polls or elections.

Actions in the News

A limited array of activities are likely candidates for coverage. The list is headed by conflicts and disagreements among government officials, particularly friction between the president and Congress. A large number of these conflicts concern economic policies.

Stories about government policies and ceremonies also provide frequent story material. These generally deal with policymaking rather than policy operation. Government personnel changes, including campaigns for office, are another news focus.

Several types of conflict action are routinely reported. These include violent and nonviolent protest, much of it about governmental activities, crimes, scandals and investigations, and impending or actual disasters. When the nation is involved in war, they also include a large number of war stories. Finally, two aspects of normal social change receive substantial coverage from time to time. They are major national ceremonies, like inaugurations or moon landings, and major social, cultural or technological developments, like the entry of women into positions previously closed to them, or major advances in the fight against cancer.

Characteristics of the News

The criteria for newsworthiness and the news production constraints (both discussed earlier) also contribute in a general way to the shape of American news, regardless of the subject under discussion. Several features stand out.

Effects of Stress on Novelty and Entertainment. The requirement that a story be new and exciting means that some news drowns out other news that may be of more lasting significance. For instance, eight times as much space and time is devoted to sports news than to news about local community problems such as school finance or housing.[28] Sensational news certainly drowned out other news of importance in March 1977, for example, when the media focused on the terrorist activities of a Moslem sect in Washington. A remarkable presidential press conference occurring at the same time was all but swamped. In this conference, President Carter proposed a $1.5 billion youth employment bill, a Youth Conservation Corps, a new approach to peace in the Middle East, new procedures for the withdrawal of American troops from South Korea, and a new atomic weapons agreement with the Soviet Union. As James Reston commented in the *New York Times,* "It is hard to remember any time since the last World War when an American President made so much news in a press conference or anywhere else . . . but nobody could hear him for the noise and the headlines about the terrorists."[29]

The emphasis on the novel also leads to stress on trivial aspects of serious stories. Complex issues are presented in the form of simplified human interest stories. The reasons for inflation are hardly explained by showing pictures of a housewife paying high prices in the supermarket or a homeowner struggling to pay the mortgage, but judging from attention patterns, audiences enjoy these stories.

The search for novelty and entertainment produces news that focuses on the present and ignores the past and future. The here and now is what counts. The news also tends to be fragmented and discontinuous. It is aired as it is received, so that background needed to place a story in context is often missing. Clarifications are usually buried in the back pages. On television, snippets of news may be presented together to drive home an easily understandable theme, such as "Washington is in a mess" or "the inner city is decaying." The theme may come through, but the individual news item is blurred.

Fragmentation makes it difficult for audiences to piece together a coherent narrative of events. More background and interpretation would help, but would also increase the chance for subjective interpretations by news commentators. A few papers, such as the *Christian Science Monitor,* do cover fewer stories in more detail. People who read *Monitor* stories carefully acquire a better background for understanding social issues, but they miss out on other news for which there is no space. They may also get skewed information if newspeople misinterpret the significance of complex events.

Effects of Stress on Familiarity and Similarity. The need for stories that involve familiar people and events close to home also has a number of consequences for the shape of news. There is, first, a circular aspect to such coverage; familiar people and situations are covered minutely, which makes them even more a part of the audience's life and therefore even more worthy of publicity. The reverse is also true.

During the 1976 presidential election campaign, for instance, Senators Hubert Humphrey and Edward Kennedy, who were frequently in the news, became candidates in many people's minds, even though they never entered the race officially. Senators Lloyd Bentsen and Fred Harris, though they were official entrants, received less media attention and remained unfamiliar. They were forced to abandon the quest.

Familiar people may become objects of prying curiosity into the details of their private lives. These details may take up an inordinately large amount of time and space in the mass media. For example, when Mayor Daley of Chicago died in 1977, the media provided a minute-by-minute account of his last moments. People were told about his blood pressure, about the emergency medical procedures performed, and about the manner in which his family was told about his death. For several days, much of the news in the Chicago area was taken up by these minutiae, to the exclusion of more significant stories. The important story, obscured initially, was that the mayor's death had launched a major power struggle for control of Chicago's politics.

Another important consequence of the criteria of newsworthiness is that American news is very parochial, compared with news in other countries. Foreign coverage will be treated more fully in Chapter 9, but here we should say that this neglect of news about foreign people and cultures leaves Americans deficient in their understanding of international affairs.

Again, there is a circularity involved. If, for instance, events in Afghanistan are rarely covered, stories about Afghanistan require a lot of background to make sense to Americans. Except during a crisis, this may take more scarce time and space than the media are willing to give to any story. Therefore, much of the foreign coverage in American media is about people to whom Americans feel culturally close and whose policies are somewhat familiar, like the English, the Canadians, and the Australians and people in Northern European countries. Foreign news concentrates on situations that are easy to report, which often means violent events, like revolutions, major disasters, and the like. This type of coverage conveys the impression that most foreign countries are always in serious disarray.

Neglect of Social Problems. Despite the ascendancy of social responsibility journalism, the constraints of news production still force the media to neglect major ongoing social problems such as alcoholism, drug addiction, environmental pollution, or care of the elderly and disabled. The pattern changes when a dramatic event takes place, such as a rash of deaths in old folks' homes or a big welfare fraud case. If a reporter investigates and finds that six elderly people starved to death because of neglect or that a few clients prosper on welfare, the spot-lighted incident may then lead to a series of reports on food in retirement homes. The recent deaths provide the element of novelty and entertainment. After that novelty has worn off, interest dims and media attention flags, even if much news still remains to be reported.

Social problems also are neglected because most media staffs are inadequately trained to cover them. Appraisal of the administration of nursing homes or prisons or pollution control programs requires technical knowledge. Specialized reporters who have expertise in such areas as urban affairs, or science, or finance are as yet available only in the larger news organizations. Even then, a science reporter can hardly be expected to be an expert in all fields of science. Nor can a reporter skilled in "urban problems" be expected simultaneously to master the intricacies of a major city's budget, its transportation system, and its services to juveniles. Since most news organizations throughout the country lack the trained staffs to discuss major social problems constructively, politicians can easily challenge the merits of media stories criticizing their policies.

Then, too, most of the public, judging from media use patterns, is not very interested in social problems or the hazards of alcohol and tobacco use. For those people who are interested and might be in a position to combat such problems, media silence makes it more difficult to rouse public support.

Effects of Emphasis on Conflict and Violence. The heavy news emphasis on conflict and bad news is most prevalent in big city media. It has three major consequences. First, and perhaps most far-reaching in its impact, emphasis on negative news events may create dangerous distortions of reality. This is particularly true with crime coverage. Media stories rarely mention that many neighborhoods are relatively free of crime. They convey the impression to many people that the whole city, but particularly inner city areas, are dangerous jungles. The impression may become a self-fulfilling prophecy. In the wake of crime publicity, many people have avoided the inner city.They even shun comparatively safe neighborhoods after a single, highly publicized crime. The empty streets then make crime more likely.

Studies of people's perceptions of the incidence of crime and the chances that they will be attacked indicate that their fears are geared to media realities. In the world of television, one has a 30 to 64 percent chance of being involved in violence; in the real world, the chance is only one-third of one percent.[30] Similarly, heavy media emphasis on air crashes and de-emphasis of automobile accidents have left the public with distorted notions of the dangers of each mode of transportation.

A second result of the emphasis on news involving conflict is the perception of many people that violence is the only acceptable way to settle disputes. Some argue that by bringing conflict into the open, media may promote its resolution, but clearly they may also make it worse.[31] This often happens when media dramatize a conflict by highlighting its more sensational aspects and oversimplifying it, picturing it as a confrontation between two clearly defined sides. It is the hawks against the doves in war, the victors or losers in a legislative battle, the communists versus anticommunists in a struggle abroad. Even when there is little actual confrontation in a situation the media often structure it as a battle and call it a clash or a feud or a fight. Yet divergent viewpoints expressed by parties or unions or members of a legislature may not mean at all that they are locked in battle.

Average people, when presented with clashing claims, often feel confused and find it extremely difficult to determine where the truth lies. They have neither the facts nor the time to explore the issues. They are also left with the disquieting sense that conflict and turmoil reign nearly everywhere. This impression is likely to affect people's feeling toward society in general. They may contract "videomalaise," characterized by lack of trust, cynicism, and fear.[32] The impact of such feelings on the climate of political action and the conduct of politics in the United States is a subject for speculation.

CAMERA FOCUS SHAPES MEANING

A tight shot (insert) exaggerates crowd size.

Finally, the popularity of violence stories has encouraged groups who seek media coverage to behave violently or sensationally to enhance their chances for publicity. One example comes from a lengthy strike by a union of Chicano workers against a Texas furniture company. During the first year, the nonviolent strike received very little publicity. To attract media coverage, the leaders therefore decided to stage noisy marches to the Capitol on the first and second anniversaries of the strike. Moderate language in appeals to the company and city authorities was replaced by fighting words. City councilors were called "rednecks" and challenged to stop the union's marches. This language created a confrontation, brought city police to the scene, and heightened tensions. Celebrities, including Senators Edmund Muskie of Maine and Birch Bayh of Indiana, and farm labor leader Cesar Chavez were invited to enter the fray. These maneuvers broke the year-long dearth of media coverage. No longer peaceful, the strike finally received ample publicity. In turn, this created sufficient pressure to bring about a settlement.[33]

A taste for conflict is not the same as a taste for controversy, however. The fear of offending members of the mass audience, or wire service subscribers, or affiliated station managers, through stories dealing with controversial subjects like abortion or corruption in the church, often keeps such problems out of the media, especially network television. If they are reported, the treatment is generally bland, carefully hedged, and rarely provocative. In fact, the world which television in particular presents to the viewer generally lags behind the real world in its recognition of controversial social changes. The civil rights struggle, women's fight for equality, and changing sexual mores all were widespread in real life long before they became common on the television screen, or received serious attention in the print media. Newspapers can afford to be more daring than television because normally there is no other daily paper in the same market. Moreover, the nature of the medium makes it easier for the audience to ignore stories they find distasteful.

Support for the Establishment

The gatekeeping process also yields news that basically supports current American political and social institutions. Although the media expose official misbehavior and inefficiencies, they display a favorable attitude toward the established American power structure and its methods of operations. They treat its symbols and rituals, such as the presidency, the courts and elections, and patriotic celebrations with a high degree of respect, which lends legitimacy to them. They cast a negative light on anti-establishment behavior, such as inflammatory speeches by militants or looting during a riot. Obscenity and profanity in public places usually are edited out of news events.

Generalized support for the establishment and the status quo is not unique to the media, of course.[34] Most institutions within any particular political system go along with it if they wish to prosper. People on their staffs have been socialized to believe in the merits of their political structures. In the media, moreover, they cater to advertisers and audiences who firmly support the American political system. Staff members whose personal ideologies differ nevertheless go along with established norms, to avoid conflict with their bosses, advertisers, or affiliated stations which may refuse to carry offensive programs.[35] People desperately want to believe that their government is competent, honest, and working hard to solve the problems. They do not welcome exposés which destroy these comforting myths. Media support for the establishment thus helps to raise respect for it and perpetuate it.

Support for the establishment is further strengthened by media reliance on government information and press releases. In the United States, the bulk of news, particularly when it comes from beyond the local communities' boundaries, comes from officials and agencies of the government.[36] Official viewpoints are likely to be particularly dominant when reporters must preserve access to their special beats, like the Pentagon or Justice Department, or when story production requires government assistance in collecting or gaining access to data. For instance, when military personnel are needed to transport correspondents to war zones, or when film producers need demonstrations of moon-flight research, the resulting stories are apt to support official views.[37]

Government officials and agencies are also used routinely for verification of information. Reporters generally equate official position and rank of sources with accuracy. The higher the official level and rank, the better. The assumption that official sources, like police departments, or Department of Agriculture spokesmen, or presidential press aides are reliable is, of course, debatable. Many private groups have complained that such reliance deprives them of the chance to publicize their own, more accurate, versions of stories and that it results in one-sided reporting, tilted toward support of the establishment.

An interesting illustration of establishment support is provided by a study of media coverage of the Durham, N.C., city council. A team of researchers at Duke University[38] observed city council sessions and then examined the newspaper reports about them. The sessions had been rather disorderly with little work done for much of the time. Council members had been observed "dozing off to sleep just as a vote is being taken on a crucial issue" and "smacking with abandon on a large wad of gum while the intricacies of a public housing dispute are discussed."[39] The mayor had cracked a number of jokes about the issues under consideration. The audience had screamed and had booed council proposals. Finally, toward the end of the lengthy sessions, when everybody was tired, a few resolutions were passed.

The published reports of the sessions conveyed a quite different impression. Nothing was said about the unprofessional behavior. Council members were quoted only for their meaningful remarks and not for their often pointless or facetious comments. They were described respectfully, each designated by official title. The stories made it appear that the city council sat down at the appointed time, immediately went about its business, and completed it promptly and efficiently without interruptions by the audience. This impression was conveyed by indicating the precise time the sessions were called to order, outlining the agenda topics, quoting a few of the arguments made during the debates, and then indicating the final decisions. Decisionmaking appeared to be a careful, deliberate, logical process, with the likely consequences of these decisions fully explored. Of course, nothing could have been further from the truth.

The type of reporting practiced in Durham is quite typical of reports of meetings in other places. Most Americans knew little about the conduct of meetings during the Nixon administration until the unexpurgated Watergate tapes provided a realistic inside view. People in public life frequently behave in ways that do not meet the highest standards of decorum and honesty. But newspeople normally wink at this type of behavior, at least while the actors are in high office. For instance, the relationship between a Mafia-linked show girl, Judith Campbell Exner, and President John F. Kennedy did not surface until the mid-1970s.

Such protective conventions have been relaxed somewhat in the post-Watergate era, but it is doubtful whether the change will last.

Newspeople commonly ignore personal misconduct and scandals, but they often draw the line when matters of official conduct become involved. For instance, the sex scandal surrounding Representative Wilbur Mills, a powerful and highly respected member of Congress, was publicized when Mills became embroiled in a public incident involving police action. In earlier years, even that might have brought only casual mention. Representative Wayne Hays of Ohio received media coverage because he paid his mistress by putting her on the government payroll. That made the private affair a public concern about which the public was entitled to be informed. But the more usual practice is to give public officials an aura of dignity and to put the results of their efforts into a context of rationality and coherence, regardless of the actual facts in the situation.

Failure to disclose private and public misbehavior by government officials and sugar-coating of political reality is both detrimental and beneficial to the public interest. It is detrimental if politicians neglect the public business or behave irresponsibly. Such stories should be told. The fear of publicity might have salutary effects and voters might be put on guard. There are, however, situations in which covering up official misconduct may be helpful if negative publicity about public officials is unnecessarily harmful.

APPRAISING THE NEWSMAKING PROCESS

Do newspeople do a good job in selecting news and entertainment categories to be covered, the proportion of time and space to be allotted to each of these categories, and the individual offerings to be included in them? It depends on the standards that the critic is applying. If one contends that news can and should be a *mirror of society* that faithfully reproduces a teacup version of life, the newsmaking process leaves much to be desired. With its emphasis on the exceptional, rather than the ordinary, its focus on a limited number of regular beats to the exclusion of other sources of news, and its preference for conflict and bad news, it pictures a world which is far from reality.[40] If one adopts the classical — albeit debatable — American notion that the media should be the eyes and ears of intelligent and aware citizens who are interested primarily in news which is of major *social* and *political significance* to their community and country, one must again find fault with the gatekeeping process. Obviously, much space and time is given to trivia and many significant developments are ignored or reported so briefly that their meaning is lost. Often the human interest appeal of a story is emphasized over its chief substance or meaning.

Having said that, it becomes a very controversial matter to name specific significant events that failed to receive the amount and kind of

coverage they deserved. What is and is not significant, as well as grada-
tions and ranks in significance, depends on the observer's world view
and political orientation. Much of the published criticism of the media
consists of polemical works which take the media to task for omitting
the author's areas of special concern. But what is one person's intellectual meat is another's poison. Conservatives decry the emphasis on civil
rights, misdeeds of the CIA and FBI, and the lack of support for defense
spending. Liberals complain that the media legitimize big business and
the military and neglect social reforms and radical perspectives.

Frequently, there is the additional charge that the choices made
about inclusion and exclusion of media fare and about story focus and
tone were dictated by political bias. These charges have been particularly common when the media have featured controversial public policy
issues such as the dangers of atomic energy generation, or the merits of a
new weapons system, or when political campaigns or demonstrations
were covered.

A number of content analyses of such events definitely refute the
charges of political bias if bias is defined as lopsided coverage of one candidate or selected issue or deliberate slanting of news. Instead, these
analyses show that media lean toward covering a balanced array of issues in a neutral manner, and include contrasting viewpoints.[41] But
these analyses have usually involved situations in which bias charges
could be anticipated and media personnel could therefore be expected to
take exceptional care to treat the situation even-handedly. It is possible,
therefore, that future studies of different situations may still turn up
deliberate political bias.

When coverage is imbalanced, the reasons generally spring from the
newsmaking process itself, rather than politically motivated slanting.
For instance, candidate Ronald Reagan received more coverage of his
campaign activities during the 1980 primaries than candidate Philip
Crane, who campaigned far more vigorously. Reagan was a familiar,
newsworthy figure, and Crane was not. Events in Chicago are reported
more fully than similar events in Denver because the networks have a
permanently leased wire from Chicago to New York, but not from Denver to New York. The New Hampshire primary receives disproportion-
ately ample coverage because it happens to be the first in a presidential
election.

Inevitably the stories chosen represent a small, unsystematic sample of the news of the day. In this sense, every issue of a newspaper or every television newscast is a "biased sample" of current events. Published
stories often generate follow-up coverage, heightening the bias effect. Attempts to be even-handed may lead to similar coverage of dissimilar
events, thereby introducing bias.

Besides evaluating news as a mirror of society and a reflection of socially and politically significant events, one can also evaluate it from the
standpoint of audience preferences. By and large the media gatekeepers

appear to be doing well by that standard. People like their products well enough to consume them on a scale unheard of in the past. Three out of every four adults claim to read newspapers regularly; nearly all homes have radio and television, which most adults use. In the average household, the radio is turned on for three hours a day and television for seven. Millions of viewers, by their own free choice, have switched from other pre-television age sources of diversion to watching shows condemned as "trash" by social critics. These same people ignore shows and newspaper stories which have the critics' seal of approval.

Overall, if one views the media simultaneously from all three perspectives, one can say that they have developed a balanced approach. Most newspapers and broadcast enterprises try to mirror at least a portion of the world. Most also see it as their function to present some serious political and social information and analysis. At the same time, most cater to the audience's appetite for easily digested entertainment and diversion. The end product cannot fully satisfy anyone.

SUMMARY

What is *news* depends on what a particular society deems socially significant and/or personally satisfying to media audiences. The prevailing political and social ideology therefore determines what type of information will be gathered and the range of meanings which will be given to it. News collection is structured through the beat system to produce the desired information.

Beyond the larger framework, which is rooted in America's current political ideology, overt political considerations for news selection are rare. Instead, the profit motive and technical constraints of news production become paramount selection criteria. These criteria impose more stringent constraints on television than on print media because television deals with larger, more heterogeneous audiences and requires pictures to match word stories. Television, unlike newspapers which have no competition in the local market, must compete with several other electronic outlets for attention.

The end products of these various constraints on newsmaking are news media which support the American political system in general, but emphasize its shortcomings and conflicts — because journalists see themselves as watchdogs of public honesty and because conflict is exciting. News is geared primarily to attract and entertain rather than educate the audience about politically significant events.

The pressures to report news rapidly while it is happening often lead to presentation of disjointed fragments and disparate commentary. This leaves the audience with the impossible task of weaving the fragments into a meaningful tapestry of interrelated events.

The end product of the gatekeeping process is inadequate, if judged in terms of the information needs of the ideal citizen in the ideal democracy. This is especially true of television, which provides little more than a headline service for news and which mirrors the world like the curved mirrors at the county fair. Reality is there, but badly out of shape and proportion.

But if one concedes, as I do, that most of us only faintly resemble the ideal citizen, and that most look to the media for entertainment, rather than enlightenment, a different appraisal suggests itself. By and large, American mass media do serve the general public about as well as that public wants to be served in practice, rather than theory. Entertainment is interspersed with a smattering of serious information. Breadth of coverage is preferred over narrow depth. In times of acute crisis, as we shall see in Chapter 8, the media can and do follow a different pattern. Serious news displaces entertainment, and the broad sweep of events turns into a narrow, in-depth focus on the crisis. Short of acute crisis, superficiality prevails most of the time.

NOTES

1. Ron Powers, *The Newscasters* (New York: St. Martin's Press, 1977), p. 1.
2. Ibid., p. 234.
3. Popularity of specific newspaper stories or television programs is assessed through audience surveys. These are done most systematically for television, where major rating services like A. C. Nielsen and the American Research Bureau (ARB) use viewer diaries and electronic devices to monitor the shows being watched. Advertising rates are based on audience size for particular radio and television shows. A 1 percent increase in audience size can mean as much as $1 million additional advertising income. For newspapers, rates are based on paid circulation, which is monitored by an independent agency, the Audit Bureau of Circulations. Audiences are rarely asked whether they would like to substitute different programs for existing fare.
4. Malcolm Warner, "Decision-Making in Network Television News," pp. 158-167 in Jeremy Tunstall, ed., *Media Sociology* (Urbana: University of Illinois Press, 1970). Also see David L. Altheide, *Creating Reality: How TV News Distorts Events* (Beverly Hills, Calif.: Sage 1977).
5. The share of the networks in television gatekeeping has increased steadily. In 1957, the networks produced roughly 41 percent of evening programming. This increased to 96 percent by 1968. Tracy A. Westen, "Barriers to Creativity," *Journal of Communication* 28 (Spring 1978): 38.
6. Quoted by Powers, *The Newscasters*, p. 31.
7. Peter Braestrup, *Big Story* (Garden City, N.Y.: Anchor Books, 1978).
8. George Gerbner, "Ideological Perspective and Political Tendencies in News Reporting," *Journalism Quarterly* 41 (August 1964): 495-508.
9. The social systems framework for mass communications analysis is sketched out in Phillip J. Tichenor, George A. Donohue and Clarice N. Olien, "Mass Communication Research: Evolution of a Structural Model," *Journalism Quarterly* 50 (Autumn 1973): 419-425.
10. David Morgan, *The Capitol Press Corps: Newsmen and the Governing of New York State* (Westport, Conn.: Greenwood Press, 1978), pp. 44-47.
11. Powers, *The Newscasters*, p. 30.
12. Quoted in Ibid., p. 79. The evidence on whether or not editors and reporters

assess their audiences' tastes properly is mixed. Ralph K. Martin, Garrett J. O'Keefe, and Oguz B. Nayman, in "Opinion Agreement and Accuracy Between Editors and Their Readers," *Journalism Quarterly* 49 (Autumn 1972): 460-468, say they do. Leo Bogart, in "Changing News Interests and the Mass Media," *Public Opinion Quarterly* 23 (Winter 1968-69): 560-574, holds to the contrary.

13. Edward Jay Epstein, *News from Nowhere* (New York: Vintage Books, 1974), pp. 17-18.

14. G. Ray Funkhouser, "Trends in Media Coverage of the Issues of the '60's," *Journalism Quarterly* 50 (Fall 1973): 533-538.

15. Somewhat similar feelings are harbored even toward the casts of soap operas. People whose lives are confined largely to their homes often adopt soap opera people as part of their family. They avidly follow the trials and tribulations of these people and may even try to model themselves after them.

16. A study of 149 small and large newspapers reports the following news space allocations: Local, 75 percent; Sports, 6 percent; National, 4 percent; Women's, 4 percent; International, 3 percent; Editorial, 3 percent; State, 3 percent; Financial, 2 percent. The measurements refer to space in column inches of total newshole. Dan Drew and G. Cleveland Wilhoit, "Newshole Allocation Policies of American Daily Newspapers," *Journalism Quarterly* 53 (Fall 1976): 434-440.

17. Robert W. Clyde and James K. Buckalew, "Inter-Media Standardization: A Q-Analysis of News Editors," *Journalism Quarterly* 46 (Summer 1969): 349-351.

18. Leon V. Sigal, *Reporters and Officials: The Organization and Politics of Newsmaking* (Lexington, Mass.: D. C. Heath, 1973), pp. 119-130.

19. The phrase is from Stanley K. Bigman, "Rivals in Conformity: A Study of Two Competing Dailies," *Journalism Quarterly* 25 (Autumn 1948): 127-131.

20. Joseph S. Fowler and Stuart W. Showalter, "Evening Network News Selection: A Confirmation of News Judgment," *Journalism Quarterly* 51 (Winter 1974): 712-715.

21. Sigal, *Reporters and Officials,* p. 66.

22. Joseph R. Dominick, "Geographic Bias in National TV News," *Journal of Communication* 27 (Fall 1977): 94-99.

23. Robert Rutherford Smith, "Mythic Elements in Television News," *Journal of Communication* 29 (Winter 1979): 75-82.

24. Ben Bagdikian, *The Information Machines* (New York: Harper & Row, 1971), pp. 99-100.

25. David M. White, "The Gatekeeper," *Journalism Quarterly* 27 (Fall 1950): 383-390, replicated by Paul B. Snider, "Mr. Gates Revisited," *Journalism Quarterly* 43 (Autumn 1967): 419-427. See also James D. Harless, "Mail Call," *Journalism Quarterly* 51 (Spring 1974): 87-90.

26. Drew and Wilhoit, "Newshole Allocation Policies of American Daily Newspapers," pp. 434-440.

27. Herbert J. Gans, *Deciding What's News: A Study of CBS Evening News, NBC Nightly News, Newsweek & Time* (New York: Pantheon Books, 1979), pp. 8-31. Also see Gaye Tuchman, *Making News: A Study in the Construction of Reality* (New York: Free Press, 1978).

28. Sandra William Ernst, "Baseball or Brickbats: A Content Analysis of Community Development," *Journalism Quarterly* 49 (Spring 1972): 86-90.

29. *The New York Times,* May 11, 1977.

30. George Gerbner, Larry Gross, Marilyn Jackson-Beeck, Suzanne Jeffries-Fox and Nancy Signorielli, "Cultural Indicators: Violence Profile No. 9," *Journal of Communication* 28 (Summer 1978): 176-207. Small-town newspapers

are more apt to highlight the positive, telling what is good, rather than what is bad, because conflict is less tolerable in social systems where most of the leaders constantly rub elbows.

31. Clarice N. Olien, George A. Donohue, and Phillip J. Tichenor, "The Community Editor's Power and the Reporting of Conflict," *Journalism Quarterly* 45 (Summer 1968): 243-52, present evidence that media watchdog functions increase as differentiation and pluralism increase in a social system. Also see Bruce Cole, "Trends in Science and Conflict Coverage in Four Metropolitan Newspapers," *Journalism Quarterly* 52 (Fall 1973): 465-71.
32. The term is Michael J. Robinson's in "American Political Legitimacy in an Era of Electronic Journalism: Reflections on the Evening News," in Richard Adler, ed., *Television as a Social Force: New Approaches to TV Criticism* (New York: Praeger, 1975), pp. 97-139.
33. Stephen E. Rada, "Manipulating the Media: A Case Study of a Chicano Strike in Texas," *Journalism Quarterly* 54 (Spring 1977): 109-113.
34. A strong attack on status-quo support is contained in Herbert J. Schiller, *The Mind Managers* (Boston: Beacon Press, 1973). Also see Claus Mueller, *The Politics of Communication* (London: Oxford University Press, 1973).
35. Social forces are "more important than reporters' personalities in shaping the news," according to Warren Breed in "Social Controls in the Newsroom," *Social Forces* 33 (1955): 326-35. Reporters think otherwise. See Ruth C. Flegel and Steven H. Chaffee, "Influences of Editors, Readers, and Personal Opinions on Reporters," *Journalism Quarterly* 48 (Winter 1971): 645-51.
36. Sigal, *Reporters and Officials*, pp. 119-130.
37. A comparison of war movies made with and without Pentagon aid showed that aided movies depicted the military in a more favorable light. Russell E. Shain, "Effects of Pentagon Influence on War Movies, 1948-70," *Public Opinion Quarterly* 38 (Fall 1972): 641-647.
38. David L. Paletz, Peggy Reichert, and B. McIntire, "How the Media Support Local Government Authority," *Public Opinion Quarterly,* 35 (Spring 1971): 80-92.
39. Ibid., pp. 83-84.
40. George Comstock and Robin Cobbey, "Watching the Watchdogs: Trends and Problems in Monitoring Network News," in William Adams and Fay Schreibman, eds., *Television Network News: Issues in Content Research* (Washington: George Washington University, 1978), 47-63.
41. Ibid., pp. 53-55.

READINGS

Adams, William, and Schreibman, Fay, eds. *Television Network News: Issues in Content Research.* Washington: George Washington University, 1978.

Altheide, David L. *Creating Reality: How TV News Distorts Events.* Beverly Hills, Calif.: Sage, 1977.

Bagdikian, Ben. *The Information Machines.* New York: Harper & Row, 1971.

Epstein, Edward Jay. *News from Nowhere.* New York: Vintage Books, 1974.

Gans, Herbert J. *Deciding What's News: A Study of CBS Evening News, NBC Nightly News, Newsweek & Time.* New York: Pantheon Books, 1979.

Morgan, David. *The Capitol Press Corps: Newsmen and the Governing of New York State.* Westport, Conn.: Greenwood Press, 1978.

Powers, Ron. *The Newscasters.* New York: St. Martin's Press, 1977.

Sigal, Leon V. *Reporters and Officials: The Organization and Politics of Newsmaking.* Lexington, Mass.: D.C. Heath, 1973.

4

Press Freedom and the Law

Should the press be barred from some judicial trials? Most newspeople say "no." But 53 percent of the public believes it should, to protect the rights of accused persons. This is what Harris poll interviewers learned in a national survey conducted in April 1979. By a 1 percent margin, the poll respondents also indicated that media reports about open trials should be free from judicial restraints and prohibitions. Fifty-four percent of those interviewed believe, furthermore, that courts should not order reporters to turn over confidential story notes, even if these notes are needed by parties involved in a criminal trial.

The nearly even split among the public on questions of freedom to gather information and publish it without restraint and freedom to conceal information to protect personal rights reflects perplexing dilemmas faced by democratic societies. How can freedom of the press to report all news be reconciled with protection of society from the dangers of unrestrained publication? How can the right to compel needed testimony be squared with the media's need to protect news sources? In this chapter, we shall look at various facets of these and related dilemmas.

We shall begin by probing the problems which arise when a free press claims the exclusive right to decide what to publish and what to omit. This right often clashes with popular demands for newspaper space and air time to publicize social and political causes. Next, we shall look at the problems which the press itself faces in gaining unrestrained access to information which it needs as raw material for news, when government claims the right to conceal this information. Finally, we shall examine barriers to publication imposed to safeguard private and public interests.

The constitutional basis for most of the laws and court decisions about free access to the press and freedom to gather news and publish it is the First Amendment. It guarantees that, "Congress shall make no law . . . abridging the freedom of speech or of the press." This makes the news business the only private industry in America that is expressly protected by the Constitution. However, the dimensions of this protection have remained in flux throughout American constitutional history.

The Founding Fathers granted this special protection to the press because they believed that the right to collect and disseminate information and opinions is the bedrock on which a free society is built. If some restraints are needed to protect society from harmful information, they must generally come through punishment after publication, not through "prior restraint." Publication can be prevented only if it "will surely result in direct, immediate, and irreparable damage to our nation or its people."[1] The belief in the political importance of a free press has stood the test of time and still remains a cornerstone of American democracy. Therefore, anything that affects the interpretation or the scope of this basic right is a matter of major political significance.

ACCESS TO THE MEDIA

The notion of government "by the people" would seem to require that the people have a right to make their voices heard. Ralph Nader's consumer protection movement or Howard Jarvis' tax revolt could never have gathered widespread support throughout the country without mass media publicity. What would have happened if the media had refused to tell these stories? Did Nader or Jarvis have a right to publicity for his views and for his organizing activities?

The answer is "No." In the absence of such a right, it is very difficult for most people, other than journalists or major public figures, to gain access to the media. Jerome Barron, a lawyer interested in civil liberties, in a book entitled *Freedom of the Press for Whom — The Right of Access to the Mass Media*,[2] accuses the media of fighting for broad rights of free expression for themselves, while denying these rights to the public. Media personnel decide what stories are publicized and whose views are presented. This leaves a large number of people who want to proclaim their views without a suitable public forum.

Barron argues that the First Amendment right to publish freely should be open to all individuals and groups, not only to news professionals. If individuals have a special cause or feel that some of the situations depicted by the mass media are not presented accurately, or that certain information is omitted, they should have an opportunity to use the mass media to state their views. Without this right, they may be doomed to political ineffectiveness.

Print Media Access

What rights of access to the mass media do individuals in private and public life have? To answer this question accurately, a distinction must be made between the print media and the electronic media. American courts have generally held that the freedom of the print media to determine what they will or will not print, and whose views they will or will not present, is nearly absolute. As long as the media stay clear of deliberate libel and slander and do not publish top secret information, they may make publishing decisions unhampered by legal restraints.

The freedom of the press to publish or suppress information is delineated in the case of *Miami Herald Publishing Company v. Tornillo,* decided in 1974.[3] The case involved the constitutionality of a Florida statute which provided a right of reply to persons running for public office who had been personally attacked by a newspaper. A candidate who was attacked on the editorial page had the right to reply on the editorial page in a format similar to the attack. If the attack appeared in the news pages, the candidate had the right to equal space, type, and position there. The law had been passed to deal with the problem of attacks published very late in a campaign, giving candidates little time for a rebuttal. The consequence might be loss of the election.

The case arose in 1972 when Patrick Tornillo, Jr., leader of the Dade County Teachers Union, was running for the Florida State Legislature. Just before the primary, the *Miami Herald* published two editorials objecting to Tornillo's election because he had led a recent teachers' strike. Tornillo demanded that the paper print his replies to the editorials. The paper refused. After Tornillo lost the primary decisively, he brought suit against the paper.

The case went through the Florida court system, with conflicting decisions by various courts. Finally, it reached the United States Supreme Court in 1974. That Court ruled unanimously that newspapers can print or refuse to print anything they like. Editors have an unlimited right to decide what goes in or what stays out of the paper. No one, including a candidate whose reputation has been damaged, has the right to demand space in a newspaper. Therefore the Florida statute granting a right to reply was unconstitutional. The decision reaffirmed what had been the thrust of the law all along. Private citizens may request that a story be printed, and that request may be granted. But they have no right to demand publication.[4]

Electronic Media Access

The rules are different for the electronic media because they are viewed as semi-monopolies. Unlike the print media business, which is open to anyone, entry into the electronic media business requires a license. To assure fair public access to this limited resources, the laws regulating the electronic communication media make provisions for their use by the public.

Access rights fall under three categories: the equal time provision, the fairness doctrine, and the right of rebuttal. These access rights are provided through Section 315 of the Federal Communications Act of 1934 and its amendments and interpretations. The equal time provision requires that broadcasters who permit a candidate for political office to campaign on their stations must give equal opportunities to all other candidates for the same office. Under the fairness doctrine, broadcasters who air controversial issues of public importance must provide reasonable opportunities for the presentation of conflicting viewpoints. The right of rebuttal requires that an attack on the honesty, character, or integrity of an identified person or group entitles the target of the attack to a reply. The broadcaster must notify the targets about the broadcast and must supply a transcript or summary. Thereafter, a reasonable opportunity to respond must be provided. All of the regulations under Section 315 which mandate public access are subject to one very important implied condition: the rights arise only after the station has broadcast the information in question.

The Right to Equal Time. Under the equal time rule, a station need not allow candidates for political office to broadcast. But if it gives or sells time to one candidate for a specific office, it must give equal time to all of the candidates for the same office. Even if there are 15 candidates for the same office, and most of them have few backers, they all have a right to equal time. By the same token, whenever the station denies time to all candidates for the same office, none of them have a right to demand access under the campaign coverage provisions of Section 315.

Stations faced with the all or none alternative of the equal time rule for candidates often opt for "none," particularly for state and local offices. This avoids the problem of cluttering their programs with a large number of campaign broadcasts which would be of little interest to their listeners and costly to the station in lost advertising revenues. It also keeps many viable candidates off the air who might otherwise have had exposure.

To make lengthy debates between mainline candidates for major offices possible, without running afoul of the equal time provisions, Congress suspended these provisions in 1960 to permit the Kennedy-Nixon debates. A different tactic was used in 1976 to facilitate the Carter-Ford debates. The equal time rule was circumvented by staging the debates as public meetings which were then covered by the news media like regular news. Routine newscasts are not subject to the equal time rule.

Billing the 1976 presidential debates as public meetings arranged by the League of Women Voters and covered by the press like any newsworthy event was obviously a subterfuge which strained the intent of the law. Several minor-party candidates, eager to be included in the debates, sued on the ground that this circumvention of equal time provisions was an illegal ruse. But the courts ruled against them. Had the objectors prevailed, it would have been impossible to achieve the main purpose of the debates: to allow the public a leisurely view of the leading candidates, side by side, matching their political wits in three 90-minute sessions.

The curbs on political dialogue engendered by the equal time rule have led to widespread dissatisfaction with Section 315. Many observers believe that it has done more political harm than good and that efforts to evade it by subterfuge have been regrettable. It has also blocked important presidential messages from reaching the public. For instance, when President Ford set forth his farm policy in a speech to the Future Farmers of America in 1976, the networks shied away from full-length coverage because it might involve them in an equal time allotment for the Democratic candidate. Normally, they would have broadcast a presidential speech outlining major policy proposals.

The Right to Fair Treatment. The fairness doctrine has a broader reach than the equal time provision because it is not limited to candidates for political office. Under the fairness doctrine, reasonable time must be given for the expression of opposing views if any controversial public issue is discussed.

Like the equal time provisions, the fairness doctrine has given rise to a number of problems; most importantly, it impoverishes public debate by suppressing controversy. The media frequently shy away from programs dealing with controversial public issues to avoid demands to air opposing views in place of revenue-producing programs.

When controversial programs have been aired, it has been difficult to decide who has the right to reply. For instance, when President Nixon justified America's incursion into Cambodia during the Vietnam War, three groups immediately demanded time to broadcast counter-arguments. One was a group of Democratic senators; another was the Democratic National Committee. The third was a group of business executives organized to oppose the Vietnam War. The three groups differed in their assessment of the errors committed by the president and none wanted to yield to any of the others.

The media finally gave air time to the Democratic National Committee to speak for the opposition. Members of the Republican National Committee then claimed that the Democratic National Committee had used its time for political propaganda unrelated to the Cambodian situation. Therefore they asked for time to oppose the views expressed by the Democrats. The whole affair became almost ridiculous. The courts finally settled the problem of choosing among opponents. They ruled that no group has the right to expound its particular brand of opposition. Rather, it is up to the media to decide which opposing group will be heard.

This decision gives the media a great deal of control over the types of opposition views which will be aired. If media personnel favor certain views they can select a group which is in accord with these views. Furthermore, the most prominent groups who wish to be heard are most likely to be selected. For instance, if a group of senators and prestigious business people are competing with members of a student organization to speak for the opposition, it is unlikely that the students will be selected as spokesmen. Groups who hold unconventional views or are on the extreme right or left of the political spectrum are also unlikely choices. This sharply reduces their chances for changing the existing power structure.

The media can avoid the problem of air time for opposing views entirely by including opposing views on the issue in question in their regular news programs. For instance, when official American Vietnam War policies became matters of controversy, media spokesmen argued successfully that opposing viewpoints had been fully aired in regular newscasts. Generally, such media contentions have been sustained by the courts if they are supported by reasonably good evidence. The courts have also ruled against an automatic right to oppose statements made during presidential news conferences, as long as the media air contrary views in news analyses immediately after such conferences.

The media thus retain a substantial degree of control over the array of viewpoints which receive a hearing. However, the pressures and litigation which they have faced have made them more receptive to airing opposing views voluntarily, particularly after presidential talks and news conferences. The temper of the times has thus curbed editorial freedom, even though legal rights remain unchanged.

Is there a right of reply to contentious statements made in commercials? A number of groups, such as the oil industry, conservation buffs, and the drug industry have used commercials to carry controversial messages regarding public policies. But the law is very unclear about the right of reply because the courts have spoken with forked tongues.

The landmark case, *Banzhaf v. Federal Communications Commission*, which seemed to indicate that there was a right to reply, has turned out to be the exception, rather than the rule. It concerned television advertisements for cigarettes, before such commercials were banned from television. John W. Banzhaf, III, a young Manhattan lawyer and antismoking activist, accused the cigarette companies of promoting the glamour of cigarette smoking without advertising its dangers. Since smoking has become a life and death public health issue, he demanded the right to present views opposed to smoking. The networks countered that opposition to smoking had been adequately presented by commercials and stories from the heart institute, the lung association, and the cancer institute. The Supreme Court held that smoking involved such an extraordinarily important health issue that, contrary to usual rules, broadcasters must balance cigarette commercials with antismoking spots.[5] But the decision did not supply a yardstick to determine which issues are exceptional enough to warrant time for counter-commercials. All subsequent claims for counter-commercial time have been refused.

The Right of Rebuttal. The final access issue to be discussed is the right of rebuttal for a personal attack, which arises when individuals are assailed on radio or television in a way which damages their reputation.

The controlling case in this area of communication law is *Red Lion Broadcasting Co. v. Federal Communications Commission,* decided in 1969. It set up a rather broad scope for the right of reply.[6] The *Red Lion* case arose because a book about conservative Senator Barry Goldwater written by Fred J. Cook, a very liberal newsman, was attacked by the Reverend Billy James Hargis on a program conducted and paid for by the ultraconservative Christian Crusade. Fred Cook asked for broadcast time, free of charge, to reply. The station was willing to sell him reply time, but refused to grant it free of charge. It argued that it could not be responsible for the content of all programs for which various groups had bought television time. If the station were forced to grant free rebuttal time for statements on such broadcasts, it would be impossible in the future to sell time to private broadcasters who might air controversial right or left-wing views.

In the *Red Lion* case, to the delight of proponents of ready access to the airwaves by the public, the courts sided with the plaintiff. Cook was granted the right to rebuttal, free of charge, on the ground that maligned individuals deserve the right to reply and that the public has the right to hear opposing views. It was a hollow victory for supporters of free access, however, because it led to sharp curtailment of air time for controversial broadcasts.

The *Red Lion* case is one of many examples of political manipulation of the regulatory process. Cook's protest had been paid for and orchestrated by the Democratic National Committee as part of an effort to generate an avalanche of demands for rebuttal broadcasts to conservative radio and television programs. The hope was that stations would then cancel these broadcasts to avoid the costs of free rebuttal time.[7] This did, indeed, happen. The Christian Crusade, for example, by 1975, had been dropped by 300 of its 350 stations. Since 1969, the courts have retreated somewhat from their broad support for the right of rebuttal because of its chilling effects on broadcasting controversial subjects. The flood of rebuttal requests also mired the FCC in a morass of claims and counterclaims which it could not process with its limited resources.

Reform Proposals. To halt the deleterious effects on programming and the flood of FCC proceedings, strong demands have been voiced in Congress and by many broadcasters and communication scholars to do away with all the access provisions linked to Section 315 — equal time, fairness, and right of rebuttal. The pleaders contend that there is no longer any reason to consider electronic media as semi-monopolies, in contrast to presumably competitive print media. In fact, print media in the age of one-newspaper towns face less competition than electronic media, with their competing networks and competition among multiple radio and television outlets. For this reason, the electronic media should be just as free as the print media to make publishing decisions. The quality and fairness of their programming decisions and their success in presenting a wide array of viewpoints on controversial issues should be judged from a long-range perspective, at license renewal time, rather than case by case. Renewal of a station's license should hinge on adequate performance over the entire three-year period.

Such proposals, proponents claim, would encourage stations to air controversies while still providing a balance of views over a period of time.[8] Opponents point to the fact that even with Section 315, many controversial programs are aired. They warn that removal of access protections will leave the public at the not-so-tender mercies of media gatekeepers. As Jerome Barron has remarked plaintively, "The myth says that if the press is kept 'free,' liberty of discussion is assured. But, in how few hands is left the exercise of 'freedom'!"[9]

Problems of the Status Quo

Apart from the right to reply to a personal attack, to request time to express opposing views when controversial matters of public interest are aired, and the right of rival candidates to equal broadcast time, there are no access rights for individuals. If a person or group wants to bring its message to public attention through the mass media, there is no way to do it if the media are unwilling.

The television networks, which command the widest national audience, have been very restrictive even in displaying high-quality public information programs produced by professionals outside their own organization. An example was a series on Cuban leader Fidel Castro, produced by former press secretaries for President John Kennedy and Senator George McGovern. Although they had excellent original film of substantial public interest, the networks refused to buy it except for a 30-second news spot, until a follow-up interview by a network reporter could be added.

People in public life who want access to the mass media to explain their views face problems quite similar to those of private individuals. Although the media are likely to be more sympathetic to their requests, there are many occasions when coverage is denied. For instance, Governor Dan Walker of Illinois (1972-1976) asked the media in his state repeatedly to broadcast his speeches dealing with important public policies, such as appropriations for educational programs. The broadcast media refused his requests, saying that they had amply covered his policies in regular news broadcasts. They did not want to give him air time because it might force them to allot time for opposing views. When the governor challenged their right to deny air time in court, the judge supported the broadcasters. Not even a governor, the court ruled, has the right to demand air time to explain his policies to the public.

Prior to the Nixon years, presidential requests for air time were routinely granted. This is no longer the case. Several speeches by Presidents Ford and Nixon were not broadcast at all because the media considered them partisan political statements. Others were carried by only a limited number of stations, forcing the president to compete against regular entertainment broadcasts. This reduced audiences sharply, compared to broadcasts which are carried simultaneously on all stations. On still other occasions, presidential speeches have been deferred until late evening, denying the president access to prime time audiences.

The question of access rights to the airwaves has also been raised in connection with efforts to assure that broadcasts are made available to suit the needs of population groups whose concerns are different from those of the general public. For instance, several public interest groups have objected to the lack of programs for young children, and have asked for increases, even though such programming would be of little interest to the majority of listeners and viewers. The FCC has concurred that children constitute an important special audience whose needs for distinctive programming have to be met. Stations have been reluctant to add such programs because revenues from children's programs are comparatively low, particularly since the FCC as a result of lobby pressures has reduced the amount of advertising permitted on children's programs from 12 minutes per hour to 9 minutes. This rule is intended to protect immature viewers from the seduction of advertising.

Other audiences whose right to access for special programs has been recognized sporadically include blacks, Hispanics, and lovers of classical music. Occasional rulings have forced the electronic media to set aside time for broadcasts geared to such groups whose interests would be disregarded if the forces of the economic marketplace were given full rein. The FCC has further protected the interests of these groups by giving preference in license applications to stations whose output is likely to serve neglected clienteles.

Other Approaches to Media Access

Access to the mass media through independently produced programs, individual requests for air time, and FCC rulings that support the interests of minority audiences has been only moderately successful. Some other routes to gain access are even less satisfactory. Letters to the editor are an example. Due to lack of space, most papers publish only very few letters. The *New York Times,* for instance, receives more than 60,000 letters a year and publishes 4 to 5 percent of them, limiting length strictly. Even with these stringent controls, space devoted to letters equals space for editorials in the *Times.* Editors select the letters to be published, using a variety of criteria that generally exclude average people. Letters that are unusual or sent by someone well known are most likely to be printed.

Another avenue to access is the use of paid advertisements. A number of labor unions, business enterprises, lobby groups, and even foreign governments have placed advertisements in newspapers and on the air to present their sides of disputes and public policy issues. This route is usually open to those who can afford the steep purchase price, which may run into thousands of dollars for full-page advertisements and national broadcast exposure. However, print and electronic media have occasionally refused to print advertisements or sell air time. For instance, in the 1970s, power companies were unable to buy air time to tell their version of the energy crisis, even when they offered to pay for rebuttal time which might be demanded by opponents.

Access to air time was also denied in 1975 to the Republican National Committee, which wanted to buy three half-hour slots on national television to explain the party's philosophy and goals to the public. The networks' right to refuse to sell time was upheld by the courts, as long as the policy had been used even-handedly for all similar organizations. The courts have also upheld the right of newspapers to refuse to sell advertising space, as long as refusal is not used to discriminate against particular groups. However, the newspaper decisions have not been as clear-cut as the television decisions. In some instances, courts have ordered papers to accept controversial advertising as long as advertising space for announcements of various types was for sale.

Most people who would like to publicize their views lack the substantial sums of money which advertising costs. This was the problem for Peter Kiger, a young draft resister, who wanted to publicize his reasons for opposition to the draft.[10] Since he earned less than $50 a week, the cost of newspaper and television advertising was way beyond his means. The cost of a full-page ad in the *New York Times* then was $7,200. One minute on a television news broadcast ranged from $1,500 to $3,000. Kiger and his friends hit upon the strategy of notifying the media where and when they would publicly burn their draft cards. Sure enough, nearly three dozen radio, television, and newspaper reporters came at the appointed time. The ensuing free publicity reached well over 2 million people. But the story had an unhappy ending for the protesters. Officials from the Justice Department, who had learned about the burning, set legal proceedings in motion which, ultimately, led to Peter Kiger's conviction for illegal draft card burning. While sympathetic to his plea that the illegal act was his only chance for media coverage, the judge did not consider it to be an adequate defense.[11]

The rise of lobby groups eager to assure broad access rights to people with minority viewpoints and FCC sympathy with their pleas have made broadcasters more sensitive to pressures for access by political activists. But even if radio or television station management is willing to grant access to such people, it is still faced with the problem of insufficient time to air every claimant's view on the electronic media. Despite the multiplication of television and radio channels promised by technological advancements, there will never be enough channels —or even newspaper pages — to publicize all important views. Nor do concerned citizens have the time or capacity to listen to all views and put them into proper perspectives. In fact, the capacity to broadcast and publicize already far exceeds the audience's capacity to listen and assimilate.

ACCESS TO INFORMATION

Special Access for the Media?

The right to publish without restraint means little if information cannot be obtained. This raises the question whether the media do and should have a special right of access to places where they wish to gather information. Recent United States Supreme Court decisions have ruled against special access rights. In *Zemel v. Rusk*,[12] for instance, a citizen sued to claim his right to a passport to visit Cuba and learn about conditions there. The Court upheld the State Department's ban on Cuban travel and ruled that neither ordinary citizens nor media personnel have a right to gather information. In the Court's words: "The right to speak and publish does not carry with it the unrestrained right to gather information."[13] Similarly, in *Branzburg v. Hayes*,[14] a case involving a newsman's right to refuse testimony before a grand jury because he wanted to protect his sources, the Court said, "It has generally been held that the First Amendment does not guarantee the press a constitutional right of special access to information not available to the public generally."[15] The press had argued that its status as the fourth branch of government, surveying the political scene for the public, entitled it to special rights of access.

The decision denying such rights excludes journalists from access to many politically crucial events and thus deprives the public of important, albeit sensitive, information. Closed White House and Camp David meetings provide many examples. Other events which are often barred to the media are pretrial hearings and grand jury proceedings. Grand jury proceedings determine the sufficiency of evidence of wrongdoing to justify indictments. Because they frequently involve very high political stakes, news about such proceedings has repeatedly been leaked to newspeople by participants eager for publicity. The press also has no right to attend conferences of the Supreme Court where it would learn why the justices had decided to hear certain cases and refused to hear others. Media people may be barred from attending sessions of legislative bodies which are closed to the general public. Such sessions ordinarily deal with secret information which requires protection or with matters which might prove embarrassing to legislators.

Newspeople have no right to be admitted to sites of crimes and disasters when the general public is excluded. Nor do they have the right to visit prisons and interview and film inmates, even for the purpose of investigating prison conditions and rumors of brutality. In three recent cases, the Supreme Court stressed the availability of general information when it upheld the right of prison authorities to deny special access to reporters.[16] This may indicate that the Court might grant access in situations where information about prison conditions was totally lacking.

Many of the decisions regarding access to information have been highly controversial, as shown by 5 to 4 divisions in the Supreme Court in such cases as *Branzburg v. Hayes, Pell v. Procunier,* and *Saxbe v. Washington Post Co.*[17] This clash of views among the justices makes media access rights a very fluid and exciting area of legal development at this time. A great deal of pressure has also been exerted on Congress to pass legislation that would clear up some of the uncertainties. Advocates of broadened access rights have been especially vocal.

By custom, though not by law, newspeople often receive preferred treatment in gaining entry to public events. Press passes assure media access to the best observation points for affairs like inaugurations of chief executives, moon shots, or political conventions. In many instances the media are admitted while the general public is kept out. Examples are accident and crime locations. But access is purely at the discretion of the public authorities in charge.

In wartime, military officials often do not want news personnel in certain war zones. They keep them out by denying access to transportation to these areas. This is tantamount to denial of access to news, without any legal recourse. Through such tactics, media can be effectively shut out from reporting many crucial political events, such as conferences in inaccessible places, briefings in airplanes, or inspections in underground mines.

Access to Government Documents

General Rules. Government documents are another extremely important source of political information to which access is frequently obstructed. The *Freedom of Information Act,* signed by President Lyndon B. Johnson on July 4, 1966, and broadened by amendments in 1974, ostensibly opened many governmental files to the news media and the general public.[18] But, since it is burdensome to apply for access under the act, it has not been used very widely by news personnel to compel government agencies to release information. By and large, reporters have been content to cover more readily available current news, rather than digging into government files to unearth past happenings.

Despite the Freedom of Information Act, many types of public documents remain unavailable to reporters. Federal and state information access policies were examined in 1974 by Elsie Hebert, a journalism professor.[19] She was able to get data from 38 states and the federal government. The remaining 12 states declined to provide data about their freedom of information policies. The study disclosed that there are wide variations. Some states are more liberal than the national government under the Freedom of Information Act in giving out information; others lag far behind. Most state laws provide for access to "public records." But the states define "public record" differently. The narrow common law definition has been broadened piecemeal, state by state.

For instance, laws which have been passed obviously constitute a public record. But it is not so clear that a "public record" is requested if citizens ask for the minutes of the meetings which preceded passage of a law, or tapes of the proceedings, or exhibits that a legislative committee considered before passing the law. In many states the term "public record" does not encompass any information at all about the genesis of laws and regulations.

In many jurisdictions applicants for information must demonstrate a special need for a particular set of data. Newspeople and private citizens cannot go into a record center and say "I would like to examine all your records on public health matters." They must indicate exactly what they want and why they want it. General interest is insufficient. How much interest and the kinds of interest that must be demonstrated are determined by administrators.

A widely used rule of thumb about access to information is that disclosure must be in the public interest and must not do excessive harm. It should be denied if the harm caused by opening the records is greater than the possible benefit. Accordingly, if a reporter requested the records of welfare clients for a story on welfare cheating, this request would probably be denied because it is embarrassing to many people to have others know that they are on welfare. Since there are no precise guidelines for determining what is in the public interest and what degree of harm is excessive, the judgments of public officials who control documents are supreme. In many states, legislatures, unwilling to leave access policies to the discretion of administrative officials, have listed the kinds of records that may or may not be disclosed. But that approach is unsatisfactory because legislatures cannot possibly foresee all the contingencies that may arise. Release of innocuous records may be stopped simply because the law has not provided specifically for their release.

Certain types of documents are routinely barred from disclosure. While the reasons are usually sound, the consequences of closed access may spell harm to the public's interests. For example, examination questions and answers for various tests given by governmental agencies are usually placed beyond public scrutiny. If questions and answers to civil service examinations were published, the value of these examinations might be totally destroyed. On the other hand, if the fairness and appropriateness of examination questions for public jobs are in doubt, bars to public scrutiny of questions and answers may be harmful. Likewise, favoritism in grading exams of the protegés of the powerful is a widely practiced tactic which is difficult to expose without access to graded examinations. A scandal in Chicago about the real estate broker exam grades earned by Mayor Daley's sons is a graphic case. It came to public attention, as do many closed records, through a series of "leaks" by disgruntled public employees.

Other data that are frequently kept from the reach of media personnel are records containing information which could give advantage to business competitors. Examples are bids for work to be performed for the government. In most states, the law requires competitive bidding and mandates that contracts, with some exceptions, must go to the lowest bidder. Because corruption is common in awarding government contracts, reporters often are very much interested in what has been bid or what promises have been made in return for contract awards. Without access to the records, investigative reporting of suspected fraud or corruption is impossible. On the other hand, secrecy is warranted because it really is not fair to publicize the details of a bid, allowing another firm to underbid by a few dollars and get the contract. Behind the cloak of secrecy, a lot of dirt can be swept under the rug.

The important fact to understand about the access problem is that some restraints on access are essential for the protection of individuals as well as the public. At the same time, restraints make betrayals of the public trust easier for potential offenders. Finding the right balance between protection of individuals, and protection of the interests of the public through media access, is an extremely difficult and controversial task.

Historical and National Security Documents. Another area of limited access concerns the records that major public officials keep of their administration. Generally, these records are unavailable to the media and the general public until 30 years after the death of the public official. The 30-year limit was selected to assure that most people whose private and public lives were entangled with that of the official would be dead by that time and spared possible embarrassment. Exceptions to the 30-year rule arise when official papers are classified as public, rather than private. Since the dividing line between personal and public papers is uncertain, exceptions frequently are contested in court. Former President Richard Nixon sued unsuccessfully to recover control of many of his records which had been released to the media.

The closure of the private records of public officials is part of the privacy protection afforded to all individuals, but it serves a public purpose as well. Assurance of confidentiality of uninhibited discussion in policymaking is essential. Without it, people will posture for an audience rather than freely address themselves to the substance of the issues which are under consideration. The danger of inhibiting free discussion also explains why deliberations prior to legislation or court decisions are generally closed to public scrutiny.

Documents concerning matters of national security often are unavailable for publication. Examples are information about prospective negotiations or about sensitive past negotiations. News about specific new weapons adopted by the United States, or stories indicating that security warning devices are not operating properly may also be restricted. However, in some cases such information is available in open files and can be pieced together into a coherent story. Government efforts to stop publication of this kind of story have been unsuccessful in recent years. This happened in 1979 when the government obtained an injunction to prohibit a Wisconsin magazine, *The Progressive,* from publishing an article, culled from open documents, describing how a hydrogen bomb is made. The injunction delayed publication for six months — an unusual instance of prior restraint. It was lifted when the government decided to drop the case after other publications had printed a letter disclosing most of the same information the magazine article had contained. The government's chances of winning the case in the Supreme Court had appeared to be slim. Of course, the bulk of instances of security censorship never reach the lawsuit stage, leaving an enormous number of documents outside the public's reach. In 1974, for instance, the Department of Defense alone classified more than 14,000 documents as top secret, more than 800,000 as secret, and nearly 2.5 billion as confidential. None were available for unrestricted review.

The main problem with security censorship lies in the determination of what information is truly sensitive and must be protected and what information should remain available to media personnel and the public. The media, and, to a lesser degree, Congress as well, have been trying to expand the range of information which is made available for publication. The president and executive agencies, charged with protecting national security, have bent over backward to protect information which might compromise security in any way.

The most graphic recent case which illustrates this fight is the *Pentagon Papers* case. Daniel Ellsberg, an aide to the National Security Council, the president's top security policy planning agency, testified in court that he had become disillusioned about United States military activities in Vietnam. He allegedly believed that foreign policy information contained in a study commissioned by the Defense Department about America's gradual entrapment in the Vietnam War had been improperly classified as top secret. Its release, he thought, would turn people against the war. He copied the information surreptitiously and gave it to prominent newspapers for publication. Since the war was still in progress, the executive branch considered this a criminal security breach and sued Ellsberg and the media which printed the information. The Court, in *New York Times Co. v. U.S.*[20] absolved the media, ruling that the government had been overly cautious in classifying the information as top secret. In the Court's view, publication did not harm the country. A case brought against Ellsberg for leaking the information was also dismissed because evidence had been collected through a burglary.

The decision did not end the public controversy. There is no agreement as yet about whether or not what was disclosed in the *Pentagon*

Papers damaged the foreign interests of the United States. Those who concurred with the Supreme Court pointed out that much of the information released had already been available. Dissenters countered that the information had never been compiled and had not heretofore been published in prominent sources like the *New York Times* and *Washington Post.*

Prior to the Nixon years, when a government agency had decided that certain information needed to be kept from the media, the courts usually refused to review the decision. This has obviously changed. Many people still believe that decisions to disclose or withhold security-related information to the media and the public should be made by the legislative and executive branches rather than the courts. They contend that the agencies which deal with military and foreign policy security information are infinitely better qualified to assess matters of public security than judges whose training is narrowly legal. Wise decisionmaking about disclosure of information involving national security issues is particularly difficult because the clamor of the media to obtain certain information in the "public interest" and the government's contention that it requires protection are often both self-serving. The "public interest" may be simply the reporters' interest in furthering their careers or the publisher's interest in making money, or the government's interest in shielding itself from embarrassment.

At times, security issues are resolved through informal cooperation between government and the media. When the CIA urged journalists throughout the country to suppress a story made available to them about secret American efforts to raise a sunken Russian submarine and study it, most of them complied. Similarly, in 1975 the Ford administration decided against the use of legal measures to stop the *New York Times* from publishing a report that American submarines had tapped Russian underwater cables off the coast of Vladivostok in the Soviet Union. Instead, it asked the *Times* to delay the story until the submarines had left Russian waters and to publish a restrained version of the venture. The *Times* complied, laying itself open to charges of subservience to government officials. Had the *Times* refused to cooperate, a serious confrontation between the government and the paper would have been likely.

Executive Privilege. The doctrine of executive privilege is deeply intertwined with the question of the limits of secrecy. Chief executives have the right to conceal information which they deem sensitive. This right extends to all their personal communications to their staffs about public matters. The courts have, in the past, generally upheld executive privilege, but decisions since the Nixon years suggest that it may be whittled down in the future.

Silence by various governmental departments and agencies also sharply restricts political news available to the media. Undisclosed information frequently concerns failures, incidents of malfeasance, malfunctions, or government waste. Agencies guard this type of news zealously because disclosure might harm the agency or its key personnel. Except for the ever-present opportunity to get information through leaks, reporters find it difficult to penetrate the walls of silence erected by publicity-shy agencies. Instead, they find it easier to rely on press handouts or publicity releases supplied by the agency, or on secondary reports from agency personnel. This handout information reflects their sources' sense of what is and is not news, rather than the reporters' own news judgment.[21]

Private Industry Documents

While the problem of government secrecy as a restraint on information collection is formidable, it is small compared to the problem of access to news stories covering the private sectors of society. Many enterprises whose operations affect the lives of millions of Americans as much or more than governmental agencies keep their operations shrouded in secrecy. If General Motors or International Telephone and Telegraph or General Mills wants to exclude reporters from access to information about their business practices, they may do so with impunity. So may drug companies, repair shops, or housing contractors.

There is no Freedom of Information Act covering unpublished records of private business, except for the reports which they have made to the government about sales or inventory figures, or customer lists. As noted earlier, many of these reports are closed to the public on the grounds that business cannot thrive if its operational data are made available to its competitors.[22] Moreover, the chances that withheld information will be disclosed through leaks are infinitely less in business than in government.

INDIVIDUAL RIGHTS VERSUS THE PUBLIC'S RIGHT TO KNOW

Thus far we have been concerned mainly with barriers to the free flow of information imposed by the mass media to protect editorial freedom, or by government to shield potentially sensitive information. We now turn to a discussion of barriers to circulation of information imposed by individuals or on behalf of individuals to protect rights such as the right to privacy, the right to an unprejudiced trial, the right to work freely, and the right to a good reputation.

Privacy Protection

How much may the media publish about the private affairs of people in public and private life without infringing on the right of privacy? How much is excluded from public scrutiny because of privacy rights?

The answer depends on the status of the people involved. Private individuals enjoy broad protections from publicity; people who have become public figures because their lives are of interest to the public or because they are public officials do not.

In general, state and federal courts have been fairly lenient in permitting the media to cover details about the personal affairs of people whose lives have become matters of public interest. The right to publish freely under these circumstances holds a preferred position over the right of privacy.

The trend of recent decisions is epitomized by a 1975 Georgia case in which a young woman had been raped and murdered. To protect their privacy, the family wanted to keep her name out of stories discussing the crime. The news media did not honor the family's request and published gruesome details of the crime, naming the victim. The family sued for invasion of privacy, claiming that there was absolutely no need to disclose the name and that Georgia law prohibited the release of the names of rape victims. The United States Supreme Court disagreed and overturned the Georgia law. It held that crime was a matter of public record, making the facts surrounding it of public interest and publishable despite protests by victims and their families.[23]

Circumstances may make private individuals into public figures. In 1975, for example, Oliver Sipple, a young man in a crowd of people watching President Ford, prevented an assassination attempt on the president by grabbing the gun of a would-be assassin. Newspeople who interviewed him checked his background and discovered that he was part of the San Francisco homosexual community. Although this had nothing to do with his impromptu action in protecting the president, it was publicized. The disclosure caused Sipple great personal difficulties. He brought suit for invasion of privacy, but the courts denied his claim, saying that he had become an "involuntary public figure" by seizing the gun and had thus forfeited his right to privacy.

Individuals may also lose their right to privacy when they grant interviews to reporters. Once the interview is given, reporters are free to round the story out with observations which were not part of the interview. They also are free to publish those facts which were told to them in confidence. If reporters, without malice, misrepresent some of the facts, this, too, is tolerated. The rationale is that the public is entitled to a full story, if it gets any story at all, and that reporting should not be unduly inhibited by fears of privacy invasion suits.

Many privacy invasion cases involve unauthorized photographs of people in public life. Jacqueline Kennedy Onassis, the widow of President Kennedy, has gone to court to sue one particularly obnoxious photographer for taking photographs of her private life. The court ruled that even though she was no longer the first lady, she remained a public figure of whom pictures could be taken and printed without her consent. The Court ordered the photographer to stop harassing her.[24]

To strengthen privacy protection, the courts have in recent years permitted subjects of unwanted investigative reporting to use trespass laws to stop the media. An example is the judgment which the fashionable Le Mistral Restaurant won against CBS in 1976 for trespass after reporters had entered the premises and filmed a story showing violations of New York's health code.[25]

Fair Trial and the Gag Rule

The broad scope of disclosure permitted about most people in public life should be contrasted with the limited scope of disclosure which the courts permit about persons accused of crimes. The right of accused persons to be protected against publicity which might influence judge and jury and harm their case has been zealously guarded by the courts. This is true even though scientific evidence proving that media publicity actually influences the parties to a trial is scant.[26]

Judges have the right to prohibit the mass media from covering some or all of a court case before and during a trial, even when the public is allowed to attend courtroom sessions. No evidence need be brought that publication of the information covered by the "gag" order would impede a fair trial. Gag orders may even extend to rulings of judges by which they tell the media to refrain from covering the case. Thus the fact of judicial suppression of information may be hidden.

The question of the permissible scope of media coverage of court cases was brought to wide public attention by two murder cases, *Shepherd v. Florida*[27] in 1951 and *Sheppard v. Maxwell* in 1966.[28] In these cases, the United States Supreme Court held that the defendants, convicted of murder, had not had a fair trial because the media had publicized the cases widely. As Justices Jackson and Frankfurter put it in the Florida case, "the trial was but a legal gesture to register a verdict already dictated by the press and the public opinion (it) generated." The convictions were therefore overturned.

Gag orders interfere with the media's ability to report on the fairness of judicial proceedings. They also run counter to the general reluctance of American courts to condone "prior censorship." Nonetheless, the courts have upheld gag laws as a necessary protection for accused persons.

Numerous reporters have gone to jail and paid fines rather than obey gag rules because they felt that the courts were overly protective of the rights of criminal suspects and insufficiently concerned with the rights of the public to know. A 1976 decision, *Nebraska Press Association v. Stuart,*[29] upholds, to a certain degree, the reporters' views. In that case, the Supreme Court reversed a gag order on coverage of a murder trial which had been in effect for several months. The Court suggested that careless reporting which interferes with the rights of defendants should be forestalled by judicial maneuvers other than gag laws.

For instance, trials can be moved to different jurisdictions if there has been excessive publicity locally. Suits can also be brought against media enterprises or individual reporters who have acted irresponsibly. Irresponsible or illegal reporting might consist of publicizing testimony from closed sessions of the courts, taking unauthorized pictures, or bribing court personnel to leak trial testimony.

The policy on gag laws is still unclear, however. Some lower courts have refused to comply with Supreme Court directions or have evaded the spirit of decisions. For example, there have been a number of instances in recent years where judges, instead of gagging the press, have placed gags on all the principals in a court case, including the plaintiffs and defendants, their lawyers, and the jury, prohibiting them from talking about the case, particularly to members of the press. In an increasing number of cases, judges have barred access to information by closing courtrooms to all observers during pretrial proceedings as well as trials. The Supreme Court in 1979 upheld their right to do so at will if the parties to the case agree.[30]

Since open pretrial proceedings and open trials are essential in a democracy, particularly when public figures are involved or when police or prosecutor misconduct is suspected, it is worrisome when the doors are shut on such cases as the murder trial of W. A. (Tony) Boyle, the former president of the United Mine Workers, accused of murdering a rival union leader.[31] The same holds true when gag orders prohibit the media from covering cases of official corruption, like the conspiracy and fraud trial of a South Carolina state senator.[32]

Shield Laws

Digging into the affairs of public officials and other prominent citizens and exposing the activities of criminal or dissident groups often requires winning the confidence of informants and promising to conceal their identity. Newspeople are hampered in their prepublication research work if a court or legislative body demands to know the identity of their sources, wants to examine undisclosed bits of information, and issues subpoenas for them. If reporters disclose the information, they break their word. Their sources are likely to dry up, whether they are public officials who have leaked confidential information, or underworld informers or crime victims or political dissidents.

Shield laws have become particularly urgent at a time when law enforcement agencies find it very difficult to penetrate dissident and deviant groups. Therefore, they use subpoenas to compel testimony from journalists, making them unwitting agents of the government. Shield laws are also needed to protect the physical safety of sources who disclose organized criminals or terrorist activities.

Generally speaking, the U.S. Supreme Court has held that newspeople, like ordinary citizens, do not have the right to protect their

Reprinted, courtesy of the *Chicago Tribune*

sources in the face of a subpoena. They have no special right to be warned about a court-approved search of their premises to discover evidence which might reveal their sources and the information provided by them.[33] Nor may they shield records or editorial deliberations from judicial scrutiny if these records are needed to prove deliberate libel.[34] Recognizing the ill effects which these common law-based rules have on investigative reporting of crime and corruption, more than half of all American states have passed shield laws to protect reporters from forced testimony. Federal legislation has also been proposed. Shield laws give journalists the same rights as lawyers, doctors, and clergy to shield their sources' identity and information. They may also bar searches of news offices to discover leads to criminal activity.

Shield laws usually do not assure absolute protection. When, for example, the right of reporters to withhold the names of their sources clashes with the right of other individuals to conduct a lawsuit involving serious matters, such as gathering evidence for a murder or conspiracy trial or a libel suit, state shield laws must yield. For example, actress Judy Garland sued New York *Herald Tribune* columnist Marie Torre to learn the names of sources of unfavorable information which had appeared in Torre's column. The information was needed for a breach of contract and slander suit.[35] The court ordered the reporter to reveal the information. Likewise, the court ordered *New York Times* reporter Earl Caldwell to testify before a grand jury about his sources. Caldwell had won the confidence of members of the Black Panther party and had reported their activities and views.[36] Caldwell refused. So did a fellow *New York Times* reporter, Myron Farber, in 1978 when ordered to make notes of his investigation into a series of deaths in a New Jersey hospital available to the physician charged with murdering the patients. Both reporters were fined and jailed.

Some journalists have argued for a federal shield law to protect all newspeople throughout the country. Others, fearing that such a law would provide conditional shielding only, prefer to do without shield laws of any kind. They contend that the First Amendment constitutes an absolute shield. These differences of opinion have taken steam out of the pressure for a federal shield law. Members of the judiciary also deny that shield laws are needed, but for different reasons. In the words of Justice Byron R. White, "From the beginning of our country, the press has operated without constitutional protection for press informants and the press has flourished." Hence absence of shield laws has "not been a serious obstacle to either the development or retention of confidential news sources by the press."[37]

The power of congressional committees to compel testimony is equal to the power of the courts, raising similar shielding questions. A recent case involved reporter Daniel Schorr, who had received secret information about the proceedings of a congressional committee investigating CIA activities. He refused to tell the committee the name of the source who had leaked the information. Although the committee had the power to cite Schorr for contempt of Congress and punish him accordingly, it chose not to do so. Insiders saw this decision as evidence of the general trend, in the post-Watergate era, to permit shielding when this eases investigative reporting of government misconduct.[38]

Libel Laws

The trend towards facilitating investigative reporting predates the Watergate case. Changes in libel law are a case in point. Libel suits, even when they were lost in court, always had a dampening effect on reporting. All that changed substantially for cases involving public officials in 1964 with the decision in *New York Times v. Sullivan.*[39] In that case, an action for libel was brought by the police chief of Montgomery, Alabama, in the wake of *Times* charges of mishandling of civil rights demonstrations. The United States Supreme Court absolved the newspaper, ruling that a public official must be able to show that a story containing libelous information was published "with knowledge that it was false or with reckless disregard of whether it was false or not."[40]

Courts since 1964 have been lenient in construing what is "reckless" behavior in story verification procedures because they know that media must publish quickly if a story is to have news value.

The "Sullivan rule" has made it very difficult for public officials to bring suit for libelous statements made about them. Malicious intent and extraordinary carelessness are hard to prove, even when journalists are required to open their files to the attacked official and to report the rationale for printing the attack. By the same token, the Sullivan rule has made it much easier for media to publish adverse information about public officials, true or false, without the need for extensive checking of the accuracy of the information prior to its publication.

A number of cases have tested the range of the Sullivan rule. *Time Inc. v. Hill*,[41] a privacy invasion case, extended the rule beyond people in public office, to people whose experiences have made them public figures. Therefore a crime victim could not sue for libel even when *Time* magazine published fictionalized facts from a play about the crime which put the victim into a false light.

Seven years later, the Court adopted a more restrictive view of a "public figure." In *Gertz v. Robert Welch*,[42] it held that a prominent lawyer, whose name had been much in the news, was not a public figure and could therefore sue for libel. The Court indicated that a person who had not deliberately sought publicity would be deemed a public figure in exceptional circumstances only. What these circumstances are remains unclear.[43]

To summarize the confusing developments in the battle between freedom of the press and the right of individuals to be protected from harmful publicity: the courts have pulled back from the position which made individual rights, except the right to a fair trial, largely subordinate. They have done so by distinguishing the rights of private individuals from those of public figures and by construing the category of "public figures" more narrowly. This leaves private individuals with substantial rights to bar the media from publishing potentially embarrassing facts, so long as those facts are not a matter of public record. By and large, laws protecting private individuals do not help people in public life very much. The only protection for public figures from unscrupulous exposure by the media is the code of ethics by which most journalists abide, most of the time.

Other Restrictions on Publication

As discussed in Chapter 1, all governments prohibit the publication of certain information on the ground that the public interest would be harmed. The United States is no exception. The areas where censorship is most prevalent are national security connected with external dangers, national security connected with internal dangers, and obscenity. In each category, there is a good deal of agreement that certain types of information should not be publicized, but very little agreement about where the line ought to be drawn between permitted and prohibited types of material.

It has been even more difficult to get agreement in specific cases on whether or not security censorship was in the public interest. We have already discussed the controversy surrounding the release of the Pentagon papers and the government's initially successful efforts to prohibit publication of a magazine article detailing, on the basis of available but dispersed information, how a hydrogen bomb might be manufactured. Additional foreign policy examples will be presented in Chapter 9.

News concerning internal security matters primarily involves investigations of potentially subversive groups and reports on civil disturbances. Several relevant cases are discussed in Chapter 8. Such news also involves media portrayal of asocial behavior that might lead to imitation. Various attempts to limit the portrayal of crime and violence, either in general, or on programs to which children have access, are examples. They are discussed in Chapter 5.

Closely related to restraints on the publication of crime and violence are restraints on publication of obscene materials and broadcasts of offensive language. It is feared that such broadcasts may corrupt members of the audience, particularly children, and lead to imitative behavior. Though the 1970 report of the President's Commission on Obscenity and Pornography casts doubt on the claim that such broadcasts are socially dangerous, many foes of obscenity and "dirty" words remain unconvinced.

In addition, proponents of obscenity restraints argue that publication of such materials, particularly in visual form in movies and on television, offends community standards and should therefore be prohibited by law. This argument rests on the notion that the public, as represented by generally self-selected spokesmen, should have the right to prohibit the dissemination of material that offends the sense of propriety of many citizens. Despite the popularity of pornography, as shown by the millions of citizens who go to pornographic movies and stage shows and read pornographic magazines, laws in many places bar free access to such information. The United States Supreme Court has repeatedly approved such restrictions.

Another example of protective censorship is the ban on cigarette advertising on radio and television, in effect since 1971. It is designed to protect susceptible individuals from being lured into smoking by seductive advertisements. Pressures for additional areas of protective censorship have been considerable and range from pleas to stop liquor and sugared cereal advertisements to requests to bar information dealing with abortion or drug addiction. Legislatures and the courts have rejected most of them. But the future is unclear. Some of these matters have become election issues. If candidates have committed themselves to censoring abortion or drug information, for example, they may have to follow through on their promises by working for appropriate laws after election.

SUMMARY

In a democratic society, citizens have the right and duty to inform themselves and to express their views publicly. The press, as the eyes and ears of the public, shares these rights and must be protected against restraints which could interfere with its ability to gather information and disseminate it freely.

In this chapter we have seen how these important basic principles have been modified to meet the realities of political life in the United States. Despite legislation such as the Freedom of Information Act of 1966, much information about governmental activities remains shrouded from the eyes of the public. Either it has been classified as secret for security reasons, or it belongs to a broad list of information categories which are closed to the public because their release could embarrass individuals or lead to undesirable business practices. The public and press are also excluded from many governmental meetings if the participants so desire. Executive sessions of legislatures, grand jury sessions, or pretrial proceedings in the courts are examples.

Nearly all of these exclusions have been challenged in the courts because they constitute restrictions on the right of access to information. The courts have ruled that most of them are compatible with constitutional guarantees of free speech and press. They have also ruled, for the most part, that news professionals enjoy neither greater rights to access to information than does the general public, nor greater freedom to protect their access to information by refusal to disclose their sources.

The right to publish information is also limited. Here the public is most seriously restricted because newspeople claim the exclusive right to determine what to publicize through the media and what to omit. The power of print media to refuse a forum to most citizens is nearly absolute, aside from social pressures which mandate that stories of widely recognized public concern be published. Under current rules and regulations, the electronic media must grant equal access to the air to political candidates for the same office, to people who hold opposing views on a controversial issue which has been advocated in a broadcast, and to people whose reputations have been attacked in broadcasts.

Even when access to a media forum is assured, the right to publish is not absolute. Public policy considerations, such as the need to safeguard external and internal security and the need to protect the moral standards of the community, have led to news suppression. The scope of permissible censorship has been the subject of countless inconclusive debates, many culminating in split and conflicting court decisions.

The right to publish also conflicts on many occasions with the rights of individuals to enjoy their privacy, to be protected from disclosure of damaging information, true or false, and to be safeguarded from publicity that might interfere with a fair trial. The courts have been the main forum for weighing these conflicting claims and the scales have tipped erratically from case to case. Two trends stand out from the haze of legal battles: the right to a fair trial generally wins out over the freedom to publish, and private individuals enjoy far greater protection from publicity than do people in public life. However, shifting definitions of what makes a private person a public person have blurred this distinction along its edges.

When we look at the massive restraints on the rights of access to information, the rights of access to publication channels, and the right to publish information freely, we may feel deep concern about freedom of information. Is there cause for worry? Taking a bright view, one can point out, as Justice Byron White did in the 1972 *Branzburg* case, that "the press has flourished. The existing constitutional rules have not been a serious obstacle" stopping the press from investigating wrongdoing.[44] The press as watchdog may be chilled by legal restraints, but it is not frozen into inaction. From the perspective of the mass media and the public, that may be small comfort as long as so many current judicial trends point towards greater, more chilling restraints, rather than less.

NOTES

1. Justice Potter Stewart in *New York Times Co. v. U.S.*, 403 U.S. 713 (1971).
2. Jerome Barron, *Freedom of the Press for Whom — The Right of Access to The Mass Media* (Bloomington, Ind.: Indiana University Press, 1973).
3. 418 U.S. 241 (1974).
4. The case is discussed fully by Fred W. Friendly, *The Good Guys, the Bad Guys and the First Amendment: Free Speech vs. Fairness in Broadcasting* (New York: Random House, 1976), pp. 192-198.
5. *Banzhaf v. Federal Communications Commission*, 405 F. 2d 1082 (D.C. Cir. 1968); certiorari denied, 396 U.S. 842 (1969).
6. 395 U.S. 367 (1968).
7. Friendly, *The Good Guys, the Bad Guys, and the First Amendment*, pp. 32-42.
8. Ibid., pp. 199-236.
9. Barron, *Freedom of the Press for Whom*, p. 5.
10. Ibid., pp. 117-121.
11. *U.S. v. Kiger*, 421 F. 2nd, 1396 (2d Cir. 1970); cert. denied, 398 U.S. 904 (1970).
12. *Zemel v. Rusk*, 381 U.S. 1 (1965).
13. Id.
14. *Branzburg v. Hayes*, 408 U.S. 665 (1972).
15. Id. at 684.
16. *Pell v. Procunier*, 417 U.S. 817 (1974); *Saxbe v. Washington Post Co.*, 417 U.S. 843 (1974); and *Houchins v. KQED, Inc.*, 438 U.S. 1 (1978).

17. These and related cases are discussed more fully in John J. Watkins, "Newsgathering and the First Amendment," *Journalism Quarterly* 53 (Autumn 1976): 406-416. Citations in notes 14 and 16.
18. The act was an amendment to the 1946 Administrative Procedure Act — 5 U.S.C.A. 1002 (1946) — which provided that official records should be open to people who could demonstrate a "need to know" except for "information held confidential for good cause found." (Sec. 22) The 1966 amendment stated that disclosure should be the general rule, rather than the exception, with the burden on government to justify the withholding of a document. Governmental decisions to withhold information could be challenged in court. (5 U.S.C.A. Sec. 552 and Supp. 1, Feb. 1975).
19. Elsie Hebert, "How Accessible Are the Records in Government Records Centers?" *Journalism Quarterly* 52 (Spring 1975): 23-29.
20. 403 U.S. 713 (1971).
21. A comparative view of government secrecy is presented by Itzhak Galnoor, ed., *Government Secrecy in Democracies* (New York: Harper & Row, 1977).
22. Richard B. Kielbowicz, "The Freedom of Information Act and Government's Corporate Information Files," *Journalism Quarterly* 55 (Autumn 1978): 481-486.
23. *Cox Broadcasting Corp. v. Cohn,* 420 U.S. 469 (1975).
24. *Gallella v. Onassis,* 487 F. 2nd 986 (1973).
25. *Le Mistral Inc. v. Columbia Broadcasting System,* 402 N.Y.S. 2nd 815 (1978).
26. Interestingly, the courts maintain the fiction that judges can command jurors to strike improper information presented in court from their memory. Presumably, judges are unable to do the same for media information which jury members might have received outside the court room.
27. 341 U.S. 50 (1951).
28. 384 U.S. 333 (1966).
29. 96 S. Ct. 279 (1976).
30. *Gannett Co. Inc. v. De Pasquale,* 47 LW 4902 (1979).
31. *Philadelphia Newspaper Inc. v. Jerome,* 434 U.S. 241 (1978).
32. *Sigma Delta Chi v. Martin,* 434 U.S. 1022 (1978).
33. *Zurcher v. The Stanford Daily,* 436 U.S. 547 (1978).
34. *Anthony Herbert v. Barry Lando and the Columbia Broadcasting System Inc.,* 441 U.S. 153 (1979).
35. *Garland v. Torre,* 259 F. 2nd 545 (1959).
36. *Caldwell v. U.S.,* 434 F. 2d 1081 (9th Cir. 1973).
37. *Branzburg v. Hayes,* Id. at 699.
38. However, Schorr lost his job with CBS as a result of the incident. By suspending Schorr, the network discouraged this kind of coverage, even though Schorr's right to shield his sources was not challenged.
39. *New York Times v. Sullivan,* 376 U.S. 254 (1964).
40. Id. at 279-80.
41. 385 U.S. 374 (1967).
42. 418 U.S. 323 (1974).
43. *Time Inc. v. Firestone,* 424 U.S. 448 (1976); *Hutchinson v. Proxmire,* 99 S. Ct. 832 (1979) and *Wolston v. Reader's Digest,* 47 LW 4840 (1979).
44. *Branzburg v. Hayes,* Id. at 699.

READINGS

Barron, Jerome. *Freedom of the Press for Whom — The Right of Access to the Mass Media.* Bloomington, Ind.: Indiana University Press, 1973.

Friendly, Fred W. *The Good Guys, the Bad Guys and the First Amendment: Free Speech vs. Fairness in Broadcasting.* New York: Random House, 1976.

Galnoor, Itzhak, ed. *Government Secrecy in Democracies.* New York: Harper & Row, 1977.

Schmidt, Benno C., Jr. *Freedom of the Press vs. Public Access.* New York: Praeger, 1976.

Simons, Howard, and Califano, Joseph A., Jr., eds. *The Media and the Law.* New York: Praeger, 1976.

5

Media Impact on Individual Attitudes and Behavior

In the prime time evening hours, on September 10, 1974, NBC broadcast a television drama called "Born Innocent." It was a story about Chris, a teenaged girl, who was sexually abused by fellow inmates in a children's reformatory. Three days later, on September 13, 1974, a group of children quarrelled while playing on a secluded San Francisco beach. Four of the youngsters assaulted a nine-year-old girl in a manner reminiscent of the "Born Innocent" scene. The parents of the abused youngster sued NBC, charging that the telecast inspired the crime. The courts rejected the principle of media liability but did not rule on whether television is "a school for violence and a college for crime," as the plaintiffs had claimed.

The suit dramatized anew the many puzzling questions so often asked about the impact of mass media on children and adults. Does violence in television fiction and news programs cause violence in real life? How much do people learn from the media? What do they learn? Are people's attitudes and values influenced by what they read and see? What political effects spring from the interaction of Americans with the mass media which paint a picture of the world around them?

In this chapter we will try to shed light on such questions, beginning with an examination of the influence media have on general attitudes towards society and politics. We will deal first with the assimilation of attitudes as an unintended byproduct of media exposure. By and large, newspeople do not try to teach attitudes and values, nor do people try to learn them. Rather, "incidental" learning of the basic world view of society springs from exposure to single, dramatic events, or from the incremental impact of the total information flow over prolonged periods of time.

In later sections of the chapter, we will look at more deliberate attempts to learn. We will examine the ways in which various types of people choose the media to which they will pay attention, and the sorts of things they learn or fail to learn. Finally, we will seek some tentative an-

Reprinted, courtesy of the *Dayton Daily News*

swers to the question posed at the start — to what degree does exposure to the mass media influence behavior?

DIFFERENTIAL EFFECTS OF PRINT AND BROADCAST NEWS

As we have done before, we will talk about mass media effects in general, rather than about the separate effects of television or radio or newspapers or magazines. The reasons are twofold. First of all, researchers have found it extraordinarily difficult to separate the effects of various types of media. In today's America, nearly every individual is exposed to all the media in combination, either through direct exposure, or indirectly, through contacts with people who have been exposed. If we know that Americans in space suits have walked on the moon, if we view this as a scientific miracle that raised the sagging prestige of the United States abroad and at home, if we feel pride about the venture and yet some unease about its high price tag, do all or part of these thoughts come from television, from newspapers, or from conversations with others? It is well-nigh impossible to disentangle such strands of information.[1]

Demographic differences in media use further confound the picture. The finding that heavy newspaper users tend to be better informed than abstainers is hard to interpret when print media users generally enjoy higher socioeconomic status and better formal education than television buffs. These facts, rather than reliance on newspapers, may explain why they absorb more political information.

Television appears to be a more potent stimulus than print sources for stirring emotions and creating politically relevant mental images. Again, exceptions are numerous, and research is fragmentary. Television's greatest political impact, compared to newspapers, flows from its ability to reach millions of people simultaneously with the same images. Print media could never reach many of these people because 23 million American adults are functionally illiterate. What these people now learn about politics may be fragmentary and hazy, but it represents a quantum leap over their previous exposure and learning.

We can summarize the research on the differential effects of various media by saying that they present stimuli which vary substantially in nature and content. It would therefore be surprising if their impact were identical, even when they deal with the same subjects. But research is still too undeveloped to provide adequate answers about the effects of stimulus variations and about the process by which individuals mesh a variety of media stimuli. Instead, we shall assess the end product — the combined impact of all print and electronic media stimuli.

THE ROLE OF MEDIA IN POLITICAL SOCIALIZATION

Before considering the role that mass media information plays in shaping our attitudes towards society, we need to assess the political importance of these attitudes. Political socialization — the learning, accepting, and approving of customs and rules, structures and environmental factors governing political life — is important because it affects the quality of interaction between citizens and their government. Political systems do not operate smoothly without the support of most of their citizens. Much of the public must be willing to abide by laws, rules, and regulations, and willing to render services, such as paying taxes or working in the military forces.

Citizen support is most readily obtained if citizens are convinced of the legitimacy and capability of their government and if they feel strong emotional ties to it. If political socialization fails to instill such attitudes, laws of all types, such as energy conservation, anti-inflation measures, or traffic regulations may be unenforceable. Refusal to pay taxes may force sharp curtailment of governmental activities. If citizens hold government in contempt or regard it as illegitimate, civil disobedience, revolution, or civil war may result.

In societies where government relies on popular participation through elections and through continuous surveillance of governmental activities, political socialization must equip citizens with sufficient knowledge to participate effectively. If it fails to do this, elections at best become a sham where people go through the motions of making a choice without understanding what this choice means. At worst, elections become a mockery in which clever politicians manipulate an ignorant electorate. Likewise, surveillance of governmental activities is impossible if people lack a grasp of the nature of government and public policies.

Childhood Socialization

Since political socialization starts in childhood, it is first conveyed by parents and other people in the small child's environment. From their families children usually learn basic attitudes towards authority, property, decisionmaking, veneration for political symbols, and similar matters. When children enter the more formal school setting, teaching about political values becomes quite systematic. At this point, too, children learn much new factual information about their political and social world.

The people who teach children rely heavily on mass media for much of the information and value structure which they transmit. Hence children receive a great deal of media-based information indirectly from the very beginning of their development. Children's direct contacts with the media are equally abundant. In the United States, millions of babies watch television. Most grade-school youngsters spend 27 hours a week in front of the television set — more time than in school. Most of the programs they see are intended for adults and differ from children's limited personal experiences. If children can understand the message, its impact is likely to be great since, lacking the built-in corrective of personal experience, they take it at face value.

Recent research convincingly demonstrates the high impact which the mass media have on children's political socialization. When high school students are asked for the sources of information on which they base their attitudes about subjects such as economic or race problems, or war and patriotism, they mention the mass media far more often than they mention their families, friends, teachers, or personal experiences.[2] Comparisons of youngsters who use the media heavily with those who are light users confirm that school age children gain substantial information from the media and that this influences their attitudes towards society. Heavy mass media users, particularly those who read newspapers, know most about current political events and show most interest in them.[3] Yet, this finding of the substantial effect of media runs counter to those of earlier socialization studies, which designated parents, and in later studies, teachers, as the chief socializers.

Several reasons account for the changed emphasis which has made the mass media "the new parents." The first is the increasing pervasiveness of television, which makes it easy for even the youngest children to be in touch with mass media images. This pervasiveness dates back only to the early 1960s.

The second reason involves deficiencies in measurement. Much of the early research counted only direct media influence, which was quite limited. Indirect influence, through media exposure of parents and teachers, was ignored, sharply reducing findings of media effects.

Finally, research designs have become more sophisticated. In the early studies, children were asked to make their own general appraisal of learning sources. A typical question might be: "From whom do you learn the most, your parents, your school, or newspapers and television?" Recent studies have asked more specific questions. For instance, Gary Coldevin, a Canadian researcher, asked high school students in Canada and the United States what they knew about such subjects as immigration policy, government in general, or education policy. Then he asked them to state arguments for and against certain policy positions. Only after the students had written down their ideas were they asked for the chief sources of facts and, separately, about the chief sources of evaluations for these issues. In nearly every case, the mass media were the chief sources of information and evaluations for U.S. as well as Canadian students. However, the media were slightly less important and parents and schools slightly more important as sources of evaluations than as information sources.[4]

What children learn from the mass media and how they evaluate it depends heavily on their stage of mental development. According to Jean Piaget[5] children between two and seven years of age are keenly aware of the objects they see and hear. But they do not independently perceive the connections among various phenomena or draw general conclusions from specific instances. Many of the lessons presumably taught by media stories therefore elude young children. Complex reasoning skills are fully developed only at the teenage level. Children's interests in certain types of stories also change sharply with age, as do their attention and information-retention spans.[6] Given these variations, valid research of mass media impact on children means focusing on narrow age spans. Such research has been comparatively rare.

We do know that children are likely to be highly supportive of the political system during their early years, when they learn basic facts about prominent political figures.[7] The president and the policeman are next to father and God. By their teenage years, youngsters have often become quite disillusioned about authority figures. This skepticism diminishes as education is completed and the youngster enters the work force. What role the media play in this transformation is unclear. It is also unclear to what extent children and adolescents imitate behavior depicted by media stories, how long they remember stories, and how long the effects of exposure last.

Adult Socialization

The pattern of heavy media exposure continues throughout life. The average American spends nearly three hours a day watching television, two hours listening to radio, twenty minutes reading a newspaper, and ten minutes reading a magazine. Time spent with the mass media has jumped by 40 percent since the advent of television, mostly at the expense of other leisure time activities.[8] On an average day, 80 percent of all Americans are reached by television and newspapers. On a typical evening, the television audience is close to 100 million people, nearly half the entire population.

This massive exposure contributes to the lifelong process of political socialization and learning. The mass media form "the mainstream of the common symbolic environment that cultivates the most widely-shared conceptions of reality. We live in terms of the stories we tell — stories about what things exist, stories about how things work, and stories about what to do. . . . Increasingly, media-cultivated facts and values become standards by which we judge."[9] Once basic orientations towards the political system have been formed, attitudes usually stabilize and later learning largely supplements and refines earlier notions. Established attitudes filter subsequent experiences. Major personal or societal upheavals may lead to more or less complete resocialization and revised political ideas. Short of drastic changes, the need to cope with information about new events and about gradually shifting cultural orientations also forces the average person into continuous learning and gradual readjustments. But the basic value structure generally remains intact, even when attitudes are modified.[10]

Much of what the average person learns about political norms, rules, and values, about events in the political universe, and about the way people cope with these happenings, comes, of necessity, from the mass media. Those with the widest exposure to political news in the mass media generally are most aware of political issues and have more political opinions about these issues. Personal experiences are severely limited compared to the range of experiences that come to us directly or indirectly through the media.

Most media content is not explicitly political. It is nonetheless full of implicit messages about the social order and political activities. These convey information that leads to formation of politically significant attitudes. In fact, surveys show that only one-half to two-thirds of the adult public exposes itself regularly to any explicit political news. Only a very small proportion of this audience pays any serious attention to such news.

People's opinions, feelings, and evaluations about the political system may spring from their own processing of facts supplied by the media, from attitudes, opinions, and feelings explicitly expressed by the media, or from a combination of the two. It is important to distinguish between learning of facts and learning of opinions. The media play a very large role in conveying information, and a much smaller role in conveying attitudes. Many people who use the media for information and as a point of departure for formulating their own appraisals reject attitudes and evaluations which are supplied explicitly or implicitly by media stories.

An incident in mid-July 1979 will demonstrate the distinction between fact and opinion learning. President Carter requested the resignation of his entire cabinet and top White House staff. The announcement came unexpectedly. The White House said little about the reasons for the request and the rationale for accepting five resignations and rejecting the rest. As a result, there was a great deal of speculation in newspaper and television stories about the motives for the massive shake-up. Editorial writers evaluated the purged and unpurged officials and reflected about their own feelings of confidence in the president. Interviews with readers and viewers showed that many accepted the facts presented by the media but drew their own conclusions about the political forces which were in play and the wisdom of the president's actions. Others accepted both facts and judgments about the situation.

Generally, people are most prone to accept the views of newspeople in those areas where they have little personal experience and lack guidance from their social contacts. When they have direct or vicarious experiences to guide them and, particularly, when they have already formed firm opinions grounded in their value structures, they are least likely to be swayed by the media.

While we can and do form our own opinions on many issues, particularly those concerning local problems, opinion formation is impossible in many instances.[11] We rarely have enough information and understanding to form our own views about the many complex national and international issues that succeed one another with bewildering rapidity. This puts us at the mercy of the media, not only for information, but also for interpretation. Even when we think that we are forming our own opinions about familiar issues, we are more dependent on the media than we realize. If they fail to supply adequate information, our opinions rest on an unsound foundation.

The 1976 presidential debates provide an excellent example of the effectiveness of media opinion guidance in even comparatively simple evaluations. A telephone survey conducted immediately after the second debate showed that viewers, by a 9-percent margin, judged President Ford to be the debate winner. Following media commentary, which strongly attacked a statement Ford had made about Eastern Europe, viewers in increasing numbers called Carter the winner. Within 24 hours, Carter's lead over Ford had risen to 42 percentage points.[12] A number of the later interviewees commented that they had originally judged Ford to be the winner, but felt that they must have been wrong because the media judged otherwise.

Many graphic examples of the persuasive power of the media come from advertising research, which has documented how messages can affect people's perceptions of unfamiliar products and activities and change consumer behavior. Broadcasting may even lead to major changes in religious beliefs. Radio and television crusades to convert people to various Christian faiths attract more than 130 million Americans each week, and thousands phone program hosts to declare their conversion.

DIFFERENCES IN MEDIA USE AND SOCIALIZATION

Inasmuch as various groups within the population differ in their cultural environment, their economic interests, and their psychological make-up, it is not surprising that they also differ in the types of media to which they expose themselves. We will outline some of these differences and the effects which they are apt to have on political socialization. To take advantage of the best available data, we shall use racial differences as our primary example. Tables 5-1 through 5-4 demonstrate that the picture is extremely complex. For instance, one cannot talk about characteristic media exposure and impact patterns for nonwhites and whites without specifying sex, age, education, income, region, and city size as well. Additional variations come from such commonly ignored factors as lifestyle and social setting, family size, personality characteristics, and social and job pressures.

Of course, the mere fact that individuals belong to a certain demographic category or social group does not mean that they necessarily share the media exposure characteristics of that category or group. For many individuals group ties, in particular, may be weak, so that they have little impact on behavior. Group influence may also be weakened for people who are subject to conflicting group pressures. For instance, college students whose peer group revels in left-wing underground newspapers may also be exposed to conservative media fare in their homes. Predicting their media exposure and impact patterns from their group affiliation would therefore be difficult.

Race

Within the American cultural context, blacks and whites diverge in political knowledge and attitudes. Although we lack firm proof, available evidence suggests that different media exposure patterns are a partial explanation.[13] Tables 5-1 through 5-4 present survey data of whites and blacks differentiated according to demographic variables. Although these data are from 1970, recent surveys show the same general patterns. However, newspaper reading and radio listening by black men has increased in comparison to black women, and radio listening overall has increased sharply for blacks.

Table 5-1 "Yesterday" Newspaper Reading, Whites and Nonwhites (in Percentages)

	Whites	*Nonwhites*
By Sex		
Men	80 (73.3)*	59 (62.2)
Women	80 (71.5)	63 (56.6)
By Age		
18-24	75	58
25-34	78	70
35-49	84	70
50 and over	79	49
By Income		
$10,000 and over	87	77
$5,000 — $9,999	78	74
Under $5,000	69	44
By Education		
Some college or more	87	85
High school graduate	84	71
Less than high school graduate	72	53
By Region		
South	75	56
North and West	82	66
By City Size		
Central Cities		
500,000 and over	81	72
50,000 — 499,000	86	63
Metropolitan-Suburban	83	70
Nonmetropolitan	73	40

*N =13,862 for whites, 1,460 for blacks. Available 1978 Simmons figures are in parentheses.

SOURCE: W. R. Simmons, Inc. 1970, in Leo Bogart, "Negro and White Media Exposure: New Evidence," *Journalism Quarterly* 49 (Spring 1972): 15-21 at 17.

Tables 5-1 through 5-4 reprinted by permission of *Journalism Quarterly* and Leo Bogart.

Most importantly, the tables show that blacks and whites present different news exposure patterns. Blacks, for example, pay considerably less attention to newspapers than whites. Fifty-nine percent read a daily newspaper, compared to 72 percent for whites. Unemployed blacks were half as likely as unemployed whites to read a daily newspaper. Since newspapers are the medium which supplies the most ample amounts of standard political news, average black citizens lacked this information. In turn, this made it less likely that they would share the political images and judgments of their white fellow citizens.

Blacks rely less on the mass media for political information than is true for whites. For example, only 22 percent of blacks polled in a low-income Los Angeles neighborhood said that they relied on print media for most of their political information, and only 23 percent said that they relied on radio or television. Many named interpersonal sources such as their families or public agencies instead. By comparison, 40 percent of the whites mentioned print media as major sources of political news, and 43 percent mentioned radio and television. Hispanics found print and electronic media even less useful for keeping themselves politically informed. Only 12 percent of the Hispanics said that they got most of their political information from newspapers, and only 5 percent called radio or television their most important sources. Such alienation from the community's major political communications sources may affect the political integration of Hispanics and blacks into the majority culture.[14]

Nonwhites also choose different papers and stations as their preferred news sources from those used by whites. This happens most often when media oriented to their racial group are available. Minority groups who use ethnically oriented media primarily are apt to live in different

Table 5-2 Prime Time TV Viewing, Whites and Nonwhites

	Whites (hours per week)	Nonwhites (hours per week)
By Sex		
Men	8.8 (8.8)*	8.4 (7.7)
Women	10.2 (8.9)	10.0 (8.8)
By Age		
18-34	8.9	10.4
35-49	9.3	9.1
50 and over	10.2	8.0
By Income		
$10,000 and over	8.9	10.0
$5,000 — $9,999	9.7	9.5
Under $5,000	10.1	8.8
By Education		
Some college or more	8.1	8.5
High school graduate	9.8	11.2
Less than high school graduate	10.1	8.7
By Region		
South	9.1	8.9
North and West	9.5	9.6
By City Size		
Metropolitan Central City	9.8	10.0
Metropolitan Suburban	9.4	8.3
Nonmetropolitan	9.3	8.5

* Available 1978 Simmons figures are in parentheses.

SOURCE: W. R. Simmons, Inc. 1970, in Bogart, *Journalism Quarterly,* p. 19.

Table 5-3 TV Viewing in Daytime and Fringe Time, Whites and Nonwhites

	Whites *(hours per week)*	*Nonwhites* *(hours per week)*
By Sex		
Men	9.8	10.8
Women	13.4	19.1
By Age		
18-34	10.4	15.5
35-49	10.6	16.0
50 and over	13.6	14.3
By Income		
$10,000 and over	9.6	12.5
$5,000 — $9,999	12.2	16.6
Under $5,000	14.7	15.0
By Education		
Some college or more	9.1	14.2
High school graduate	11.5	16.4
Less than high school graduate	13.5	15.0
By Region		
South	12.3	14.5
North and West	11.6	16.1
By City Size		
Metropolitan Central City	11.5	15.6
Metropolitan Suburban	11.1	16.3
Nonmetropolitan	12.4	13.9

SOURCE: W. R. Simmons, Inc. 1970, in Bogart, *Journalism Quarterly,* p. 21.

communication and socialization environments from people in the majority culture. Substantial differences among racial groups in attitudes towards governmental bodies and in trust in government and feelings of political efficacy lend credence to the belief that diverse media images, combined with life experiences, produce distinct socialization patterns.

Blacks and whites also extract different information from the same media. Blacks are more apt than whites to believe that factual, as well as fictional, stories presented by the media are true to life. Therefore the images which many blacks form about life styles or societal patterns are more likely to mirror the distortions found in media presentations.[15] A study of information diffusion of six assassinations showed that each racial group dwelled heavily on news which dealt with its own race. While all blacks and whites had heard about the deaths of Martin Luther King and the Kennedys, a substantially larger number of blacks (10 to 24 percent) knew about the assassinations of black leaders Medgar Evers and Malcolm X. Similarly, many more whites than blacks knew about the death of white Nazi leader George Lincoln Rockwell.[16]

There are many possible explanations for variations in media use and socialization patterns. Most blacks in the 1970s belonged to different social groups than did whites and had life settings quite unlike those of the white middle-class to whose tastes most media catered. The social status of many older blacks also kept them alienated from the northern urban culture in which they found themselves, often after a childhood in a rural southern setting. Hence they were less interested in news that focused heavily on city life and politics. For the many blacks whose schooling had been poor, deficient reading skills made newspaper reading unattractive.

Some researchers have questioned whether the apparent differences between blacks and whites are based on race-linked cultural differences or spring from the fact that the black population is more frequently poor and educationally deprived. Bradley Greenberg and Brenda Dervin,[17] for instance, contend that within the subculture of poverty, blacks and whites use the media in similar ways. Accordingly, they believe that it is more accurate to talk about differences in media habits and socialization on the basis of economic and educational stratification. Other scholars argue that race and its cultural consequences are indeed important factors in media exposure and impact. Leo Bogart,[18] for example, found racial differences in media use patterns regardless of socioeconomic status. The kinds of data on which Bogart based his analysis appear in Tables 5-1 through 5-4. The current unresolved issue thus revolves around the cause of subcultural differences, rather than their existence. If they are linked to race, they may be long-lasting. If they are linked to socioeconomic status, they may change with rising incomes, education, and occupational status.

Age, Sex, Socioeconomic Status, and Location

The tables also show differences in newspaper reading, radio listening, and television viewing when people are grouped by sex, age, income, education, region and city size, as well as race. For instance, men and women differ sharply in daytime television viewing; age has a bearing on newspaper reading; and Southerners listen to substantially less radio than do Northerners. Program preferences vary as well. For instance, women over 50 are the heaviest viewers of television news, followed by men over 50. Twelve to 17-year-olds are last on the trail in news watching. Men far exceed women in following sports coverage, while women spend substantially more time on television drama.

Differences in media use patterns are particularly pronounced between income levels. People of higher income, who usually are better educated than poorer people, use print media more and television less

Table 5-4 Radio Listening, Whites and Nonwhites

	Whites (hours per week)	Nonwhites (hours per week)
By Sex		
Men	13.7 (23.7)*	15.9 (31.6)
Women	17.5 (22.0)	17.4 (30.6)
By Age		
18-34	17.2	17.5
35-49	16.0	17.9
50 and over	14.0	14.6
By Income		
$10,000 and over	15.7	20.9
$5,000 — $9,999	17.0	17.1
Under $5,000	13.4	15.1
By Education		
Some college or more	13.4	15.7
High school graduate	17.4	18.0
Less than high school graduate	15.4	16.4
By Region		
South	12.7	14.2
North and West	16.7	19.9
By City Size		
Metropolitan Central City	16.0	18.5
Metropolitan Suburban	16.0	20.3
Nonmetropolitan	15.0	11.6

* Available 1978 Simmons figures are in parentheses.

SOURCE: W. R. Simmons, Inc. 1970, in Bogart, *Journalism Quarterly*, p. 18.

than the rest of the population. For instance, 47 percent of all high school graduates read newspapers for at least 3 hours per week, compared to 33 percent of the grade school educated.[19] Upper income people also are more prone to use a variety of media. Among the upper economic groups, 57 percent are multimedia users compared to 27 percent in the lower economic groups. Thus, the well-to-do have potentially much more information and a greater variety of information available to them. This helps them to maintain and increase their influence and power in American society.

In part, the poor pay less attention to print media because these media carry less information of interest to them. For instance, the urban poor need consumer information on prices, goods, and services more than coverage of new business regulations or city politics. Yet the media rarely supply this kind of information. By contrast, television and radio programs appeal to the poor because they carry a great deal of light entertainment fare which allows them to escape from the grim reality that surrounds their lives.

Unifying Forces

We must not carry the notion of vastly different communications environments for various population groups too far, however. The bulk of media entertainment and information is similar throughout the country. The same network television programs are broadcast on the East Coast and the West Coast, in big cities or small towns. Differences among individual networks are slight. Hence television comes close to being a single, nationwide source of news and commentary. Radio is more diverse, but even there, many radio news programs are little more than national wire service reports. Insofar as newspaper stories are based on wire service information, they too are fairly uniform everywhere.

In Chapter 3 we saw that news media cover basically the same categories of stories in the same proportions. There are variations, of course. For instance, newspapers on the West Coast are more likely to devote their foreign affairs coverage to Asian affairs than newspapers on the East Coast, which concentrate more on Europe and the Middle East. Tabloids like the *New York Daily News* put more stress on sensational crime and sex stories than does the staid *New York Times*. Still, news sources everywhere provide a large common core of information and interpretation that imbues their audiences with a shared structure of basic values and information.

CHOOSING MEDIA STORIES

Uses and Gratifications Theories

General patterns of media use do not tell us why people pay attention to specific stories. A number of theories have been formulated to explain how and why such individual choices are made. Currently, one of the most widely accepted of these theories is the "uses and gratifications" approach. Put most simply, proponents of this approach contend that individuals ignore personally irrelevant messages and pay attention to the kinds of things they need and the kinds of things which they find gratifying, provided the expense in time and effort seems reasonable.[20]

Uses and gratifications may be behavioral, emotional, or intellectual.[21] For instance people pay attention to stories which help them in making political decisions, such as voting or participating in protest demonstrations. They use the media to gain a sense of security from knowing what is happening in their political environment and also to attain a feeling of social adequacy to take part in future arguments and conversations. They feel gratified if the media reinforce what they already know and believe. They also use the media to while away time, to participate vicariously in exciting ventures, and to reduce loneliness.

Special subcultural needs may lead to significant variations in attention patterns. For instance, a Jewish person may be particularly attentive to news from the Middle East and other places which concern Israel. A person of Polish ancestry may look for news that affects the Polish community. If a woman favors increased job opportunities for women, she is apt to notice stories about women's expanding presence in the business world.

What people actually select depends very much on life style circumstances and the context in which information exposure occurs. What is useful and gratifying in one setting may be less so in another. When people change their life styles, such as moving from daytime to nighttime work, or trading a desk for a travel job, media patterns may change drastically. The changes are needed to bring about closer accord with people encountered in the new environment.[22]

Life style also determines the time available for media use and hence the quantity of news that can be selected. In early adulthood, when people begin their careers, or when they are raising children, the demands of home and job may leave very little time for attention to the media. The cost of newspaper and magazine subscriptions may be prohibitive on a tight budget. Conversely, older people whose home and job duties have become light, and whose financial obligations are decreasing, frequently have much more time for reading or watching television. Life style also determines what media are readily available. People may expose themselves to media which are of little interest to them, when this is convenient or socially appropriate.

Selective Exposure Theories

While people pick up what is personally useful and gratifying for them, they ignore many other bits of information, regardless of political and social significance. Most of these omissions are random. People simply fail to notice certain information or have no time or inclination to pursue it, even when it comes to their attention. But there are systematic omissions as well. According to various cognitive balance theories, people avoid information that is disturbing to their peace of mind, runs counter to their political and social tastes, or conflicts with information, attitudes, and feelings they already hold. Social scientists explain this type of selective exposure by pointing out that people are uncomfortable when they are exposed to ideas that differ from their own or that question the validity of beliefs they already hold. To avoid such discomforts, people select information that is congruent with their beliefs.

Selectivity diversifies socializing influences and lays the groundwork for differential attitudes towards politics. It also reduces the already slim chances that an individual's cognitions, attitudes, and feelings will be altered once they have become established. This then helps to explain the considerable stability we see in basic orientations such as party allegiance, conservatism or liberalism, and isolationism or interventionism.

Over the years, scholars have repeatedly examined the various selective exposure phenomena and have modified their theories in accordance with more complete research findings. Scholars now believe that selective exposure occurs to a lesser extent than they thought initially. Many people find it too bothersome to select news sources carefully, particularly when using electronic media. When television news, for instance, carries stories which are objectionable to a viewer, there is no easy way to screen out the undesired stories and still watch the rest of the broadcast.

Some folks are actually curious about discrepant information or pride themselves on being open-minded and receptive to all points of view. For instance, Democrats may want to hear what Republicans are saying if for no other reason than to find out how the opposition is stating its case. They may also want to determine what counter-arguments need to be formulated. Many people actually enjoy news about something that differs from their own ideas, even if it contradicts them. At worst, exposure to discrepant information is not as universally painful as thought. It can be ignored, overlooked, or distorted. The source can be discredited and the message met with disbelief.[23]

Much of the evidence for markedly selective exposure has come from settings in which available media supported the preferences of the audience. No choice was necessary. Selection was "de facto," rather than deliberate. For example, unionized workers whose friends and associates are also highly involved with unions are likely to encounter a lot of pro-union information at home and at work. They do not have to make a special effort to seek out pro-union or reject anti-union information. In fact, anti-union information may be unavailable. Genuine, rather than de facto selective exposure appears to be most prevalent for those personality types who recognize dissonance, find it painful, and therefore feel constrained to resolve it by reconsidering already established attitudes and opinions.

Agenda-Setting Theories

If selection of news items were entirely determined by individual uses and gratifications, news selection patterns would show infinite variations. This is not the case. The similarities in the environment of the average American impose a common structure on news selection patterns. We have already mentioned similarity in news supply, springing from gatekeeping practices, as a powerful unifying force. Media also tell people in fairly uniform fashion which individual issues and activities are most significant and deserve to be ranked highly on the public's agenda of concerns.[24] Importance is indicated through clues such as banner headlines or front-page placement in newspapers or first story placement on television. Frequent and ample coverage also implies significance.

Many of us readily adopt the media's agenda of importance. We look at the front page of the newspaper and expect to find the most important stories there. We may watch the opening minutes of a telecast eagerly and then allow our attention to slacken. Consequently, agenda-setting by the media leads to uniformities in exposure as well as in significance ratings of news items. When the media make events seem important, politicians are likely to comment about them and to take action. This enhances widespread belief in the importance of these events and assures even more public attention.

Proof of the agenda-setting influence of media comes from many recent studies.[25] For instance, in a 1976 study, several thousand responses given by small panels of voters over the period of a year revealed quite similar judgments about the salience of many current issues to their per-

Table 5-5 Personal, Talk and Public Issue Agendas (in Percentages)*

Issue	Personal Agenda				Talk Agenda				Public Agenda			
	Women		Men		Women		Men		Women		Men	
	O**	Y	Y	O	O	Y	Y	O	O	Y	Y	O
Social services, crime control	15%	16%	10%	14%	17%	21%	10%	15%	10%	11%	9%	12%
Foreign affairs, defense	16	8	4	15	7	5	7	11	0	1	1	1
Economy: taxes, jobs, prices	55	65	56	55	43	53	49	40	70	74	71	69
Life styles, race issues	3	7	5	4	2	8	5	2	5	7	5	1
Resource conservation	3	4	8	3	2	1	6	2	2	0	3	1
Feelings about politics	1	0	13	6	2	1	5	6	1	0	1	0
Current political affairs	3	0	2	1	7	2	11	5	5	2	5	7
Miscellaneous, D.K., N/A.	4	0	2	2	20	10	8	20	6	5	6	8

* N=2,342 replies.
** O stands for older women and men, over age 40.
Y stands for younger women and men, under age 40.

SOURCE: Doris A. Graber, "Agenda-Setting: Are There Women's Perspectives?" in Laurily Keir Epstein, ed., *Women and the News* (New York: Hastings House, 1978), p. 18.

Tables 5-5 through 5-9 reprinted by permission of Hastings House, Publishers, from *Women and the News,* © 1978 by Laurily Keir Epstein.

sonal lives. The list of issues mentioned by the panelists corresponded to cues in their news sources. It reflected the issues about which they talked most and to which they claimed to pay most attention in the media.[26]

However, agenda-setting varied in potency. The audience followed media guidance, but not slavishly. From comparisons of media agendas with public opinion polls and reports about political and social conditions, we know that media guidance is most important for new issues that have not been widely discussed and for issues beyond the realm of personal experience.[27]

Prominent media coverage does assure that an issue will be noticed, but it does not guarantee that the audience will assign it the same relative rank of importance which media play has indicated. Likewise, information which is useful or gratifying to the audience will be noted even if it is on the back pages, receives minuscule headlines, or is a brief item at the tail end of a newscast.[28]

Table 5-5 demonstrates the broad resemblance of the concerns and priorities that people express to the problems emphasized by the media. Under the heading "Personal Agenda," the table presents issues which the respondents designated as "most important" to them personally when asked: "Of the various problems and issues now facing the United States, which is most important to you personally?" The table also records which issues people talked about most (Talk Agenda) and which issues people believed were most important to the community (Public Agenda). The table is divided according to age and sex to capture the differences attributable to these characteristics. The need for raw material for conversation with friends and associates is a particularly strong force towards selecting stories of common appeal.

LEARNING PROCESSES

Media-Audience Interaction

Thus far we have talked about news selection processes, noting the forces that make for diversity and for uniformity. We now need to examine briefly what happens after the news has been selected. Communication research tells us that the early models which depicted a straight stimulus-response relationship were incorrect. There is no "hypodermic effect" where information presented by the media is transferred, unaltered, into the minds of the audience. Rather, media and audience interact, so that the images conveyed by the media stimulate perceptions in audience members that reflect each individual's perceptual state at the time the message was received. Items of news are selected, interpreted, and integrated, following a number of culturally determined reasoning rules. For instance, in Marxist societies, most political events are viewed as expressions of economic force. Hence Marxist observers interpreted racial rioting in the United States in the late 1960s as proletarian uprisings, whereas most Americans viewed them as protests against racial injustice and its consequences.

In the United States, much subcultural diversity is maintained within the matrix of basic uniformity created by the shared dominant culture. The fact that most political images absorbed by average Americans come from the mass media, rather than individualized direct experiences, is also a homogenizing influence. Coherence springs, too, from the human effort to organize perceptions into internally consistent images which are meaningful from the perceiver's perspective.[29] As Walter Lippmann explained long ago:

> For the most part we do not first see, and then define, we define first and then see. In the great blooming, buzzing confusion of the outer world, we pick out what our culture has already defined for us, and we tend to perceive that which we have picked out in the form stereotyped for us by our culture.[30]

Because individuals pick up information that is related to things they already know or in which they are interested, numerous "knowledge-gap" studies show that political elites and other well-informed people tend to absorb a great deal more mass media information than people who are poorly informed.[31] It is not functionally advantageous for the poorly informed to acquire knowledge for which they see no purpose. This explains why information-poor population groups, although they spend a lot of time with the mass media, generally extract far less political information from this experience than do more politically sophisticated audiences. The upshot is that the knowledge gap between the privileged and underprivileged is increased. Those with the least political knowledge are likely to remain politically impotent. Moreover, the knowledge gap between the privileged and underprivileged makes mutual understanding more difficult. Improved public education, which might shrink the gap, remains a distant goal.

Transient Influences

Many transitory factors impinge on news processing. Our frame of mind may be accepting or critical. Our attention may be focused totally on the media source or partly on a simultaneous game of backgammon. Examination time at school or the year-end rush at work may eat up the time normally devoted to media.

The other people present when news is received or discussed are also significant. For instance, if one watches or talks about a presidential inauguration with friends who are making fun of the way the president talks and acts, the occasion loses solemnity and becomes trivial. If one watches or talks about the event with a group who admire the president, one comes away feeling inspired. We cannot predict the effect of media messages without knowing the group context in which exposure or conversation took place.[32]

How a person interacts with information also depends on the format of the information. If news reports are conflicting in fact or opinion, if they are overly long or overly short, if they are repetitious, dull, or offensive, their effect is apt to be diminished. The total communications matrix also affects the influence of its parts. Print news impact may be blunted by prior television and radio presentations which have removed the edge of novelty.

Source credibility and appeal are other significant factors in news processing. Once President Nixon had lost his credibility and respect in the wake of Watergate disclosures, his statements were suspect for most Americans. His manner and bearing were more closely watched for clues to his general state of mind. Partisanship, too, may play an important role in source appraisal. It may cast a rosy glow over fellow partisans and a pall over the opposition.

Perceptual and Image Factors

When new information reaches people, it is combined with existing beliefs. Does the new shape the old or the old shape the new in the final images? Research on the impact of media information on images of political candidates supplies some answers. Images are largely "perceiver-determined" for those aspects for which the audience already holds stereotyped beliefs. For instance, people assume that Democratic presidential candidates will pursue policies typically associated with Democrats. They read or view the news in that vein, picking up bits of information that fit and ignoring those which do not fit. The same is likely to hold true for information about Big Business or Big Labor, the Arab world, or the Soviet Union.

Information about aspects of events or people that are not widely known or stereotyped leads to "stimulus-determined" images. What the media present then determines largely what is perceived. Candidates' personalities, assessments of their capabilities, and appraisals of the people with whom they surround themselves, for example, usually are stimulus-determined.[33] Likewise, when the media describe present-day China, when they cast doubt on the safety of nuclear energy production, or when they discuss the merits of a new wage insurance plan, the images they create are dominant.

The general rule that media are most influential in areas where the audience knows least does not apply to specialized publications. Professional journals, for instance, often have a strong impact on their readers' images of professional matters. This happens because of the high credibility of the sources, which makes audiences for these publications subordinate their own expert views to those of the experts whose views they read.

LEARNING EFFECTS — KNOWLEDGE AND ATTITUDES

Measurement Problems

What kinds of politically relevant knowledge, attitudes, feelings, and behaviors spring from people's contact with the media? The answer is difficult because the precise impact of particular stories is nearly impossible to measure in most circumstances, given the limitations of currently available measuring instruments. Some of these problems were discussed in Chapter 1. There we pointed to the difficulty of isolating media influence when it is one of many factors in a complex environment.[34] For instance, when we find rising levels of cynicism about government in the United States following the disclosure of the Watergate scandal in the Nixon administration, we cannot say for sure that the disclosure stories were responsible. It is possible that cynicism was produced primarily by the experience of paying higher prices in the grocery store, facing fuel shortages at the gas station, or living through a public transit strike. Research can strongly implicate the Watergate scandal, but it cannot yet bring positive proof. Until we can trace an individual's mental processes and isolate the components that interact and combine to form mental images and reactions to these images, we cannot fully assess the impact of media.

Our inability to trace mental processes also keeps us from understanding just what is learned from media. Research up to now has focused on very small facets of learning, such as learning of specific facts about political candidates or about a limited number of public policies. Even within such narrow areas, testing has been severely limited. It has zeroed in on learning of explicit messages rather than assessing total knowledge gain. For instance, election coverage of a presidential candidate teaches more than facts about the candidate. It may inform the audience about the role played by White House correspondents and about living conditions in other cities. Because researchers have focused on campaign stories, such learning, however important it may be, is overlooked. Much of the incidental learning may actually be subconscious. People are unaware that they have learned something new and may even be unable to retrieve it readily.

At times, information recall is delayed. For example, in one experiment, soldiers saw information films of armies in other countries. Questions were asked right after the film showing and again six weeks later. Some things that were not recalled in the initial interviews surfaced in the later ones. We do not know how commonly such sleeper effects occur and how much learning remains unmeasured as a consequence.

Many assumptions about learning that seem intuitively correct remain untested, but we continue to judge media practices as if they were true. Among others, these include the assumption that people deduce important social lessons from specific stories presented by the media.

For instance, we believe that adults as well as children often model their behavior after the behavior of characters they encounter in the media. We assume that unfavorable stereotypes will hurt the self-esteem of the groups so characterized, and so we urge newspeople to present these groups in a better light. News reports and dramatic shows presumably teach people how lawyers or policemen or hospitals conduct their business. We assume that people watching these shows are motivated to aspire to such professions, and, conversely, we worry that the distortions in the portrayal of these roles may mislead inexperienced people who regard them as models.

But while we assume these effects, and while there is every reason to believe that many are quite common, most of them remain unmeasured. An important exception is the Cultural Indicators project conducted since the mid-1960s at the University of Pennsylvania's Annenberg School of Communications. The investigators study trends in network television dramatic content and the conceptions of social reality produced in viewers. Findings from this project confirm that heavy viewers of television drama (more than four hours daily), more than light viewers of the same demographic background and similar circumstances, see the world as television paints it and react to that world rather than to reality. For instance, heavy viewers, exposed to large doses of crime in television drama, believe that the dangers of becoming a crime victim are far greater than they actually are.[35] They fear crime more and are more mistrustful and suspicious than light television viewers.

Another neglected research sphere concerns forgetting. We know that much that is learned from the media is evanescent. When Iran is engulfed by revolution or Philadelphia rocked by a patronage scandal, the salient names and facts are on many lips. But after the crisis has passed, this knowledge evaporates rapidly. How rapidly, or with what residue, we do not know.

Factual Learning

Given these limitations, what *do* we know about the extent of political learning from the mass media? The data that follow come from a 1976 research project in which the information supply and political learning of four small panels of adults living in Evanston, Illinois, Indianapolis, Indiana, and Lebanon, New Hampshire, was monitored intensively throughout an entire year.[36] The investigators found that the panelists in the "Three Sites" Project became aware of a large number of the topics featured by the media, but that the mix of topics varied from person to person. Four broad topic areas were mentioned by nearly every panel member as receiving "a lot of coverage" in 1976. These were the economy in general, government spending, busing for school desegregation, and national defense. Unemployment, corruption in government, and the drop in the prestige of the United States received nearly

Table 5-6 Recall of Specific Information on Unemployment and Inflation (in Percentages)

	Unemployment							
	Ford				Carter			
*Responses**	*Women*		*Men*		*Women*		*Men*	
	O**	Y	Y	O	O	Y	Y	O
Statistics	0%	0%	0%	2%	4%	0%	2%	11%
Policy data	12	8	9	12	3	4	3	5
General information	41	38	44	43	43	41	48	35
Don't know	47	55	47	43	50	55	46	48

	Inflation							
	Ford				Carter			
*Responses**	*Women*		*Men*		*Women*		*Men*	
	O	Y	Y	O	O	Y	Y	O
Statistics	1%	0%	1%	0%	0%	0%	1%	0%
Policy data	1	2	2	0	3	2	6	6
General information	38	34	39	42	34	29	29	27
Don't know	59	63	59	58	63	69	64	67

N = 1,716 replies.

* "Statistics" signifies that the respondent was able to cite precise figures for unemployment and inflation rates and/or rate changes.

"Policy data" means that the respondent was able to refer to specific proposals made by Ford or Carter to cope with the inflation or unemployment problem.

"General information" means that the respondent knew whether general trends were changing or stable, and knew whether action was planned, without being able to give specifics.

**O stands for older women and men, over age 40; Y stands for younger women and men, under age 40.

SOURCE: Graber, *Women and the News*, p. 22.

as much mention. Sixteen other topics were recalled by a somewhat smaller majority of the panel members as receiving a lot of media attention as well, including such diverse issues as the Middle East, alcohol and drug addiction, abortion, and dirty campaign tactics. This is an impressive array of politically important topics to be remembered by an average mass media audience.

By and large, however, people did not seem to gain much specific knowledge. They recognized details if they were mentioned to them, but failed to recall them without such assistance. For instance, the panelists in the Three Sites Project were asked during the height of the 1976 presidential campaign what they knew about the positions taken by presidential candidates Gerald Ford and Jimmy Carter on the issues of inflation and unemployment. Both of these issues were personally very important to the panelists and had been discussed by them with friends and associates. Most of them planned to vote for one of the candidates. Yet as Table 5-6 indicates, specific knowledge about the issues was abysmally small. Half of the answers were "don't know's." Specific information about each policy was contained in less than 10 percent of the answers on unemployment and less than 5 percent of the answers on inflation. Women, especially those under 40 years of age, recalled much less information than the men.

More generally, when people were tested on their recall of prominent news stories to which they had been exposed several weeks earlier, men, on the average, recalled specific details for only 14 percent of the stories for which they were tested throughout the year. For women, the figure was even lower: 5 percent. Table 5-7 tells the story. It also shows that the rates of recall varied, depending on the nature of the story, with different patterns for age and sex groups.

As one would expect from uses and gratifications theories, the disparities between men's and women's recall patterns conform to their different life styles. It became clear upon further questioning that most women, unlike men, lacked focused interests such as gathering information to help with their jobs or a penchant to learn more about prominent people. Rather, women tended to remember interesting or touching details about disparate stories without having a particular use for the story.[37] Stories about crimes and accidents were recalled most readily by both women and men. The chief reasons for forgetting stories or not paying attention to them at all were unplanned inattention, lack of interest in the subject matter, or unwillingness to struggle with complex matters.

That the average individual learns so few facts has disturbed many people because it is one of the axioms of democracy that good citizens must be well informed. Many older studies show even less knowledge than the Three Sites Project. They judge informedness largely by ability to name prominent politicians and to recite facts from the United States Constitution. Such factual information tests are inappropriate for judging political knowledge and competence. What really matters is that citizens understand major political issues and not that they can recite names of political figures or the length of the term of a U.S. Supreme Court Justice. Are people aware of major political issues and their significance? Are they able to place them in the general context of current politics? When these genuinely important questions are asked, the picture of public political competence brightens considerably.

We have already noted that people are aware of a wide range of current issues. Moreover, when interviewers probe for understanding, rather than knowledge of specific facts, they often find considerable

Table 5-7 Percent of Stories for Which Specific Details Were Recalled*

	Women		Men	
Story topic	O**	Y	Y	O
Women's issues	0%	4%	8%	20%
Medical/health care	2	2	11	9
Education	6	2	11	6
Economy in general	3	3	2	0
Unemployment	13	5	9	15
Inflation	8	3	8	14
Celebrities	18	4	13	18
Entertainment	0	10	14	16
All news stories (including group above)	5	4	14	13

*N = 5,421 stories.
**O stands for older women and men, over age 40; Y stands for younger women and men, under age 40.

SOURCE: Graber, *Women and the News,* p. 25.

political insight. For instance, people who cannot define either "afffirmative action" or "holocaust" may have fairly sophisticated notions about these matters. Panelists in the Three Sites and other projects who had very little formal education knew about the nature of persecution in Nazi Germany and fully understood the burdens faced by people hampered in finding a job because of their race or sex.[38]

Learning General Orientations

Many media stories may leave the audience with politically significant feelings. These may persist long after facts are forgotten. Although many details of the assassination of John F. Kennedy have been forgotten, Americans retain feelings of sympathy, grief, shame, and moral indignation. Often stories that impress few factual memories on people's minds may leave them nonetheless with generalized feelings of trust or distrust. A large number of prominently featured stories of serious governmental corruption, for instance, may lower the public's esteem for governmental integrity. This was demonstrated by a national survey in 1974 which showed that people who had been exposed to newspapers that had criticized the government severely on numerous counts trusted government significantly less than respondents exposed to more favorable newspapers. People who had not gone beyond grade school seemed to be particularly susceptible to erosion of trust in the wake of mass media criticism.[39] A number of laboratory and field experiments demonstrate similar linkages, positive as well as negative. Favorable publicity enhances esteem for government, unfavorable publicity diminishes it. Cynical people, in turn, tend to participate less than others in activities such as voting and political action.[40]

Media stories may produce an overpowering sense of a world out of control or reassurance that all is going well. Either one of these feelings may make people quiescent because they become fearful of interfering with crucial government actions or else complacent about the need for public vigilance. Fear that dissension weakens the government may decrease tolerance for dissidents. These are the chief points made by the writings of political scientist Murray Edelman.[41] Edelman points out that political quiescence leads to acceptance of mismanagement by politicians, poor laws, and poor administrative practices. If this is true — as the real life evidence adduced by Edelman indicates — this is a significant political effect.

On a more personal level, for millions of people, the media are a way to keep in touch with their environment. This helps to counter feelings of loneliness and alienation because information becomes a bond between individuals and others in their environment who share this information.[42]

The media may also arouse desires that are potentially explosive for good or ill. They provide models for the good life and, directly and indirectly, advertise a lot of products and services which everyone is expected to desire. By creating wants and expectations, as well as dissatisfactions and frustrations, the media may become powerful stimulants for social change for the society at large or for selected individuals within it. Whether this change is considered positive, negative, or a mixture of both depends on sociopolitical preferences.

Deterrents to Learning

Even granting that media exposure produces a great deal more political enlightenment than is generally revealed through survey research, still, the average individual's political knowledge and understanding is quite limited. Lack of motivation for political learning and distrust for the media, as well as deficiencies in the information supply, provide explanations. Most people do not need detailed knowledge of current affairs for either their job or their social relationships. They would rather discuss sports, or the weather, or gossip than politics, which they see as a touchy topic. So they scan the news for major crises but do not try to remember specific facts. When people sense that events have a large impact on their lives or when they need information to make voting choices, political interest and learning perk up quickly and often dramatically.

Occasionally, serious radio and television programs become highly popular. Most of them involve themes of corruption, violence, or other wrongdoing, which may account for their popularity. Examples are

"Sixty Minutes," which probes a variety of social ills, "Roots," which examined black history, and "Helter Skelter,"which dealt with an actual California murder case. These are exceptions, however.

Like a strawfire, widespread public interest in most political crises dies almost as quickly as it flares. For instance, attention to stories about the Watergate scandal peaked only briefly. Most people tired of the matter after a few weeks and began to complain that it usurped too much media time. Attention spans are erratic and brief even though most Americans believe that, as good citizens, they ought to be well informed about political news and feel guilty, or at least apologetic, if they are not.[43]

Learning is further inhibited by the fact that many population groups are alienated from the media. Some white ethnics and police and union members, for instance, consider most mass media to be opposed to them. They believe that the media lie and distort, either in general, or in certain particulars. Overall, public opinion polls in the late 1970s showed a steady erosion of public confidence in the trustworthiness of the media. On a scale ranging from "a great deal" to "some," to "very little," Gallup and Harris polls found high confidence in television and newspapers in less than 20 percent of the public.

The presentation of media information also contributes to the difficulty people experience in learning from the media. First of all, there is the sheer bulk of new information. People are deluged, day after day, with important and trivial news, most of which is touted as "important." The constant crisis atmosphere numbs the interest and creates jaded boredom.

The fact that stories are told in disconnected snippets further complicates the task of making sense out of them and integrating them into existing knowledge. This is especially true when stories are complex.[44] People who feel that they cannot understand what is happening are discouraged from spending time reading or listening.[45] Featuring conflicting stories and interpretations, without giving guidance to the audience, is another deterrent to learning.

Television news, which is the most widely used source of news, deters learning because it carries little information. The average half hour television news program covers the equivalent in words of one newspaper page. If several newscasts are watched, about half the material is repetition. Even within a single newscast, a large proportion of every item is background information that must be furnished to put the item into perspective for viewers seeing it for the first time. Moreover, as Tony Schwartz points out in *The Responsive Chord,* most television programs are not designed primarily "to get stimuli across, or even to package . . . stimuli so they can be understood and absorbed." Rather, television tries "to evoke stored information . . . in a patterned way,"[46] to make use of what the audience already knows. These deterrents to learning are not outweighed by such positive factors as the interest generated by the picture and sound combination and the high confidence in familiar newscasters.

The format of television news also impedes learning. News items are tightly strung together with few pauses to allow for information absorption. Such pauses are essential for learning. In their absence, it is not surprising that half the audience, after the lapse of a few hours, cannot recall a single item from a television newscast.

Some social scientists even contend that the availability of television, per se, has destroyed learning incentives because television takes the place of personal interactions and real life experiences. People who participate in life passively, watching the world through a television set, do not need to acquire information for talking with others and do not learn through action.[47]

Having said this much about slim knowledge and the reasons for it, we still can end the discussion of political learning and socialization from the mass media on a positive note. Compared to other people in the world, Americans rank quite high in political information levels. With increasing education of the population, which heightens the need for and salience of information, this record should improve even further. Americans are also well socialized into the American system. Despite the negative publicity given to political stories, the underlying support for the political system and culture that pervades the news is shared by most Americans. They may be disappointed and cynical about particular leaders or policies, but relatively few question the legitimacy of the government, object to its basic philosophies, or reject its claims to their support.

LEARNING EFFECTS: BEHAVIOR

If the media shape people's political knowledge, attitudes and feelings, they obviously influence political behavior since it is based, to a great extent, on attitudes and feelings. In this chapter, we will examine media impact on two areas of specific behavior: imitation of crime and violence, particularly among children, and stimulation of development in underdeveloped regions. Both are areas of great political concern. In Chapter 6 we will discuss the effects of media coverage on voting behavior. And in Chapter 8 we will turn to the impact of the media on behavior in various societal crises.

Crime and Violent Behavior in Children

Many Americans, including many social scientists, believe that violence and crime portrayed in the media, particularly in television entertainment, will lead to learning and imitation. Children in particular are presumed to be highly impressionable. Since crime and violence are serious problems in American society, much public and private money and effort have been spent to investigate the possible link between exposure and behavior. Several Surgeon Generals' commissions have produced a bookshelf of information to support corrective legislation, should it be needed.[48]

What have these studies revealed? Despite the strong inclination of many of the researchers to find that crime fiction causes asocial behavior, the evidence is mixed. As the "Born Innocent" incident discussed at the start of this chapter demonstrates, some children obviously do copy violent behavior. This is especially true when they have watched aggression that was left unpunished or was rewarded and when countervailing influences from parents and teachers were lacking.[49] But most children do not become more violent after exposure to violence in the mass media. They lack the predisposition, and, usually, the opportunity for violence and their environment discourages asocial behavior. In fact, exposure to crime makes some children more sympathetic towards the suffering of crime and violence victims.[50] A crude cause and effect model is therefore obviously invalid.

At this time, we do not know the percentage of imitation-prone children in the vast child population exposed to televised violence. We do know that the wide dispersion of television throughout American homes makes it almost certain that the majority of susceptible children will be exposed. We also know that many other triggers to violence might arouse these children, even in the absence of television. Whatever the source of arousal, even if the actual number of seriously susceptible children is tiny and statistically insignificant, the social consequences may still be profound.

Other confounding factors in assessing the impact of television fare on children are age-linked comprehension differences. Younger children may not be able to comprehend many of the events presented by the media in the same way that older children do. Several studies of preschool age and early grade-school-age children suggest that much of what adults consider to be violent does not seem so to children. Cartoon violence is an example. When an enemy drops Donald Duck on his head, or shoots Mickey Mouse, or flattens Mrs. Flintstone with a boulder, most children view it as funny make-believe.[51] For them, it is not a behavior model for action in the real world. If this is true, many of the programs which adults consider as potentially dangerous may actually be harmless.

Children not only see things differently from adults, but they also draw different inferences. The complex social reasoning which adults often ascribe to even young children does not develop until youngsters reach their teens. For instance, after seeing a series of shows with the implied message that the big bully who hits everybody always wins, children presumably conclude that similar behavior on their part will yield similar results. Yet, while young children often imitate what they have seen, they are rarely able to generalize or respond to implied messages.

Until we understand better how the average child at various stages of development interacts with the stories presented by the media, we cannot completely assess media effects on subsequent behavior. Nor can we plan program content with any assurance that it will encourage approved or inhibit disapproved behaviors.

Behavior Change in Adults

What about imitation of socially undesirable behavior by adults? The same broad principles apply as in the case of children. Imitation of the behavior depends on the setting at the time of exposure and on the personality and attitudes the viewer brings to the situation. Widespread societal norms seem to be particularly important. For instance, studies by the presidential Commission on Obscenity and Pornography found that exposure to aberrant sexual behavior led to comparatively little imitation. In fact, there was some evidence that greater availability of obscene and pornographic materials might reduce sex crimes and misdemeanors because vicarious experiences were substituted for actual ones.[52] By comparison, there was a great deal more evidence that exposure to criminal behavior encourages imitation. The difference in effects appears to lie in general social attitudes which in 1970 were more tolerant of violence than of aberrant sexual practices.

Given our lack of knowledge about the precise linkage between exposure to information and corresponding behavior, legislative tampering with media offerings appears premature. It will take a great deal more research and experimentation to determine which offerings are harmful for most people and how media fare can be presented to produce desirable results and avoid undesirable ones. Even assuming that this goal could be reached — which may be an unrealistic assumption — it is questionable whether a democratic society should attempt to manipulate the minds of its citizens or protect them from temptations to violate social norms.

Socioeconomic Modernization

The assumed potential of the media to guide people's behavior has led to great efforts to use media as tools for social and political development. The results have been mixed — some successes and many failures. We will try to explain why this is so.

Creation of Psychic Mobility. The hope of using the media to bring about industrialization, improved social services, and greater political participation in underdeveloped areas of the industrialized nations, such as parts of the American South, or in Third World nations, ran very high at mid-century. The psychological key to human and subsequent material development was assumed to be a personality characteristic that political scientist Daniel Lerner labeled "empathic capacity." The media were thought to be the stimuli; when media present new objects and ideas, they presumably stimulate people to empathize and imagine themselves as involved with these objects and ideas. For instance, when the media show how slum dwellers have converted old tires into sandals, or how flood victims have purified their polluted water supply, audience members begin to wonder "How would this work for me?"

Before the age of mass media, such "psychic mobility" was generated when people came into direct contact with strangers whose life and production styles differed. Such contacts usually were limited to relatively few people. Changes, therefore, diffused very slowly to wider groups. The mass media made it possible for the first time in human history to reach millions of people with comparative ease and to expose them to developmental stimuli. Transistor radios and satellite television have opened even remote and inaccessible regions to modern communication and brought news of current life styles directly to people's homes.

Social scientists who assign to the media a major role in modernization have made three assumptions. First, they believe that the mass media are, indeed, able to create interest and empathy in things that people have never experienced before. Secondly, they contend that the mass media not only present people with alternatives to their current life styles; they also present graphic examples of new practices which are readily understood and copied. For instance, they can show people how to build a modern structure or how to prepare food or how to raise children. Thirdly, they argue that development, once started, creates an incentive for more and more people to become more skilled and informed. Where formal education is not readily accessible, the media provide information and enhance the capacity to learn. Proof of the validity of these assumptions is seen in the fact that advances in media development in many regions have been followed by advances in urbanization, industrialization, per capita income, and literacy.

Psychological Barriers to Modernization. While many poverty areas have shown measurable progress with the media apparently serving as a catalyst, modernization has been far slower and more sporadic than expected. A number of psychological and physical obstacles have kept the dreams of the development theorists from coming true. Most damaging has been outright individual or community hostility to change or unwillingness to alter long-established patterns. In this situation, mass media may actually become a negative reference point; people condemn the modern life style depicted by the media.

For instance, when several federal government agencies attempted to improve poverty conditions in Knox County, Kentucky, where per capita income was one-fourth of the U.S. average, they found great resistance in tightly knit, homogeneous communities in the county. Mass media programs designed to change health, childrearing, and employment practices fell on deaf ears. In more heterogeneous communities, success was moderate.

In the absence of overt hostility to change, people may still be totally uninterested in changing. This has been called the "housewife syndrome," because it happens most frequently with women who are isolated in their homes. It may spring from insecurity about ability to cope with changes and reluctance to further complicate a difficult life. Women and men exhibiting this mental state cannot be reached by the mass media without the intervention of a trusted person such as a priest or physician or family member. Mass media influence then becomes a "two-step" flow reaching its targets through selected opinion leaders.

Putting modern skills into words and concepts that uneducated people can understand has also turned out to be exceedingly hard. For instance, teaching people new ways to keep baby food pure, or to apply for aid from a government agency, or to construct cinderblock houses, all involve concepts and terminologies which may be tough to grasp for people who have little or no education. The disparity in social background between the journalists and their audiences complicates the problem of communication further. It creates "heterophily" — a gap in social background, which complicates communication — rather than "homophily" — similarity in background, which eases it.

Changes that require adopting new social values or abandoning old habits are the most difficult of all and the least likely to occur. For example, people whose religious and social values favor large families are unlikely to be persuaded by mass media information that they should settle for small ones. Ingrained habits, like driving without seat belts, are almost as resistant to change. For example, in the 1970s, the Insurance Institute for Highway Safety broadcast advertisements in a number of cities about the importance of wearing seat belts. Even though these public service commercials were shown on prime time television more than 100 times each month, roughly 70 percent of the people who had seen and agreed with them did not use car seat belts.[53]

Adoption of Changes. How can the mass media bring about socially desirable changes? We will outline the steps involved in change and indicate how the mass media fit into the picture.

The first step involves awareness of the possibility for change. Here the media are especially helpful. Radio can inform people about new energy-saving devices or new child raising methods. Television and movies can show new technologies and new styles of political participation.

The second step is understanding how to accomplish the suggested changes. For example, people may be aware that there are ways to get public assistance, but they may not know how to apply for it. Mass media usually fail to supply detailed information. On the average, only a third of all stories which might inspire action of various types, such as environmental protection or energy conservation, contain implementing information.[54] Unless this gap is filled, the chain which leads to the adoption of innovations is broken.

The third step involves evaluation. People assess the merits of the innovation, given their circumstances, and decide whether they want to adopt it. Innovations often fail to take root because prospective users consider them bad, inappropriate, too risky, or too difficult. Media messages alone are not persuasive enough, so it may be crucial to have a trusted person urge or demonstrate adoption of the innovation.

The fourth step is trial. The effect of the media in getting people to try innovations is limited. Factors beyond media control are more important, such as social and financial costs of the change as well as the audience's willingness to change. Generally, young men are most receptive to innovations; older people are most skeptical and cautious.

Trials may be followed by adoption. The media contribute most to this phase by encouraging people to stick with the changes which they have made part of their life and work styles. For example, adoption of birth control is useless unless it is continuous. The same holds true of many health and sanitation measures or improved work habits. To assure continuity, mass media must cover a topic regularly, stressing long-range goals and reporting progress.

It has been difficult to predict which media campaigns designed to change behavior will succeed and which will fail. A number of carefully planned projects to motivate poor people or elderly shut-ins to listen to vitally needed information about nutrition, medical care, and social security benefits have failed. On the other hand, campaigns to get people to study pesticide labels more carefully, to learn about employment for the mentally retarded, or to win support for environmental protection programs have met with success. Despite careful study, the explanation for the differences has eluded researchers thus far in most of these cases.[55]

In some instances, mass media efforts to mobilize people for change have produced unanticipated attitude and behavior changes. For instance, when television was introduced in several Canadian Eskimo communities, programs were designed to show the audience how to modernize their living conditions and to acquaint them with Canadian affairs generally. Instead of the anticipated results, Eskimo adults in the television communities turned their eyes to the past. Rather than aspiring to further modernization of their life styles, they wanted to return to traditional Eskimo ways. It is not clear whether this attitude, which was not apparent in localities without television, sprang from nostalgia for the past or aversion to the life style changes foreshadowed by television. Yearning for traditional life styles went along with a spectacular rise in aspirations for a modern life style for their children.[56]

The success of the mass media in bringing about change hinges above all on the receptivity for change. Ongoing efforts to use the media to modernize underdeveloped areas or bring socially helpful information to the poor, the elderly, or the handicapped must therefore concentrate on identifying the specific circumstances under which success is most likely. Responding to locally initiated requests, rather than designing information campaigns from the outside, and integrating local traditions into modern approaches, seem to hold the most promise for future success.[57]

SUMMARY

This chapter began with a discussion of the role which the mass media play in political socialization — the learning and accepting of norms and rules, structures, and environmental factors that govern political life. Contrary to earlier findings of limited impact, evidence presented in this chapter suggests that the mass media play a major part in this process. Given the importance of continuous political socialization, this alone, quite aside from other political functions, makes the mass media a tremendously powerful political force.

However, the impact of the media on political socialization and other aspects of political learning is not uniform for all members of the media audience. We therefore examined how individuals of different life styles and circumstances interact with mass media information. We noted the impact which psychological, demographic, and situational factors have on perceptions and their political consequences.

While many factors contribute to diversity in socialization and learning, there are also powerful unifying forces. As a result of these, most Americans are exposed to similar information and develop roughly similar outlooks on what it means and ought to mean to be an American and live one's political life in the American way.

We also looked at some major theories which explain why and how individuals select the information to which they expose themselves and which they commit to memory. Factual learning of specific media information is sparse. Nonetheless people become aware of many political problems and sense their basic significance, even without remembering details about them. Equally important, exposure to the media produces politically significant moods such as apathy, cynicism, fear, trust, acquiescence, or support. These moods condition people's participation in the political process, which may range from total abstinence to efforts to overthrow the government by force.

The media may also produce or retard behavior that affects the quality of public life. We assessed the role of the media in fostering socially undesirable behavior, particularly the controversy over the impact of crime and violence in the media on the behavior of children and adults.

We also looked at the role that media play in political and social development of poor and industrially backward population groups. We found that media influence is greatest in informing people and creating initial attitudes, and it is least effective in changing attitudes and ingrained behaviors.

Given the many largely uncontrollable variables that determine what influence media offerings will have on individual behavior, we concluded that concerted efforts to manipulate media content to foster societal goals are risky at best. They could set dangerous precedents for inhibiting the free flow of controversial ideas or for using the media as channels for government propaganda.

NOTES

1. Impact differences between print and electronic media are discussed in Peter Clarke and Eric Fredin, "Newspapers, Television and Political Reasoning," *Public Opinion Quarterly* 42 (Summer 1978): 143-160; Lee B. Becker, Idowu Sobowale, and William E. Casey, "Newspaper and Television Dependencies: Their Effects on Evaluations of Public Officials," *Journal of Broadcasting* 23 (Fall 1979): 465-475; and Robert D. McClure and Thomas E. Patterson, "Print vs. Network News," *Journal of Communication* 26 (Spring 1976): 23-28.
2. Gary Coldevin, "Internationalism and Mass Communications," *Journalism Quarterly* 49 (Summer 1972): 365-368.
3. M. Margaret Conway, A. Jay Stevens and Robert G. Smith, "The Relations Between Media Use and Children's Civic Awareness," *Journalism Quarterly* 52 (Autumn 1975): 531-538; Steven H. Chaffee, L. Scott Ward and Leonard P. Tipton, "Mass Communication and Political Socialization," *Journalism Quarterly* 48 (Winter 1970): 647-659.
4. Sidney Kraus and Dennis Davis, *The Effects of Mass Communication on Political Behavior* (University Park: Pennsylvania State University Press, 1976), pp. 8-47, contains a good review of the political socialization literature. Also see the mass communications chapters in Stanley Renshon, ed., *Handbook of Political Socialization* (New York: Free Press, 1975).
5. Jean Piaget, *The Language and Thought of the Child* (New York: Harcourt Brace, 1926).
6. George Comstock, Steven Chaffee, Natan Katzman, Maxwell McCombs, and Donald Roberts, *Television and Human Behavior* (New York: Columbia University Press, 1978), pp. 261-287.
7. This research is summarized in Comstock et al., *Television and Human Behavior,* pp. 172-287.
8. Alexander Szalai, et al., eds., *The Use of Time* (The Hague, Netherlands: Mouton, 1972); and John P. Robinson, *Changes in Americans' Use of Time: 1965-1975,* Report, Cleveland State University, August 1977.
9. George Gerbner et al. "Cultural Indicators: Violence Profile No. 9," *Journal of Communication* 28 (Summer 1978): 176-207, at 178, 193. Also see George Gerbner et al., "The Demonstration of Power: Violence Profile No. 10," *Journal of Communication* 29 (Summer 1979): 177-196.
10. George Comstock, "The Impact of Television on American Institutions," *Journal of Communication* 18 (Spring 1978): 12-28.
11. L. Erwin Atwood, Ardyth B. Sohn, and Harold Sohn, "Daily Newspaper Contributions to Community Discussion," *Journalism Quarterly* 55 (Autumn 1978): 570-576; Harold G. Zucker, "The Variable Nature of News Me-

dia Influence," in Brent D. Ruben, ed., *Communication Yearbook 2* (New Brunswick, N.J.: Transaction Books, 1978): pp. 225-240.

12. Frederick T. Steeper, "Public Response to Gerald Ford's Statements on Eastern Europe in the Second Debate," in George F. Bishop, Robert G. Meadow, and Marilyn Jackson-Beeck, eds., *The Presidential Debates: Media, Electoral and Policy Perspectives* (New York: Praeger, 1978) pp. 81-101. For additional evidence of changes in political opinions produced by commentary, see Michael J. Robinson, "The Impact of 'Instant Analysis,' " *Journal of Communication* 27 (Spring 1977): 17-23.

13. Comstock et al., *Television and Human Behavior*, pp. 307-309.

14. Frederick Williams, Herbert S. Dordick, and Frederick Horstmann, "Where Citizens Go for Information," *Journal of Communication* 27 (Winter 1977): 95-99.

15. Comstock et al., *Television and Human Behavior*, pp. 295-306.

16. Sheldon G. Levy, "How Population Subgroups Differed in Knowledge of Six Assassinations," *Journalism Quarterly* 46 (Winter 1969): 685-698.

17. Bradley Greenberg and Brenda Dervin, "Mass Communication Among the Urban Poor," *Public Opinion Quarterly* 34 (Summer 1970): 224-235.

18. Leo Bogart, "Negro and White Media Exposure: New Evidence," *Journalism Quarterly* 49 (Spring 1972): 15-21. Also see George Comstock and Robin E. Cobbey, "Television and the Children of Ethnic Minorities," *Journal of Communication* 29 (Winter 1979): 104-115 and sources cited there.

19. Carl E. Block, "Communicating with the Urban Poor: An Exploratory Inquiry," *Journalism Quarterly* 47 (Spring 1970): 3-11.

20. Charles Atkin, "A Conceptual Model of Information Seeking, Avoiding, and Processing," pp. 205-242 in Peter Clarke, ed., *New Models for Mass Communication Research* (Beverly Hills, Calif.: Sage, 1973).

21. Lee B. Becker, "Two Tests of Media Gratifications: Watergate and the 1974 Election," *Journalism Quarterly* 53 (Spring 1976): 28-33.

22. Doris A. Graber, Three Sites Project, unpublished research.

23. Lewis Donohew and Philip Palmgreen, "A Reappraisal of Dissonance and the Selective Exposure Hypothesis," *Journalism Quarterly* 48 (Autumn 1971): 412-420.

24. Percy H. Tannenbaum "The Indexing Process in Communication," *Public Opinion Quarterly* 19 (Fall 1955): 292-302.

25. Donald L. Shaw and Maxwell E. McCombs, *The Emergence of American Political Issues: The Agenda-Setting Function of the Press* (St. Paul: West Publishing Co., 1977), and sources cited there.

26. Doris A. Graber, "Agenda-Setting: Are There Women's Perspectives?" in Laurily Keir Epstein, ed., *Women and the News* (New York: Hastings House, 1978), pp. 15-37.

27. Zucker, "The Variable Nature of News Media Influence," p. 227.

28. The importance of personal and contextual factors in news selection and evaluation is discussed in Lutz Erbring, Edie Goldenberg and Arthur Miller, "Front-Page News and Real World Cues: Another Look at Agenda-Setting by the Media," *American Journal of Political Science* 24 (February 1980): 16-49.

29. David Krech and Richard S. Crutchfield, "Perceiving the World," in Wilbur Schramm and Donald F. Roberts, eds., *The Process and Effects of Mass Communication*, rev., ed. (Urbana: University of Illinois Press, 1971), pp. 235-264.

30. Walter Lippmann, *Public Opinion*, (New York: Harcourt Brace, 1922), p. 31.

31. Phillip J. Tichenor, George A. Donohue, and Clarice A. Olien, "Mass Media Flow and Differential Growth in Knowledge, *Public Opinion Quarterly* 34 (Summer 1970): 159-170.
32. Eliot Freidson, "Communications Research and the Concept of the Mass," in Schramm and Roberts, *The Process and Effects of Mass Communication,* pp. 197-208.
33. Roberta S. Sigel, "Effect of Partisanship on the Perception of Political Candidates," *Public Opinion Quarterly* 28 (Summer 1964): pp. 488-496.
34. A brief review of recent effects studies is in Comstock, *Journal of Communication,* 1978. Also see Kraus and Davis, *The Effects of Mass Communication on Political Behavior.* A general discussion of learning factors is presented in Albert Bandura, *Social Learning Theory* (Englewood Cliffs: Prentice Hall, 1977).
35. The chances of becoming a crime victim are one-third of one percent in real life, but 30 to 64 percent in TV life.
36. Doris A. Graber and Young Yun Kim, "Why John Q. Voter Did Not Learn Much From the 1976 Presidential Debates," in Brent D. Ruben, ed., *Communication Yearbook 2* (New Brunswick, N.J.: Transaction Books, 1978), pp. 407-421.
37. Goal oriented information seeking is discussed in Charles Atkin, "Instrumental Utilities and Information Seeking," in Clarke, *New Models for Mass Communication Research,* pp. 205-242.
38. "Nazi Era Illuminated by 'Holocaust' Program," *The Sampler* 12 (Fall 1978): No. 1.
39. Arthur H. Miller, Edie N. Goldenberg, and Lutz Erbring," Type-Set Politics: Impact of Newspapers on Public Confidence," *American Political Science Review* 73 (March 1979): 67-84.
40. Michael J. Robinson, "Public Affairs Television and the Growth of Political Malaise: The Case of 'The Selling of the Pentagon,'" *American Political Science Review* 70 (June 1976): 409-432.
41. Murray Edelman, *Politics as Symbolic Action* (Chicago: Markham, 1971).
42. Comstock et al. *Television and Human Behavior,* pp. 289-309. Tables 5-1 through 5-4 present data on media use in communities of various sizes.
43. Graber and Kim, "Why John Q. Voter Did Not Learn Much from the 1976 Presidential Debates," pp. 414-419.
44. James W. Tankard, Jr. and Stuart W. Showalter, "Press Coverage of the 1972 Report on Television and Social Behavior," *Journalism Quarterly* 54 (Summer 1977): 293-298; Philip Palmgreen, "Mass Media Use and Political Knowledge," *Journalism Monographs,* No. 61 (May 1979): 20-33.
45. Edwin Diamond, *The Tin Kazoo: Television, Politics, and the News* (Cambridge, Mass., MIT Press, 1975).
46. Tony Schwartz, *The Responsive Chord* (Garden City, N.Y.: Anchor Press, Doubleday, 1973, p. 25.
47. Jarol B. Manheim, "Can Democracy Survive Television?" *Journal of Communication* 26 (Spring 1976): 84-90.
48. None of these studies focuses on the effects of exposure to nonfictional violence in the media, since the first amendment would be a strong bar to censorship of news. Surgeon General's Scientific Advisory Committee on Television and Social Behavior, *Television and Growing Up: The Impact of Televised Violence* (Washington, D.C.: U.S. Government Printing Office, 1971); Richard A. Dienstbier, "Sex and Violence: Can Research Have It Both Ways?" *Journal of Communication* 27 (Summer 1977): 176-188.
49. George A. Comstock, *The Evidence on Television Violence* (Santa Monica, Calif.: Rand Corporation, P-5730, 1976).

50. Herbert H. Hyman, "Mass Communication and Socialization" in W. Phillips Davison and Frederick T. C. Yu, eds., *Mass Communication Research* (New York: Praeger, 1974), pp. 36-65.
51. Robert P. Snow, "How Children Interpret TV Violence in Play Context," *Journalism Quarterly* 51 (Spring 1974): 13-21.
52. Commission on Obscenity and Pornography. *Report of the Commission on Obscenity and Pornography* (New York: Bantam Books, 1970). Also see Dienstbier, "Sex and Violence," pp. 177-180.
53. Leon S. Robertson, "The Great Seat Belt Campaign Flop," *Journal of Communication* 26 (Autumn 1976): 41-45.
54. James B. Lemert et al., "Journalists and Mobilizing Information," *Journalism Quarterly* 54 (Winter 1977): 721-726.
55. Rodolfo N. Salcedo, Hadley Read, James F. Evans and Ana C. Kong, "A Successful Information Campaign on Pesticides," *Journalism Quarterly* 51 (Spring 1974): 91-95; Dorothy F. Douglas, Bruce H. Westley and Steven H. Chaffee, "An Information Campaign that Changed Community Attitudes," *Journalism Quarterly* 47 (Autumn 1970): 479-487.
56. Sheldon O'Connell, "Television and the Canadian Eskimo: The Human Perspective," *Journal of Communication* 27 (Autumn 1977): 140-144; and Gary O. Coldevin, "Anik I and Isolation: Television in the Lives of Canadian Eskimos," *Journal of Communication* 27 (Autumn 1977): 145-153.
57. Everett M. Rogers, "The Rise and Fall of the Dominant Paradigm," *Journal of Communication* 28 (Winter 1978): 64-69; Wilbur Schramm and Daniel Lerner, eds., *Communication and Change: The Last Ten Years — and the Next* (Honolulu: University Press of Hawaii, 1976).

READINGS

Altheide, David L., and Snow, Robert P. *Media Logic*. Beverly Hills, Calif.: Sage, 1979.

Comstock, George A. *The Evidence on Television Violence*. Santa Monica, Calif.: Rand Corporation, 1976.

Comstock, George; Chaffee, Steven; Katzman, Natan; McCombs, Maxwell; and Roberts, Donald. *Television and Human Behavior*. New York: Columbia University Press, 1978.

Krauss, Sidney, and Davis, Dennis. *The Effects of Mass Communication on Political Behavior*. University Park: Pennsylvania State University Press, 1976.

Schramm, Wilbur, and Lerner, Daniel, eds. *Communication and Change: The Last Ten Years — and the Next*. Honolulu: University Press of Hawaii, 1976.

Winick, Mariann Pezzella, and Winick, Charles. *The Television Experience: What Children See*. Beverly Hills, Calif.: Sage, 1979.

6

Elections in the Television Age

In the fall of 1978, as the story goes, Illinois Senator Charles Percy's reelection campaign was in trouble. Alex Seith, the Democratic challenger, had pulled ahead and the polls were predicting a Seith victory. Then, during the final days of the campaign, Chicago's media saved the day for Charles Percy, killed Seith's 1978 chances, and dimmed his prospects for future election wins. The turn of the tide began with three tough columns by famed Chicago *Sun Times* columnist Mike Royko. Royko linked Seith to corrupt machine politicians allied with the Chicago crime syndicate and blasted him for racist appeals to black voters.

Percy, sensing the punch that these columns carried, reprinted them as full-page newspaper advertisements and mailed them throughout the state. Seith's strength in the polls began to drop sharply. Then, just four days before the election, another media event delivered the knockout punch. Percy and Seith got into a verbal brawl in the lobby of a Chicago television station, just before they were scheduled for a joint broadcast. Walter Jacobson, the station's news anchor and commentator, through artful questioning kept the lobby battle going after the candidates were before the cameras. Later on that night it became part of a 75-minute news special. It created an image of a dignified, senatorial Percy defending himself against an undeserved attack by a vicious, unprincipled challenger who had made a fine art of hitting below the belt. The voters sided with Percy.

That, at any rate, is the story among Chicago's political pundits about the changing fortunes of candidates Percy and Seith. It takes its place among many others that document the strong impact media interpretations can have on the fate of political candidates. The trouble with the Percy-Seith story, and most of the others, is that it does not prove beyond a doubt that the media stories turned the tide. Other things were happening at the time, including Percy's concerted efforts to make his messages to the voters more pleading and personal. Although the link between media and elections has been studied more thoroughly than other media-politics linkages, we still lack definite answers for most cause-effect questions like those posed by the Percy-Seith contest.

THE STATE OF RESEARCH

Understanding the role of the mass media in elections is hampered by imbalances in research. Presidential elections have been extensively studied, but we know little about the media's role in congressional elections, and practically nothing about their impact on local, judicial, or school board elections. There is evidence that the role of the mass media varies substantially, depending upon the particular office being contested, even when the manner of coverage is fairly constant.[1]

Even at the presidential level, little comparative research has been done to point up differences in the role of the media as candidates and issues change. Nor has the influence of such factors as incumbency, three-way competition, or major national crises been thoroughly investigated. It stands to reason that the impact of the media will vary depending on the type of coverage and the interests of voters. Comparable studies in Canada, Britain, France, Germany, and elsewhere are plagued by similar problems.

Another serious obstacle to understanding is the dearth of analyses of media content. Media effects have been inferred largely by assuming that people have been exposed to media election information, or by asking general questions about their usual media habits. Election news content and its setting within the context of general news have been examined only rarely because content analysis is very costly. High costs have also discouraged studying media and other political influences throughout the entire campaign, from the preprimary period to the primaries, the nomination stages, and the final election. Consequently, the potentially most crucial stages in the campaign have been largely ignored.

A shortage of good data also prevents us from isolating the effects of political advertising on political campaigns. Candidates and their supporters spend a large share of their campaign budgets on political commercials displayed on bumper stickers and on billboards, printed in newspapers, or broadcast with clockwork regularity on radio and television. The precise impact of these advertisements on target audiences is unknown because it is difficult to untangle effects of commercials from the effects of other types of campaign publicity.

One of the few studies that has systematically investigated the impact of television commercials is *The Unseeing Eye*,[2] by Robert McClure and Thomas Patterson. They report that, during the 1972 presidential campaign, major campaign issues were covered more extensively in television commercials than in network newscasts. For instance, between September 18 and November 6, 1972, more than 65 minutes of television time was used to tell about Nixon's policies on Vietnam, China, Russia and America's allies. The average television network spent only 15 minutes on these stories.[3] Most viewers remembered more from the commercials, which took five minutes or less air time each, than from the general flow of television news. This appeared to be particularly true for people who did not read newspapers and were poorly informed to begin with. Simplicity of content, expert eye-ear appeal, and repetition of the message combined to produce this result.

Although people learned about campaign issues, the commercials apparently failed to influence viewers' evaluations of the candidates. Ultimate voting choices were not altered. The claims that television commercials can manufacture fairyland candidates and make them believable to credulous audiences apparently are vastly exaggerated.[4] Commercials are perceiver-determined. People see in them pretty much what they want to see — attractive images for their favorite candidate and unattractive ones for the opponent. If attempts to glamorize political actors and hide their weaknesses succeed, the effect lasts for only a short time. Commercials of opposing candidates see to that.

Provided that the McClure-Patterson findings remain firm after further studies in other elections, one can conclude that television commercials add substantial chunks of information to the flow of news about campaign issues. However, they deal primarily with the same issues that are already covered by newspapers and television. Even though commercials present strong images of candidates and their positions, these images fail to penetrate most viewers' protective shielding of preconceived political ideas and preferences. The effects of commercials on images and voting thus differ only moderately from the effects of regular news coverage. What we shall say about the nature and impact of newspaper and television coverage of elections therefore applies to most aspects of television commercial news as well.

THE CONSEQUENCES OF MEDIA POLITICS

This is truly an era of "new politics." The advent of television and its ready availability in every home, the spread and improvement of public opinion polling, and the use of computers in election data analysis have combined to bring about major political changes that have vastly enhanced the role of the mass media in elections. What are these major changes wrought by the new technologies?

Decline in Party Influence

Foremost among the changes is the decline of the influence of political parties, particularly in presidential elections. In the 1940s, when social scientists first investigated the impact of the mass media on the outcome of presidential elections, party allegiance was the most important determinant of the vote. It was followed by group allegiance, assessment of the candidate's personality, and consideration of issues, in that order.

Since the full flowering of the electronic age, the order has been reversed. The candidate as a personality has become the prime consideration at the presidential level. Second are issues associated with the candidate, followed by party affiliation and group membership.[5] When voters base their decisions on candidate personality or issues, the media become more important because they are the chief source of information about these matters.

Correspondingly, political parties take on less importance. When voters can see and hear candidates in their own living rooms, they can make choices that differ from those made by the party. Split ticket voting has become common. The candidates can defy party control because television gives them direct access to voters. More candidates can enter the race and campaign on their own strengths, raising their own money, and building their own organizations. New candidates, with the aid of the media, can gain a wide following rapidly. This new independence of voters and candidates makes primary and general election races more crowded and less predictable than in the past. Party regulars who have groomed themselves over long periods of time for positions of power may find themselves bypassed.

Party affiliation remains very important at the state and local level where the average person knows little about most candidates and media information is scanty, particularly on television. This is not true, however, when candidates run without overt or covert party designation and endorsement or when candidates of the same party compete against each other in primary elections. When party choice criteria are lacking, and personal experience or advice from opinion leaders is unavailable, people turn to the media for guidance, either positively or negatively. Some will follow the paper's or station's expressed or implied endorsements; others will take them as cues to vote the opposite way. In either case, what the media say about the candidates becomes the information base for decisionmaking.

Media as Kingmakers

A second and related important consequence of the new politics is the sharp increase in the power of media personnel to influence the selection of candidates and issues. As is true of actors, candidates' successes hinge as much on the roles into which they are cast as on their acting ability. In the new politics, media people usually do the casting for presidential hopefuls, whose performance is then judged according to the assigned role. Strenuous efforts by campaign directors and public relations experts to dominate this aspect of the campaign have not been very fruitful.

Casting occurs early in the primaries when newspeople, on the basis of as yet slender evidence, must predict winners and losers in order to narrow the field of eligibles. This allows them to concentrate on the front-runners and makes their tasks more manageable, but it often forces those who have been labeled losers out of the race. As *New York*

Times political writer R. W. Apple conceded after appraising the candidates' chances in January 1976, "Such early calculations are highly speculative. . . . But early calculations have a life of their own, because they are the backdrop against which politicians and the media tend to measure the performance of the various candidates in their early confrontations."[6]

For instance, in the 1976 Democratic primaries, when almost a dozen candidates were running, the media covered Jimmy Carter far more heavily and favorably than other candidates. Coverage began months before the primaries, with above average numbers of newspaper stories, assiduously sought out by the Carter campaign staff. Ample television coverage followed after the New Hampshire primary in February, where Carter received 30 percent of the Democratic vote. NBC's Tom Pettit called Carter "the man to beat." *Time* magazine labeled his campaign as the only one "with real possibilities of breaking far ahead of the pack." It featured him on its front cover, as did *Newsweek*. Along with the front cover picture in *Time* went a 2,630-line feature story, compared to 300 lines devoted to all other Democrats in the race. Television news and newspaper front-page coverage were equally generous, giving Carter three and four times the attention his opponents received.

Senator Henry Jackson and Representative Morris Udall, who did well in the early Democratic primaries, between them got less than a third of the coverage which Carter received. Subsequent primary defeats, such as Carter's poor showing in Massachusetts in early March, were characterized as exceptions that merely slowed his momentum, rather than as disastrous defeats. Gallup Poll ratings in early February that gave Carter only five percent of the national vote were ignored.[7]

Carter earned his "winner" spurs because he had managed to outrun the expectations newspeople had established for his political success. Such expectations, based on poll results, projections from past campaigns, and more or less educated guesses, are the uncertain yardsticks by which newspeople measure winners and losers. Carter won his prized and priceless status after less than five percent of the primary delegates had been selected. The emphasis which the media placed on these early victories created the kind of psychological momentum that enhances a candidate's chances for winning successive primaries and getting the nomination. The winner image becomes a self-fulfilling prophecy, because supporters and money flow to the front-runner.

The media role as kingmaker or destroyer of the dreams of would-be kings is often exercised over a long span of time. Image-making for the 1976 and 1980 elections began on a massive scale more than a year before the first primary. Senators who receive favorable publicity over many years may gradually come to be thought of as likely nominees. On the basis of such media boosts, people may decide to vote for them irrespective of an official party nomination. Public support in 1968,

1972, 1976, and 1980 for Senator Edward Kennedy of Massachusetts as a presidential contender is a case in point.

Media giants like the late publisher Henry Luce are often able to use their personal influence and the power of the media under their control to support nominations for their favorites. For instance, Luce enticed popular war-hero Dwight Eisenhower to run for the presidency in 1952 and put Luce publications like *Time* and *Life* at his service. As discussed in Chapter 1, Kyle Palmer and the Chandler family, through their control of the *Los Angeles Times,* were instrumental in getting Richard Nixon a seat in the House of Representatives in 1946 and a U.S. Senate seat in 1950.

On the other hand, Senator Thomas Eagleton's crushed chances for the vice-presidency illustrate the problems faced by public officials whose public and private difficulties make headlines. When the media reported that the Missouri senator had a record of traffic arrests and treatment for a mental breakdown, Senator George McGovern, who had chosen him as his running mate in the 1972 election, felt forced to drop him from the ticket. Publicity for even trivial incidents may nip presidential aspirations. Stories about Senator Edmund Muskie's tears over an insult to his wife, and Governor George Romney's offhand remark that he had been "brainwashed" by the military establishment, are examples.

Media images are also vastly important during the general election campaign. For instance, a media event, the Kennedy-Nixon television debates of 1960, helped to remove public impressions that John F. Kennedy was too young and inexperienced to be president. Kennedy was apparently able to demonstrate through debates that he was capable of coping with the presidency. No other medium could have equaled the impact of television.

In fact, politicians were so awed by the risks of television debates that they shied away from a repeat performance for 16 years. When debates were scheduled again in 1976, the impact was less dramatic. Candidates Gerald Ford and Jimmy Carter both lacked the Kennedy charisma that had generated so much audience appeal. In all-important visual attractiveness, they were fairly well matched. No Prince Charming here, battling against a sweaty, gray-looking opponent. Still, many political observers believe that President Ford might have won reelection in 1976, had he been able to look substantially more presidential than Jimmy Carter in the debates.

Similarly, President Lyndon Johnson saw his chances for a second term diminish sharply because he was unable to use the media effectively to make a good case for his Vietnam policies. A comparison of his statements justifying his policies with the statements that were publicized shows that the bulk of his most telling messages were never transmitted. Media message selection had gutted the case he needed to win to make him a strong second term candidate.[8]

Television-Age Recruits

A third important consequence of the new politics is the change it has wrought in the types of candidates likely to be politically successful. Because television can bring the image of candidates for high national and state office directly into the homes of millions of voters, political recruiters have become extremely conscious of a candidate's ability to look impressive and to perform well before the camera. The pool of available recruits has been altered, eliminating people who are not telegenic. Scholars have mused that Abraham Lincoln's rugged face would not have passed muster in the television age. President Harry Truman's "Give 'em Hell, Harry" style would have backfired if presented to nationwide groups, rather than small gatherings. Franklin Roosevelt's wheelchair appearances would have spelled damaging weakness, as did George Wallace's in the 1970s. Roosevelt, in fact, was keenly aware of the harmful effects that a picture of himself in a wheelchair might have and never allowed photographs to be taken while he was being lifted to the speaker's rostrum.

Actors and celebrities from other walks of life, who are adept at performing before the public, now have a much better chance than ever before to be recruited for political office. Governor Ronald Reagan, a former actor, and Senator John Glenn, an ex-astronaut, are examples of typical television-age recruits whose chances for public office would have been small in an earlier era.

Candidates who are short on television performance skills now spend considerable time with professionals to remedy their shortcomings. In recent years, television advisers have become regular members of presidential and gubernatorial staffs. Names of media experts like Gerald Rafshoon, Tony Schwartz, David Garth, Charles Guggenheim, or Joseph Napolitan have become as well-known as the political bosses of yesteryear.

Largely because of the high costs of television, media exposure has become an exceedingly expensive aspect of political campaigns. Media time and production costs can take 30 to 50 percent of the total spent by all candidates and parties in elections at all levels. In 1976 total campaign spending was $540 million.[9] In 1976, partial public funding of presidential elections was introduced. Both Carter and Ford accepted such funding, which was tied to a spending limit of no more than $21.8 million in the general election. Of this amount, Carter spent $10.3 million on total media costs, of which $7.6 million went for television time alone. The Ford campaign spent $10.8 million on media advertising ($6.3 million for TV time).

Given the high campaign expenses, even when federal funding is available, the ability of a candidate to raise money remains a strong consideration. Wealthy candidates have an advantage because they can draw on personal resources. Activities and statements likely to alienate donors are shunned. While there is evidence that the best-financed candidates do not always win, folklore says they do. Hence falling behind in the race for money to finance media exposure is a sharp brake on political aspirations. The political consequences that spring from such financial considerations are enormous.

Campaigning For the Media

A fourth major aspect of the new politics is the fact that mass media coverage has become the pivot around which campaigns turn. Campaigns are arranged for the best media exposure before the largest suitable audience. To attract media coverage, candidates concentrate on press conferences, talk show appearances, or trips to interesting locations. Even when candidates meet voters personally through rallies, parades, or shopping center visits, they generally time them to attract the media and dovetail with publication schedules. This means that campaigns are tailored to suit media coverage opportunities.

Incumbents have a distinct advantage over challengers in this effort to attract coverage because journalists need exciting stories, preferably from candidates of proven newsworthiness. The official status of incumbents makes them intrinsically attractive. Therefore they usually get

Reprinted, courtesy of the *Chicago Tribune*

more and better coverage and are able to dictate time and place. When an incumbent president schedules a meeting for reporters in the White House Rose Garden, ample coverage is assured. There even is a quasi-incumbency status for promising candidates. Once they have attained wide recognition as front-runners, newspeople compete for their attention. Their power to grant or withhold it can be translated into influence over quality and quantity of coverage.

Candidates often plan their schedules to dovetail with media plans. For instance, when it became apparent during the 1976 prenomination period that the media would cover the January presidential caucuses in Iowa as an early weather vane for the campaign, candidates hurriedly re-arranged their schedules to make a good Iowa showing. Morris Udall, who had planned to campaign only in New Hampshire, Massachusetts, and Wisconsin, felt that "Iowa justifies the expense. It will be covered like the first primary always has been in the national press. If we can emerge as the clear liberal choice in Iowa, the payoffs in New Hampshire will be enormous."[10] Udall committed $80,000 of his scarce funds and 10 days of valuable time to the Iowa effort, but the anticipated payoffs did not materialize. Nonetheless, 1980 hopefuls responded in similar manner to prospective media coverage for straw polls and caucuses in places like Iowa, Florida, and Maine, where campaigning might otherwise be light.

To keep a favorable image of their candidate in front of the public, campaign managers arrange newsworthy events to familiarize potential voters with their candidates' best aspects. In 1972, for instance, Senator McGovern's campaign aides put him into settings where he was surrounded by small groups of friendly people. They did not involve him in large rallies where cameras might be able to focus on dissenters and hecklers. In fact, newspeople who wanted a balanced picture were hard put to find unfavorable footage.

Most television producers do not like "talking heads," which means merely showing the faces of speakers, even though talking is the staple of campaigners. Candidates therefore engage in some fairly meaningless activities merely to provide attractive pictures. Most of these pictures are deliberately packed with symbols to convey stock messages quickly and easily. In fact, over the years, a complete language of picture stereotypes has developed, and candidates adapt their own styles to fit into this mold. For instance, showing candidates with old people, or black workers, or college students proclaims affinity for these groups. Showing candidates in informal settings, surrounded by family members, attests to their being "regular" folk and good family people.

Most major campaign events are now staged as prime-time live-coverage television spectacles. Nominating conventions are the biggest single media event of a presidential campaign, aside from presidential debates. Both major parties now select the convention city with an eye to effective television coverage. No longer are delegates allowed to ramble on in long speeches or to engage in lengthy spontaneous demonstrations of support. Rather, convention managers try to keep a tight rein on speakers and demonstrations to make certain that desirable images are conveyed and that major presentations appear when the television audience is likely to be at a peak. For their part, media people try to structure the flow of their words and pictures to cover unfolding events and still tell a coherent dramatic story with a central theme, a beginning and ending, and a climax. The theme may be that the favorite contender is unbeatable, or that a battle is shaping up between party liberals and conservatives, or that the whole nominating process resembles pandemonium.

Structuring and staging campaign activities to make them newsworthy by the standards of modern American media has not necessarily made them more trivial than they have been in the past. But it has made it more certain that they will remain trivial, aiming for glitter and excitement more than substance. As California governor Jerry Brown's campaign manager put it, "newsworthy" means featuring disagreement, conflict, and contrast. It means painting campaign participants as heroes and villains. It means making one's point briefly, at the start of a speech, and using popular, emotionally stirring symbols. It means tailoring one's speech to the needs of the moment and capturing the audience's fancy.[11] Noteworthy by its absence from this definition is any mention that newsworthy means saying something important or enlightening for the audience.

Since conflict is deemed attractive and memorable, journalists often help campaigners to create confrontations by asking questions that point up existing conflicts or that may lead to new battles. During the 1980 presidential campaign, for instance, the media encouraged challengers to attack President Carter's energy policies and his handling of cabinet appointments. When journalists select the battlegrounds for the presidential contest, they shape the political agenda not only during the campaign but afterwards as well. Campaign statements may be construed subsequently as commitments to action.

Because campaign stories are judged by general news criteria, minor candidates do not get much coverage. They have no chance to win the fight; therefore they simply are not "big news" to the mass audience. Lack of coverage, in turn, makes it extremely difficult for them to become well known and increase their chances of winning elections. This is an example of unintentional bias built into media coverage in favor of established political forces.

MEDIA CONTENT

We are now ready to examine the kind of press and television coverage that recent presidential elections have received. We shall focus on the media's evaluation of candidates' qualifications and issue positions in two close contests, 1968 and 1976, and on the landslide 1972 election. Was enough information made available about the issues likely to require decisions by the new president? Were sufficient criteria supplied to enable voters to decide which of several policy options would best suit their priorities? Were people informed about each viable candidate's positions on the issues? Did they receive sufficient information about each candidate's personality, experience, and ability to evaluate her or his likely performance as president? All of these questions assess the adequacy of the information supply for making rational voting choices.

To mesh the preferences of the general public for simple, dramatic stories with the need to present sufficient information to make rational election choices possible poses an extremely difficult task for the media. Information that may be crucial for voting decisions may also be unappealing to much of the potential audience, which will therefore ignore it. Hence newspeople feel compelled to feature exciting, humanly touching aspects of the election, even when they are trivial, without totally neglecting essential, unglamorous information needed for decisionmaking. Any evaluation of how the media perform their task must take these conflicting demands into consideration.

Patterns of Coverage

The information on mass media output comes from a content analysis of newspapers and national and local television newscasts for the last 30 days of the presidential campaign in each of the three years.[12] Content analysis of 1976 election news from January to October showed few major differences in news coverage patterns between the early and late parts of the campaign.[13] Therefore we shall talk about election coverage in general for the entire campaign.

Prominence of Election Stories. Election stories constituted roughly 13 percent of all newspaper political news during each presidential election year, and 15 percent of television political news. This makes election stories major foci of news attention, on a par with foreign affairs news and crime coverage. But it does not give them a dominant position. It is quite possible to read the daily paper without encountering election news and to come away from a telecast with the impression that election stories are just a minor part of the day's political developments.

Treatment of election stories in terms of such prominence criteria as headline size, front page or first story placement, and picture treatment substantiates this feeling. Election stories received average treatment in all these categories. Election stories were preferred in one important repect, however; they were, on the average, longer in the space or time allotted to them than other stories and so provided more detail than an average story.

Uniformity of Coverage Patterns. One of the most striking findings in all three presidential election years was the uniformity of patterns of coverage. Media personnel everywhere selected the same kinds of stories and emphasized the same types of facts, despite the wealth of diverse materials available to them. The only difference was that smaller newspapers carried fewer election stories and that news stories varied in the evaluation of candidates, issues, and campaign events. Newspapers in small or large communities, endorsing Republicans or Democrats, all showed the same patterns. Television news was also uniform. [14]

The finding that election news patterns are uniform is politically very significant. It means that Americans everywhere have a similar information base for political decisionmaking. There are benefits as well as drawbacks to this situation; the same topics are aired but the same ones are also neglected. Joint knowledge is marred by joint ignorance.

A uniform information base obviously has not produced uniform political views throughout the country. Hence the differences in political concerns must be attributed to the outlook which the audience brings to the news, rather than the news itself. This accords with the findings reported in the previous chapter that the impact of news frequently is perceiver- rather than stimulus-determined.

Of the factors that encourage uniform coverage, common professional socialization of journalists is apparently the most important. As we discussed in Chapter 3, newspeople share a sense of what is newsworthy and how it should be presented. Pack journalism also is the rule in reporting elections, as Timothy Crouse pointed out so vividly in *The Boys on the Bus: Riding with the Campaign Press Corps.*[15] Several other possible explanations can be ruled out, such as universal use of wire service stories, quotes from the same speeches, or shared columnists. Only roughly one-fourth of all campaign stories were based on similar wire service stories or relied on quotes to make their main points. Papers that used very few wire service stories for campaign coverage still showed the same news patterns. The small percentage of campaign stories that were based on the writings of columnists (15 percent) involved a wide array of writers.

Uniform coverage patterns might also be produced if the media followed what has been called the "campaign model" of reporting.[16] In this model, the rhythm of the campaign, as produced by the candidates and their managers, determines what is covered. Reporters dutifully present whatever campaign managers supply. Comparisons of campaign activities with media coverage show that this model does not prevail. Instead, press coverage conforms to an "incentive model." Whenever exciting stories provide an incentive for coverage, they are published in a rhythm dictated by the needs of the media and the tastes of their audiences. This means that when candidates step up their campaign activities, coverage does not necessarily follow suit. For instance, media coverage lags behind the acceleration of campaign activity just prior to nominations and primary and general elections.

The incentive model also explains the handling of news substance. Producing exciting stories means concentrating on conflicts, real or manufactured, keeping score about who is ahead or behind in the race and who has won a particular round in the battle, and digging out tidbits about the personal and professional life and foibles of the actors in the political drama. It means shunning election stories that are complex and stuffed with statistics and strange names.

Election coverage by specialized media further illustrates the use of the incentive model. News patterns differ from those in the general audience media. For instance, papers geared to Hispanic audiences focus on the aspects of the campaign which are of primary concern to Hispanics, ignoring most of the rest. Business and labor publications put extraordinary emphasis on economic news, which is totally lacking from general audience publications.

Political and Structural Bias. Does election coverage give a fair and equal chance for all viewpoints to be expressed in a manner that allows the media audience to make informed decisions? Are the perennial charges of bias leveled by disappointed candidates merely reactions to coverage which does not suit their whims, or are they evidence that newspeople always show favoritism?

The answer is that media people try very hard to produce balanced coverage for all candidates for the same office. This holds true for print journalists, who have no legal obligation to keep coverage balanced. It also holds true for broadcasters, who are obliged to give equal coverage for special election programs, but who are free to indulge in unequal exposure in regular news programs. There are no universally accepted standards of fairness and balance, but generally, newspeople construe it as rough parity among the number of stories about each candidate and rough parity in the balance of overtly favorable and unfavorable stories. Fairness does not mean discussing the candidates from the same perspectives, covering similar proportions of their campaign appearances, or giving their stories similar time, space, or placement.

Implementing the prevailing notions of fairness and balance may be impossible. For instance, in the McGovern-Nixon campaign of 1972, George McGovern was a new face on the presidential scene, challenging an incumbent who lacked rapport with most newspeople. McGovern was saying all sorts of newsworthy things while Nixon stayed out of the media limelight claiming to be too busy in the Oval Office. Quite naturally, the media quoted Senator McGovern more often than President Nixon. Having their statements publicized is usually advantageous to candidates because their stories are told in their own words, rather than in the words of a newsperson. On the other hand, Nixon received more coverage overall because the manifold activities of an incumbent president are always highly newsworthy.

One may question whether it is fair to attempt to balance coverage when the situation surrounding the candidates is not comparable.

Reducing an incumbent president's coverage to that accorded to a challenger seems unfair and inappropriate; so would expansion of the challenger's coverage to presidential proportions. Likewise, when McGovern met more often with reporters and used more quotable phrases than his opponent, it would have been unfair to suppress these quotes for the sake of balance. Imbalanced coverage, in these instances, resulted from "structural bias," which is caused by the circumstances of news production. This differs from "political bias," which would involve slanting the news for partisan reasons. Structural bias, though devoid of partisan motives, may nonetheless have profound effects on the perceptions people form of the campaign.[17]

McGovern also benefitted from the fact that newspeople drew primarily on Democrats as sources for their stories, even though the vast majority of newspapers had editorially supported Nixon. Campaign stories in 1972 reflected this Democratic slant but again, structural and news judgment considerations, rather than political bias, are the explanations. More news was available from Democratic than Republican sources and it was more exciting because candidate McGovern had worked hard to make it more exciting.

Explicit bias, by contrast, is highly unusual. Outright editorial comment in news stories is practically nil. Veiled criticism is somewhat more common and can be detected in 1 to 4 percent of the stories when one considers all types of media and all types of elections. Editorials, of course, are biased, as it is their function to express opinions.

As part of the editorial function, many news sources also endorse candidates. Just as Senator McGovern's favorable media coverage did not prevent a Nixon landslide win, so have editorial endorsements failed to alter election outcomes drastically at the presidential level. Even though Republican presidential candidates have received the bulk of endorsements in this century, the people have elected more Democratic presidents. Endorsements for less exalted offices have been more influential, particularly in elections when voters had little information available to make their own decisions.[18] Highly respected papers like the *Los Angeles Times,* the *Baltimore Sun,* or the *Washington Post* can be extraordinarily successful in promoting the election of candidates they have endorsed. These three were credited, respectively, with sending Richard Nixon into the House of Representatives in 1946 and the Senate in 1950, electing Harry Hughes as Maryland governor in 1978 over a better known incumbent, and winning the mayoral primary in Washington, D.C., in 1978 for City Councilman Marion Barry, who had been trailing in the polls. At the presidential level, news coverage tends to be evenhanded, regardless of the candidate favored by the endorsement. Below the presidential level, there is some evidence that media give more coverage to their endorsed candidates than to those they have not endorsed.

As mentioned earlier, the effort to keep coverage balanced does not extend to third-party candidates. Anyone who runs for the presidency outside of the Republican or Democratic party is out of the mainstream of newsworthiness and slighted or even totally ignored by the news profession. Exceptionally newsworthy third-party candidates like George Wallace of the American Independent Party and Robert La Follette of the Progressive Party were notable exceptions. Newsworthiness considerations also account for the sparse coverage of vice-presidential candidates. Although the office is extremely important, because vice-presidential candidates fairly often become president, that possibility always seems remote until it happens. Hence these candidates receive very little media attention. Ninety-five percent of the coverage goes to the presidential contenders and only 5 percent to their running mates.

Substance of Coverage: Candidates

We now turn to specific coverage characteristics. How are candidate qualifications and positions delineated, and how are campaign events and issues described and analyzed?

Judging from the highly consistent patterns of the 1968-1976 period, it is clear that the media discuss the qualifications of the candidates more amply than campaign events and issues. For instance, in 1976 newspapers devoted 61 percent of the coverage of both presidential candidates to personal qualifications, and 39 percent to events and issues. Comparable 1972 and 1968 figures for personal qualifications were 64 and 56 percent. Actually, emphasis on issues was somewhat greater than these figures indicate since a moderate portion of the discussion of presidential qualities related to presidential ability to cope with issues.

The presidential qualifications highlighted by the media fall into two broad groups: those that are generally important in judging a person's character, and those more specifically related to the tasks of the presidency. Personal capacities include personality traits such as integrity, reliability, and compassion. They also encompass style characteristics, such as forthrightness or folksiness, and image characteristics, such as the ability to appear productive and fiscally responsible. Professional capacities include the capacity to conduct foreign and domestic affairs, ability to mobilize public support, and a flair for government reorganization. The candidate's political philosophy is also a professional criterion.

Within these broad categories some 40 qualities were mentioned repeatedly in all the news sources, in quite similar proportions. Only ten qualities were stressed heavily, and these involved primarily personal capacities. In fact, in 1968 and 1976, 77 percent of the presidential qualifications which were discussed involved personal rather than professional capacities. In 1972 the figure dipped to 62 percent.

Over the years, candidates were most frequently assessed in terms of their trustworthiness, strength of character, and compassion. As one wit has phrased it, the crucial question is, "Would you buy a used car from him?" For the media, and, as we shall discuss later, the public as well, this question of trustworthiness has been paramount because of the tremendous amount of unchecked power in the hands of American presidents. Style and presidential image characteristics are important as well, but pale before the prominence given to personality traits.[19]

When it comes to professional capacities — the very qualities which one might argue deserve the fullest discussion and analysis — media coverage was comparatively scanty and narrowly focused in all three elections. Only four qualifications were mentioned fairly frequently. Two broadly phrased qualifications were the capacity to handle foreign affairs, which has always been deemed a key presidential capacity in the twentieth century, and the capacity to handle domestic affairs. The ability to extricate the country from foreign wars and make peace was mentioned often in 1968 but not thereafter. The ability to maintain law and order and cope with crime, on the other hand, was mentioned frequently during all three elections.

Table 6-1 shows the percentages of newspaper comment devoted to various presidential qualities in 1968, 1972, and 1976. The table illustrates the basic similarities in patterns in all three elections. It also

Table 6-1   Presidential Qualities: Percentage and Rank Order of Newspaper Mention in Three Elections*

Personal Capacities	1968 Percentage	Rank	1972 Percentage	Rank	1976 Percentage	Rank
Personality Traits	37	(1)	24	(2)	36	(1)
Presidential Image	18	(3)	25	(1)	25	(2)
Style	22	(2)	13	(4)	16	(3)
Totals	77		62		77	
Professional Capacities						
Capacities	12	(4)	17	(3)	7	(5)
Relations with Public	7	(5)	7	(6)	3	(6)
Philosophy	2	(6)	11	(5)	10	(4)
Organizational Policies	2	(7)	3	(7)	2	(7)
Totals	23		38		22	

*These percentages are based on the following numbers of newspaper comments: 6,486 for 1968; 20,363 for 1972; 17,423 for 1976.

shows that very limited information was made available about the candidates' basic political philosophies, their ideas about government organization, and their abilities and willingness to communicate with the public. This information could have been obtained from the candidates' campaign literature or interviews.

One might expect some differences in patterns of media coverage because the 1968 race was a three-way contest that featured a cast of strangers to the presidential office, while 1972 and 1976 were contests between an incumbent and a single challenger. Specifically, one might expect that with a professional record available for the incumbent in the latter years, coverage would lean more heavily toward professional qualities. That was true in 1972, but not in 1976. One must therefore conclude that even when an incumbent is involved and there is ample opportunity to assess professional qualifications, media personnel prefer to focus on personal qualifications.

While media output in all three years contained references to the same kinds of qualities and even the same specific qualities, profiles of individual candidates varied. Tables 6-2 and 6-3 tell the story, distinguishing between comments made by the candidates themselves, as cited in the media, and comments made about them by reporters. For instance, in 1968, when neither Humphrey nor Nixon had served as president, the media quoted Nixon's remarks about professional capacities more amply than Humphrey's. Humphrey's emphasis was more on significance of personality traits. In reports *about* the candidates, this pattern was reversed. Variability in patterns of emphasis was even greater when one looked at coverage of specific qualities, rather than quality groupings. One must wonder about the impact of such disparate coverage, which makes it very difficult for the electorate to compare and evaluate the candidates on these important dimensions.

Another hurdle to effective comparison is that many remarks reported about the candidates are contradictory. Bound by current codes of objective reporting and neutrality in electoral contests, the media rarely give guidance to the audience on judging conflicting claims. Moreover, choices must often be made between lesser evils. Newspaper stories in particular tend to depict candidates as deficient in the qualities essential for the presidency. As Figure 6-1 indicates, the percentage of negative comments has risen over the past three elections. Normative comments, which prescribe that candidates *ought* to have certain qualities, have dropped correspondingly, while positive comments have dropped only slightly.

Tables 6-4 and 6-5 show that there were considerable differences among the candidates in the proportions of positive, negative, and normative comments that the media reported by and about them. In general, in quotes by Republicans, positive comments predominated, while the opposite was true for Democrats. A partial explanation is the fact that Republicans were incumbents in 1972 and 1976, praising their own

Table 6-2 Presidential Qualities Mentioned *by* the Candidates and *about* the Candidates: A Comparison of 1968, 1972, and 1976 Newspaper Coverage (Percentage of mention)

	1968 Press		1972 Press		1976 Press	
	Humphrey	Nixon	Nixon	McGovern	Ford	Carter
Quality	%	%	%	%	%	%
Comments by the candidates*						
Personal						
Personality traits	45	29	18	23	33	35
Presidential image	12	19	25	24	25	27
Style	22	26	11	13	17	15
Totals:	79%	74%	54%	60%	75%	77%
Professional						
Capacities	10	15	16	16	10	9
Relations with public	9	7	12	9	4	4
Philosophy	2	3	11	11	9	8
Organizational policies	1	2	6	3	2	2
Totals:	22%	27%	45%	39%	25%	23%
Comments about the candidates**						
Personal						
Personality traits	40	43	22	28	37	36
Presidential image	19	15	25	25	27	23
Style	23	19	12	15	14	21
Totals:	82%	77%	59%	68%	78%	80%
Professional						
Capacities	11	11	16	15	8	7
Relations with public	4	8	10	5	3	3
Philosophy	3	2	11	11	8	9
Organizational policies	0	1	5	1	3	1
Totals:	18%	22%	42%	32%	22%	20%

*These percentages are based on the following numbers of comments by the candidates: Humphrey 955; 1968 Nixon 975; 1972 Nixon 2,625; McGovern 3,520; Ford 1,718; Carter 1,561.

**These percentages are based on the following numbers of comments about the candidates; Humphrey 970; 1968 Nixon 1,536; 1972 Nixon 9,913; McGovern 3,583; Ford 6,044; Carter 4,187.

record, while Democratic challengers were attacking it. In stories about the candidates, patterns of praise and condemnation did not follow party lines. Overall, the balance between positive and negative comments made for a confusing picture.

Television coverage trends were similar to newspaper trends, although television, especially at the local level, remained more positive

Table 6-3 Presidential Qualities Mentioned *by* the Candidates and *about* the Candidates: A Comparison of 1972 and 1976 Television Coverage (Percentage of mention)

| | 1972 TV | | 1976 TV* | |
| | Nixon | McGovern | Ford | Carter |
Quality	%	%	%	%
Comments by the candidates**				
Personal				
Personality traits	33	24	6	50
Presidential image	23	24	6	13
Style	19	22	4	11
Totals:	75%	70%	73%	74%
Professional				
Capacities	15	19	21	24
Relations with public	6	5	4	0
Philosophy	3	6	0	2
Organizational policies	1	0	2	0
Totals:	25%	30%	27%	26%
Comments about the candidates***				
Personal				
Personality traits	33	30		
Presidential image	20	22		
Style	14	16		
Totals:	67%	68%		
Professional				
Capacities	23	20		
Relations with public	6	5		
Philosophy	3	4		
Organizational policies	0	2		
Totals:	32%	31%		

*Data based on written abstracts rather than actual broadcasts. Comments about the candidates are not reported because they are too sparse.

**These percentages are based on the following numbers of comments by the candidates: Nixon 221; McGovern 508; Ford 62; Carter 81.

***These percentages are based on the following numbers of comments about the candidates: Nixon 715; McGovern 349.

throughout than the print media. This finding challenges theories that attribute the greater political cynicism of television fans to greater negativism in television news.[20] On the whole, television resembles newspaper patterns in concentrated form. If newspapers stress personality qualities heavily, television stresses them even more. If they concentrate remarks on comparatively few qualities, television concentrates on even fewer. The usual one- or two-minute story gives little chance for in-depth portrayals. It does permit creation of simple, graphic images which viewers can readily absorb and use as a basis for decisionmaking.

To conserve their limited time, television newscasters create stereotypes of the various candidates early in the campaign and then build their stories around these stereotypes. Creation of fresh images for each broadcast would make coverage of new events impossible. During the 1972 primaries, for instance, television stereotyped Senator Hubert Humphrey of Minnesota, a former presidential candidate and vice presi-

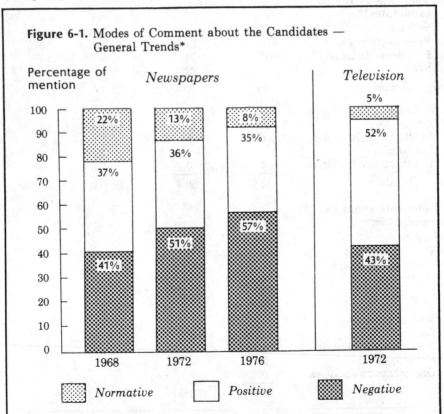

Figure 6-1. Modes of Comment about the Candidates — General Trends*

*Percentages are based on presidential qualities mentioned in 6,486 newspaper stories in 1968, 20,363 newspaper and 1,623 television stories mentioned in 1972, and 17,423 newspaper stories mentioned in 1976. *Positive* = Candidate has the desirable quality; *Normative* = Candidate ought to have the desirable quality; *Negative* = Candidate lacks the desirable quality.

Table 6-4 Modes* of Comment, *by* the Candidates and *about* the Candidates, in 1968, 1972, and 1976 Newspaper Coverage (Percentage of mention)

	1968 Press		1972 Press		1976 Press	
	Humphrey %	Nixon %	Nixon %	McGovern %	Ford %	Carter %
Comments by the candidates**						
Positive	37	40	93	31	59	31
Normative	17	24	3	12	2	2
Negative	46	36	3	57	39	66
Comments about the candidates***						
Positive	43	34	40	34	38	38
Normative	16	18	5	7	4	4
Negative	41	48	55	58	58	58

*Three modes are used: *Positive* = Candidate has the desirable quality; *Normative* = Candidate ought to have the desirable quality; *Negative* = Candidate lacks the desirable quality.

**These percentages are based on the following numbers of comments by the candidates: Humphrey 955; 1968 Nixon 975; 1972 Nixon 2,625; McGovern 3,520; Ford 1,718; Carter 1,561.

***These percentages are based on the following numbers of comments about the candidates: Humphrey 970; 1968 Nixon 1,536; 1972 Nixon 9,913; McGovern 3,583; Ford 6,044; Carter 4,187.

dent, as "the politician of the past." Television's Humphrey had old supporters, was linked to the unpopular Johnson presidency, and represented the old politics confronted by the new. Senator Edmund Muskie of Maine was stereotyped as the "front-runner," and Senator George McGovern was depicted as the "anti-establishment populist." Alabama Governor George Wallace was "the creator of division and discord" who was trying to ride into the presidency on the school busing issue.

A few examples from television broadcasts during the 1972 primaries indicate how television produces these kinds of images. Relevant passages are italicized. Here is a typical one on Hubert Humphrey as "the politician of the past."[21]

The filmed report on Humphrey begins with the reporter's comment: "While Senator McGovern flew off to New Mexico, Senator Humphrey stumped the state from San Francisco to San Diego in *the sort of wind-up that has become traditional in California campaigns.* And perhaps nothing illustrated the difference between the two campaigns more than that McGovern has done the unusual, the unexpected, while *Humphrey has followed the old paths and done the things that have brought him victory in the past.*" An applauding, mainly black crowd is shown with Humphrey at the front of the room behind a podium. "His cam-

Table 6-5 Modes* of Comment, *by* the Candidates and *about* the Candidates, in 1972, and 1976 Television Coverage (Percentage of mention)

| | 1972 TV | | 1976 TV** | |
| | Nixon | McGovern | Ford | Carter |
	%	%	%	%
Comments by the candidates*				
Positive	90	67	27	16
Normative	5	2	0	0
Negative	6	31	73	84
Comments about the candidates**				
Positive	45	70	—	—
Normative	5	3	—	—
Negative	50	27	—	—

*Three modes are used: *Positive* = Candidate has the desirable quality; *Normative* = Candidate ought to have the desirable quality; *Negative* = Candidate lacks the desirable quality.

**Data based on written abstracts rather than actual broadcasts. Comments about the candidates are not reported because they are too sparse.

***These percentages are based on the following numbers of comments by the candidates: Nixon 221; McGovern 508; Ford 62; Carter 81.

****These percentages are based on the following numbers of comments about the candidates: Nixon 715; McGovern 349.

paign has been hampered by lack of money, and a shortage of workers. *The old coalition, labor and the blacks, has not jelled this time* and the California Poll this week showed him trailing McGovern with both groups. Even Humphrey's own poll, released yesterday, showed him trailing McGovern among blacks. Because of that, *Senator Humphrey has had to spend a great deal of time appealing to past loyalties.*"

Then the camera zooms in on Humphrey who says: "*I remember marching with Dr. Martin Luther King Jr.* on that day in August 1963, down Pennsylvania Avenue. I wasn't hiding out. I was down there marching. I was sitting there on the steps with him on the Lincoln Memorial, and I brought him on over to the White House." At this point, the reporter cuts in: "*Senator Humphrey has been a national leader for a long time.* That may help him with some voters, but it could cost him votes among *other people who view him as the politician of the past.*"

Senator Muskie suffered because in the early primaries the media pictured him as "the front-runner," who could be expected to win by wide margins. Candidates try to peg their goals low to avoid the risk of falling below predictions. But the press often takes this decision out of their hands. If they then fail to live up to expectations, they are automatically "losers." The problem which this image created for Muskie became quickly apparent in the New Hampshire primary. As the first primary in presidential election years, New Hampshire receives plentiful, nationwide billing as the harbinger of successes and failures to come. Proportionate to the number of delegates elected, it receives at least 10 times the coverage of later primaries. Muskie polled 38 percent of the New Hampshire vote, compared to 37 percent for McGovern. Despite his one percentage point lead, the media called him a loser because the size of the lead did not comport with the front-runner image.

Here is how one broadcaster handled the "defeat" of front-runner Muskie in the New Hampshire primary. "Edmund Muskie's presidential campaign took off and flew like a paper airplane built by somebody who does not know how to build paper planes. It went straight up, did a strange, unexpected loop, and came straight down again. And now Muskie is working desperately at the controls, trying to avoid a crash and trying to avoid an appearance of panic."

While winner Muskie received the loser label, loser McGovern received the winner label. Right after the New Hampshire primary a broadcaster noted that George McGovern "was leaving New Hampshire feeling, he said, like a winner. Numerically he had not won, but compared to what people had expected of him, compared to what they had been writing about him, and saying about him for two years, compared to all of that, he felt he had won." The upshot of such a victory could be tremendous. "Momentum in politics means the money comes in, volunteers start calling, the staff works with new zeal, the candidate is lifted. Momentum is fragile and very important. And George McGovern feels that he and his campaign as they head to Florida now have it."

Television is the most widely used medium for campaign information and reaches nearly every voter, so the potential impact of such typecasting is vast. This is particularly true during the primaries, when party cues are unavailable. Candidates with a loser image lose momentum and may well be finished because funds dry up, as does the enthusiasm of actual and potential campaign workers.

During the general election, when party cues are available, typecasting is less potent, even though earlier images do persist from the primaries of previous campaigns. Once Jimmy Carter had been tagged as "fuzzy," there was, according to his press secretary Jody Powell, "no way on God's earth we could shake the fuzziness question . . . no matter what Carter did or said. He could have spent the whole campaign doing nothing but reading substantive speeches . . . and still have had that image in the national press."[22] The general feeling in such cases seems to be that leopards do not change their spots.

Substance of Coverage: Issues and Events

Issue and events coverage, as already pointed out, has usually lagged behind that of personal characteristics. This balance bothers social scientists, who contend that the electorate ought to judge the candidates on their issue positions. It also runs counter to the common impression that the print media put primary emphasis on issues, leaving it to television to show off personalities. Actually, electronic and print media display surprisingly similar patterns, although television lags behind print media in the range and depth of issue coverage.

The overriding consideration in choosing issues, as in other political coverage, is newsworthiness rather than intrinsic importance. In fact, the amount of coverage for particular issues often seems to be in inverse proportion to their significance. For instance, during the 1976 campaign, Ford's blunder about political freedom in Eastern Europe captured enormous amounts of media attention. So did Carter's indelicate remark about the ethnic purity desirable for neighborhoods and his comments on sexual conduct during an interview with *Playboy* magazine.

During the 1968, 1972, and 1976 campaigns, three major features stand out in coverage of issues and events. Most significantly, the media devote the bulk of their stories to campaign hoopla and the horse-race aspects of the contest. Second, they slight political, social, or economic problems facing the country and say little about the merits of the solutions proposed, unless these issues can be made exciting and visually dramatic. Finally, information about issues is patchy because the candidates and their spokesmen address only issues that will help their campaign. Newspeople rarely investigate neglected issues on their own. The issue positions of vice-presidential candidates remain virtually unexplored, for example.

Figure 6-2 shows the proportions of stories allotted to various types of issues and events during the final month of the campaign. Stories about campaign incidents dominate, except in 1968 when election-related Vietnam War stories captured the most coverage. In 1972 and 1976, emphasis on foreign affairs campaign issues dropped sharply. Next to campaign events, election issues concerning general domestic politics normally receive the heaviest coverage. They consist of reports about the candidates' views concerning ongoing activities of government at all levels. Such stories, which are available from regular beats, are generally tied to familiar names and widely salient events. Therefore they require little background information, and pictorial coverage is easily arranged. All of these considerations make it very tempting to report them.

Social problems, like poverty or the plight of the elderly, usually lack novelty and are complex to describe. They frequently involve highly controversial and emotionally charged policies about which candidates and media keep silent for fear of alienating large segments of the public. Such issues therefore receive scanty coverage in election stories, except

Figure 6-2. Newspaper and Television Issue Coverage in the 1968, 1972, and 1976 Presidential Campaigns

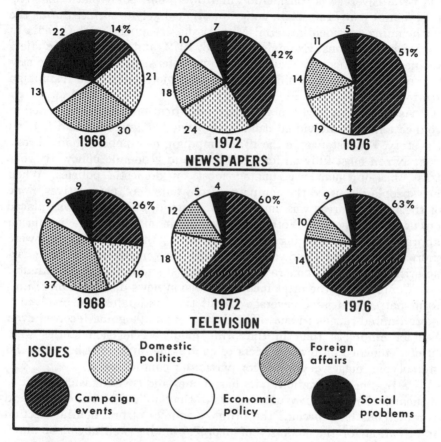

Percentages are based on the following numbers of issues: 1968 press: 3,538; TV: 1,346; 1972 press: 11,187; TV: 963; 1976 press: 11,027; TV: 1,355.

when they erupt in violence, as happened in 1968 when racial tensions turned into racial riots.

Coverage of economic issues, like unemployment, inflation, and taxes, is also limited because these issues are hard to explain and dramatize and rarely produce exciting pictures. Skimpy coverage may seem puzzling because these are issues with which the average voter is intimately concerned.[23] The explanation is that most people, though concerned, are unwilling to wrestle with a difficult subject that newspeople have not yet learned to simplify and dramatize. Rather than risk writing complex campaign stories that most of the audience would probably ignore, newspeople prefer to feature the horse-race glamour of campaign events.

Overall, some 25 issues surfaced fairly constantly in the press and some 20 on television in the 1968, 1972, and 1976 campaigns. Typically, only half of these received extended and intensive attention, so that media issue coverage is considerably narrower than party platforms. The media omit many important policy questions likely to surface during the forthcoming presidential term. Many issues reappear in the media in successive elections. Examples for 1968, 1972, and 1976 were the effectiveness of the incumbent administration, defense policies, race and ethnic relations, the meaning of public opinion polls, and campaign strategies.

As was the case with presidential qualifications, issues discussed in connection with individual candidates varied. Figures 6-3 and 6-4 tell the story. For instance, in the 1972 campaign, newspapers quoted President Nixon most fully on foreign affairs and economic policy. By contrast, his opponent was quoted most on domestic policies. When newspeople discussed the campaign, from outsiders' perspectives, none of these policy areas was emphasized. Instead, chief stress was placed on campaign hoopla. Voters received little aid from the media in appraising and comparing the candidates on the issues. So they were more likely to rest their voting decisions on general personality characteristics, which were more amply presented and far easier to evaluate.

Compared to the print media, television news displayed more uniform patterns of issue coverage for all the candidates and involved a more limited range of issues. The drama of campaigning received even heavier emphasis than in the print media. Television stories were briefer, touched on fewer aspects of each issue, and contributed to the stereotypic images developed for particular candidates.

Stripping information to its bare bones and covering what is left as a theatrical event apparently appeals to the public. Television news and commercials have become the primary sources of presidential election information for the majority of people, ranking well ahead of newspapers. Television images of the candidates are more appealing because they are far simpler and more positive, with fewer conflicting appraisals than their newspaper counterparts. Readers who find newspaper coverage confusing and depressing can turn to television for a simpler and more encouraging image of the unfolding electoral scene.

Adequacy of Coverage

How helpful are the media for making rational voting decisions? On the basis of three elections, one would have to say that appraisal of candidates and issues is quite difficult for the voter. Information is ample on personal qualifications of the major mainstream candidates and on day-to-day campaign events. It is sketchy and often confusing on most professional qualifications, on substantive issues, and on the policy options involved in these issues. Most primary contenders, candidates of minor parties, and the vice-presidential candidates are largely ignored. The prevalence of negative information makes it seem that all of the

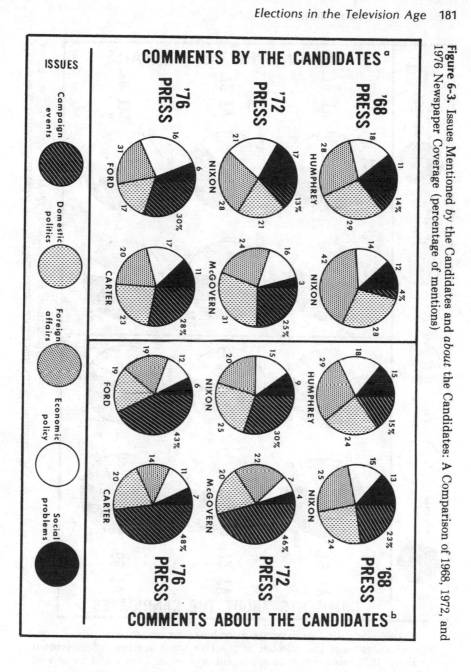

Figure 6-3. Issues Mentioned *by* the Candidates and *about* the Candidates: A Comparison of 1968, 1972, and 1976 Newspaper Coverage (percentage of mentions)

[a] These percentages are based on the following numbers of comments by the candidates: Humphrey 625; 1968 Nixon 647; 1972 Nixon 858; McGovern 1,455; Ford 779; Carter 783.

[b] These percentages are based on the following numbers of comments about the candidates: Humphrey 597; 1968 Nixon 902; 1972 Nixon 4,446; McGovern 2,116; Ford 3,455; Carter 2,661.

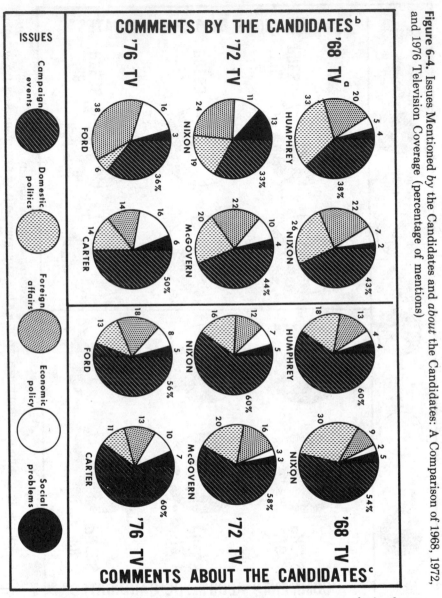

Figure 6-4. Issues Mentioned *by* the Candidates and *about* the Candidates: A Comparison of 1968, 1972, and 1976 Television Coverage (percentage of mentions)

[a] 1968 and 1976 television data are based on content analysis of story logs which reduces the number of positive identifications of individual speakers. 1972 television data are based on content analysis of audio and video features of videotapes.

[b] These percentages are based on the following numbers of comments by the candidates: 1968 Humphrey 55; Nixon 54; 1972 Nixon 75; McGovern 139; 1976 Ford 61; Carter 64.

[c] These percentages are based on the following numbers of comments about the candidates: 1968 Humphrey 112; Nixon 106; 1972 Nixon 412; McGovern 154; 1976 Ford 399; Carter 263.

candidates are mediocre, or even poor, choices. This negative cast appears to be a major factor in many voters' decisions to stay home on election day.

The deficiencies of media coverage are most noticeable during the primary period when a large slate of same-party candidates is running in each primary. The media solve the dilemma of covering multiple candidacies by giving uniformly skimpy treatment to all candidates except for those designated as front-runners. For instance, during the spring and summer primaries in 1976, 70 percent of all mentions of presidential qualities and 77 percent of all mentions of issues and events referred to the campaigns of Republicans Gerald Ford and Ronald Reagan and Democrat Jimmy Carter. The remainder were divided among ten less-favored candidates. Remarks about personal qualifications generally are so scant in primary election coverage compared to the general election that the balance between discussion of qualifications and issues is reversed. In 1976, for example, 61 percent of all primary commentary referred to issues and events and only 39 percent to presidential qualities, despite the need to acquaint voters with a host of unfamiliar personalities. Moreover, horse-race and hoopla news predominated, taking up 65 percent of issue coverage, at the expense of more substantive matters. Only 20 percent of the coverage was devoted to domestic and foreign affairs and only 15 percent to economic and social problems.

Although it would be unfair to blame low voter turnout in primary elections on inadequate election news, interviews with voters show that poor coverage plays a significant part. People find election stories interesting, but they do not feel that these stories prepare them adequately to make choices. Media images depict campaigns as tournaments where voters sit on the sidelines and watch the bouts, waiting to see who is eliminated and who remains. Winning and losing are all important, rather than what winning and losing means in terms of the political direction of the country in general or the observer's personal situation in particular. Taking its cues from the media, the audience accepts election news as just another story, rather than as an important tale about real life with very direct impact on its own welfare.

MEDIA EFFECTS

Learning About Candidates and Issues

What do people learn from campaign coverage? It varies, of course, depending on such factors as interest in the campaign, prior political knowledge, a felt need for information, and political sophistication. But certain general trends emerge from national surveys like those conducted biannually by the Survey Research Center at the University of Michigan, and from intensive interviews of smaller panels of voters like those conducted by the author of this book.

The foremost impression from such interviews with voters is that people learn very little specific information in a presidential campaign. The fact that most are interested in the campaign may not mean that they want to learn a great deal about it beyond who is winning and losing, how the candidates look, and how they go about fighting political battles. Interest in the campaign competes with interest in other events and issues. In 1976, for instance, a panel of voters who kept diaries on the important news stories that came to their attention throughout that election year devoted only 11 percent of their entries to election stories. When asked to name "major current events or issues," 38 percent of the panelists never named the primary election during four interviews conducted during the primary season.

Turning to what is learned, a comparison of election information supplied by the media with information mentioned by survey respondents about candidates and issues shows roughly similar patterns. The similarity is greatest for people who use the media most and who rely most heavily on newspapers. However, there are differences in emphases and specificity between media and public images. The public mentions fewer issues and qualities than the media and is much hazier about image content. For instance, when asked about the reasons for voting for a candidate, the respondent may say, "I like him," but may be unable to name any specific reasons. A query about the issues that figured in the voter's appraisal of the candidates is likely to elicit a broad reference to foreign or domestic policy in general, rather than mention of specific issues. Facts and figures are rarely recalled, and a good deal of misinformation surfaces when specifics are mentioned. Complex policy positions are remembered far less often than positions involving simple yes or no choices.

Overall, three out of four answers people give when asked what they have learned about candidates and issues or why they would vote or refrain from voting for a certain candidate concern personality traits. People are interested in the human qualities of their elected leaders, particularly their trustworthiness, principled character, strength, and compassion. Newspeople provide ample data on these traits. In fact, as Table 6-6 shows, when the public appraises the candidates, its emphases parallel those of the media.

The table records answers given by several thousand respondents in a nationwide survey who were asked for good and bad points about each candidate that might affect their voting choices. In addition to the qualifications discussed by the media, and general comments about liking or disliking candidates, people also mentioned party allegiance and a variety of reasons concerned with their own personal and economic interests as reasons for casting their vote. In many instances, people ignored much available media information. They made their choices, first, commonly on the basis of quick judgments about personality or vague feelings of party allegiance, and then acquired information to justify the choice.

Table 6-6 Presidential Qualities Mentioned by the Public and by Newspapers in 1976

| | Likes | | Dislikes | | Newspapers |
| | Carter | Ford | Carter | Ford | 1976 |
	%	%	%	%	%
Personal Comments					
Personality Traits	49	38	39	18	36
Presidential Image	15	37	21	24	25
Style	5	4	16	10	16
Totals:	69	79	76	52	77
Professional Capacities					
Capacities	21	17	16	43	7
Relations with Public	1	—	—	—	3
Philosophy	9	4	8	5	12
Totals:	31	21	24	48	22

The percentages are based on responses to the question, "Now I'd like to ask you about the good and bad points of the two major candidates for president. Is there anything in particular about (name of candidate) that might make you want to vote for him? Is there anything about (name of candidate) that might make you want to vote against him? What is that? Anything else?" Survey data from 1976 Election Survey, Center for Political Studies, Survey Research Center, University of Michigan.

N = 2,182 for Carter likes, 2,337 for Ford likes; 2,125 for Carter dislikes; 1,747 for Ford dislikes. N = 17,423 mention of qualities for 1976 newspapers.

In 1976 fully 43 percent of the people in a nationwide poll could comment on only one candidate's strengths and weaknesses. Such limited information prevented them from comparing candidates and choosing accordingly. Less than 20 percent could state three or more likes or dislikes about either candidate. Appraisals commonly were limited to one or two statements. Positive and negative comments about candidates were evenly balanced with a slight tilt towards the positive. This, of course, differs from the more negative tone found in campaign news. As in the media, respondents who bothered to learn about several candidates often evaluated them along different dimensions. This reduced the chances for comparisons. During the 1976 primaries, for instance, Ford was appraised more on his issue stands and personality traits and Carter more on his style and image characteristics. Ronald Reagan was judged largely on his political philosophy.

The issues people mentioned as important in the campaign represented a much abbreviated and imprecise version of media issue coverage. As Table 6-7 indicates, people put substantially greater stress on economic and social issues than did newspeople. This is not surprising;

people have personal experience with these issues that is more salient to them than any media reports. It does not require media coverage to tell the public that inflation, unemployment, poverty, crime, race relations, and environmental pollution are serious problems needing attention from presidents. Nor is it surprising that people put much less emphasis on the campaign hoopla that the media cover so plentifully. These events are so trivial that people make little effort to remember them, although they find them fleetingly entertaining.

Knowledge Base for Voting

Many social scientists worry about the public's limited preparation for voting and feel the media do a poor job, particularly in covering issues. But the blame and worry are largely misplaced. While election news definitely stresses personality traits over issues, it does supply a fair amount of issue coverage. Voters who want to base their decisions on the candidates' stands on specific issues can usually find that information. When voters are poorly informed about issues, the chief reason is that elections are not important enough for them to take the time and make the effort to learn.

Given the realities of politics, the average voter's choice to concentrate heavily on personal qualities of the candidates can be defended as sound and rational. Forming opinions about complex issues like arms limitation or monetary policies is time-consuming and difficult, particularly when experts differ about the merits of conflicting policy recommendations. People therefore ignore most issues, paying attention to only a few major ones, like the Vietnam War, law and order problems, the Watergate scandal, or inflation and energy shortages.

Table 6-7   Comparison of Percentage of Mention of Issues and Events by Newspapers and Rated and Unrated Survey Responses, 1976*

	Papers	Television	Rated Responses	Unrated Responses
Campaign events	51%	63%	0%	0%
Domestic politics	19	14	5	5
Foreign affairs	14	10	5	7
Economic policy	11	9	75	63
Social problems	5	4	14	23

*Unrated responses are based on multiple answers to a question asking for important national problems. Rated responses specify the most important national problem.

N = 11,027 for newspapers, 1,355 for television, 2,263 for rated responses and 5,575 for unrated responses. Survey data come from the 1976 Election Survey of the Center for Political Studies, Survey Research Center, University of Michigan.

Interest in issues is also diminished because the issue stands discussed during the campaign generally refer to the past. Voters do not know what kinds of issues and issue configurations will actually come up during a candidate's term. Moreover, candidates may be unable to keep their promises because of an obstreperous Congress, lack of money, or other problems that no one can anticipate.

The kind of thing that most people *can* judge, often quite expertly, is a candidate's general ability and integrity. Through personal experience people learn to pick a doctor, clergyman, or repairman without understanding medicine or religion or machines. They know how to judge people in terms of trustworthiness, integrity, and general competence. The information that media provide most plentifully is geared toward such decisionmaking.

Although the media furnish most people with more information than they are willing to use, they fall short of supplying the needs of political elites. In a society where much of the mass public still depends on opinion leaders to appraise and select candidates and to assess the merits of prospective public policies, these leaders need more information about issues and candidates than most mass media currently offer. Opinion leaders and mass publics alike would benefit from greater clarity of presentation in the daily press, more point-by-point comparisons of candidates and policies, and more ample evaluations of the political significance of differences found among candidates and their programs.

That so little specific knowledge is "learned" should not blind us to the fact that conclusions drawn from facts may be retained. Voting choices often match approval of a candidate's policy positions, even when voters do not remember the candidate's stands or the specifics of the policy.[24] In such cases, media facts may have been converted into politically significant feelings and attitudes, and the facts forgotten. Such long-range, cumulative general impressions are likely to have more profound impact than short-term memory. For instance, a general impression over a series of elections that one's party is fielding candidates of poor caliber may ultimately kill off party allegiance. The negative appraisals that candidates receive from each other and from the media may leave a residue of disappointment with politics that drives people away from the polls.

Voting Behavior

Does campaigning change votes? When we ask this perennial question, so dear to the hearts of campaign managers, public relations experts, and social scientists, the answer hinges on the interaction between audiences and messages. Crucial variables include the voter's receptivity to a message urging change, the potency of the message, the appropriateness of its form, and the setting in which it occurs. A vote change is most likely when voters pay fairly close attention to the media and are ambivalent in their attitudes toward the candidates. Messages are most potent if they concern a major and unpredicted event, such as the Watergate scandal, and if individuals find themselves in social settings where a change of attitudes will not constitute deviant behavior. This is a fairly uncommon combination of circumstances, which explains why changes of voting intentions are comparatively rare. The talk about "electronic ballot-stuffing" is therefore not realistic.

Even though media-induced vote changes are rare, this does not make them unimportant. Many elections at all levels are decided by very small percentages of votes, often less than 1 percent. The media may also have a crucial impact on election outcomes whenever they are able to stimulate or depress voter turnout. This is a more likely consequence of media publicity than changes in voting choices.

Overall, the most important influence of the media on the voter does not lie in changing votes, once predispositions have been formed. The most important influence lies in shaping and reinforcing predispositions and influencing the initial selection of candidates. When newspeople sketched out the Jimmy Carter image and dubbed him a potential winner during the 1976 primaries, ignoring most of his rivals, they made "Jimmy-Who?" into a viable candidate. Millions of voters would never have cast their ballot for the obscure Georgia politician, had not the media thrust him into the limelight as a likely winner.

Through focusing the voters' attention on selected individuals, their characteristics, and the issues for which they stand, the media also determine to a large extent what the crucial issues will be on which the competence of candidates will be judged. Media interpretations of the significance of issues further shape the perceptual environment in which the election takes place. All this occurs usually, though not always, very early in the campaign, and often long before formal campaigning starts.[25]

President Carter's chances for reelection in 1980 therefore hinged in no small manner on the images which the media created about his presidency in the previous four years. In the same manner, Watergate stories created public moods that doomed many Republicans in the 1974 elections; and media coverage of the handling of Chicago's snow emergencies in 1979 broke decades of Democratic machine control over Chicago voters. Newspeople shape national election outcomes by molding the images of political reality which lead to voting decisions, rather than by suggesting voting choices to an electorate that prefers to make its own choices. They "play less of an independent part in creating issues, sketching imagery, and coloring perceptions of the candidates than in getting attention for their candidacies. Newsmen do not write the score or play an instrument; they amplify the sounds of the music makers."[26] Although voters pay most concentrated attention to media coverage just before elections, the crucial attitudes that determine voting choices may already be so firm that the final vote is a foregone conclusion.

SUMMARY

We have examined the general consequences of the larger part played by the media, especially television, in recent campaigns. Three results are striking: the smaller contributions of political parties and other political actors; the domination of campaign strategies and schedules by media demands; and the emergence of media as kingmakers in political recruiting, particularly at the presidential level.

We also scrutinized the kinds of election coverage provided by newspapers and television throughout the campaign. This included a look at general coverage patterns and the problem of political and structural bias, as well as a look at the substance and slant of coverage and the manner of presentation. Heaviest emphasis is on personal, rather than professional, qualities of the candidates and on campaign events, rather than substantive issues. Stories are chosen for their newsworthiness rather than their educational value.

Lastly, we examined the effects of media output on the people who are exposed to it. Although the public complains about the skimpiness and shallowness of election coverage, it absorbs only a small portion of available news. This does not necessarily lead to lack of political understanding or irrational voting, however. The bits of information that people absorb permit informed choices based on appraisal of a chosen candidate's character. We also pointed out that minute changes brought about by the media in final voting decisions or voter turnout may alter the outcome of a close election and the course of political life.

Much of what was said in this chapter contradicts past claims that the media have only a very limited influence on elections. This older view rests on the election studies undertaken in the 1940s and 1950s, which are now badly out of date. The early research was concerned primarily with changes in the final vote decision. But the profound impact of media on elections becomes apparent only when one casts the net much wider, to include effects on all phases of the election campaign, from the recruitment and nomination stages to the strategies that produce the final outcome. One must also look at political learning during campaigns and at the information base that supports the voting decision, regardless of the nature of that decision. Finally, one must recognize that television, in particular, has changed the rules for the election game, especially at the presidential level. Candidates and media are inextricably intertwined. Those who aspire to elective office must play the "new politics," which is "media politics."

NOTES

1. A good review of the literature on presidential elections is presented in Herbert Asher, *Presidential Elections and American Politics* (Homewood, Ill.:

Dorsey Press, 1976). Reports on campaigns at other levels include John Carey, "How Media Shape Campaigns," *Journal of Communication* 26 (Spring 1976): 50-57, which covers congressional campaigns; John W. Windhauser, "Reporting of Campaign Issues in Ohio Municipal Election Races," *Journalism Quarterly* 54 (Summer 1977): 332-340; Leonard Tipton, Roger D. Haney and John R. Baseheart, "Media Agenda-Setting in City and State Election Campaigns," *Journalism Quarterly* 52 (Spring 1975): 15-22; and Jules Becker and Douglas A. Fuchs, "How the Major California Dailies Covered Reagan vs. Brown," *Journalism Quarterly* 44 (Winter 1967): 645-53, which deals with a gubernatorial contest.

2. Robert McClure and Thomas Patterson, *The Unseeing Eye* (New York: G. P. Putnam's Sons, 1976). Also see C. Richard Hofstetter and Cliff Zukin, "TV Network News and Advertising in the Nixon and McGovern Campaigns," *Journalism Quarterly* 56 (Spring 1979): 106-115.

3. McClure and Patterson, *The Unseeing Eye*, p. 104.

4. Joe McGinniss, *The Selling of the President, 1968* (New York: Trident Press, 1969), p. 31.

5. Walter DeVries and V. Lance Tarrance, *The Ticket Splitters* (Grand Rapids: Eerdmans, 1972).

6. F. Christopher Arterton, "Campaign Organizations Confront the Media — Political Environment," in James David Barber, ed., *Race for the Presidency: The Media and the Nominating Process* (Englewood Cliffs, N.J.: Prentice Hall, 1978), p. 21.

7. Ibid., p. 22; also Michael J. Robinson, "TV's Newest Program: The 'Presidential Nominations Game,'" *Public Opinion* (May-June 1978): 41-46.

8. Walter Bunge, Robert Hudson and Chung Woo Suh, "Johnson's Information Strategy for Vietnam: An Evaluation," *Journalism Quarterly* 45 (Autumn 1968): 419-425.

9. Herbert E. Alexander, *Financing the 1976 Election* (Washington, D.C.: Congressional Quarterly, 1979), pp. 166, 372, 373, 411.

10. Arterton, "Campaign Organizations Confront the Media," pp. 16-17, quoting an aide to Morris Udall.

11. J. D. Lorenz, *Chicago Tribune*, Feb. 12, 1978, "An Insider's View of Jerry Brown."

12. The newspaper sample consisted of 20 newspapers from communities of different size and political orientation from all parts of the country. The sample is broadly representative of the American press, although slightly skewed towards papers which media critics consider above average in performance. The papers were the *New York Times, Philadelphia Inquirer, Boston Globe, Bangor Daily News, Chicago Tribune, Cleveland Plain Dealer, Detroit Free Press, Topeka Daily Capital, Houston Chronicle, Miami Herald, Raleigh News & Observer, Atlanta Constitution, Los Angeles Times, Seattle Daily Times, Denver Post, Salt Lake City Tribune, Chicago Daily Defender, National Observer, Wall Street Journal*, and *Washington Post*. Papers were selected with the assistance of a panel of editors to be representative of the American press. Criteria for sample selection included sectional representation of all sections of the U.S., diversity of community size, representation of high and low population density regions, diversity of endorsement and audience political affiliation, reflection of various types of newspaper competition ranging from near-monopoly status to highly competitive markets, and inclusion of papers designed for special interest audiences. The television sample comes from the early evening national news presented by ABC, CBS, and NBC, as well as local Chicago area CBS and NBC newscasts. Tapes and abstracts for coding were made available by the Vanderbilt Television News Archive, described in Fay C. Schreibman,

"Television News Archives: A Guide to Major Collections;" in William Adams and Fay C. Schreibman, eds., *Television Network News: Issues in Content Research* (Washington, D.C.: George Washington University, 1978), pp. 89-110.

13. Doris A. Graber, "Media Coverage and Voter Learning During the Presidential Primary Season," *Georgia Journal of Political Science* 7 (Spring 1979): 19-48.

14. Content analysis studies during congressional and even local campaigns show the same patterns. See Carey, "How Media Shape Campaigns," and Windhauser, "Reporting of Campaign Issues."

15. Timothy Crouse, *The Boys on the Bus* (New York: Ballantine, 1972).

16. C. Richard Hofstetter, *Bias in the News: Network Television Coverage of the 1972 Election Campaign* (Columbus: Ohio State University Press, 1976), pp. 39-41.

17. Wenmouth Williams Jr. and William D. Semlak, "Structural Effects of TV Coverage on Political Agendas," *Journal of Communication* 28 (Autumn 1978): 114-119; Hofstetter, *Bias in the News*, pp. 32-36.

18. Michael Hooper, "Party and Newspaper Endorsements as Predictors of Voter Choice," *Journalism Quarterly* 46 (Summer 1969): 302-305; G. Cleveland Wilhoit and Taik Sup Auh, "Newspaper Endorsements and Coverage of Public Opinion Polls in 1970," *Journalism Quarterly* 51 (Winter 1974): 654-658.

19. The eight most frequently mentioned qualities are, trustworthy, principled, compassionate, inspirational, forthright, strong, administratively competent, and capable in foreign affairs.

20. Michael J. Robinson, "Public Affairs Television and the Growth of Political Malaise: The Case of the 'Selling of the Pentagon,' " *American Political Science Review* 70 (June 1976): 409-432.

21. All quotations of network news coverage of Democratic presidential candidates are taken from Marc F. Plattner, "Introduction," and James R. Ferguson, "Network Coverage of the Major Democratic Candidates," pp. 2-12, 14-89 in the Alternative Educational Foundation's *Report on Network News' Treatment of the 1972 Democratic Presidential Candidates* (Bloomington, Ind., 1972). Reprinted by permission.

22. F. Christopher Arterton, "The Media Politics of Presidential Campaigns," in James David Barber, ed., *Race for the Presidency: The Media and the Nomination Process* (Englewood Cliffs, N.J.: Prentice Hall, 1978), p. 36.

23. Richard Scammon and Ben Wattenberg, *The Real Majority* (New York: Coward McCann, 1970).

24. Richard W. Boyd, "Popular Control of Public Policy: A Normal Vote Analysis of the 1968 Election," *American Political Science Review* 66 (June 1972): 429-449; Philip E. Converse, "The Concept of Normal Vote," ch. 2 in Angus Campbell et al., eds., *Elections and the Political Order* (New York: John Wiley, 1966).

25. Arthur T. Hadley, *The Invisible Primary* (Englewood Cliffs, N.J.: Prentice-Hall, 1976).

26. Leon V. Sigal, "Newsmen and Campaigners: Organization Men Make the News," *Political Science Quarterly* 93 (Fall 1978): 465-470.

READINGS

Asher, Herbert. *Presidential Elections and American Politics.* Homewood, Ill.: Dorsey Press, 1976.

Barber, James David. *Race for the Presidency: The Media and the Nominating Process.* Englewood Cliffs, N.J.: Prentice Hall, 1978.

Hofstetter, C. Richard. *Bias in the News: Network Television Coverage of the 1972 Election Campaign.* Columbus: Ohio State University Press, 1976.

McClure, Robert, and Patterson, Thomas. *The Unseeing Eye.* New York: G. P. Putnam's Sons, 1976.

McGinniss, Joe. *The Selling of the President.* New York: Trident Press, 1969.

Nimmo, Dan, and Savage, Robert L. *Candidates and Their Images.* Pacific Palisades, Calif.: Goodyear, 1976.

7

Relations Between Media and the Branches of Government

Walter Cronkite once remarked that, "Politics and media are inseparable. It is only the politicians and the media that are incompatible."[1] There is a love-hate relationship between government officials and the media. To perform their functions adequately, each needs the other. But they have conflicting goals and missions and operate under different institutional constraints. To retain public support and maintain its power, the government wants to influence what information is passed on to the public and to other officials. It wants to be able to define situations and project images in its own way to accord with its social and political objectives.

THE ADVERSARY RELATIONSHIP

Newspeople often see the world from a different perspective and want to define the situation accordingly. They view themselves as critics of government who take special pains to expose wrongdoing. They also want to present exciting stories that attract a large audience. This often means prying into matters that government officials would like to hide because they involve conflict, controversy, corruption, or simple wheeling and dealing. Government wants its portrait taken in its Sunday best, from the most flattering angle. The media, however, want to take candid shots, showing government in awkward poses and off its guard.

We now want to look at the interrelationship of government and the media from a closer focus, concentrating on the three branches of the national government. Casual as well as systematic observations readily establish that the media devote a great deal of attention to the affairs of the national government. A year-long content analysis of three Chicago newspapers in 1976, for instance, showed that 27 percent of all news stories dealt directly or indirectly with the presidency. Of these, 2 percent focused on the president, another 2 percent dealt with the federal bureaucracy, 10 percent covered foreign affairs, which are largely a presidential function, and 13 percent concerned domestic policies involving the president and Congress. If one adds the 10 percent of the stories devoted to the 1976 presidential election, the total comes to 37 percent.

Like the president, Congress was covered either directly or indirectly by 27 percent of all stories. Of these, 3 percent were explicit coverage. Substantial ancillary publicity was obtained through the stories concerning domestic policy (13 percent) and national problems, such as the state of the economy (2 percent), business and labor (6 percent), and environment and transportation (3 percent). Five percent of all stories focused on the judiciary, primarily Supreme Court coverage. National television averaged 10 percent more coverage of the presidency than the newspapers, if one includes election stories, 3 percent less coverage of congressional business, and 2 percent less coverage of the courts.[2]

We shall begin our analysis at the level where the marriage between government and the media is most encompassing — the presidency. Most of what is said about the presidency also applies, though to a lesser degree, to other chief executives such as governors and mayors.[3]

THE MEDIA AND THE EXECUTIVE BRANCH

Role of Media

The media perform four basic functions for presidents and other chief executives. First of all, they supply executives with information about current events and the political settings for their policies. They highlight problems which may then spur executive action. Not infrequently, media provide daily news faster than bureaucratic channels. John F. Kennedy, for instance, would read the *New York Times* before starting on his official day because stories about foreign affairs often reached him 24 hours earlier through the *Times* than through State Department bulletins which had to be coded initially and then decoded.

Second, the media give the president a feel for the major concerns of the American people. They do this directly by reporting on public opinion and indirectly by featuring the stories likely to shape public discussion and public opinion. Public officials assume that newspeople are in touch with popular concerns because they want to write stories that are meaningful to their readers and viewers. Readers and viewers, in turn, take their cues about what is important and worthy of discussion from the media.

Third, media furnish chief executives with channels to convey their messages to the general public as well as to political elites within and outside of government. These channels, to which presidents have access almost at will, provide unparalleled opportunities to explain presidential policies and to attack the positions taken by opponents. Political elites need such information as much as or more than the public, because there is no effective internal communication system to link government officials who are dispersed throughout the country with each other and with Washington.

Fourth, the media allow chief executives to remain almost continuously in full public view on the political stage, keeping their human qualities and professional skills always on display. Newspapers, television, and radio supply running commentary about a president's daily routines. Coverage of personal life may be minute. For instance, when President Eisenhower had a heart attack in Denver in 1955, presidential news secretary James Hagerty held five news briefings a day, seven days a week, for three weeks. The media dutifully reported even the most intimate details of the president's condition, including the color of his morning toast and the bowel movements recorded on his medical chart. The purpose of this coverage was more than selling human interest tidbits. It was to reassure the public that it was fully informed about the president's disability and his fitness to continue his official functions. Human interest stories help to forge links of human concern between people and their leaders and may contribute to the relation of trust which turns people into willing followers.

Impact of Media

An outline of the functions that media perform for the executive branch fails to convey the full story about the political significance of the relationship. Media coverage is the lifeblood of politics because it shapes the political perceptions which form the reality on which political action is based. Media images define situations for nearly all participants in the political process because direct contact with political actors and situations is limited.

As we saw in previous chapters, the age of television politics that began in the mid-fifties has vastly enhanced media impact and hence media power. In the past, a story might have caused ripples on the sea of politics when thousands of people in one corner of the country read it or heard it on the radio. Now that same story can cause political tidal waves when millions throughout the country see and hear it simultaneously. A politician now can visit with millions of potential followers in their living rooms, creating the kinds of emotional ties which hitherto came only from personal contact.

A large share of the millions who watch these spectacles are people who have never before paid serious attention to politics. Lyndon Johnson was right when he called the rising power of television the major change in political life between his early days in Congress and his presidency 30 years later. "You've given us a new kind of people," he told a television filming crew, and new kinds of politicians as well. Obviously displeased with some of the consequences, he complained: "Teddy, Tunney. They're your creations, your puppets. No machine could ever create a Teddy Kennedy. Only you guys, they're all yours. Your product."[4]

In the process of attracting new participant-observers to politics and creating new types of politicians, television also has tipped the political scales of power in favor of the presidency. This follows from what have been called the first and second laws of "videopolitics": "Television alters the behavior of institutions in direct proportion to the amount of coverage provided or allowed," and "the more coverage an institution secures, the greater its public stature and the more significant its role."[5]

We have already described how strongly media in general, and television in particular, influence who becomes eligible for presidential office and how profoundly they affect the conduct and outcome of elections. After elections, the success of presidential policies, the length, vigor and thrust of a president's political life, and the general level of support for the political system depend heavily on the images that the media convey.

Support for the Vietnam War, for instance, ebbed after television news had shown American marines leveling Vietnamese villages and after it had reported the massacres of Vietnamese civilians by American troops. Television news provided "greater receptivity to darker news about Vietnam. . . . It was the end of the myth that we were different, that we were better."[6] Three years later, after Walter Cronkite announced that the war could not be won, Lyndon Johnson considered it hopeless to try to recapture public support for the war. Accordingly, he decided to abandon the venture. As David Halberstam put it: "It was the first time in American history a war had been declared over by an anchorman."[7] While it is difficult to prove conclusively that Vietnam War coverage had the massive effects which Halberstam claims, circumstantial evidence supports the verdict.

There is also evidence that media coverage can increase public support for a presidential policy. This is particularly important in national emergencies when substantial congressional and public acceptance is vital. For instance, in August 1964, only 42 percent of the American public supported President Johnson's Vietnam policies, raising doubts about his ability to continue to raise men and money for the war. These doubts were apparently dispelled when approval ratings of his Vietnam policy rose to a comfortable 72 percent after he broadcast an explanation.

Similarly, President Nixon's dispatch of troops to Cambodia in April of 1970 won a 50 percent approval rating after he explained it on television. Prior to the broadcast, only 7 percent of the public had approved. Favorable ratings for President Carter's foreign policy jumped by 34 percentage points — from 22 percent to 56 percent — after the news media announced that the 1978 Camp David meeting had produced a peace settlement between Egypt and Israel. Such steep rises may be short-lived, however, because memories fade quickly. Following the Camp David stories, the ratings dropped steadily by about 4 percentage points a month, until the trend was reversed by a new announcement of Mideast successes six months later.

On the other hand, media coverage may also stir opposition to presidential policies. The effects of television coverage of Vietnam war scenes have been mentioned. Television also gave respectability to vocal opponents of the war by covering antiwar lobbies and teach-ins pitting academicians against officials. Many observers believe that publicizing problems created by school busing for racial integration has kept alive and strengthened opposition to federally mandated school integration.

The media frequently raise damaging issues that presidents and other public officials would prefer to hide. The Watergate scandal of 1973, which led to the resignation of President Nixon, is a prime recent example of an issue put at the top of the public agenda by constant media prodding, despite presidential efforts to downplay it. The seemingly endless list of scandals and reports about malfeasance have included misdeeds of the Central Intelligence Agency, corruption in the General Services Administration, shady dealings by Bert Lance, Carter's confidant and former head of the Office of Management and Budget, and the capers of the president's brother, Billy Carter.

By highlighting problems, requesting governmental action, or reporting demands for action, media stories may lead to new policies or major changes in existing policies. For instance, in 1968 a documentary called "Hunger in America" painted the government's food assistance program to the poor as totally inadequate. Agriculture Secretary Orville Freeman called the telecast shoddy journalism and asked for equal time to reply, but the federal food stamp program was liberalized and expanded shortly after the broadcast. Congress increased funding for food stamps, and the Senate called for an investigation into problems of hunger in America. The Nixon administration subsequently credited the telecast with setting the wheels of governmental action into motion.

There have even been instances where the threat of potential publicity has been used by media personnel to force presidents to act. In one reported incident in 1950, publisher Philip Graham of the *Washington Post* forced the White House and Department of the Interior to integrate Washington swimming pools by threatening to publish a story about rioting in the capital which the paper had previously withheld.[8]

Sensational adverse publicity can also kill programs. For instance, sharp curbs on the production of nuclear energy were made nearly inevitable by the publicity following an accident at a nuclear plant at Three Mile Island, Pennsylvania, in 1979. Welfare programs like Head Start's pre-kindergarten training for poor children or financial aid for minority businesses have been decimated by coverage of inefficient management and corrupt handling of money.

Media publicity can also be crucial in determining whether a candidate for high appointive office will pass Senate scrutiny. President

Carter's nominee for attorney general, Griffin Bell, almost missed Senate confirmation in 1977 because of adverse press reports about his racial views. During the Nixon administration, the Senate refused to confirm two prospective Supreme Court justices. In each instance, knowledgeable observers thought that highly unfavorable media publicity was instrumental in the defeat. In the case of one of the nominees, G. Harrold Carswell, the most damaging piece of evidence was a 1948 speech in which Carswell had praised segregation. The speech was unearthed by a reporter for a Jacksonville, Florida, television station affiliated with the *Washington Post*.[9]

A Rocky Marriage

Direct and Mediated Transmission. Audiovisual and print images about government are conveyed in two modes: directly or indirectly. Direct conveyance allows government officials to transmit their messages verbatim, and often live, with a minimum of intrusion of media editorializing. President Truman was the first to use the direct mode by broadcasting his entire State of the Union message in 1947 to a nationwide radio and television audience. In January 1961, President John F. Kennedy initiated live telecasts of news conferences. The president,

Reprinted with permission from the *Minneapolis Tribune*

more than any other public official, enjoys opportunities for virtually uncontrolled access to the American people. As we saw in Chapter 4, political leaders competing with the president for power and public support have tried for matching privileges with only minimal success.

Of course, even live television and radio broadcasts are not totally devoid of shaping by the media because camera angles and other photographic techniques slant all presentations somewhat. Likewise, a print news story describing a presidential news conference followed by a published transcript involves some shaping by media personnel. But it is minimal, compared to the large leeway that newspeople usually have in choosing and interpreting information about the presidency.

Indirect or mediated transmission — the shaping of news presentations by journalists — lies at the heart of the problems of the rocky marriage between media and government because it bestows more power upon the media than governments like to surrender. It permits media personnel to pick and choose among the information given to them, supplement it with information gathered from other, possibly hostile sources, and present it in a framework of their own choosing. It allows them to evaluate people and policies at will and criticize an administration, often when its popularity is already on the downgrade. This has given rise to the charge that mediated coverage is used deliberately, or at the least, inconsiderately, to hurt public officials and their policies.

Media Goals and Tactics. Media personnel refute the charge that they go out of their way to show incumbent administrations in a bad light. They contend that they are looking for lively, significant stories that will earn them the respect of their colleagues and the acclaim of their readers and viewers. They also see themselves as guardians of the public interest, helping to keep or make government more honest and efficient. Newspeople believe that they have a duty to report wrongdoing by public officials. They contend that the actors who produced the unfortunate situation, not the newspeople who reported it, should be blamed. Politicians who attack the media for reporting bad news are accused of resembling the ancient Greeks who often killed bearers of bad tidings. This is what newsman William J. Small had in mind when he entitled his book on government and the media *To Kill a Messenger*.[10]

As we have seen, many of the stories journalists choose to cover deal with socially undesirable or unusual behavior. When this is coupled with the intent to ferret out government misbehavior, it is inevitable that many negative stories will emerge. It is therefore true that media personnel assigned to the presidential beat regularly feature harsh criticism of presidential programs, particularly if it is voiced by politically influential opponents. Media also try to present the most stirring story possible, often accenting a comparatively minor point.

Strains in the Relationship. Chief executives have generally been unhappy with the coverage which they have received from the media.

All presidents profess to believe in a free press and claim to run an "open" administration. But they rapidly develop a distaste for news about their administration. As President Kennedy told a 1962 news conference, midway into his term, he was "reading more and enjoying it less."[11]

A classic attack on the press occurred on November 13, 1969, in Des Moines, Iowa, when Vice President Spiro Agnew lashed out at the media for their instant adverse commentary on a televised address by President Nixon. Agnew charged that a tiny, anonymous group of men, based in New York and Washington, who represented nobody but their own privileged fraternity, took it upon themselves to impugn the truthfulness and capabilities of the elected head of the nation. He challenged the networks to give the American people "a full accounting of their stewardship," warning that "we would never trust such power over public opinion in the hands of an elected government — it is time we questioned it in the hands of a small and unelected elite."[12] Media people were outraged, but the many people who called stations to comment on the address sided with Agnew two to one.[13]

Such presidential displeasure is readily understandable. Media coverage deprives presidents, to varying degrees, of control over the definition of political situations. It forces them to talk in clichés and quotable oversimplifications and, in the process, to put themselves on record in ways which may narrow their options for future action. When secret activities are disclosed, such as an impending military intervention, or a planned price freeze, publicity may actually force their hand. Bargaining advantages may be lost through premature disclosure of news. Trivia, conflict, and public wrongdoing may receive undue emphasis. Worst of all, media bring things to light that executives would prefer to shield permanently or to disclose in their own way.

When battle lines are drawn, the media may have the advantage. Skilled reporters can stack the cards against politicians. The public, which is the jury, may be more willing to believe reporters, regarding politicians as more self-serving. It may believe that media stories, however exaggerated, must contain at least some truth. Columnists like Jack Anderson who specialize in probing misdeeds of the high and mighty, have large and loyal bands of followers. In surveys recording trust in American institutions, the media regularly rank slightly higher than governmental institutions.

In practice, despite mutual suspicion that governments manipulate and lie and the press distorts and entraps, open battles are comparatively rare. Each side holds strong cards and is fully aware that it needs the other. The president controls valuable information which the media need and must publish quickly while it is fresh. There is little time to check the facts or consult other sources to balance what the president has said. Even when outside information sources are available, "official" sources are preferred.

In fact, the president *is* the story in many instances. If presidents deny reporters the privilege of direct access, this story cannot be covered first-hand. Alienating the prime newsmaker and prime source of governmental news is a major catastrophe for any news organization.

The media, for their part, can withhold or force publicity. They can stress the positive or accent the negative. The upshot of such an evenly matched situation is a good deal of fraternizing and cronyism among these two "enemies," often to the dismay of those who would have the press be pure. Each side works hard to cultivate the other's friendship. This may reduce journalists' zeal to investigate government misdeeds. Indeed, charges of collusion have been made when media, time and again, have suppressed news at the request of government departments or the White House. Many of these instances have concerned questions of national security. Examples are the squelching of TV documentaries in 1962 about a German attempt to tunnel under the Berlin Wall[14] and the delay in 1980 in publicizing the fact that American diplomats were hiding in the Canadian embassy in Tehran to escape capture by the Iranian militants. Reports about the forthcoming Bay of Pigs invasion of Cuba in 1961 were also held back. With the wisdom of hindsight, President Kennedy acknowledged later that the news suppression might have been a mistake. Publicity might have averted the ill-fated venture.[15]

Cycles in the Relationship. The warmth of the relationship between the media and the chief executive often runs in three distinct phases.[16]

Initially, there is a honeymoon period. This is a time of cooperation, when the media convey the president's messages about organization of the new administration, appointment of new officials, and plans and proposals for new policies. At this early stage, few policies and proposals have as yet been implemented, so that there is little opportunity for adverse criticism. Presidents and their advisers, eager to get their story across, make themselves readily available to the media and supply them with ample information.

The honeymoon period ends when the administration becomes vulnerable to criticism because it has embarked on controversial programs and because its officials have left a trail of actions to praise or condemn. Attacks on President Carter's plans for energy conservation and criticism of his White House staff and cabinet members midway through his first term of office are examples. By mid-term, too, top officials have become immersed in their work and often delegate contact with the media to lower-level officials, particularly those charged with press relations. The administration, stung by adverse publicity, tries to manipulate the media. The media, in turn, try to develop more unofficial sources to supply them with the information that they do not get from the top.

If the rifts between media and the executive branch become particularly severe, there often is a third period in which both sides retreat from their mutually hostile behavior to a more moderate stance. Frequently this coincides with a race for re-election, when newspeople try harder to provide impartial coverage and presidents are more eager to keep newspeople happy. Relations between President Ford and the news media, for instance, brightened considerably during his 1976 campaign to retain the presidency.

Administrations differ considerably in their ability to get along with the media. In recent history, the Kennedy administration was particularly good at press relations, while the Nixon administration was especially bad. In fact, there has been speculation that Nixon's Watergate problems would have been only a minor scandal, had he been able to charm the press in the Kennedy manner.

Likewise, there is considerable variation in relationships between the executive and media in various parts of the country. Frictions are greatest between the Washington press corps and the White House because they are most strongly interdependent, and familiarity breeds a certain amount of contempt. The northeastern seaboard press, in general, has a reputation of being more critical than its colleagues in the rest of the country.

For this reason, most presidents occasionally circumvent the eastern press by scheduling news conferences in other parts of the country and by making major policy pronouncements away from the East Coast. As Jeb Stuart Magruder wrote in his account of the Nixon years, "We were involved in media politics, and we were seeking not only to speak through the media in the usual fashion — press releases, news conferences — but to speak around the media, much of which we considered hostile, to take our message directly to the people. . . ."[17] Similarly, President Carter adopted a policy of visiting small communities throughout the country to bask in the adulation of local audiences and local media for the benefit of nationwide television audiences.

Presidential Goals and Tactics. Just as newspeople seek to control the substance and tenor of news, so presidents and their staffs attempt to manipulate what is published. Three approaches are used, along with carrot-and-stick tactics. First, presidents try to influence reporters to present favorable news in a manner that meets with presidential approval. Second, they try to shape the flow of news to make good publicity more and bad publicity less likely. Finally, they pace and arrange their work schedules to produce opportunities for favorable media coverage. Because presidents are constantly surrounded by people who must have news to earn their pay, and who hunger for the special scoops that may bring them distinction, management of reporters is not unduly difficult.

Chief executives woo reporters through offering them good story material in general, as well as occasional scoops. They cultivate their friendship by making themselves accessible, treating reporters with respect, and arranging for their creature comforts. To keep reporters in line, presidents may threaten them directly or obliquely with withdrawal of privileges. These may include accommodations on the presidential plane, special interviews, or answers to their questions during new conferences. Presidents may attack individual reporters or their organizations for undesirable reporting, as President John F. Kennedy did when he found David Halberstam's reports about Vietnam in the *New York Times* objectionable. The *Times* did not follow Kennedy's suggestion to remove Halberstam from Vietnam, and he later won a Pulitzer prize for his reporting there. Kennedy also dispatched General Maxwell Taylor, chairman of the Joint Chiefs of Staff, to complain personally to publisher Henry Luce about reporters who had made inaccurate statements about the Bay of Pigs disaster. It was to no avail — no heads rolled in consequence.[18]

By way of managing the flow of news, presidents try to push the least controversial and sensitive stories rather than the most controversial and sensitive ones that reporters want. They may prohibit their staffs, on pain of dismissal, from expressing public disagreement with presidential politics. The Carter administration insisted that members of the White House staff clear any appearances on televised talk shows with the president's top advisers. When approval was withheld, appearances had to be canceled. Criticism by the eastern press has been averted by withholding advance copies of speeches and timing them late enough in the evening so that eastern morning papers could not cover them adequately.

Presidents may also space out releases so that there is a steady manageable flow of news. If they want emphasis on a particular story, they may withhold competing news that breaks simultaneously. Sometimes a barrage of news is released or even created to distract attention from sensitive developments. For instance, when the media began to zero in on the Watergate scandal, President Nixon went on a whirlwind trip to the Middle East and the Soviet Union. The major purpose, critics charged, was to create news to distract attention from problems at home.

Numerous examples of efforts to arrange activities so as to provide the chance for favorable publicity have already been cited. They include the scheduling of campaign activities, the heightening of suspense by news blackouts prior to major pronouncements, and the manufacturing of pseudo-events. Timing speeches for broadcast at popular television hours and when there are no competing sports events or television spectacles is another example. Political successes may be coupled with political failures in hopes that publicity for the success will draw attention away from the failure. An example is the announcement of the opening of formal relations with the People's Republic of China late in 1978, which reportedly was timed to take the edge off possible failure by the Carter administration to clinch a Mideast peace settlement between Israel and Egypt.

The president may also control the newsflow from administrative departments by requiring that publicity and interviews be cleared through the White House to avoid conflicting pronouncements on matters such as unemployment statistics or oil conservation policies. A president may assist newspeople in prying loose information from agencies, like the Deparment of Defense, that have a tight information policy or may make access more difficult through obstructive rules and regulations.

News management may even go to the point of deceiving the press in order to get a smoke-screen message in front of the public. For instance, during the 1961 Bay of Pigs invasion, spokesmen for the executive branch told Miami reporters that 5,000 troops had been dispatched. This news was intended to encourage Cubans to rise up in support of a large invasion force. In actuality, only 1,000 troops had been sent. When the troops ran into trouble, officials circulated stories that only a few hundred American troops had been involved and that their chief mission had been to land supplies for anti-Castro guerrillas in Cuba, rather than to invade the country. When reporters discovered that they had been used to spread false stories, they were furious. The inevitable result was a credibility gap between government and the media and between the media and the public.

In a more indirect way, presidents can shape the news by controlling appointments to the FCC and other public agencies concerned with the media. Financial life lines can be controlled through the Office of Management and Budget, which screens budgetary requests of the FCC, the Corporation for Public Broadcasting, and similar bodies. Control can also be wielded through the Justice Department, which can challenge FCC decisions such as the approval of a merger between the American Broadcasting Company (ABC) and the International Telephone and Telegraph Company (ITT). In that case, the Justice Department carried a series of appeals through the courts and ultimately to the Supreme Court. The antitrust division in the Justice Department has also discouraged various media business combinations. Presidents may even involve themselves directly in media policymaking through White House study commissions and task forces.

Institutionalizing Media Access

Organization and Personnel. Because the relationship between the executive branch and the media is so continuous and pervasive, it has become routinized and institutionalized. In 1970, President Nixon created the first permanent agency within the White House to plan communications policy. His Office of Telecommunications Policy took strong stands on a number of policy issues. The Carter administration renamed the office the National Telecommunications and Information Agency (NTIA) and reduced its power and functions. The bulk of policy planning was switched to the Commerce Department where the position of assistant secretary for National Telecommunications and Information Administration was created, and to the Office of Management and Budget. Only a small policy planning staff remained in the White House to advise the president. Such diffusion of control has been typical in communications policy, to the detriment of strong executive leadership. Moreover, the divorce of planning from operations has made it more difficult to plan wisely and to implement policies.

Other White House media agencies have included the Office of the Press Secretary and the Office of Media Liaison. By custom, the press secretary meets almost daily with the White House press corps to make announcements and take questions. These briefings supply reporters with the White House interpretation of events. The Office of Media Liaison sets up meetings between the president and groups of editors, publishers, and non-Washington reporters twice a month. White House reporters are excluded from these meetings and do not get transcripts until those in attendance have had a chance to file their stories. This device gives the president an opportunity to get publicity beyond the control of the often hostile Washington press corps. As part of the White House staff, there is also a press release office and a research office that provides information on what the president has said in the past. Furthermore, press secretaries are attached to other parts of the presidential establishment, such as the National Security Council.

In addition to the press secretary, President Carter in 1978 appointed Gerald Rafshoon, a media specialist who had handled advertising and media coverage during Carter's 1976 campaign, as special assistant for communication. Rafshoon was to structure the president's activities so that he and his programs could project a desirable image for media coverage.

On the media side, the White House press corps consists of some 70 newspeople who cover the president regularly. Many have considerable experience and reputations to match. Major newspapers like *The New York Times, Washington Post, Los Angeles Times, Chicago Tribune,* and *Philadelphia Inquirer* have full-time reporters exclusively assigned to the president. So do a number of newspaper chains, like the Scripps-Howard papers, the Hearst press, and the Newhouse papers. Other papers send their Washington bureau chiefs to the White House when there is news of special interest to their region.

The major broadcast networks have three or four reporters each at the White House on a regular basis; smaller networks have one. There are also regular representatives from the weekly news magazines and several periodicals, as well as photographers and their supporting staffs. Much of the photographic coverage of the president, however, is handled by White House staff photographers.[19]

Better than 70 percent of the country's dailies have no regular Washington correspondent or part-time "stringer" to cover the White

House. The same holds true for 96 percent of the country's television stations and 99 percent of the radio stations. These papers and stations rely heavily on White House wire service news. The two major American wire services, AP and UPI, each have three full-time reporters accredited to the White House. They cover the beat continuously, including all presidential trips. Other news organizations alternate coverage of out-of-town presidential trips, taking turns assigning a reporter to the "pool" of reporters. Two foreign wire services, the British Reuters and the French Agence France-Presse, also have one regular reporter each assigned to the White House.

Much of the time of the White House press corps is spent waiting for news from the president's staff. Reporters often find this frustrating and even humiliating. Their press passes give them unlimited access solely to the White House press room. Other parts of the White House and executive offices are open only by special appointments, which are given out selectively. For public ceremonies in the East Room or Oval Office or Rose Garden, reporters usually are escorted as a group. Some have likened this to being herded like cattle. Many also object to the hero worship and protectiveness that they sense in the president's staff and to the frequent occasions when presidents make personal or public moves without first alerting the press corps.

Forms of Contact. The release of news by chief executives or their aides takes a number of routinized forms. Most of these represent a concerted effort to control news output. The most common is the *news release.* This is a story prepared by government officials and handed to members of the press, usually without an opportunity for questions. It can be used verbatim, and officials hope that it will be. To make sure that the release appears at the most opportune time, it often has a date line that stipulates the earliest time when it may be published. If an administration wants to give the appearance of great activity or to distract reporters' attention from areas of undesired publicity, it may publish a flood of releases simultaneously. The Carter administration also initiated a program of taping 30 to 40-second radio spots to be distributed to stations around the country on request. In this way, stations receive the news in a ready-made version controlled directly by the White House.

In a *news briefing* reporters have an opportunity to ask the press secretary questions about the news releases. But since officials furnish the news for the briefing, they control the substance and tone of the discussion. Most press secretaries, as well as members of the press, believe that daily news briefings are unnecessary and could just as well be covered by press releases; but the briefings have become traditional.

Although a *news conference* may appear to be a wide-open question period, most are in fact heavily controlled by the official to be questioned. They are a form of political theater, staged, directed, and partially written by top executives to cast themselves into praiseworthy roles. Seemingly spontaneous answers are often carefully prepared by experts on the president's staff and rehearsed during extensive briefings that precede news conferences.

Presidents usually decide when to call a news conference and when to skip it. Once it is called, they generally make an opening statement that sets the tone for a good part of the conference. They may also plant questions by letting it be known ahead of time that certain types of queries will receive very interesting answers. Pierre Salinger, John Kennedy's press secretary, and Bill Moyers, Lyndon Johnson's press secretary, both used this tactic.

Presidents generally know which reporters are likely to ask sympathetic or hostile questions. By recognizing friendly reporters for questions and controlling follow-ups, presidents can largely dictate the subject and tone of a news conference. But no president has been able to squelch embarrassing questions entirely or to deny reporters the chance to use their questions as opportunities to express their own views about controversial issues.

Some news conferences are off-the-record "backgrounders." They are called by high officials to give newspeople important information that may not be publicized at all or may not be attributed to its source. Various forms of vague attribution may be permitted, such as the euphemism "government sources say" or "it has been reported by reliable sources," or even, more specifically, "the White House discloses" or the "Defense Department indicates."

Government officials like the backgrounder because it permits them to bring a variety of policy ideas before the public without openly identifying with them. Secretary of State Henry Kissinger used backgrounders to submit foreign policy options to public debate and to warn foreign countries that their behavior was unacceptable to the United States. For instance, to discourage the Soviet Union's support of India in a war with Pakistan, Kissinger told reporters in a backgrounder that Russia's policy might lead to cancellation of President Nixon's Moscow trip. Had the statement been officially attributed to Kissinger, it would have constituted a threat that might have destroyed detente with the Soviet Union.

Reporters, on the other hand, are somewhat more ambivalent about backgrounders. They do like having access to news which might otherwise be unavailable, but they dislike being prevented from giving the source of the information so that the story can be placed in its proper perspective. At times they have evaded the prohibition on source disclosure by refusing to attend a background briefing and then reporting the story as told to them by reporters who attended.

Besides these formal encounters between reporters and the president or White House staff, there are countless informal contacts in work and social settings. Frequently, the most probing stories about White

House activities come from reporters not ordinarily assigned to cover the president. The regulars would be too vulnerable to retaliation by the White House if they wrote unusually critical reports.

Top government officials and occasionally the president may also appear on shows such as "Meet the Press" and "Face the Nation." Questioning there can resemble a hostile inquisition, but executive officials participate because these shows provide an excellent opportunity to present the administration's position to a nationwide interested audience. Besides, if questioning becomes excessively harsh, the audience often feels sorry for the targets and sides with them.

An even less formal release of news occurs through leaks — the surreptitious release of information by governmental sources who wish to remain anonymous. Leaks frequently involve information which the officials in question may not be authorized to release or which they may not wish to release formally. Leaks may destroy the timing of political negotiations; they may alienate the parties whose secrets have been betrayed; and they may cause substantial political harm by disclosing politically sensitive matters. Although presidents frequently leak confidential stories, they passionately hate news leaks by others. Since the source is hidden, personal confrontation and punishment are impossible. All recent presidents have therefore used federal investigative agencies like the FBI and CIA to find the sources of news leaks.[20]

A typical leak occurred in 1970, when a memorandum by Defense Secretary Melvin Laird warned U.S. commanders to keep silent about the willingness of the United States to sign a treaty with the Soviet Union to abandon the antiballistic missile (ABM) system. Silence would preserve negotiating strength. The memo was leaked by an unidentified official, and the *Washington Post* printed it in full, while the *New York Times* wrote a story about it. American negotiators were furious, because their negotiating ability had been impaired by the leak. The harm which leaks may cause must be weighed against their benefits. In a system in which the executive maintains tight control over the more formal channels of news flow, they provide a valuable counterbalance.

THE MEDIA AND CONGRESS

Nature of Coverage

Image versus Reality. Political folklore has it that the presidency basks in the limelight of publicity at all times while Congress is in the shadows. Astute political observers have claimed that the television age has permanently altered the balance of political power to make the president dominant and the legislature inferior. As Senator J. William Fulbright of Arkansas told Congress in 1970, "Television has done as much to expand the powers of the President as would a constitutional amendment formally abolishing the co-equality of the three branches of government."[21]

When one probes beyond these impressions to the underlying facts, the situation is not quite so clear. As Table 3-2 in Chapter 3 shows, over a period of a year, even a presidential election year, Congress and the president receive roughly the same amount of coverage, with a slight edge for Congress, if we combine stories dealing with the body in general and with individuals in it and exclude campaign stories. On an average, 2.8 percent of all stories covered the president directly, compared to 3.1 percent for Congress. Furthermore, television coverage has occasionally weakened the presidency, as happened most conspicuously with the Watergate story. Why, then, is there the impression of vast presidential predominance?

There are several reasons. Most importantly, the presidency is a single-headed body, readily personified, filmed, and recorded in the visible person of the chief executive. This gives the media and media audiences a single, familiar, easily dramatized focus of attention. The president is like a superstar, surrounded by a cast of supporting actors. As the symbolic personification of the nation, presidents can command national television or radio time almost at will, often at prime time, and simultaneously on all major networks. One recent study showed that over a 10-year period, 44 out of 45 presidential requests for coverage were granted, compared to 3 out of 11 for the Democratic congressional leadership.[22]

By contrast, Congress is a many-headed hydra with no single widely familiar personal focus. Its activities are conducted simultaneously in more than 100 locations on Capitol Hill. No single member can command nationwide media coverage at will. Even well-known senators and representatives are viewed as spokesmen for their own or their party's views, or as potential presidential candidates, not as spokesmen for Congress as an institution. Their celebrity status usually has little to do with their legislative activity in Congress. In fact, there has never been a single spokesman for Congress in general, or even for the Senate or House because senators and representatives are loathe to designate one of their number as *primus inter pares*. Consequently, most stories about Congress deal with individual members or legislative activity on specific issues, rather than the body as a whole.

Another reason why stories on Congress escape wide attention lies in the nature of its work. The legislative branch deals primarily with planning for action, making compromises among conflicting interests, and working out legal details. Stories about the executive branch that describe what is actually done are far more memorable than reports about the laborious process of hammering out legislation. Besides, the most interesting aspect of the legislative process, the forging of broad guidelines for policy, is usually reported by the media as part of the work of the executive branch.

Congress itself has recognized that legislative floor sessions would present an unedifying, boring spectacle and therefore resisted live radio and television coverage of most sessions until the late 1970s. Prior to 1979 only selected committee hearings were televised, primarily those involving spicy topics such as labor racketeering, communists in government, or high-level corruption. They became highly dramatic morality plays, with their casts of sinners brought to justice and congressional knights battling evil before the public. Members like Senators Harry Truman and Estes Kefauver and beetle-browed Sam Ervin were catapulted into the national limelight by such hearings. Many of the targets of the investigations, on the other hand, were harmed by the damaging publicity, even when they were officially exonerated of any misdeeds. Few ordinary congressional sessions could provide comparable drama.

In 1979, the prohibition on televising House floor sessions imposed by Speaker Sam Rayburn in 1951 was lifted. The action was prompted in part by the desire to do everything possible to counterbalance the political advantages reaped by the executive branch from heavy media publicity. House sessions began to be telecast, albeit with restrictions. Fearful of negative publicity, the House retained control over filming and specified that only the member speaking should be shown. Thus the typical scene of the near-empty chamber and inattentive members is not part of the coverage. Commercial, cable, and public television are allowed to plug into the House system to show the procedures live or on tape. They are not permitted to do their own taping. Senate floor sessions remain off-limits except for special occasions such as the Panama Canal Treaty debate of 1978 and the 1979 debate on the Strategic Arms Limitation Treaty (SALT).

The verdict about the long-range consequences of coverage is not yet in, though it is doubtful that televised sessions will change the publicity balance between the president and Congress. For the reasons outlined already, Congress is not likely to become a first rate "show." A few interesting and unexpected results of congressional coverage have been reported, however. Representatives themselves apparently are among the most avid watchers because the television cameras permit them to monitor many sessions that they previously missed. They keep up on floor action and issues reported by committees other than their own.

In time, the chance to appear on television and gain valuable publicity may even lure more representatives to the chamber, just as televised committee hearings have attracted above average congressional attendance. The added publicity may also make incumbent representatives even more unbeatable for re-election than they are now. As Sam Rayburn had feared, broadcasting may also make it more difficult in the future to reach legislative compromises after representatives have publicly committed themselves to definite positions.

Broadcasting of congressional sessions apparently has reduced the power of lobbyists, who now have competition in their efforts to convince the public of the rightness of their views. Interested observers are tuning in to congressional sessions and realizing that many issues are far more complex than lobbyists had led them to believe.[23]

Criteria and Organization for Coverage. Newspeople assigned to the congressional beat use general criteria of newsworthiness and gatekeeping to decide who and what will be covered and who and what will be ignored. Exciting novel or controversial topics that can be made personally relevant to the public and that can be simply presented have precedence over complex, mundane ongoing problems, like congressional reorganization or the annual farm bill. Orderly, dispassionate debate usually is passed over in favor of purple rhetoric and wild accusations which can produce catchy headlines. Heated confrontations are more likely to occur in the more intimate committee hearings than in full sessions. In fact, the chance of headlines may provoke them when they might not otherwise occur.[24] Accordingly, committee hearings attract most extensive coverage, particularly on television.

Congress is a regular beat, and major media organizations like the *Washington Post* and the *New York Times,* major newspaper chains like Gannett, Hearst, and Knight, and the television networks and wire services have full-time reporters covering it. Some are specialists in various policy areas. Among wire service reporters, some concentrate on news from various regions, covering, for instance, members of Congress from western states and committees dealing with problems affecting these states. There are also Washington "stringer" bureaus whose reporters serve assorted subscriber news services throughout the country. Specialized news services like Congressional Quarterly cover the congressional beat in detail for professional audiences. In all, more than 2,000 correspondents are accredited to the press galleries in the House and Senate. About 400 of these cover Congress exclusively.[25]

Much information about Congress published by news sources without a regular reporter on the Hill originates in congressional press releases and written reports. These are gathered and distributed by wire service reporters who are unable to attend and report directly about the many hearings occurring simultaneously. Wide use of these documents permits congressmen to tell their stories in their own words. It gives an advantage to members of Congress whose offices can turn out interesting releases.[26]

In general, senators get more play than representatives, even though an equal number of reporters cover both houses. On network television, stories about senators outnumber those about representatives two to one. This happens because senators have greater prominence and prestige, and their larger constituencies make them of interest to a wider audience. Senators from large states also are more likely to have staff to turn out good press releases and other publicity, particularly if they want to increase their eligibility as presidential candidates.

Unlike the president, neither senators nor representatives enjoy automatic coverage of whatever they say and do, even though they issue frequent press releases and call occasional news conferences. However, on certain topics, such as tax policy or investigation of executive activities, congressional spokesmen, rather than the president, are routinely sought out. Additionally, many members of Congress receive regular local coverage through their own news columns, radio, or television programs.

Functions of Media

An outline of the functions performed by Congress for the national media and by the national media for Congress parallels the outline for press-presidency relations. But there are major qualitative differences in the relationship. Neither Congress nor the media feels the need for the services of the other as keenly as on the presidential level. The media can afford to alienate some legislators without losing direct access to congressional news. Similarly, legislators can often ignore national publicity and rely on publicity in their district instead. News about national events and national public opinion is also somewhat less important to most members of Congress than to the president. Senators and representatives are most keenly interested in news relevant to their own constituency. The home media are particularly important to them as sources of news and as channels for transmitting messages back to the district while they are at work in Washington.

National as well as local media also provide senators and representatives with a forum to express their views on political issues and to attract public support for themselves and their causes. Publicity reassures people that their lawmakers are aware of problems and trying to cope with them. It may produce action to remedy publicized abuses such as faulty tires, unnecessary surgery, or pesticides in food. Publicity by itself may bring about reform without the need for legislation or judicial action.

For a few members of Congress, media attention may provide a springboard to higher office, including the presidency. Once members achieve visibility, their fame often grows by its own momentum. They become regulars on interview shows, and their opinions are solicited when important national issue are debated. However, they rarely receive the intimate personal coverage that presidents get. For most members, media attention may do little more than make them visible for lobby groups. This may lead to financial support from these groups for re-election or research support for pet projects. It may also produce vocal attacks and increased support for the opposition.

For run-of-the-mill congressmen, national publicity is not particularly important. They do need favorable media attention in their districts to let their constituents know what they are doing and to pave the

CONGRESSMAN
O. ZILTCH

TAYSK-L
19CHICA-O
TRIBUNE

THE BUCK
STARTS HERE

'THERE'S A NEWSMAN HERE WANTING TO ASK IF YOU KNOW
ANYTHING ABOUT THE REPORT THAT SOME CONGRESSMEN
HAVE RECEIVED MONEY FROM SOUTH AFRICA!"

Reprinted, courtesy of the *Chicago Tribune*

way for re-election. In most instances, local publicity is not particularly difficult to obtain. Several dozen national legislators own mass media outlets. The best known of such owners was Lyndon Johnson, who had extensive broadcast properties in Texas. Even non-owners can get many of their press releases into the local press if they are well done. Newsletters mailed directly to constituents help round out the picture.

All legislators have full- or part-time media consultants. Senators and representatives also have studios available on Capitol Hill where they can produce, at low cost, videotapes, films, and audiotapes for distribution to their constituencies. Seventy-five percent of the House membership and 80 percent of the Senate use these facilities to make broadcasts for hometown distribution. Local broadcasters normally are eager to feature these programs in their "public service" time slots.

A Cautious Marriage

Just as the functions which media perform are similar for the executive and legislative branches, so is the love-hate relationship. But it, too, is less ardent. Senators and representatives competing with peers for media attention bemoan lack of coverage of their pet projects and pronouncements despite their efforts to attract media attention. They complain that reporters treat them as if they were scoundrels conspiring to defraud the public. They point to the fact that they receive more negative coverage than the presidency or the Supreme Court.[27] They resent the cross-examinations that reporters love to conduct with a prosecutor's zeal and an air of infallibility. They charge and can prove that trivia and scandals and official misconduct are covered and dissent is stressed, while congressional consensus and activities of major significance are often ignored. They blame the media for the declining prestige of Congress.

The media, in turn, complain, with justification, about efforts of legislators to manage the news through their professional publicity staffs. They point to the lack of candor and to their exclusion from many congressional activities. Broadcasters resent the constraints put on them when they want to cover congressional sessions.

But senators and representatives realize that they need the media for information and for the publicity that is crucial to their work. They know that the media discreetly ignore their personal foibles as long as no official wrongdoing is involved. Newspeople, in turn, realize they need individual legislators for information about congressional activities and as a counterfoil and source of leaks to check the executive branch. Members are valuable for comments that personalize otherwise dull stories. Congress often creates major story topics for the media when it investigates ongoing problems like auto or mine safety. For such problems, a congressional inquiry becomes the catalyst that turns an everyday event into a newsworthy story. The story may then ride the crest of publicity for quite some time, creating its own fresh and reportable events until it recedes into limbo once more. Newspeople do not want to dry up these sources; they do not want to bite the hand that feeds them the news.

Congress and Communications Policy

Additionally, the media, particularly radio and television, are aware of the potential power Congress has over regulatory legislation. In the past, Congress made little use of its power to legislate communications policy, aside from the broad grant of authority to the Federal Communications Commission (FCC) in the 1934 Communications Act and supplementary laws to deal with technical innovations. Periodic attempts to supersede the act have largely floundered, but the power to legislate communications policy remains and could become important when and if strong, unified industry or consumer pressures develop in the future. Meanwhile, there is a vacuum in both policy formulation and oversight of administration, which neither the executive nor the FCC has attempted to fill.[28] Industry representatives have partly filled the void in planning for the future. They are in a strong position to push their ideas because they enjoy a near monopoly over the basic information needed to make policy.

The communications subcommittees in the Commerce committees of both houses control communications policy largely indirectly through the power of investigation, which has been used frequently but with few dramatic results. Likewise the Appropriations committees wield the power of the purse in a dilatory way. The Senate has used confirmation hearings only occasionally to impress its views on new FCC commissioners. Most presidential nominees have been routinely confirmed, and appointments represent political rewards to the faithful.[29] But there is always the possibility for more active control, and media people pay deference to that possibility.

Congressional control over media also includes matters such as postal rates and subsidies, legislation on permissible mergers and chain control of papers, and laws designed to keep failing newspapers alive. Copyright laws, which affect print and electronic media productions, are also involved. So are policies and regulations about telecommunication satellites, broadcast spectrum allocations, and cable television.

Laws regulating media procedures likewise may occasionally have a strong impact on media content and policies. For instance, FCC encouragement of diversification of programs are largely responsible for the development of a sizable number of FM rock music stations. These stations were able to provide alternatives to more conventional programs. Congressional scrutiny of documentaries may chill investigative reporting. Examples are investigations of a documentary on drug use at a major university and scrutiny of the accuracy of charges of illicit public relations activity by the Pentagon. Former Senator John Pastore, D-R.I., who was deeply concerned about television violence, was instrumental in creating the Surgeon General's Advisory Committee on Television and Social Behavior, which investigated violence in television shows in preparation for congressional action.

Congressional failure to act may also have far-reaching consequences for the mass media. For instance, failure to regulate cable television has left the FCC and the courts in control of this medium. Last but not least, members' ownership of media outlets or purchase of media time makes them part of the media fraternity or valued clients who may receive kid-glove treatment.

Because of their dependence on Congress, the media treat congressional leaders and Congress as an institution with a fair amount of deference and respect. Media critic Ben Bagdikian has even charged that the media have become an effective propaganda arm for Congress. He credits them with making it virtually certain that any incumbent who is willing to run will be re-elected. "Most of the media are willing conduits for the highly selective information the member of Congress decides to feed the electorate."[30] This claim is obviously exaggerated; many factors unrelated to media coverage contribute to the re-election patterns. Besides, the media often present unfavorable publicity and do turn down the bulk of press releases submitted by senators and representatives. For example, in the Third Congressional District in Wisconsin papers published only 7 percent of the available news release copy from their representative in 1973. Senatorial publicity fared even worse. Many papers published no news releases at all; the most generous papers published no more than 30 percent of the news release copy they received.[31] Nonetheless, there is some truth to Bagdikian's charges because media generally report the proceedings of governmental bodies in ways that reflect more coherence and dignity than the facts warrant.

THE MEDIA AND THE SUPREME COURT

Nature of Coverage

Of the three branches of government, the federal judiciary receives the least publicity for its officials. Aside from initial appointments to the federal bench, justices are rarely in the limelight in a way which would be comparable to chief executives or members of the legislature. Judges infrequently grant interviews, almost never hold news conferences, and generally do not seek or welcome media attention, primarily because they fear their impartiality might be compromised.

Neither do the courts as institutions receive much coverage. There are exceptions, of course. Speeches of justices have been telecast and reported when they addressed public bodies like the American Bar Association. On rare occasions, there have been special features about the courts. For instance, in 1968, Supreme Court Justice Hugo Black took part in a one-hour television program in which CBS reporters Eric Sevareid and Martin Agronsky asked him questions about the workings of the Court. While the show had a sizable audience, it was outdistanced by far by a competing telecast on NBC which featured French movie queen Brigitte Bardot.

Although justices are not very newsworthy because they generally do not become embroiled in open battles about policies or election to office, their products — judicial decisions — do make the news. This is particularly true of U.S. Supreme Court decisions, which frequently have major consequences for the political system. A decision like *Baker v. Carr*[32] in 1962, which led to massive changes in electoral districting in the United States, or the case of *Brown v. Board of Education*,[33] which ruled that separate schooling of children of different races was unconstitutional, are examples. In fact, many decisions are so newsworthy that advance word is leaked to the press occasionally, to the dismay of the judges.

Impact of Coverage

Publicity about Supreme Court decisions informs public officials at all governmental levels, as well as the general public, about the substance of selected Court decisions. Choices about which decisions to cover and which to ignore are made by newspeople since Supreme Court justices do not generally issue press releases or hold news conferences. This significant responsibility is assigned to a small corps of reporters because court beats tend to be covered comparatively lightly. At the Supreme Court, full- and part-time staff combined number about 50 people. Of these only the correspondents for the major wire services and four major newspapers are full-time.

Court coverage is difficult; the reporters must digest a large number of voluminous and often contradictory opinions supporting or dissenting from a given decision. This must be done quickly and without guidance from the judges who rendered the opinions. Advice from outside commentators is usually unavailable initially since they are not allowed to preview the opinions. Leaks of advance information are very rare. The Supreme Court does have a press office, which provides small quantities of reference materials and bare bones records of the Court's activities. In addition, brief analyses of important pending cases are available to the media through publications sponsored by the legal profession.

Because of the shortage of skilled reporters, much court reporting, even at the Supreme Court level, is imprecise and sometimes outright wrong. Justice Felix Frankfurter once complained that editors who would never consider covering a baseball game through a reporter unfamiliar with the sport regularly assigned people unfamiliar with the law to cover the Supreme Court. This situation has improved considerably in recent years, but it is far from cured.

Baker v. Carr and the school prayer cases[34] furnish examples of imprecise reporting. An analysis of stories about these two decisions in 63 metropolitan daily papers[35] showed that headlines were misleading and coverage was sketchy and uninformative. Ill-informed statements by well-known people opposing the court's decision made up the major part of the stories. Several stories contained serious errors. For instance, it was reported that the prayer decision outlawing classroom prayer in public schools was based on the religious freedom clause of the Constitution, when, in fact, it was based on the establishment of religion clause. Arguments made in lower courts were erroneously attributed to Supreme Court justices. Moreover, the media concentrated heaviest coverage on the prayer decision, which was relatively easy to grasp and which presented an emotionally stirring story. They slighted the duller reapportionment decision, which was of far greater political significance because it forced states to reapportion legislative districts on a massive scale to meet the one-person, one-vote requirement.

The thrust of complaints about sketchy, inaccurate reporting is the same as for coverage of the presidency and Congress. However, reporting of court activities seems to be more superficial and flawed than its presidential and congressional counterparts.[36] The reasons are not difficult to understand. The volume of decisions is huge, frequently coming all together near the end of a Court term. The subject matter is often highly technical, difficult for reporters to understand and make understandable. With notable exceptions, stories about judicial decisions lack the potential to become front-page, exciting news. They are hard to boil down into catchy phrases and clichés. The Court beat tends to be understaffed. All of this makes it very difficult for assigned reporters to prepare interesting, well-researched accounts.

The information supplied to the public may produce respect for the court and compliance with its rulings. It may also have the opposite effect. For instance, widespread adverse publicity about Supreme Court decisions outlawing prayer in the public schools has encouraged individuals and entire school systems to ignore the ban. It also has led to an abortive movement to pass a constitutional amendment to permit prayers in the public schools. Justice Tom Clark, one of the participants in the prayer decision, complained that popular misunderstanding of the decision caused its unpopularity. He blamed inadequate reporting for the misunderstanding.

Public reactions to Court decisions, in turn, may affect future decisions of the Court. Justices themselves are influenced in their work by what they read and hear from the media. Media reports of crime waves or price-gouging by business, or public opposition to aid for parochial schools are likely to influence subsequent Court decisions and set boundaries to jucidial policymaking.

Publication of decisions by the Supreme Court and lower courts is by no means the only significant judicial news. General news about crime and the work of the justice system is also important in creating images of the quality of public justice. Here a plentiful media diet is available. For example, a 1976 survey of Chicago newspapers and television stations, as well as national network broadcasts, showed that crime and the justice system in general were discussed in 25 percent of all newspaper stories, 20 percent of all local television stories, and 13 percent of all national television stories. Even if we subtract the large number of stories reporting individual crimes from the totals, the figures are still impressive, particularly when compared with stories allotted to other social problems. Stories about health issues and minorities combined, for example, received less than a third of the coverage given to crime and the justice system. Like stories about other governmental activities, crime and justice system stories tended to focus on sensational events often at the expense of significant trends and problems in the legal system that might benefit from greater public concern.[37]

Judicial Censorship

While there is ample coverage of crime and justice system news in general, there are a number of prohibited areas. The Supreme Court bars reporters from all of its deliberations prior to the announcement of decisions. On the few occasions when information about a forthcoming decision has been leaked ahead of time, justices have reacted with great anger and have curtailed the contacts between newspeople and court personnel. Television cameras are barred from the Court and proceedings may not be broadcast directly.

Below the Supreme Court level, courts in most states also bar radio and television reporters from covering trials and other proceedings. The rationale for this restriction is that electronic equipment might produce a carnival atmosphere that would intimidate participants and harm the fairness of the proceedings. Sensational coverage of the Lindbergh kidnapping trial in 1935 originated such bans. Now, however, they appear to be on the decline. By 1980, six states permitted electronic coverage of judicial proceedings in state, though not federal, courts, and 13 more were considering lifting their bans.

Restraints on live audio and visual coverage are not the only limitations on judicial publicity. Courts also limit the information that may be printed about a trial in the interest of fairness. These types of restrictions, and the Supreme Court's support for them, have been discussed in Chapter 4.

Communications Law

Justices are also of interest to media personnel for their views on communications law. Because the public interest standard established for the FCC is vague, and judges have clashed over the interpretation of the First Amendment free press provisions, federal courts are frequently asked to interpret compliance with constitutional and statutory restraints. Media lobbies have therefore tried to influence the appointment of federal judges. In appeals from FCC licensing and rules change decisions, they have tried to have the cases submitted to sympathetic judges and have often provided testimony.

In an average year, 15 to 20 appeals involving various aspects of communications policy are brought from the FCC to the courts, most often to the Court of Appeals for the District of Columbia. The law permits any person who is "aggrieved" or whose interests are "adversely affected" by the orders of the FCC to seek a court review, and these provisions have been loosely interpreted. Such liberal access policies to the courts have enhanced concern about the potentially large role of courts in communications policymaking. However, in the past the majority of FCC rulings have been upheld in the Court of Appeals. This holds true even more for the limited number of cases which have reached the Supreme Court. While influence over the FCC itself thus seems more important for policy impact than control over the courts, it is difficult to gauge how much impact the prospects of judicial review have on FCC activities. Agencies frequently modify their behavior to avoid reversals by the judiciary.

The vagueness of the power grant to the FCC provides immense leeway to the courts as well as the agency. "If 'the public interest' leaves the FCC in a trackless normative wilderness in which it is free to make up the rules of the game, the court's discretion to pass on those rules for reasonable or substantial correspondence with record evidence is not less broad."[38]

SUMMARY

In this chapter, we have examined the relationship between the media and the three branches of the national government. Coverage is ample, but the goals of the media differ from those of government officials. Officials want stories that cover them and their work accurately and favorably. They also wish to dominate the news sifting process so that published news mirrors their sense of what is important and unimportant.

Newspeople want stories that are newsworthy, judged by the usual criteria. They believe that their publics are more interested in exciting events and human interest tales than in academic discussions of public policies, their historical antecedents, and their projected impact, expressed in statistics. Newspeople also feel a special mission, like Shakespeare's Mark Antony, "to bury Caesar, not to praise him." And, like Brutus, they claim that their criticism is not disloyalty. They do not love the government less; they only love the nation more.

Each side in this tug of war uses wiles and ruses as well as clout to have its own way. The outcome is a see-saw contest in which both sides score victories and suffer defeats, but each is most attuned to its own failures rather than its victories. The public interest is served in equally uneven fashion. If we equate it with a maximum of intelligible information about important issues and events, media presentations fall short. But coverage is good in that it is continuous, often well-informed, with sufficient attention to audience appeal to make dry information palatable. Investigative reporting has brought to light many shortcomings and scandals which might otherwise have remained hidden. The fear of exposure by the media has undoubtedly kept government officials from straying into many questionable ventures, although this effect is hard to document. On the negative side, fear of media coverage and actual publicity have probably inhibited desirable actions.

Since the contacts between officials of the national government and the media are so constant, a formal institutional structure has been established to handle these interactions. We have described the fairly elaborate set-up at the presidential level, and the simpler arrangements for Congress and the Supreme Court. We have also indicated some of the problems which newspeople face in covering a flood tide of complex news expeditiously, accurately, and with a modicum of critical detachment and analysis.

Finally, this chapter has pointed to the as yet unsolved problems in communications policymaking. All three branches of government are involved, but there is little coordination among them. Even within the executive and the legislative branches, where most policy should be made, control is dispersed among so many different committees and agencies, that drift, rather than direction, has been the prevailing mode of operation. Few major policy decisions have been made except in times of crisis, and even then, the weaknesses of governmental structures have made it easy for industry spokesmen to dominate the decisionmaking process.

Governmental weakness in this area may be a blessing in disguise and in the spirit of the First Amendment. Since the Constitution commands that Congress shall make no law abridging the freedom of the press, it may be well to keep all communications policymaking to the barest minimum. As Chief Justice Marshall warned the nation at the start of its history, the power to regulate is the power to destroy.[39] Policymaking and regulation overlap. A uniform, well-articulated communications policy, however beneficial it may seem to many people in public and in private life, still puts the governmental imprint indelibly on the flow of information.

NOTES

1. James F. Fixx, ed., *The Mass Media and Politics* (New York: New York Times Arno Press, 1972), p. ix.
2. See Table 3-2, above, adapted from Doris A. Graber, "Is Crime News Excessive?" *Journal of Communication* 29 (Summer 1979): 81-92.
3. One of the best accounts of the effects of media coverage of the presidency is Newton Minow, John B. Martin, and Lee M. Mitchell, *Presidential Television* (New York: Basic Books, 1973). A more recent source is William C. Spragens, *The Presidency and the Mass Media in the Age of Television* (Washington, D.C.: University Press of America, 1978). Also see two books by William Rivers, *The Opinion Makers,* and *The Adversaries: Politics and the Press* (Boston: Beacon Press, 1965 and 1970). Books about the relations of individual presidents with the press include: Graham J. White, *FDR and the Press* (Chicago: University of Chicago Press, 1979), and volumes reproducing *The Nixon Presidential Press Conferences, The Johnson Presidential Press Conferences,* and *The Kennedy Presidential Press Conferences* (Pine Plains, N.Y.: Earl M. Coleman, 1976).
4. David Halberstam, *The Powers That Be* (New York: Alfred A. Knopf, 1979), p. 6.
5. Michael J. Robinson, "A Twentieth Century Medium in a Nineteenth-Century Legislature: The Effects of Television on the American Congress," in Norman J. Ornstein, ed., *Congress in Change: Evolution and Reform* (New York: Praeger, 1975), pp. 241, 256.
6. Halberstam, *The Powers That Be,* p. 49.
7. Ibid., p. 514.
8. Ibid., p. 161.
9. William E. Porter, *Assault on the Media: The Nixon Years* (Ann Arbor: University of Michigan Press, 1976), p. 61.

10. William J. Small, *To Kill a Messenger* (New York: Hastings House, 1970).
11. *Kennedy and the Press: The News Conferences* (New York: Thomas Y. Crowell, 1965), p. 239.
12. *Collected Speeches of Spiro Agnew* (New York: Audubon Books, 1971), p. 89.
13. Porter, *Assault on the Media*, p. 47.
14. Small, *To Kill a Messenger*, p. 29.
15. Ibid., p. 102.
16. Michael Baruch Grossman and Martha Joynt Kumar, "The White House and the News Media: The Phases of Their Relationship," *Political Science Quarterly* 94 (Spring 1979): 37-53.
17. Jeb Stuart Magruder, *An American Life* (New York: Atheneum, 1974), p. 101.
18. William J. Small, *Political Power and the Press* (New York: W. W. Norton, 1972), p. 162.
19. John Herbers, *No Thank You, Mr. President* (New York: W. W. Norton, 1976).
20. Small, *Political Power and the Press*, p. 163.
21. Robert O. Blanchard, ed., *Congress and the News Media* (New York: Hastings House, 1974), p. 105.
22. Alan P. Balutis, "Congress, the President and the Press," *Journalism Quarterly* 53 (Fall 1976): 509-515.
23. Effects reported by California Representative Lionel Van Deerlin's office to a panel on the "Politics of Broadcasting," International Communications Association, Philadelphia, 1979.
24. Warren Weaver, Jr., *Both Your Houses* (New York: Praeger, 1972), p. 12.
25. Blanchard, *Congress and the News Media*, p. 240. For a detailed content analysis of television coverage of Congress, see Michael J. Robinson and Kevin R. Appel, "Network News Coverage of Congress," 94 *Political Science Quarterly* (Fall 1979): 407-418.
26. Blanchard, *Congress and the News Media*, pp. 169-239.
27. Arthur Miller, Edie Goldenberg and Lutz Erbring, "Type-Set Politics: Impact of Newspapers on Public Confidence," 73 *American Political Science Review* (March 1979): 70.
28. Daniel D. Polsby and Kim Degnan, "Institutions for Communications Policymaking: A Review," in Glen O. Robinson, ed., *Communications for Tomorrow: Policy Perspectives for the 1980s* (New York: Praeger, 1978), pp. 501-514.
29. Ernest Gellhorn, "The Role of Congress," in Robinson, ed., *Communications for Tomorrow: Policy Perspectives for the 1980s*, pp. 445-457.
30. Ben H. Bagdikian, "Congress and the Media: Partners in Propaganda," *Columbia Journalism Review* 12 (January-February 1974).
31. Leslie D. Polk, John Eddy and Ann Andre, "Use of Congressional Publicity in Wisconsin District," *Journalism Quarterly* 52 (Autumn 1975): 543-546.
32. 369 U.S. 186 (1962).
33. 347 U.S. 483 (1954).
34. *Engel* v. *Vitale*, 370 U.S. 421 (1962).
35. Chester A. Newland, "Press Coverage of the United States Supreme Court," *Western Political Quarterly* 17 (1964): 15-36.
36. David C. Grey, *The Supreme Court and the News Media* (Evanston, Ill.: Northwestern University Press, 1968).
37. A detailed account of coverage of crime and justice system news is presented in Doris A. Graber, *Crime News and the Public* (New York: Praeger, 1980).
38. Polsby and Degnan, "Institutions for Communications Policymaking," p. 513.
39. *McCulloch* v. *Maryland*, 4 Wheaton 316 (1819).

READINGS

Blanchard, Robert O., ed. *Congress and the News Media.* New York: Hastings House, 1974.

Grey, David C. *The Supreme Court and the News Media.* Evanston: Northwestern University Press, 1968.

Herbers, John. *No Thank You, Mr. President.* New York: W. W. Norton, 1976.

Minow, Newton; Martin, John B.; and Mitchell, Lee M. *Presidential Television.* New York: Basic Books, 1973.

Porter, William E. *Assault on the Media: The Nixon Years.* Ann Arbor: University of Michigan Press, 1976.

Small, William J. *Political Power and the Press.* New York: W. W. Norton, 1976.

8

Crisis Coverage

You awake at 4 A.M. Outside the civil defense sirens are screaming. What could be wrong? Has it happened? Or is it about to strike? What are you supposed to do to cope with this as yet unknown menace? You turn on your radio, almost instinctively. Sounds of soft music. Just hearing them is reassuring. At least the radio is working. If there are things you must do immediately, the radio announcer will tell you. You wait for the music to stop, anxious to know what is happening. But you also hope it won't stop for a while — the longer it plays, the less chance that danger is immediate. They wouldn't play music if disaster were imminent.

Finally the announcer breaks in. A tornado has been sighted nearby. "Take shelter," says the voice on the radio. "Keep away from windows. Stay indoors until the sirens stop. There will be further news bulletins at five-minute intervals." You heave a sigh of relief as you dress quickly, pick up your apartment keys and a small transistor radio, and head for the basement. Nothing has happened yet, and if it does, officials are obviously prepared to deal with the crisis. They already woke you, warned you about the potential menace to your life and property, told you how to protect yourself initially, and promised to shepherd you through the dangers of the hours to come.

THE NATURE OF CRISIS CONDITIONS

This is just one small scenario of a common public crisis. Public crises are natural or manmade events that pose an immediate and serious threat to the lives and property or to the peace of mind of large numbers of citizens. Examples are assassinations of major public figures, terrorist attacks, particularly when hostages are taken, or major accidents, like train wrecks or spectacular fires. They trouble the public's peace of mind even when they threaten no personal harm to most observers. When such disasters happen, people expect to be informed and protected by the appropriate government agencies.

In times of crisis the media, particularly radio, become a vital arm of government. They perform their usual functions of selecting, shaping, and reporting the news to people in and out of government. But, in addition, they provide a ready channel for government officials to address the public directly or indirectly, through media personnel. These official messages keep endangered communities in touch with essential information and instructions. People are reassured and may be less likely to panic. This makes it easier to re-establish normal community life.

The rapid transmission of information and commentary is most crucial for those areas that are immediately and directly affected by the disaster and must cope with its disruptions. Our analysis of crisis coverage will focus on these types of situations. However, many of the problems faced locally also have ramifications for areas remote from the scene. The coverage of a racial riot in Los Angeles may have effects on readers and viewers in Detroit or Chicago when similar background conditions exist or similar situations occur. Publicity for airplane crashes or radiation leaks may affect the future of these industries throughout the country, not only at the disaster scene.

A dramatic example of the nationwide impact of a local event occurred in 1970 when four students were killed during an antiwar demonstration at Kent State University in Ohio. Wide publicity for the event kindled protest demonstrations on the nation's campuses from coast to coast. Classes stopped, antiwar meetings were held, and thousands of students rushed to Washington to lobby against the war and the Kent State slayings.

FOUR CRISIS SITUATIONS

Most of our examples will be drawn from four situations for which media coverage has been studied intensively. These include the assassination of President John F. Kennedy in Dallas on November 22, 1963, racial rioting in Winston-Salem, North Carolina, November 2-5, 1967, coverage of Israel's Yom Kippur War, October 6-28, 1973, and radio news during a series of floods and tornadoes.

The Assassination of John F. Kennedy

The facts of the Kennedy assassination are familiar. A young, vigorous president who had created an aura of ushering in a fresh, new breed of politics and politicians, was struck down by a sniper's bullets while traveling in an open limousine in a motorcade in Dallas. The president died in a hospital several hours after the attack. Initially, there was uncertainty about his physical condition. The extent and severity of his injuries were unknown. Rumors mushroomed that the assassination was part of a larger plot by domestic or foreign political enemies of the president to kill prominent government officials. The exact procedures which would be followed in filling the presidential office without delay were unclear. There were countless unanswered questions about the impact the disaster might have on American politics and policies. All these uncertainties compounded the grief and anger which touched millions of Americans in a very personal way.[1]

North Carolina Racial Rioting

In Winston-Salem, in 1967, a black man was arrested on the street for drunkenness. He was taken to a local police station where a white policeman clubbed him for being unruly. Several days later, the victim died of a fractured skull. Because this incident occurred in a period of racial unrest and mounting opposition to harsh police action, particularly against minority groups, the police apparently tried to hush up the story. However, rumors of the incident circulated in the black community, and a brief story did appear in one local newspaper. The National Association for the Advancement of Colored People (NAACP) planned a march to protest police brutality, but was persuaded to cancel it for fear that it would provoke rioting.

After the victim's funeral, rioting began with throwing rocks, breaking windows, and starting small fires. Ultimately 500 people were involved, and the governor called out 1,000 National Guard troops. There were rumors of bomb threats and looting and sniping. A curfew was then imposed; and the National Guard was supplied with ammunition, in case the situation got out of control. It did. Fighting lasted for four days. Fortunately there were no dead, but more than 100 people were injured, 200 people were arrested, and there was $750,000 worth of property damage.[2]

The Yom Kippur War

The Yom Kippur War started at 2:00 P.M. on October 6, 1973 with a surprise attack by Egyptian and Syrian forces on Israeli troops along Israel's frontiers. Fighting was confined to the border regions and there were no large-scale attacks on civilian populations. Though this was the fourth time in Israel's history that the country found itself at war, the suddenness of the outbreak surprised most Israelis. There had been no political and little military warning of the attack, and hence few preparations had been made to cope with the initial crisis.

On the day of the attack, people were busy with religious ceremonies of the Yom Kippur holiday, a most sacred day for members of the Jewish faith. Because of the holiday, the Israeli media were totally shut down. The wailing of the air raid sirens at 2:00 P.M. jolted the nation back to worldly affairs.

Radio and television immediately resumed broadcasting. Their initial task was to summon military units through coded information, to broadcast civil defense instructions, and to inform an anxious public about ongoing events. In the days that followed, these initial tasks were expanded to include keeping up the morale of the soldiers and the home front, directing propaganda broadcasts to the Arab world, and interpreting the war situation so that the public could put unfolding events into perspective and understand and support the policies of their government.[3]

Natural Disasters

Natural disasters are in many ways akin to first strikes in war. In the case of floods and tornadoes, the physical impact of water or wind has suddenly wiped out lives and property and disrupted communication and transportation. People are anxious about their own survival and welfare and that of their loved ones and their communities.

The cases on which our analysis of disaster coverage is based involve four flood and three storm disasters. In two of the floods, nearly the entire city was submerged in the wake of a hurricane; in the other two, flash floods wiped out part of the city. In the storm disasters tornadoes hit and destroyed major portions of towns in Georgia, Texas, and Iowa. Homes were leveled, burying people under the rubble. Telephone lines were broken; live electric wires posed hazards of electrocution and fire. Streets became impassable even to rescue vehicles. Television stations, bereft of power, stopped broadcasting.[4] In each case, radio became the major source for emergency information. It is the most likely medium to have emergency power supplies if regular power is disrupted and, thanks to transistors, it is the most likely to be received by large numbers of the public when electricity is unavailable.

MEDIA RESPONSE AND ROLE

During crises, the public becomes almost totally dependent on the media for news that may be vital for survival, and for important messages from public and private authorities. The mass media are the only institutions with the capacity to collect this escalating mass of information and to disseminate it quickly. When people become aware of a crisis, they therefore turn on their radios or television sets, often on a round-the-clock basis, to monitor the event.

The audience for crisis information is, indeed, massive and loyal. In the days immediately after the Kennedy assassination, the average television set was turned on for nearly 32 hours of broadcasts about the unfolding events. In the U.S. alone, 51 million homes were tuned in. During the Yom Kippur War, the entire Israeli population used both radio and television. Sixty-eight percent of the people listened to radio all day long to catch the hourly news bulletins.

Besides information, the public looks to the media for explanations and interpretations of the situation, since media people are often the first ones on the scene collecting reports and trying to fit them into a coherent story. Official investigations generally come much later. The media also guide the public about appropriate behavior during the crisis. This may be a warning to retreat to an air raid shelter, an announcement of escape routes, information on purification of polluted food and water, news of missing persons, or schedules to be maintained by schools and work places.

Stages and Patterns of Crisis Coverage

Stage One. The typical scenario of crisis coverage has three stages. During the first stage, the crisis or disaster strikes or is announced as impending. Media people, officials, and onlookers rush to the scene. This immediately produces a flood of uncoordinated messages, largely transmitted over the airwaves. Radio and television interrupt regularly scheduled programs with bulletins announcing the crisis, or they may preempt the entire program for reports from the scene.

During the storm and flood disasters, emergency messages generally were broadcast within minutes after the disaster struck, often by a sharply limited corps of stations which had survived the immediate impact of the disaster. The stations rapidly became information collection centers to which people would phone reports to be broadcast and which they could contact to receive information. The most important broadcasts in the early hours of the disaster were messages describing what had happened, directing people to places where aid was available, summoning National Guard units and other security forces, and coordinating appeals for survival supplies, such as food, blankets, blood donations, and medical equipment.

In the early phase the number of news broadcasts multiplies steeply. In the Yom Kippur War, radio and television doubled broadcast time to a 24-hour schedule and replaced many regular programs with war-related news and interviews. News bulletins were issued hourly on radio and five times daily on television. After a major earthquake in 1964 ravaged Anchorage, Alaska, radio stations remained on the air continuously and asked people to stay tuned in for emergency messages. Over a three-day period, one station alone broadcast 4,000 messages.[5]

Once the initial announcements have been aired, many people who have heard the broadcast will relay the information to others by word of mouth in person or by telephone. In turn, this stimulates those who have been alerted to tune in to subsequent broadcasts. For instance, when the news of the assassination of President John F. Kennedy was first broadcast, a larger than average daytime audience heard it within minutes from the media because the shooting occurred at the noon hour when many people in the East and Midwest were listening to radio during lunch. Each person who heard the news told it to five or six other people on an average.[6] More than two-thirds of the American public — nearly

150 million people — received the news within the first half hour of its happening.

The striking characteristic of this first stage is the rapidity of the communication. Television and radio can focus the public's attention almost instantaneously on the developing situation. In many cases, news about the crisis replaces most other stories. Whatever else happens in the world during the crisis days, regardless of its importance, may be totally blocked out.

At this early stage, the media are the major source of information even for public officials concerned with the crisis. Media reports serve to coordinate public activities. During the Anchorage earthquake, for example, the radio stations that were able to function became the focal point for coordinating information on casualties, property damage, and available supplies so that officials could determine the priorities for relief work. At a later stage, direct communication among officials and other affected parties may supplement or even supersede media communication.

Next to reaching the disaster site, the chief problem for newspeople during the first stage is getting accurate information. Public and private officials involved in the crisis may be reluctant to talk. Rumors abound. In the Yom Kippur War, stories about damage done by the initial attack, preparedness of the Israeli army, and advance warning about the forthcoming attack were garbled. During the Alaska earthquake, many buildings were evacuated unnecessarily because of false reports that they had been condemned or were about to collapse. The number of dead and extent of injuries were frequently exaggerated. In the Kennedy assassination and the racial disturbances, there were intimations of conspiracies to commit more violence. Newspeople were faced with many conflicting reports and not enough time to check their accuracy. If highly technical matters are involved, as happens in explosions, structural failures, and radiation disasters, it may be impossible to present a coherent story. Reporters may lack the expertise to make sense out of baffling technical data and the skill to simplify the information so that laymen can comprehend it.

If television and radio stations attempt to provide continuous coverage, they must suddenly produce a steady stream of interesting stories to fill hours instead of minutes of broadcast time. This pressure for fresh accounts leads to interviews with eyewitnesses and commentators of doubtful knowledge, who may lend a local touch without adding substance to the news. It also leads to reporting information that has not been adequately verified.[7] It encourages speculations both by reporters and by public officials. At times, these speculations involve spinning past prejudices into a web of scenarios which cast blame for the disaster or its aftermath on socially outcast groups. "Outsiders" or ethnic minorities or political deviants in the community often become the hapless scapegoats.

Stage Two. During the second stage, the media try to make sense out of the situation. At this point, generally enough time has elapsed so that patterns are emerging. For instance, in a natural disaster, the full extent of the damage has been ascertained. Names of victims and the degree of their injuries are known. Plans have been made for repair of the damage. In the Kennedy assassination, it became clear how the death occurred, even though the persons responsible for the crime were not yet known. Plans had been made for the funeral ceremonies and for the transfer of power.

In general, print media are able to do a more thorough job during this stage in pulling together the various events and fitting them into a coherent story. They have larger staffs for investigation than are available to radio and television. Print media also have more room to present background details that make the events understandable. In the hours and days following the assassination of John F. Kennedy, the *New York Times,* for instance, probed many of the questions about the motives for the assassination, the possibility of conspiracy, and the involvement of foreign agents which the Warren Commission investigated much later and at a much slower pace.

Stage Three. The third stage overlaps with the other two. It involves attempts by media personnel to place the crisis into its larger, long-range perspective and to prepare people to cope with the aftermath of the initial events and modifications in initial policies. For instance, information on evacuation routes and ways to protect people and property may be updated with an eye to ultimate restoration of normal conditions. In wartime, the third stage may involve broadcasting news, patriotic features, and action-adventure or comedy shows designed to relieve tensions and sustain morale. In the Israeli situation, it also required structuring messages so that they would not give aid and comfort to the enemy who could readily listen to broadcasts intended for Israeli consumption.

A concerted effort may have to be made to prevent panic. After the Anchorage earthquake, the mayor and other city officials made frequent radio reports describing the damage and assuring people that the situation was under control by the authorities. Similarly, after the assassination of Martin Luther King Jr., live camera facilities were set up to permit local mayors throughout the United States to communicate with city people. In Washington, D.C., for example, Mayor Walter Washington and other black leaders addressed the public repeatedly urging people to stay calm. Network tributes to Dr. King were designed to stress peaceful behavior as a genuine tribute to the civil rights leader's memory.

Following the leaking of radiation from a nuclear energy plant at Three Mile Island, Pennsylvania, in 1979, efforts to calm the population involved centralization of news releases to halt disquieting conflicting reports. All information released by government and plant officials about the disaster had to be cleared through a press center operated by the federal government's Nuclear Regulatory Commission near the site of the accident. Officials of the stricken plant protested about the censorship, but complied with President Carter's order. A formal investigation of how 43 newspapers and network evening newscasts reported the accident subsequently credited the media with providing balanced treatment in a highly confused and confusing situation.[8]

To reorient people to the new situation after the Kennedy assassination, news about Lyndon Johnson's assumption of power was featured. A greater than average effort was made to keep people informed about the whereabouts and activities of the new president and to convey the impression that the political life of the nation was continuing with as little disruption as possible.

In the storm and flood disasters, after the initial relief activities had been organized, stations switched heavily to morale-building activities. The general theme of these efforts was that the community had shown its strength by coping heroically with the disaster, and that it would now unite and rapidly build a better future. "Belmond is coming back," proclaimed the front page of the local newspaper in the Iowa town paralyzed by a tornado. "Belmond is looking ahead. It had received perhaps the cruelest blow ever dealt an Iowa town in the way of a natural catastrophe. But it is far from being beaten."[9]

Which medium — radio, television, or newspapers — performs best in crisis situations? Public opinion surveys from the Yom Kippur War provide some answers. More than half of the people who were interviewed about their media preferences said that radio had been best in providing initial information. Television was rated second best for information, but best for interpreting events. As interpreter, radio ranked second, followed by interpersonal communication and newspaper coverage, in that order. Television was also called the best medium for tension release, followed by interpersonal communication. Only 5 percent of the respondents credited newspapers with providing relief from tension.

Less educated people relied more heavily on television and interpersonal communication for news and interpretation, while the better educated relied more on radio and newspapers. Less educated people also felt the highest levels of tension and found it most difficult to get relief. Without comparable information from other crisis situations, one can only guess that these reactions to crisis coverage by various media are probably representative of what occurs in similar crises in other countries.

Effects of Media Coverage

Positive Effects. Media coverage of crisis situations usually has both positive and negative effects. On the positive side, information,

President Carter tours the nuclear power plant at Three Mile Island.

even if it is bad news, relieves disquieting uncertainty and calms people. The mere activity of watching or listening to familiar reporters and commentators is reassuring and keeps people occupied. It gives them a sense of vicarious participation, of "doing something." To maintain this quieting effect, media personnel may avoid showing gruesome crisis details. For instance, in the Kennedy assassination, photos of the president's injuries were not shown initially, though they were available. In the Three Mile Island accident, conjectures about possible effects of a nuclear explosion were avoided. Local media even rejected advertisements by merchants for "evacuation sales" and radiation detectors to lessen the chance for panic.

News stories may be able to create the reassuring feeling that grief and fear are not borne alone. After seeing the same disaster pictures and listening to the same broadcasts, people can discuss the crisis with neighbors, friends, and co-workers who have shared their experiences. This gives the feeling of mutual support. Watching the Kennedy funeral on television and witnessing the grief of his young family made people feel that they were participating with millions of others in a national catharsis of grief. Many were able to cry to relieve their personal tensions.

If the news conveys the idea that the authorities are coping properly with the disaster, this, too, is reassuring. Scenes of a train or bus or plane crash become less frightening if the police, firefighters, ambulances, and medical personnel are on the scene. Watching the mayor or governor tour a disaster site is further reassurance. Finally, directions about appropriate behavior may save lives and property and assure that the struck community continues to function.

While benefits of coverage are readily apparent in most disasters, the case is not always clear. In the riots following the King assassination, for instance, looting and rioting continued or even started up, despite broadcasts intended to cool the tense situation. The broadcasts may have reduced the amount of violence, but we don't know for sure.

Negative Effects. Media coverage may also have adverse effects. It may disturb people to the point that they cannot act rationally. People may panic in the face of crisis news, endangering themselves and others. For instance, an unplanned mass exodus of frightened people during an impending flood or wind calamity may clog roads and overcrowd shelters; it may lead to injuries and death for people caught beyond the safety of their homes and work places. Pictures of violence may lead to a terrifying multiplication effect. Audiences frequently believe that the violent act is merely one of many. One house on fire or the sight of one victim's body may lead to visions of whole neighborhoods on fire and scores of victims killed.

Statements provoking unwise reactions are more likely to be publicized in times of crisis because the exceptionally large demand for news and guidance reduces gatekeepers' vigilance. Pack journalism may run rampant when all available news is shared to provide as much coverage as possible. If mistakes are made by news sources or reporters, they appear in all the media. Dallas police, for instance, made many widely quoted comments about Lee Harvey Oswald, Kennedy's accused slayer, which would have impaired Oswald's chances for a fair trial. After the nuclear mishap at Three Mile Island, workers complained that media reports based on conflicting assessments by government officials frightened their families into needless evacuation of the area and threatened the survival of the plant and their job security.

Crisis and disaster news frequently attracts crowds of citizens and reporters to the site, making rescue and security operations more difficult. It is arguable that Jack Ruby, who killed Lee Harvey Oswald while millions of people watched on television, could never have trailed Oswald had it not been for the reporters cluttering Dallas police premises. Likewise, small disturbances have grown into large ones when people were attracted to the scene by media reports.

Media coverage may also incite riots or spur rioting which has already erupted. For instance, during the racial riots in the Watts neighborhood of Los Angeles, police reported that violence peaked wherever television cameras were in evidence. Rioters actually seemed to "perform" for the cameras. Racial rioting in which whites attacked blacks in Washington, D.C., Chicago, and East St. Louis, Illinois, in 1919 was attributed to sensational coverage of crimes by blacks against whites.[10]

Media coverage of racial riots may let people know where police forces are deployed, permitting looters and arsonists to avoid those areas. Potential riot participants use news reports to learn where most of the action is so that they can join in the fray and enlarge the disturbance. During racial rioting in Detroit, live coverage of looting and shooting seemed to arouse viewers emotionally so that some who had never thought of becoming involved in such activities took part in the violence.[11]

Even a small number of publicized riot scenes may produce adverse results because acts of violence generally are noticed and remembered much more clearly than other aspects of riot coverage. In 1967, 499 men who had been among those arrested in a Detroit race riot were asked what they had seen on television about race riots. Seventy-one percent of the respondents spoke first about seeing killings, shoot-outs, police brutality, arson, looting, rock throwing, fighting, screaming, and other violent acts. Yet the Kerner Commission, which investigated riot coverage by television, found that, overall, violent behavior constituted less than 5 percent of total coverage of race riot incidents.[12]

Planning Crisis Coverage

Because media play such a crucial role in keeping the polity going during crises, most media organizations have more or less formal plans to cope with crisis coverage problems. This is particularly true for electronic media. In one sample of 72 radio and television stations in 12 United States cities, 70 percent of the stations had plans for reporting of natural disasters and 73 percent had plans for civil disturbances.[13] The plans were generally more detailed for natural disasters because needs are more predictable and there is greater consensus about the objectives to be pursued.

Crisis coverage planning involves two aspects — preparation for the crisis and deciding how to present ongoing events. Plans to avoid crises are rare, probably because media focus on short-range happenings and because crisis prediction is difficult. Nonetheless the media have often been blamed for neglecting preventive coverage. The Kerner Commission, for example, condemned the media for its silence about the plight of blacks in the United States. It claimed that ample early coverage might have prevented violence in the mid-1960s. There is usually disagreement about whether or not specific sets of social indicators herald a crisis at some future time, so the commission's complaints seem unfair. Besides, even if newspeople could accurately forecast an impending crisis, there is no assurance that increased publicity would prevent it. As we saw in Chapter 5, publicity does not necessarily produce behavioral changes, however easy and obviously beneficial they may be.

Natural Disasters. In the radio and television stations sampled, natural disaster plans were generally predicated on the assumption that people tend to panic and that coverage must be designed to forestall this. The management of 72 percent of the stations, particularly those who had previous experience with natural disasters, assumed that panic would occur.

Preparation for predicted natural disasters may involve the publication of news tracing the path of a storm or reporting geological studies that forecast the likelihood of earthquakes in an area. Official warnings and plans in case of disasters may be publicized along with information on protective measures that individuals can take. Stories that are graphic enough to arouse a lethargic population to prepare for the disaster, however, may cause panic or may be so scary that people shut them out of their minds. Such ostrich tactics may explain why, despite frequent warnings about serious earthquake danger in Southern California, few people have taken recommended precautions.

Civil Disorders. Interviewees at 83 percent of the stations in the study mentioned above assumed that there would be a contagion effect from broadcasts in civil disturbances which would increase the number of people flocking to the scene to commit violent acts. Broadcasters with previous experience in riot situations reported that "respected members of the community, who had jobs, who lived in pretty decent homes, joined the rioting and became looters and snipers because all of a sudden there was an unleashing of . . . hatred."[14] By contrast, social scientists who study disasters deny that panic and contagion occur frequently.[15] Whether or not they are correct, the important fact is that media personnel expect these reactions and act accordingly.

An example of disaster preparation for civil disturbances is presented by the Winston-Salem case. The 1965 Watts riots formed the backdrop of media planning in Winston-Salem. The local papers, which were generally considered liberal on civil rights, decided to lay the groundwork for subsequent coverage by pointing out that the city planned to treat rioters harshly. The preparatory stories also implied that rioters would most likely be outside agitators, rather than local people.

This type of publicity was intended, first of all, to discourage would-be rioters by warning them that they faced stiff punishment, and second, to increase public support for harsh suppression of disturbances. If, as the mayor had put it, rioting would be done by "thugs and hoodlums who see a chance to profit from looting," the local community would feel no sympathy for these offenders.

The riot coverage that followed three months later was largely cast into this framework. It tried to minimize the involvement of local people and stress that of outsiders. It also tried to convey the impression that law enforcement would keep rioters from profiting by violence and looting.

The Problem of News Suppression

In natural as well as manmade crises, major policy questions are posed by plans for temporary or permanent news suppression. How much coverage should be presented immediately, at the risk of telling an inaccurate story, spreading panic, and attracting bystanders and destructive participants to the scene? What should be withheld initially or permanently? Eighty percent of the newspeople in the sample of radio and television stations mentioned earlier said that they would temporarily withhold information that might arouse troublesome reactions. Many would go further, indicating that they would withhold live coverage entirely, particularly in civil disturbances, because they believed that coverage increases the intensity and duration of crises. Such a self-imposed blackout of live television and radio coverage occurred in Winston-Salem during the first day of rioting. The story was reported solely in the print media, making it less immediate and graphic. Similarly, in 1979 television networks avoided coverage of demonstrations involving Iranian students in the United States. It was feared that coverage would spur more disturbances, further straining tense U.S.-Iranian relations and endangering American citizens held hostage in Iran.

Some news outlets have plans to delay live coverage until officials have the situation under control. Others believe that suppression of live coverage will allow rumors to spread that may be more inciting than judicious reporting of ongoing events. We do not know which of these views is most correct and how different circumstances affect reactions to media coverage of crises.

The question of suppression of coverage becomes particularly acute when a crisis involves terrorists or maniacal killers who crave publicity. Granting exposure to them by live coverage may encourage them or others to further outrages. As the *New Yorker* commented in 1977 in the wake of live coverage of terrorist acts by Hanafi Moslems in Washington, D.C., and lurid stories about a mass murderer in New York, known as Son of Sam: "By transforming a killer into a celebrity, the press has not merely encouraged but perhaps driven him to strike again — and may have stirred others brooding madly over their grievances to act."[16]

Several other rules for cautious reporting during crises have been widely adopted. For instance, in the wake of filming the Watts uprising, television newspeople learned that they must keep their equipment inconspicuous. Consequently, when rioting broke out after the death of Martin Luther King Jr., camera crews traveled to riot scenes in unmarked vehicles and kept camera equipment unobtrusive. They used available light rather than floodlights. The development of small videotape equipment that does not require floodlighting has helped immeasurably to keep coverage discreet.

Newspeople have also learned to avoid inflammatory details or language. For instance, in Winston-Salem, editors instructed reporters in advance of the crisis to identify the troubled area precisely and to indicate that surrounding areas were quiet. This was intended to reduce the multiplication effect. Reporters were asked to keep details of the incident which led to the rioting to a minimum. Exaggerated language or publication of unconfirmed reports of violence were to be avoided. The rule to follow was, "When in doubt, leave out."

In the Winston-Salem case, the media heeded these rules. The scope of rioting was minimized, for example, by reporting that, "As the rioters moved through downtown last night, most of the city went about its business as usual. Many people probably never knew what was going on."[17] The riots were described as occurring "in connection with unrest created by the recent death" rather than "murder" of a man "who died after injuries sustained when he resisted arrest and was hit" rather than "clubbed" by a police officer. A detailed story of the incident was not published until several days after the rioting ended. Wire service copy, which was used in other cities, had said that the victim died "after he was blackjacked by a white policeman."

Words like "rioting mobs" or "murder" or racial designations were largely avoided in the Winston-Salem press. Photographs showed black and white law enforcement officials working together to quell the riots, assisted by both black and white citizens. They showed arrests of looters and confiscation of their loot. There were no predictions of future trouble or further threats and no unconfirmed reports on dead and wounded and property damage. After the riots ended, most news people and community leaders felt that the press had handled the situation as planned, with good results.

Nonetheless, preparations for muted coverage, particularly in civil disturbances, raise some serious political and philosophical questions. Muted coverage generally leads to presentation of the official story only and suppression of unofficial views. The perspective of law enforcement officers, preoccupied with controlling criminal activities, becomes paramount. In fact, stories are frequently cleared first with the police.

In the Winston-Salem case, the initial stories did not show that many blacks supported the riots as a social protest against unfair treatment of blacks by the white community. The media reports suppressed or failed to vent the feelings and ideas of militant black leaders. Instead, they concentrated on showing blacks who supported the policies of the established local governing elites. In the short run, this helped keep the situation under control. The long-run effects of this kind of coverage are more problematic.

Some observers feel that muted reporting reduces the potential for post-riot hostilities among warring parties. Delayed coverage can, they feel, be more analytical and so more likely to produce reforms. Others feel that the drama of an ongoing crisis arouses public consciousness much better and faster than anything else. People will act to remedy injustice if the situation is acute. If the heat of battle is already over, action may seem pointless. A permanent news blackout will make reforms highly unlikely. These people oppose muted coverage or news suppression. They are willing to risk paying a very high price in lost lives, personal injuries, imprisonment, and property damage in hopes that immediate complete coverage will shock the community to undertake basic social reforms.

Finally there is the unresolved philosophical question about the wisdom and propriety of news suppression in a free society. The true test of genuine press freedom does not come in times of calm. It comes in times of crisis when the costs of freedom may be dear, tempting government and media alike to impose silence.

SUMMARY

In American political culture, the normal feuds of politics are suspended when the nation is in danger. While this unwritten rule has been most often mentioned in connection with foreign policy, where "politics stops at the water's edge," it applies equally as much to domestic crises of the types we have discussed in this chapter. When there is widespread danger to life and property, or when sudden death or terror have taken a large toll, when well-known leaders are in serious trouble or have fallen by the wayside, people and their government pull together far more than in normal times. Though there are many instances when sensational media coverage has hindered governmental efforts to maintain calm, it is increasingly true that the media abandon their adversary role during crises. They become teammates of officialdom in attempts to restore public order, safety, and tranquility.

In this chapter, we have described the indispensable functions that media perform during crises in diffusing vital information to the public and officials, in interpreting the meaning of events, and in providing emotional support for troubled communities. In major disasters, radio is particularly helpful because its technical requirements are most adaptable to makeshift arrangements. It can broadcast without regular electric power supplies to people who have only a pocket transistor radio and are otherwise isolated.

Because the media play such a large part in public communication during crises, the manner in which they discharge their responsibilities has been of great concern to public officials and the community at large. Information gaps, misinformation, and the dissemination of information that makes the effects of the crisis worse all have led to demands that the information flow be controlled to ease crisis management. Many media institutions have formal plans that temporarily set aside the usual criteria for publishing exciting news in the interest of calming the public.

We have questioned the wisdom of muted coverage, particularly during civil disturbances, because it may drown out explicit and implicit messages about unmet societal needs. We have not questioned the need to plan for crisis coverage. Modern society faces crises of various sorts so frequently that policy makers in the media and in government would be remiss were they to make no plans to cope with emergencies.

NOTES

1. Wilbur Schramm, "Communication in Crisis," in Bradley S. Greenberg and Edwin B. Parker, *The Kennedy Assassination and the American Public: Social Communication in Crisis* (Palo Alto, Calif.: Stanford University Press, 1965), pp. 1-25.
2. David L. Paletz and Robert Dunn, "Press Coverage of Civil Disorder: A Case Study of Winston-Salem, 1967," *Public Opinion Quarterly* 33 (Summer 1969): 328-345.
3. Tsiyona Peled and Elihu Katz, "Media Functions in Wartime: The Israel Home Front in October 1973," in Jay G. Blumler and Elihu Katz, eds., *The Uses of Mass Communications: Current Perspectives on Gratifications Research* (Beverly Hills, Calif.: Sage, 1974), pp. 49-69.
4. The incidents are reported in Jerry J. Waxman, "Local Broadcast Gatekeeping During Natural Disasters," *Journalism Quarterly* 50 (Winter 1973): 751-758 and Russell R. Dynes, *Organized Behavior in Disaster* (Lexington, Mass.: D. C. Heath, 1970), pp. 41-43, 88-89, 127-128.
5. Daniel Yutzy, *Community Priorities at the Anchorage, Alaska Earthquake, 1964* (Columbus, Ohio: Ohio State University Disaster Research Center, 1969), p. 127.
6. Schramm, "Communication in Crisis," pp. 1-25.
7. T. Joseph Scanlon, "Media Coverage of Crises: Better than Reported, Worse than Necessary," *Journalism Quarterly* 55 (Spring 1978): 68-72.
8. Deidre Carmody, "News Media Defended in Inquiry on Reports of Three Mile Island," *New York Times*, Oct. 31, 1979; Peter Sandman and Mary Paden, "At Three Mile Island," *Columbia Journalism Review* (July/August 1979): 43-58.
9. Dynes, *Organized Behavior in Disaster*, pp. 127-218.
10. Paletz and Dunn, "Press Coverage of Civil Disorder," p. 329.
11. Benjamin D. Singer, "Mass Media and Communication Processes in the Detroit Riot of 1967," *Public Opinion Quarterly* 34 (Summer 1970): 236-245.
12. Ibid., p. 238.
13. Rodney M. Kueneman and Joseph E. Wright, "News Policies of Broadcast Stations for Civil Disturbances and Disasters," *Journalism Quarterly* 52 (Winter 1975): 670-677.

14. Ibid., 672.
15. See the report on the work of the Disaster Research Center at Ohio State University reported in E. L. Quarantelli and Russell R. Dynes, eds., "Organizational and Group Behavior in Disasters," *American Behavioral Scientist* 13 (January 1970): 325-456.
16. *New Yorker,* August 15, 1977, p. 21.
17. Quoted in Paletz and Dunn, "Press Coverage of Civil Disorder, p. 336.

READINGS

Dynes, Russell R. *Organized Behavior in Disaster.* Lexington, Mass.: D. C. Heath, 1970.

Greenberg, Bradley S., and Parker, Edwin B. *The Kennedy Assassination and the American Public: Social Communication in Crisis.* Palo Alto, Calif.: Stanford University Press, 1965.

Tichenor, Phillip J.; Donohue, George A.; and Olien, Clarice N. *Community Conflict and the Press.* Beverly Hills, Calif.: Sage, 1980.

Yutzy, Daniel. *Community Priorities at the Anchorage, Alaska Earthquake, 1964.* Columbus, Ohio: Ohio State University Disaster Research Center, 1969.

9

Foreign Affairs Coverage

After eight years of acrimonious debate and many months of intensive negotiations, the 146 states who are members of UNESCO, including the United States, finally endorsed a Declaration on the Media on
November 22, 1978. The document consists of 11 brief articles and bears
the rather pompous full title, "The Declaration of Fundamental Principles Concerning the Contribution of the Mass Media to Strengthening
Peace and International Understanding, the Promotion of Human
Rights and to Countering Racialism, Apartheid, and Incitement to
War." Article III is typical in mapping out a wide area of political
responsibility for the mass media. It states that, "the mass media, by
disseminating information on the aims, aspirations, cultures and needs
of all people, contribute to eliminate ignorance and misunderstanding
between peoples." The media also "make nationals of a country sensitive to the needs and desires of others," thereby ensuring "the respect
of the rights and dignity of all nations, all peoples and all individuals."
By drawing "attention to the great evils which afflict humanity, such as
poverty, malnutrition and diseases," the media promote "the formulation by states of policies best able to promote the reduction of international tension and the peaceful and equitable settlement of international
disputes." A tall order: Can and do American media fill it? How are they
organized to do the job?

To throw light on such questions, we shall discuss the significance
which American media and Americans assign to news about foreign
countries overall. We shall also examine the types of foreign news most
common in American media. Foreign news gathering is quite different
from domestic reporting, so we shall consider the qualifications of foreign correspondents and the unique problems they face. Partly as a result of these problems, and partly because news about foreign countries
reflects American foreign policy interests, the world image as seen
through the American media is often distorted. We shall look at a number of examples and assess their consequences for American foreign
policymaking. Finally, we shall compare the American performance
with the high hopes UNESCO has for the press.

THE FOREIGN NEWS SLICE IN THE NEWS PIE

Newspeople and social scientists commonly assume that the American public is highly ethnocentric, interested primarily in what goes on in the United States. Newspaper and broadcast news editors routinely judge audience interest in foreign news to be below interest in local and national news, sports, and comics. Americans themselves profess somewhat greater interest but their claims are not matched by their behavior.[1]

A number of studies have confirmed the accuracy of the ethnocentrism assumption. For instance, when the *Indianapolis News* polled readers and editors, asking them to name the top ten stories in 1976, no foreign stories were mentioned by the readers. The editors, on the other hand, ranked six foreign affairs stories among the top ten. These included such major events as political changes in China, conflict in southern Africa, civil war in Lebanon, the murder of two United States soldiers by North Koreans, CIA foreign activities, and several earthquakes in foreign countries.[2]

The assumption of limited interest has put a heavy damper on foreign affairs news coverage. On an average, it constitutes only 11 percent of all stories in American newspapers, and about 16 percent of the stories on national newscasts. By contrast, foreign affairs news takes up 17 percent of the newspaper space in Russian papers, 23 percent of the space in the press of Third World countries, 24 percent in Western European papers, and 38 percent in papers in Eastern European countries. Foreign affairs coverage is limited even in American elite newspapers. For instance, in 1970, only 16 percent of the *New York Times* coverage was devoted to foreign affairs, compared to 22 percent in the *London Times,* 25 percent in the *Times of India,* 38 percent in Soviet *Pravda,* and 44 percent in the German *Die Welt.*[3]

Besides being limited in number, foreign news stories generally receive comparatively brief space and time and modest display. The standards which lead to publication for foreign news items are more rigorous than is true for domestic news. Foreign news must be more important, involve people of more exalted status, and entail more violence or disaster, for instance.

While interest in foreign affairs is limited, it does wax and wane with the political currents. It was exceptionally high during the Vietnam War, peaked in various Mideast crises, and crested during presidential trips to China, but ebbed sharply thereafter until the Iranian hostage crisis in early 1980.

Declining interest in foreign news is generally reflected in a drop in the number of foreign correspondents. There were 637 accredited correspondents in South Vietnam in 1968. As the war drew to a close, this dropped to 392 by 1970, and 295 in 1972. By mid-1974, there were only 35. Even though this small corps of correspondents filed relatively few stories from Vietnam, it became difficult to induce editors to use them in daily newscasts and papers because the public had presumably lost interest. When this happens, a spiral effect sets in. Presumed lack of interest leads to less coverage. Inadequate coverage further lessens interest in foreign news. An upward spiral of domestic news takes up the slack. This pattern prevails in most of the country's newspapers and television newscasts whenever foreign crises subside.

Compared to average papers and newscasts, prestige papers like the *New York Times,* the *Washington Post,* and the *Los Angeles Times* provide fairly extensive, thorough, and steady foreign affairs coverage. The country's foreign policy elites, including government officials, depend heavily on these media. A comment from a State Department official is typical: "The first thing we do is read the newspaper — *the newspaper* — the *New York Times.* You can't work in the State Department without the *New York Times.*"[4] Members of the U.S. Congress and foreign officials in the United States, particularly those concerned with foreign affairs, have made similar comments. All feel that elite newspaper reports keep them informed faster and often better than their own official sources.

What foreign affairs topics are most likely to be featured in the American press? Sociologist Herbert Gans, who examined foreign affairs news in television newscasts and in news magazines, has compiled a list of seven subjects that are most often aired.[5] They include, first, American activities in foreign countries, particularly when presidents and secretaries of state visit there. Second, foreign events receive attention when they affect Americans directly in a major way. Wars or oil embargoes are examples, along with foreign problems that replicate American problems like unemployment and inflation.

A third area of interest concerns relations of the United States with communist countries. Internal problems of these countries which relate to their political and military power are emphasized. Elections in noncommunist countries where strong Communist parties are involved, such as those in France and Italy, are also part of the routine coverage of the "communist menace." Fourth, foreign elections are covered in other parts of the world if they involve a change in the head of state. There also is a sentimental attachment for following the major activities of European royalty.

In the fifth place are stories about dramatic political conflicts. Most wars, coups d'état, and revolutions are reported; protests, as a rule, are covered only when they are violent. Left-wing coups receive more attention than right-wing coups. Disasters are a sixth area of interest, if they involve massive loss of lives and destruction of property. There is a rough calculus by which severity is measured: "10,000 deaths in Nepal equals 100 deaths in Wales equals 10 deaths in West Virginia equals one death next door."[6] In general, the more distant a nation, the more frequently a newsworthy event must happen to be reported.

The seventh area of coverage involves the excesses of foreign dictators, particularly when they entail brutality against political dissidents. The deeds of Uganda's Idi Amin and Vietnam's Nguyen Cao Ky are examples of such news.[7] Noticeably absent from American broadcasts and papers are stories about ordinary people and ordinary events abroad. These would be new to Americans, but, except for occasional special features, are not "news" in the professional dictionary of journalists.

MAKING FOREIGN NEWS

There are many similarities between newsmaking for domestic stories and newsmaking for foreign stories. To make comparisons easy, we will follow the sequence of discussion used in Chapter 3. We shall begin by looking at the corps of foreign correspondents who are the front-line echelon among foreign affairs news gatekeepers.

The Gatekeepers

Concentration of Control. A striking aspect of foreign news coverage is the extreme degree of concentration of the newsgathering process. Most foreign news for the American press is collected by only seven newspapers, the two wire services, and the three national television networks, along with an occasional story from syndicated columnists and news feature services. The papers are the *New York Times, Washington Post, Los Angeles Times, Baltimore Sun, Chicago Tribune, Wall Street Journal,* and *Christian Science Monitor.*[8]

Most coverage comes from the wire services. They ferret out the stories that make up the pool from which other gatekeepers select complete reports or find leads to pursue stories more fully. Because wire service reporters work for a vast variety of clients — UPI alone goes to 113 countries in 48 languages — their news must be bland. It emphasizes fast reporting of dramatic events, not interpretation. Interpretation and follow-up depend on other foreign correspondents.

The stories gathered by the small corps of initial gatekeepers reach a huge audience. In the mid-1970s, the *New York Times* syndicate supplied news for 330 papers in the United States and 97 abroad; the *Los Angeles Times-Washington Post* feature service supplied 290 papers in the United States and 60 abroad.[9] Subscribers generally use only a limited portion of the coverage made available by the syndicates. But what they use mirrors the interpretation of the pace-setting foreign news sources. For instance, when the *New York Times* labelled a 1958 Soviet note to Britain, France, and the United States as an "ultimatum," the American press almost universally followed the lead, even though the facts were questionable and some papers had originally adopted different interpretations.[10] "Once the main stories of the day have been identified and defined, the media can be like a stampeding herd, hard to turn toward a new interpretation of an issue." The stories chosen set the scene for follow-up stories. "The news of today sequels the news of yesterday. Only a relatively small number of journalists are able or allowed to open up new areas of concern."[11] Stereotypes become fixed; countries and leaders whom gatekeepers depict as friendly or antagonistic to the United States may retain their images long after the reality is quite different.

Surveillance of the Foreign Scene. In 1975, 676 full-time overseas correspondents served the American media, including 429 Americans and 247 foreigners. Six years earlier, there had been 929 foreign correspondents, including 563 Americans and 366 foreigners. There was thus a 27 percent decline in the foreign correspondent corps between 1969 and 1975.[12] Several reasons account for the drop in numbers. The winding down of the Vietnam War is one. The ability to dispatch correspondents quickly from an American home base to foreign countries is another. Air travel has made it possible for each American correspondent to reach and cover many more countries than ever before. However, physical mobility is not matched by the psychic mobility that would allow reporters to feel at home in more countries. Nor is it accompanied by sudden spurts in knowledge that would allow reporters to cover a new area with insight.

Table 9-1 Distribution of Foreign Correspondents in 1975

	Distribution of Americans		(Origin of Foreigners Covering U.S.)	
	N	%	N	%
Western Europe	345	51	(465)	(54)
Central/East Asia	155	23	(132)	(15)
Latin America	101	15	(77)	(9)
Middle East	54	8	(53)	(6)
Africa	34	5	(8)	(1)
East Europe, USSR	20	3	(46)	(5)
Australia/New Zealand	13	2	(33)	(4)
Canada	7	1	(42)	(5)
Worldwide	—	—	(9)	(1)

N = Americans covering foreign countries = 676; Foreigners covering U.S. = 865. Figures add to more than 100% because some correspondents cover more than one area. (Figures for foreigners covering the U.S. have been added for comparison.)

SOURCES: Foreign data from Hamid Mowlana, "Who Covers America?" *Journal of Communication* 25 (Summer 1975): 87; U.S. data from John A. Lent, "Foreign News in American Media," *Journal of Communication* 27 (Winter 1977): 49.

High costs have also led to reduced numbers. In the late 1970s, it cost up to $150,000 a year to keep one correspondent abroad, a steep price considering the limited demand for foreign affairs stories. It was much cheaper to use stringers instead of regular employees. Stringers usually are foreigners who live abroad and are paid for each story they produce.[13]

Correspondents are unevenly distributed. More are stationed in friendly countries and areas than in neutral or hostile ones. Table 9-1 tells the story. Two-thirds of the Middle East correspondents were stationed in Israel and Lebanon, for instance. Correspondents accredited to Western Hemisphere countries served primarily Canada, Brazil, and Argentina. Asian correspondents were concentrated in Hong Kong, Japan and Australia. Africa was the most understaffed, with full-time reporters in only four countries. However, their reports were supplemented through news from Reuters and Agence France-Presse, the British and French news agencies, which had more ample representation in Africa. With the decline in the numbers of foreign correspondents, the number of countries in which newsmen were stationed had narrowed as well. In 1972, 64 countries had one or more American journalists, but by 1975 this had dropped to 54 countries.

What kinds of people are these journalists who select the foreign news for American elites and publics? What are their biases? And how do they compare with the correspondents who cover the United States for the benefit of foreign nationals?

A typical American journalist abroad is a white male in his forties, college educated, with more than ten years of foreign news reporting under his belt. Many have remained at the same locations for several years, so that they are fully familiar with their areas.[14] As Table 9-2 shows, however, this does not necessarily mean language competence. In Latin America and Western Europe, reading and speaking competence with native or easy fluency exceeds 80 percent. In Eastern Europe and Africa, these figures are cut in half. The poorest showing is in Central and East Asia, where only 9 percent are able to read the intricate written characters and only 18 percent can speak the languages well. Deficient reading and speaking skills hamper American reporters in local interviews and investigations. They must depend on translated newspaper reports and on handouts to the foreign press. This sharply curbs their effectiveness as reporters.

Contacts with local people and personal ties which may supply good insights are also sparse. In Western Europe, 33 percent of the correspondents say that most of their close friendships and social contacts are with nationals of the country. In Latin America, this is true for 23 percent. The figure drops to 16 percent for Eastern Europe and 15 percent for Central and East Asia.[15] When more casual contacts are added, these figures double, but they still spell a gap in integration into the local setting.

Table 9-2 Foreign Language Fluency of American Reporters

	Western Europe		*Latin America*		*Asia*		*East Europe, Africa Middle East*	
	Read	*Speak*	*Read*	*Speak*	*Read*	*Speak*	*Read*	*Speak*
Native Fluency	62%	51%	70%	56%	3%	6%	21%	20%
Easy Facility	23	31	19	30	6	12	17	28
Partial	10	16	11	14	23	33	28	32
Slight	3	2	—	—	3	15	10	8
None	1	—	—	—	65	33	24	12

N = 174. The question was, [If English is not the local language] "How familiar are you with the language spoken in the country in which you are stationed?"

SOURCE: Adapted from Leo Bogart, "The Overseas Newsman: A 1967 Profile Study," *Journalism Quarterly* 45 (Summer 1968): 300.

By their own identification, 54 percent of American foreign correspondents lean to the left in their politics, 32 percent are middle roaders, and 14 percent consider themselves as leaning to the right. These figures closely parallel those for staff people generally in prominent American news organizations.[16]

Surveillance of the American Scene. Altogether, there were 865 correspondents from foreign countries covering the United States in 1975. As Table 9-1 shows, most of them came from nations friendly to the United States. Just as Americans receive scanty news about countries outside their friendship circle, so foreigners outside this circle receive scanty news about the United States.[17] Representation varies widely among regions as well as countries. The foreign press corps included no correspondents from black Africa. Israel was represented by 23 correspondents while the Middle Eastern Arab countries combined had only 13 journalists, including 3 from Egypt. Taiwan in 1975 had 23 registered correspondents while the People's Republic of China had none. India was represented by 10 newspeople, Pakistan by one. Canada's media sent 43, compared to 8 from Mexico, the other next-door neighbor of the United States. With the exception of Argentina and Brazil, few Latin American countries had correspondents stationed in the United States.

Foreign reporters are an extremely well-educated group. About half have advanced degrees and 13 percent have Ph.Ds. On the average, they speak three languages. Close contacts with Americans were nonetheless limited. Only 7 percent said that their best and closest contacts were Americans. In political orientation, foreign newspeople covering the

United States are further to the left than most American reporters. Seventy percent claim to be left-leaning, 14 percent prefer a middle position, and 17 percent lean to the right.[18]

It is difficult for foreign reporters to cover the United States adequately. Most correspondents are kept busy in Washington and New York. They rarely get into other parts of the country, except for spectacular events like a moon shot in Florida or a political convention in Kansas City. Thus the impressions that people in other countries receive about Americans, their views, and their policies, are largely official Washington views. The leftward orientation of most reporters produces a substantial amount of criticism of the American economic scene and interventionist foreign ventures and often makes the conduct of foreign relations rocky. Hostile coverage is only partially balanced by influx of news from American media and government broadcasts, like those of the Voice of America.

The Setting for News Selection

Cultural Pressures. As is true in covering domestic news, American correspondents abroad must operate within the context of current American politics and current American political culture. Though their own leanings may be to the left of the political spectrum, they aim for the middle ground in their stories because that is what their audiences presumably want. Keeping in touch with the American scene is deemed so important that news organizations bring their reporters back to the United States periodically to refresh their feel for the American setting.

Stories must not only reflect the American value structure, but also must conform to established American stereotypes. It is easy to place stories about a German beer festival or German war crimes because they involve well-accepted images. But tales about vodka-drinking Germans or humane Nazis would strain credibility. Stories about the problems of German youth would also risk rejection unless the problems are shared by American youth.[19] On the other hand, foreign correspondents have greater leeway than their domestic counterparts to make evaluations and interpretations because there is less concern about possibly offending foreigners than about offending domestic interest groups.

Intra-organizational norms and pressures also influence news selection. The news is gathered by a small enough group of reporters so that personal contact and cooperation are common. The wire services perform the initial gatekeeping tasks for most newspapers and electronic media. Elite papers, like the *New York Times,* then fashion the norms for presentation and interpretation which editors and reporters throughout the country adapt for their media.

Political Pressures. Overt and covert political pressures play a greater role in foreign news production than on the domestic scene. Pressures are negative — to refrain from covering certain stories, as well as positive — to give publicity which might otherwise be denied. Foreign correspondents are more or less welcome guests in the countries from which they are reporting and often must do their hosts' bidding. Many of these hosts are dictators whose political survival depends on assuring supportive coverage for their regimes and squelching unfavorable coverage. Their own newspeople are heavily censored and they treat foreigners the same. If foreign correspondents want to remain in the country, they must write dispatches acceptable to the authorities. Otherwise they face severe penalties, expulsion, confiscation of their notes and pictures, closure of transmission facilities, refusal of contact by public officials, and the like. This has led to the strange phenomenon that the most totalitarian countries often receive the least criticism while more open societies are freely attacked.

Censorship can also take the form of denying visas. In 1975 alone, visa denials were reported from 21 countries. Some countries, such as Cambodia, Laos, and Vietnam, have completely shut out all foreign reporters for years on end. Expulsions of reporters are also common.[20] Reporters may also be prevented from covering certain stories. When the Chinese city of Tangshan was destroyed by an earthquake on July 28, 1976, and more than 655,000 people were killed, reporters stationed in Peking, barely 100 miles away, were denied permission for more than a year to visit the scene.[21] At the height of the Angolan war, reporters were kept out of the battle areas and permitted to send out only official government communiqués. South Africa has made it illegal to quote "banned" people or to describe prison conditions. Elsewhere, reporters who interview dissidents are harassed.

Bureaucratic hurdles abound. In Moscow, television reporters depend on the Novosti Press Agency for camera crews and access to various sites. Cameras are made available only after a story proposal has been approved by the Foreign Ministry's Press Department. Once a proposal has been filed, no deviations are allowed. Promised camera crews frequently arrive late or not at all. Pictures often are deliberately out of focus, and transmission equipment may be disconnected if events do not proceed as planned. Reporters may even be in physical danger. They have been jailed and manhandled on many occasions in various countries and occasionally murdered. In the Nicaraguan revolution of 1979, for instance, a National Guardsman, angry over American support of revolutionary forces, shot and killed an American television reporter. The Helsinki Accords of 1975, in which many countries promised free and safe access to each other's newspeople, have done little to improve the situation.

When previously closed countries suddenly open their borders to newspeople, the foreign press may be totally unprepared to cover the area adequately. The opening of the People's Republic of China in 1972 is an example. Reporters arrived with President Nixon and Secretary of

State Henry Kissinger. During their short stay in China, they dutifully shot those pictures that the Chinese allowed them to shoot and reported those stories that the Chinese arranged for them to report. The resulting coverage was a romanticized travelogue, rather than solid political analysis.

Media Diplomacy. A recent development in foreign news production is "Television Diplomacy." It involves attempts by television correspondents in the United States and abroad to inject themselves directly into the political process and attempts by foreign leaders to use television to further their causes.

In 1979, for instance, Iran rebuffed official emissaries from the United States sent to negotiate the release of American embassy personnel held hostage by Iranian students. Instead, Iran's revolutionary leader, Ayatollah Ruhollah Khomeini, agreed to meet American television correspondents to discuss the situation with them. The upshot was a series of interviews, carefully controlled by the Iranian government by requiring prior approval of questions. To assure maximum exposure for the Ayatollah's views, Iranian leaders permitted an especially lengthy interview for the highly popular "60 Minutes" program. At the same time, they assigned low priority to an interview to be aired on low-audience public television. The Iranian embassy also bought full-page

Reprinted, courtesy of the *Chicago Tribune*

advertisements in the *New York Times* and other American newspapers to acquaint the American public with Iran's version of the hostage story. For their part, reporters used interviews with Iranian officials to suggest policies which might resolve the crisis and to elicit Iranian views and counterproposals. Placing these views before a worldwide audience made them part of the agenda of international politics.

The Middle East situation in the late 1970s also presents a number of dramatic examples. CBS anchorman Walter Cronkite became a peacemaker on November 14, 1977, during a television satellite interview, when he drew from Egypt's President Anwar el Sadat a public promise to go to Jerusalem if this would further peace. In a separate interview, Cronkite secured a pledge from Israeli Prime Minister Menachem Begin that he would personally welcome Sadat at Ben Gurion airport, should he come. With such mutual commitments, the scene was set for the historic meeting.

When Sadat arrived in Israel on November 19, anchorpersons from the three American networks were in his entourage. Among the welcoming crowds at the airport were an additional 2,000 journalists from all over the globe. Again, this was open diplomacy in the broadest sense. The event was covered live on American television and radio, giving the principals a chance to woo American television audiences. In the weeks to come, more than 30 million Americans and millions of other people throughout the world would watch and judge the peacemaking process. Television alone devoted 24 hours of broadcasts to the spectacle, supplemented by radio and print news.

Such "media diplomacy" continued when the peacemaking scene moved to the United States in the following spring. President Sadat made himself available for a televised interview immediately after arrival for the 1978 Camp David meeting. The next day he appeared before the National Press Club for a public address in which he accused the Israelis of stalling the negotiations. Israel promptly dispatched Foreign Minister Moshe Dayan on a ten-day speaking tour of major American cities to gather publicity for the Israeli side.[22] The media covered it all with relish, proud of the role newspeople had played in bringing about encounters between Israeli and Egyptian officials.

Economic Pressures. Last but not least, economic considerations of two kinds have a strong impact on news selection. There is the usual pressure to present appealing stories that attract wide audiences and keep the media profitable. This pressure is even more burdensome for foreign correspondents than for their domestic counterparts because their stories must be exceptionally good to attract large audiences. There is also the pressure to avoid or minimize huge production costs. Reporting events such as President Nixon's trip to China, or the Yom Kippur war, cost each of the networks in excess of $3 million in each case. Leasing cables for news transmission is expensive and so is telephone communication. Satellite transmission is also costly, especially for short messages. Networks therefore normally avoid satellites unless they have several important stories to transmit. Networks may pool stories to save on transmission expenses. In the process, some stories may be shut out because they cannot be transmitted cheaply and quickly while others may be included merely because they happened while satellites were in use.

Gathering the News — The Beat

On the international level, the beat system is quite similar to local beats. Originally newspapers established their foreign news bureaus in major capitals of the world, primarily in Western Europe. From there, correspondents covered entire countries, rather than particular types of stories; London, Paris, Bonn, and Rome were the main newsgathering spots. In the wake of the Vietnam War Saigon and other Far Eastern points like Tokyo and Hong Kong became important news centers. Now China is moving into focus.

The average newspaper bureau abroad has one or two correspondents, one or two film crews staffed by foreigners, perhaps a radio correspondent, and a few stringers. Correspondents from these bureaus jet to spots within easy flying range whenever the need arises. For local news, they rely heavily on national news services which exist in two-thirds of the countries of the world. Countries without such services, and without satellite transmission facilities, are far less likely to receive coverage than countries which have such facilities.

The major Western news agencies and the three American television networks have overseas news bureaus in the main news centers of the world. However, the networks rely heavily on the wire and newspaper services for nonvisual news. Seventy to 80 percent of foreign news copy read on the air comes directly from the wire services.[23] In this way "the major international news agencies and elite newspapers set the agenda for international affairs coverage by other media, including U.S. network television."[24]

The bulk of foreign affairs news for American media actually originates in Washington from various beats in the executive branch. Such stories may be hard to get because officials are reluctant to discuss foreign affairs whenever delicate negotiations or the prestige of the United States are at stake. A further common drawback to Washington stories is their lack of exciting pictures to dramatize them for television. As in domestic news, foreign correspondents prefer predictable stories like elections or summit conferences so that reporting can be planned well in advance. The decision to film particular foreign stories abroad is usually made in New York because officials there consider themselves in closer touch with the interests of American audiences, but foreign bureaus do the actual filming.

Foreign news bestows unequal attention on various countries, just as domestic news covers regions of the United States unequally. There is no correspondence, either, between size of population and amount of coverage.[25] In general, beats cover America's closest political allies and the major communist countries. Specifically, this means England, France, West Germany, Italy, and the Soviet Union in Europe; Israel and Egypt in the Middle East; and, more recently, the People's Republic of China and Japan in the Far East. Africa and Latin America are lightly covered. Asian coverage was light until the Vietnam War, when, for several years, it replaced most stories from other parts of the world.

Criteria for Choosing Stories

As is true of domestic stories, particular foreign news items are selected for audience appeal primarily, rather than political significance. As the story list on page 245 shows, this means that they must have an American angle and must deal with subjects with which Americans are deeply concerned. They also must have an appealing format. Emphasis on violence, conflict and disaster, timeliness or novelty, and familiarity of person or situation are the major selection criteria. For instance, stories from Western Europe and other culturally related areas are more likely to be published than stories from other parts of the world. When news from countries with unfamiliar cultural settings is published, the rule of "uncertainty absorption" comes into play. This unwritten rule requires that questionable information coming from remote sources must be eliminated at every stage of the gatekeeping process.[26] The impact of such cumulative biases makes it very difficult to change images of exotic countries. Stories from distant parts of the world are covered solely if they report highly exciting events such as violence and disaster, or involve major events and personalities, preferably in a negative context.[27]

An example of how story acceptability varies when proximity, familiarity, and violence scores are balanced against each other occurred in August 1979, when the roof of a sports arena under construction in Chicago collapsed. Five construction workers were crushed to death. The story took up better than half of the front page of the *Chicago Tribune,* with a massive picture, measuring 8 by 12 inches, and a total of 90 column inches of text, 20 of them on the front page alone, and three additional pictures on later pages. On the same day, a dam collapsed in Morvi, a town of 60,000 people in India. The ensuing flood demolished most of the town. An estimated 1,000 people were killed and speculations were that the death toll might rise to 15,000. That story was printed on page 9, under a headline one-fifth the size of the Chicago story. There were no pictures and the entire story took up seven column inches.[28]

The need to produce stories which are timely has led to concentration on rapidly breaking news in accessible places, regardless of its intrinsic importance. Long-range developments like programs to improve public health or reduce illiteracy or develop new political parties do not fill the bill. Pressure for timeliness and novelty also makes news presentation fragmented, with little follow-through. This gives major events an unwarranted air of suddenness and unpredictability.

News Production Constraints

The production problems for newsmaking on the domestic scene are magnified for foreign newsmaking. Staffs are smaller, research facilities are more limited, language barriers are troublesome, and transmission difficulties may be enormous. When the story reaches the audience, it must often overcome basic disinterest as well as ignorance of the setting in which it originated.

Production constraints are particularly severe for television news, which presents the bulk of foreign news to the average American. The quest for good pictures is often frustrated by restrictions on access or because facilities for taking and processing pictures are inadequate.[29] Pictures are important in providing insight into foreign affairs because they bring unfamiliar sights, which might be hard to imagine, directly into viewers' homes. Starvation in India or Nicaragua, the life style of primitive tribes in New Guinea or Australia, or street riots in Spain or Hungary are better understood if they can be visually experienced, along with supporting text.

Even words and pictures combined cannot tell the whole story if the audience is unfamiliar with the setting in which the reported events are happening. When television news showed Buddhists rioting in Saigon and Da Nang during the Vietnam War, "The pictures could not show you that a block away from the Saigon riots the populace was shopping, chatting, sitting in restaurants in total normalcy. The riots involved a tiny proportion in either city; yet the effect of the pictures in this country, including the Congress, was explosive. People thought that Vietnam was tearing itself apart, that civil war was raging. Nothing of the sort was happening."[30]

The need to keep news stories brief is particularly troubling for foreign correspondents because foreign news is often unintelligible without adequate background information and interpretation. Complexity therefore becomes a major enemy, and avoidance or oversimplification, the defensive strategy. Stories must be written simply and logically even if the situation defies logic. Usually a single theme must represent the complex story.

For instance, in January 1972 British Prime Minister Edward Heath went to Brussels to sign an agreement to bring Britain into the Common Market.[31] A four-minute mini-documentary devoted one minute and thirty seconds to the signing ceremony, explaining that Britain and three other countries were beginning a period of integration into the market. The remaining two minutes and thirty seconds were used to explain why agricultural products created the greatest stumbling block to Britain's entry. Pictures of horse and plow farmers in France and more mechanized farming elsewhere were used as backdrops. The basic theme was that each country was trying to protect its own farmers while keeping the price of farm products low for consumers. This was a gross oversimplification of the highly complex issues involved in Britain's entry, but it made an appealing story, comprehensible to the average listener and viewer.

Effects of Gatekeeping

The various gatekeeping factors result in foreign affairs coverage that lacks depth and breadth, that emphasizes the simplest of themes, and that may distort facts in the interest of timeliness. The stories that preceded United States intervention in the Dominican Republic in 1965 are a case in point.

The Dominican Republic Case. When dispatches reached the United States in late April and early May 1965 that a military coup was in progress in the Dominican Republic, American correspondents were hastily dispatched to the scene. Upon arrival, they were not allowed to visit the cities and countryside because of the military activities. Instead, they received a briefing from the American ambassador based on second-hand information. Because of the pressure to meet the earliest publication deadlines, stories were sent out before they could be verified. Since they had come from an authentic source, no disclaimers were made.

The *Los Angeles Herald Examiner* reported on April 30 that Cuban communists had arranged the insurrection and that the loss of life was horrifying. "There are about 2,000 casualties, and about half of them are dead. In one street alone, there were at least 90 people dead or dying. There are children dying on the streets with their stomachs ripped open, and nobody to bury their bodies. It is carnage. It is real civil war. The streets are almost literally running with blood."[32] One week later, on May 7, *Time* magazine still reported that "No one had an accurate count of the casualties as frenzied knots of soldiers and civilians roamed the streets, shooting, looting and herding people to their execution. . . . The rebels executed at least 110 opponents, hacked the head off a police officer and carried it about as a trophy." *U.S. News & World Report* on May 10 spoke of victims being "dragged from their homes and shot down while angry mobs shouted, 'To the wall!' — the same cry that marked the mass executions in Cuba in the early days of Fidel Castro."[33]

On the basis of such reports, President Lyndon Johnson, with the approval of the Organization of American States, sent more than 1,000 Marines to the Dominican Republic to quell the rebellion, stop the bloodshed, and halt the march of communism. When the correspondents were finally allowed to visit the cities and countryside, they discovered that none of the stories which they had reported were true. Instead of the 1,000 to 1,500 bodies which, according to President Johnson, had made the intervention imperative, there were fewer than a dozen. There was no looting either, and no display of severed heads. Only a small number of the forces seeking to overthrow the established government were communists. But by that time it was too late to undo the severe political damage done to the Dominican Republic and to the reputation of the United States.

Stereotyping the Cuban Revolution. Stress on the culturally familiar and acceptable not only leads to serious neglect of many areas of the world, but also to stereotyped judgments about foreign political systems. Once a system becomes labeled as communist or communist-dominated, stories focus on its difficulties, often exaggerating them, and neglecting its good points. Faulty policy decisions are a likely outcome. A graphic example comes from media coverage of Cuban affairs in the period before the disastrous United States-supported Bay of Pigs invasion to overthrow Fidel Castro.[34]

The Cuban revolution had received unfavorable comment in the United States almost from its start in January 1959. By November 1960, according to American press reports, the Castro government was in deep trouble. Anti-Castro guerrillas were fighting inside Cuba. Dissidents were fleeing the country and some had been executed. The U.S. press also reported repeatedly that Castro could be easily overthrown by exile groups eager, willing, and able to do so.

The negative publicity was not balanced by stories about social and economic improvements in Cuba in the wake of the revolution. A content analysis of the *New York Times, Chicago Tribune, Time, U.S. News & World Report,* and the official *State Department Bulletin* between November 1, 1960 and May 1, 1961 disclosed no mention of Cuba's massive program to combat illiteracy or improve medical care for the poor. Instead, the press was highlighting communist infiltration of the Cuban revolution, attempts to export it to other Latin American countries, executions and expropriations, defections, and mounting international opposition.

When the content of the five publications was rated on a 5-point scale, ranging from full opposition to Cuba to full support, the mean rating averaged 4.5. It barely missed a totally negative 5-point score. Table 9-3 presents the results. Government officials and citizens who read such stories in prestigious publications could readily deduce that the Cuban regime was vulnerable to attack because it was totally evil, rejected by its own people, and a menace to the United States and other countries. Such thinking made the Bay of Pigs intervention seem logical.

Many of the stories reported by the media were correct, of course. But many others were distorted and exaggerated to conform to existing

Table 9-3 Support of the Cuban Revolution in U.S. News Stories, November 1, 1960-May 1, 1961

	Full Support	*Part Support*	*Neutral*	*Part Opposition*	*Full Opposition*
New York Times	8%	1%	19%	23%	49%
Chicago Tribune	2	2	11	45	41
Time	—	—	15	3	82
U.S. News & World Report	—	—	8	28	64
Department of State Bulletin	—	—	9	—	91

N = 334 for *New York Times;* 241 for *Chicago Tribune;* 33 for *Time;* 83 for *U.S. News;* 36 for *Department of State Bulletin.*

Adapted from Jon D. Cozean, "Profile of U.S. Press Coverage in Cuba: Was the Bay of Pigs Necessary?"*Journal of International and Comparative Studies* 5 (Winter 1972): 34-35.

stereotypes. The absence of stories about positive achievements ob-scured the existence of likely sources of support for Castro. Problems of inaccurate media images are not unique to the United States, of course. Cuba's press was a mirror image of the U.S. press in presenting a highly negative image of the United States.

Distortions and Their Consequences. Just like domestic news, for-eign news neglects major social problems, particularly political and eco-nomic development issues. In 1977, only 11 percent of foreign affairs cov-erage dealt with such matters.[35] The reasons are readily apparent. Such problems are difficult to describe in brief stories, visual materials are of-ten lacking, and changes come at a glacial pace. Some of them, like the story of the European Common Market, are extremely complex. Most reporters are ill-equipped to understand, let alone describe them. When they do describe them, the focus is on their dramatic negative aspects: shortages, famines, conflicts, and breakdowns. As Rafael Caldera, former president of Venezuela, told a press conference at the National Press Club in 1970 in Washington, D.C., "the phrase 'no news is good news' has become 'good news is no news'. . . . Little or nothing is men-tioned about literary or scientific achievements," in American media or "about social achievements and the defense against the dangers which threaten our peace and development." Instead, "only the most deplor-able incidents, be they caused by nature or by man, receive prominent attention."[36]

Negative and conflictual news is more important in the United States than in many other societies. A study by George Gerbner demonstrates the difference. Gerbner compared coverage of United Nations news in the *New York Times* with a major Hungarian newspaper, *Nepszabadsag,* for one month in 1960.[37] He found that in the *New York Times,* 12 percent of the U.N. stories dealt with substantive issues and 88 percent with procedural strategies and conflicts. In the Hungarian paper, the figures were 32 and 68 percent, respectively. In the *New York Times,* 4 percent of the stories reported agreement among U.N. members, and 52 percent reported conflict. Thirty-six percent were neutral. By contrast, 39 percent of the stories in the Hungarian paper reported agreement, 7 percent reported conflict, and 54 percent were neutral.

Gerbner's findings agree with results from other investigations. The Canadian television news violence rate, for example, is half the U.S. rate. Newsworthiness criteria in the United States apparently differ from the criteria used widely elsewhere in the world.[38] Many foreign news organizations may find it comparatively easy to shun dramatic negative news because governmental subsidies relieve them of the need to secure large audiences.

Regardless of the reasons for the difference, the approach used by U.S. newspeople draws attention to conflict, rather than to peaceful settlement, and puts emphasis on procedures, rather than on the frequently duller substantive concerns. It makes most of the world outside of the United States seem chaotic. While ordinary foreign news languishes in the back pages, or is condensed into the briefest broadcast accounts, stories concerned with civil disorder and revolutions are featured prominently. Usually they are oversimplified and told from an American perspective that may be totally inappropriate. Instead of interpreting what the conflict means to the country and its people, the dominant concern ordinarily is whether the leaders are pro-West or pro-communist and how this tilt will affect the international balance of power.

Finally, the thrust of foreign news, like its domestic counterpart, provides basic support for the policies and personalities of the current American administration. The media generally accept official designations of who are America's friends and enemies and interpret their motives accordingly. When relationships change, media coverage mirrors the change. Editorials and news stories about India and the People's Republic of China provide many examples of ebbs and flows in media appraisals which matched changes in official relationships.[39]

News emphases stabilize perceptions about the international status quo. Preoccupation with the developed powers reinforces the beliefs many Americans hold about the importance of these nations. Images of less developed countries showing them incapable of managing their own internal affairs make it easy to believe that they do not deserve higher status and the media attention that accompanies it.

Support of the status quo also means that newspeople are willing to withhold news and commentary from publication when publicity would severely complicate the government's foreign policy problems.

Withholding sharp criticism of Iranian leaders during the 1979 hostage crisis to avoid angering them, and throttling information about America's breaking of Japanese military message codes during World War II are examples in which major political interests were at stake. Likewise, news of delicate negotiations among foreign countries may be temporarily withheld to avoid rocking the boat. This has happened when East and West Germans were settling scores and when the Soviet Union has expressed willingness to change course.[40]

APPRAISING THE FOREIGN NEWSMAKING PROCESS

From what we have said thus far, it is clear that foreign news in the American press does not meet the criteria which UNESCO has set out for it. It is sparse and unbalanced, focusing on the wealthier and more powerful countries. It assesses foreign countries largely in terms of U.S. interests, with little attempt to explain their culture and their concerns from their own perspective. It does not sensitize Americans to the problems of foreigners, but reinforces existing American assumptions and stereotypes instead. Major problems abroad such as hunger, disease, and poverty are ignored except when unusual disasters dramatize them temporarily.

Much of the news totally lacks a sense of history and a sense of the meaning of successive events. A good example is the widely believed story that China turned to communism because of American foreign policy failures. This interpretation ignores the long-range forces which made revolution in China inevitable. It vastly exaggerates the power of the United States to change the course of Chinese politics. The news does not even provide sufficient information to permit most Americans to understand the rationale for major foreign policies like the renegotiation of the Panama Canal treaties or the necessity for international economic cooperation.

Some stories are ignored, even if they directly involve U.S. security, until events reach crisis proportions or until there is a precipitating incident. For instance, stories about the relative military strength of the United States and the Soviet Union did not receive prominent coverage until the SALT negotiations in 1977. Before that time, news was "so spotty and lopsided that it failed to provide the essential facts for understanding U.S. defense and military issues, the Soviet definition of detente, or the forward surge in Soviet military might."[41] *New York Times'* correspondent James Reston put the problem this way:

> We are fascinated by events but not by the things that cause the events. We will send 500 correspondents to Vietnam after the war breaks out, and fill the front pages with their reports, meanwhile ignoring the rest of the world, but we will not send five reporters there when the danger of war is developing.[42]

Adds *Washington Post* assistant managing editor Phil Foisie, "We are surprised more often than we ought to be and need to be."[43] This leaves the country unprepared for twists and turns in foreign affairs that might have been foreseen and for which plans might have been made.

As with domestic news, there is also a continuous debate about whether the "right" issues have been covered in the proper way. Conservative critics complain about too much disparagement of U.S. activities to restrain communism abroad, too much sympathy for leftist regimes, and too little stress on military security. Liberal critics say the opposite.[44] Others point to distorted coverage during major foreign policy crises which, allegedly, misled the American public and harmed foreign policy. Debate about the adequacy of Vietnam War coverage has been especially heated.[45]

If one assumes that better information leads to better policies, then deficiencies in news coverage are grave. When President Carter complained that he was ill-informed about unrest in Iran prior to the overthrow of the shah in 1979, he intimated that American policymaking and public support for policies would have benefited from more accurate news. The blame in this case was put on the CIA as well as the media, which perform what has been called a "massive overt intelligence operation."[46] The Bay of Pigs story also raises questions about the chance for better policies if the media told the story more fully and avoided ideological blinders. The media's stress on conflict and on force as the solution for conflict and as a tool for conflict avoidance contributes to feelings of insecurity.

While the media are exceedingly important in providing the information base for policy formation, their explicit input into foreign policymaking is muted. When journalists give policy advice, or criticize ongoing policies, their influence is generally weaker than the position of formal government agencies. In fact, James Reston of the *New York Times* claims that press advice has great influence on American foreign policy only when things are obviously going badly, as they did in the Vietnam War.[47] When policy failures are not readily apparent and the president alleges that all is going well, contrary media claims are not likely to be believed by officials and the mass public.

EXPORTING NEWS

While the American public seems reasonably content with the foreign news which it receives, Third World countries are unhappy with the thrust of foreign news in the United States. Their disappointment about the world images presented to Americans is compounded by resentment that these images are exported to other countries. Eighty percent of the non-communist world's political and economic news comes from just four huge American enterprises — the Associated Press (AP), United Press International (UPI), the *New York Times* News Service, and the

Los Angeles Times-Washington Post News Service.[48] Most of the remainder is produced by Britain's Reuters, Agence France-Presse, and Russia's Tass. Four countries thus dominate the world's news supply.[49]

This concentration has given rise to charges of media imperialism — the dependence of domestic media systems on dominant foreign media systems.[50] Third World countries charge that Western news is not only domineering, but also corrupting for Americans, other Westerners, and Third World people. Foreign affairs journalism, according to these critics, should play an educational role in the Third World; it should inspire and mobilize people to work hard to develop their country. If freedom of the press permits and in fact fosters cynicism and dejection with the way Third World leaders manage their problems, that is deemed a luxury developing countries cannot afford at this time.[51]

Western broadcasts allegedly damage the cultural identity of poorer nations, especially those which are vulnerable because of colonial exploitation.[52] They draw people away from their own heritage and create false expectations about easily attainable affluence. Programs are designed to benefit industrial monopolies in the United States that are eager to sell their merchandise through television. They lure the rich abroad to buy luxury goods which drain their country's resources. Television entertainment programs like "Charlie's Angels," "Starsky and Hutch," or "Hawaii Five-0" contain too much violence and too many sexually explicit episodes. They corrupt young and old alike.

This Marxist interpretation of the role of the media is widely believed in the Third World. It seems quite plausible because the international news market is indeed dominated by a few giant corporations which have their headquarters in New York and other major Western cities. These organizations sell news as well as more tangible goods for profit. However, scientific proof is lacking that the Marxist interpretation of the causes and consequences of media imperialism is correct.

Early entry into the media business has given the major news producers an economic edge of size and scale which makes it well-nigh impossible for Third World nations to set up viable competing enterprises.[53] The high cost of television programming and comparatively low cost of purchasing foreign television entertainment — roughly one-fourth of the cost of original programming — has also discouraged Third World countries from creating their own television industries. Forty-five percent of the developing countries have no facilities for producing television shows. Those which do still import an average of 55 percent of their programs, particularly those shown in prime time.[54] They also rely on Western technicians and Western money for installation and maintenance.

The fact that current structures and patterns of telecommunications networks give price advantages to large producers and consumers hurts less developed countries. News transmission rates are cheaper when volume is high, making it extremely costly for poor countries to send their messages out. It also costs more to transmit news from under-developed to developed countries than vice versa. In fact, all the economies of scale benefit the rich and hurt the poor.

Dependence on foreign resources is made even worse because news producers slight Third World happenings and the program needs of people in the developing nations. Only 20 to 30 percent of the stories produced by the world's chief news suppliers deal with the Third World even though three-fourths of the world's people live there. The flow of news thus is primarily one-way — into the developing world but not out of it.

As a consequence of such dissatisfactions, and in recognition of the political importance of news, Third World countries are now trying to impose more control over their internal communication systems and over the influx of foreign news. The United States has strongly resisted this movement because it constitutes an infringement on the free flow of information. The trend towards controlled news in the developing world is making headway nonetheless.

The socialist countries, under the leadership of Yugoslavia's *Tanjug* news agency, have been pooling the reports of their national news agencies since 1975. These reports de-emphasize bad news and political skirmishes and stress positive developments almost entirely. Much time and space may be devoted to stories about purchasing a single tractor for a farm cooperative or installing a single electric generator. *Tanjug* broadcasts the daily output of Third World stories via shortwave radio from Belgrade to clients of the pool, who receive it on radio sets linked to teletype machines. In many instances, reporters from Western countries are kept out of member states so that the flow of news can be more tightly controlled.

Third World countries are also contesting the control of the United States and other Western powers over world radio and satellite facilities. Just as the domestic broadcast spectrum is limited, so is the international spectrum. In the past, frequencies were allocated on a first-come-first-served basis. This has given the developed nations, including the United States, the lion's share — nearly 90 percent — of the broadcast spectrum and the bulk of satellite facilities. Third World nations want to change this. As made clear at the World Administrative Radio Conference (WARC), which met in Geneva, Switzerland, in the fall of 1979, they want to divide the spectrum equally among all nations and bar radio and television satellite transmissions across national borders unless the receiving country has given permission.

The United States has resisted Third World demands because it is the world's number one international broadcaster.[55] It uses broadcasts as an important foreign policy strategy. United States agencies and several private broadcasters were sending 2,534 program hours weekly throughout the world in the late 1970s. (This compared with 1,998 hours for the Soviet Union.)

The Voice of America (VOA) broadcasts constitute an integral part of the federal government's foreign information program, which is handled by the International Communication Agency (ICA). These broadcasts portray American society and its problems and policies abroad and provide Western news to countries unlikely to receive it. VOA's largest service goes to the Soviet Union, to which it broadcasts 168 hours weekly in Russian, Ukrainian, Estonian, Latvian, Lithuanian, Armenian, Georgian, and Uzbek.[56] Other Eastern European countries receive 87 hours of broadcasts. The international broadcast spectrum is also used for Radio Liberty (RL) which broadcasts foreign internal news, mainly to the Soviet Union, Radio Free Europe (RFE), which does the same for Poland, Czechoslovakia, Hungary, Romania, and Bulgaria, and RIAS, Radio in the American-Sector Berlin, which covers all of Berlin and East Germany. The pressures of Third World nations, which threaten such programs, present the United States with many difficult policy problems.

SUMMARY

The quality of U.S. foreign policy and the effectiveness of U.S. relations with other countries are crucial to the welfare of people throughout the world. Sound policy and relations require a solid information base. As this chapter has shown, the foreign affairs information base on which Americans depend leaves much to be desired. The reasons are complex and, in part, inevitable. They involve the people who produce foreign policy news, the sociopolitical setting in which they must work, and the audiences to whose world views and tastes the news must cater.

Foreign correspondents are a well-trained, able group. But there are too few of them to cover the world. America's correspondents work within a narrowly controlled organizational structure consisting of a handful of giant newsgathering institutions that supply the news and entertainment needs of the United States and much of the rest of the non-communist world. If one distrusts giant information conglomerates which collect and shape the news for much of the world, the present situation is frightening.

Most Americans are reasonably well satisfied with the foreign news produced by these conglomerates. This is not true for many of the foreign clienteles, particularly in the Third World. They complain that agents of monopoly capitalism are guilty of "electronic rape" of their people through decadent entertainment and Western political and economic propaganda.

Much foreign affairs news must be produced under trying conditions. Strange locations and underdeveloped technological facilities often make a nightmare of the physical aspects of getting to the scene of events, collecting information, and transmitting it. Political difficulties compound these technical difficulties. They range from the reluctance of officials in the United States and abroad to commit themselves publicly on foreign affairs matters, to harassment of correspondents venturing into places where they are unwanted, to closing off of vast portions of the world entirely by expelling correspondents, jailing them, or refusing them entry. With so much territory to cover and such limited personnel to cover it, newspeople frequently avoid areas where news is hard to get and devote their efforts to those where public attitudes are supportive. This effectively closes off many regions from media scrutiny and contributes to unevenness of news flow from various parts of the world.

How good is the foreign affairs news which reaches the United States and other clients of Western international news transmission facilities? The picture is mixed. Foreign correspondents must produce news that is at once timely, exciting, personalized, and brief yet understandable, for an American audience which is not intensely interested in most events abroad. Given the problems of foreign affairs news production, correspondents therefore dwell heavily on negative and sensational news. They write stories from an American perspective which follows the current administration's foreign policy assumptions and the American public's stereotyped views of the world. They cover the most important countries primarily, keeping American national interests and policy objectives in mind. Despite these shortcomings, Americans can obtain a reasonably accurate view of salient political events abroad, particularly if they turn to prestige newspapers. These papers generally give thorough exposure to controversial American foreign policies. However, they rarely challenge the merits of foreign policy actions.

In recent years, television commentators have occasionally become active diplomats through interviews that set the stage for subsequent political action. Aside from these adventures, media influence on foreign policy has been largely indirect. It has been exercised primarily through surveillance activities, through the power to choose what to report and what to omit, and through the ability to interpret the meaning of events. There has been little investigative or adversary journalism except when foreign affairs were obviously going badly, as happened toward the end of the Vietnam War. Political controversy stops at the water's edge, not only for American politicians, but for American media as well.

NOTES

1. David H. Weaver and John B. Mauro, "Newspaper Readership Patterns," *Journalism Quarterly* 51 (Spring 1978): 84-91; David H. Weaver, *Recent Trends in Newspaper Readership Research* (Bloomington, Ind.: School of Journalism, Indiana University, Research Report No. 5, June 23, 1978).
2. Barry Rubin, "International News and the American Media," in Dante B. Fascell, ed., *International News: Freedom Under Attack* (Beverly Hills, Calif.: Sage, 1979), p. 192.

3. George Gerbner and George Marvanyi, "The Many Worlds of the World's Press," *Journal of Communication* 27 (Winter 1977): 55-56.
4. Bernard C. Cohen, *The Press and Foreign Policy* (Princeton: Princeton University Press, 1963), pp. 164-165.
5. Herbert J. Gans, *Deciding What's News: A Study of CBS Evening News, NBC Nightly News, Newsweek and Time* (New York: Pantheon Books, 1979), pp. 30-36.
6. Edwin Diamond, *The Tin Kazoo: Television, Politics, and the News* (Cambridge, Mass.: The MIT Press, 1975), p. 94.
7. Gans, *Deciding What's News*, pp. 30-36.
8. Rubin, "International News and the American Media," p. 187.
9. William H. Read, "Multinational Media," *Foreign Policy* 18 (Spring 1975): 55-67.
10. J. Herbert Altschull, "Khrushchev and the Berlin 'Ultimatum': The Jackal Syndrome and the Cold War," *Journalism Quarterly* 54 (Fall 1977): 545-551.
11. Rubin, "International News and the American Media," p. 214.
12. John A. Lent, "Foreign News in American Media," *Journal of Communication* 27 (Winter 1977): 46-50.
13. Rubin, "International News and the American Media," pp. 197-198.
14. Leo Bogart, "The Overseas Newsman: A 1967 Profile Study," *Journalism Quarterly* 45 (Summer 1968): 293-306.
15. Ibid., p. 299.
16. See Chapter 2.
17. Hamid Mowlana, "Who Covers America?" *Journal of Communication* 25 (Summer 1975): 86-91. Table 9-1 shows that countries most heavily covered by the U.S. send the largest number of reporters to the U.S.
18. Ibid., pp. 89-90.
19. Robert M. Batscha, *Foreign Affairs News and the Broadcast Journalist* (New York: Praeger, 1975), p. 156.
20. *New York Times*, January 14, 1976.
21. Sean Kelly, "Access Denied: The Politics of Press Censorship," in Dante B. Fascell, ed., *International News: Freedom Under Attack* (Beverly Hills, Calif.: Sage, 1979), p. 249.
22. Bob Wiedrich "Sadat Has Invented a New Diplomacy," *Chicago Tribune*, February 9, 1978.
23. Batscha, *Foreign Affairs News and the Broadcast Journalist*, p. 122.
24. James F. Larson, "International Affairs Coverage on U.S. Network Television," *Journal of Communication* 29 (Spring 1979): 147.
25. Jeff Charles, Larry Shore and Rusty Todd, "The New York Times Coverage of Equatorial and Lower Africa," *Journal of Communication* 29 (Spring 1979): 151, report, for example that only 5 out of 18 countries in that region received substantial coverage.
26. Susan Welch, "The American Press and Indochina, 1950-1956," in Richard L. Merritt, ed., *Communication in International Politics* (Urbana, Ill.: University of Illinois Press, 1972), pp. 227-228.
27. Johan Galtung and Mari H. Ruge, "The Structure of Foreign News," in Jeremy Tunstall, ed., *Media Sociology* (London: Constable Press, 1970), p. 265. Galtung and Ruge have developed a much quoted scheme for rating the newsworthiness of various types of foreign affairs events. Also see Einar Ostgaard, "Factors Influencing The Flow of News," *Journal of Peace Research* 2 (1965): 39-63.
28. *Chicago Tribune*, August 14, 1979.
29. Rubin, "International News and the American Media," p. 227.
30. Batscha, *Foreign Affairs News and the Broadcast Journalist*, pp. 67-68.
31. Ibid., pp. 136-137.

32. Paul Bethel, "Anarchy in Domingo: City Without Food, Water, Medicine in Civil War," in Alan Casty, ed., *Mass Media and the Mass Man* (New York: Holt, Rinehart & Winston, 1968), p. 218.

33. Theodore Draper, "Contaminated News of the Dominican Republic," in Alan Casty, ed., *Mass Media and the Mass Man*, pp. 212-214.

34. Jon D. Cozean, "Profile of U.S. Press Coverage in Cuba: Was The Bay of Pigs Necessary?" *Journal of International and Comparative Studies* 5 (Winter 1972): 29.

35. Gertrude J. Robinson, "Foreign News Conceptions in the Quebec, English Canadian, and U.S. Press: A Comparative Study," Paper presented to the International Communications Association Convention, Philadelphia, May 1-5, 1979.

36. Fernando Reyes Matta, "The Latin American Concept of News," *Journal of Communication* 29 (Spring 1979): 169.

37. George Gerbner, "Press Perspectives in World Communication: A Pilot Study," *Journalism Quarterly* 38 (Summer 1961): 321-322.

38. Benjamin D. Singer, "Violence, Protest, and War in Television News: The U.S. and Canada Compared," *Public Opinion Quarterly* 34 (Winter 1970-71): 611-616; also Chris J. Scheer and Sam W. Eiler, "A Comparison of Canadian and American Network Television News," *Journal of Broadcasting* 16 (Spring 1972): 156-164.

39. Lent, "Foreign News in American Media." Also see Haluk Sahin, "Turkish Politics in *New York Times:* A Comparative Content Analysis," *Journalism Quarterly* 50 (Winter 1973): 685-689.

40. W. Phillips Davison, "Diplomatic Reporting: Rules of the Game," *Journal of Communication* 25 (Autumn 1975): 138-146.

41. Ernest LeFever, *T.V. and National Defense* (Chicago: Institute for American Strategy, 1974), p. 139.

42. James Reston, *Sketches in the Sand* (New York: Knopf, 1967), p. 195.

43. Rubin, "International News and the American Media," p. 216.

44. Thomas M. McNulty, "Vietnam Specials: Policy and Content," *Journal of Communication* 25 (Autumn 1975): 173-180. Ernest W. LeFever, "CBS and National Defense," *Journal of Communication* 25 (Autumn 1975): 181-185.

45. Peter Braestrup, *Big Story: How the American Press and Television Reported and Interpreted the Crisis of Tet 1968 in Vietnam and Washington.* (Garden City: Anchor Press/Doubleday, 1978).

46. Rubin, "International News and the American Media," p. 193.

47. Ibid., p. 182.

48. Mustapha Masmoudi, "The New World Information Order," *Journal of Communication* 29 (Spring 1979): 172-185.

49. Oliver Boyd-Barret, "Media Imperialism: Towards an International Framework for the Analysis of Media Systems," in James Curan, Michael Gurevitch, and Janet Woolacott, eds., *Mass Communication and Society* (London: Edward Arnold, 1971), pp. 117, 129.

50. Media imperialism is discussed fully in Jeremy Tunstall, *The Media Are American* (New York: Columbia University Press, 1977) and Herbert I. Schiller, *Communication and Cultural Domination* (White Plains, N.Y.: International Arts and Science Press, 1976).

51. *New York Times,* August 12, 1977.

52. The impact of foreign television is assessed in David E. Payne and Christy A. Peake, "Cultural Diffusion: The Role of U.S. T.V. in Iceland," *Journalism Quarterly* 54 (Fall 1977): 523-531.

53. Boyd-Barrett, "Media Imperialism," p. 130.

54. Elihu Katz, "Cultural Continuity and Change: The Role of Mass Media," in Majid Teheranian, Farhad Hakimzadeh and Marcello L. Vidale, *Commu-*

nications Policy for National Development (London: Routledge & Kegan Paul, 1977), p. 113.

55. Kelly, "Access Denied," p. 255.
56. David M. Abshire, "A New Dimension of Western Diplomacy," in Dante B. Fascell, ed., *International News: Freedom Under Attack* (Beverly Hills, Calif.: Sage, 1979), p. 40.

READINGS

Batscha, Robert M. *Foreign Affairs News and the Broadcast Journalist.* New York: Praeger, 1975.

Casty, Alan, ed. *Mass Media and the Mass Man.* New York: Holt, Rinehart and Winston, 1968.

Cohen, Bernard C. *The Press and Foreign Policy.* Princeton: Princeton University Press, 1963.

Fascell, Dante B., ed. *International News: Freedom Under Attack.* Beverly Hills, Calif.: Sage, 1979.

LeFever, Ernest. *T.V. and National Defense.* Chicago: Institute for American Strategy, 1974.

Schiller, Herbert I. *Communication and Cultural Domination.* White Plains, N.Y.: International Arts and Sciences Press, 1976.

10

Trends in Media Policy

In Shakespeare's *Julius Caesar,* Brutus urges his fellow conspirators to act while the time is ripe.[1]

There is a tide in the affairs of men
Which, taken at the flood, leads on to fortune;
Omitted, all the voyage of their life
Is bound in shallows and in miseries.
On such a full sea are we now afloat;
And we must take the current when it serves
Or lose our ventures.

Communications policy stands on just such a threshold in the last quarter of the twentieth century. New technologies have solved old problems and made new policy directions possible, but old policy concepts linger. Unless there is a bold attempt to take control of the tides of change, the chance for a new information order may vanish.

In this chapter, we shall trace the forces for change and the obstacles to change. We shall outline some of the areas of disenchantment with mass media performance which may fuel the quest for new directions, and the steps taken by dissatisfied audiences to improve and supplement the existing information supply system. We shall also look at the major new technologies and the changes which they make possible. The potential impact of these changes on politics and policy alternatives, and the political obstacles which these policies face, will likewise be examined. Finally, we shall peer into the murky crystal ball to try to discern the general shape of future communications policies that will set the stage for the continuing interaction between the mass media and American politics.

CURRENT DISSATISFACTIONS WITH THE MEDIA

The 1960s and 1970s have been an era of political disenchantment in the United States. Many people have become dissatisfied with major political institutions and blame them for the ills of society. True enough,

"Every now and then Roger likes to cut himself off from all media."

Drawing by Joseph G. Farris © 1970 *Saturday Review* Inc.

vocal protesters have been in the minority. There are still large "silent majorities" whose silence constitutes approval of the political system or resignation to its unavoidable shortcomings. But even the silent feel that the times are out of joint, if only because of the increase of unrest.

The media, particularly television, have been among the targets of public protest. In 1979 alone, the Federal Communications Commission's Broadcast Bureau in Washington received more than 100,000 complaints from viewers about television fare.[2] Most complaints concerned the display of obscenity, excessive crime and violence, infringement of equal time and fairness provisions, undue or objectionable attention to racial and religious matters, and excessive or offensive advertising.

In addition to the formal complaints lodged with the FCC, there have been a host of less formal criticisms as well.[3] Media critics call television a vast intellectual wasteland. They chide the networks for slavish submission to the dictates of rating systems, blaming shallow programming and cheap appeals to human emotions on the desire to capture huge audiences. They complain about the small amount of social criticism and the large amount of support for the established system. Such criticism is often extended to the print media as well.

Criticism of media orientations toward politics has been two-pronged, however. Sniping from the left about the media's subservience to the establishment has been balanced by criticism from the middle and the right. They charge the media with being overly aggressive and often unfair to major segments of society, and unduly romantic about the woes and virtues of the poor, the disadvantaged, and the racially different.[4] In the process, the media allegedly undermine national security and hurt the nation's prestige at home and abroad. They demean the status of American business and labor and major professions like medicine and law. They invade the privacy of the individual and impair the fairness of the judicial process.

The merits of these charges do not concern us right now. Their gist is that the media do not serve "the public interest." That elusive concept is always measured by political yardsticks of disputed accuracy and validity. What is important to an understanding of media policymaking is the response to perceived media deficiencies. How do dissatisfied Americans cope with shortcomings of their information supply? Coping strategies can be grouped into three types: (1) various forms of informal criticism, expressed regularly or sporadically; (2) establishment and use of formal criticism mechanisms; and (3) use of alternative media.

Informal Criticism

Informal criticism has come from the journalism profession itself as well as from the general public. Professional criticism has been published in specialized journals that frequently review the output of the profession. The *Chicago Journalism Review* and the *Columbia Journalism Review* are examples. Many of these reviews have been short-lived because they could not maintain enough subscribers to pay their expenses. The *Chicago Journalism Review,* despite its widely acknowledged excellence, died an untimely death only a few years after its birth. The *Washington Journalism Review* has long been teetering on the brink of financial disaster. The degree of influence wielded by such reviews is a matter of opinion. Within narrow circles, professional reputations may be affected. But the circulation of these reviews is so limited and the pocketbook effects on the industry so negligible, that pressure to alter journalistic practices is likely to be small.

A more robust vehicle of criticism, and probably more influential than the review journals because of broader circulation, has been critical commentary by media commentators attached to newspapers and news magazines. Columnists like Les Brown of the *New York Times* or Gary Deeb of the *Chicago Tribune* have become familiar gadflies of the news business and the journalism profession. Their work supplements the efforts of several academic experts who have written critical appraisals of the mass media in recent years. Names like David Altheide, John Hohenberg, Edwin Diamond, and Herbert Schiller belong in this group.[5]

The media also have been scanned critically, if informally, at professional conventions of journalists and at the counter-conventions that they have occasionally provoked.[6] Special workshops, such as the annual Aspen Conference on Communication and Society, have focused more narrowly on specific problems and have publicized reform proposals.

Informal criticism has also come from various public interest groups. In many cases, these have been institutions organized for other purposes such as the national Parent and Teacher Association (PTA) or the American Medical Association (AMA). Others are special media action groups. The National Citizens Committee for Broadcasting or the Children's Television Workshop are examples. Their work is discussed more fully in Chapter 2. As pointed out there, their efforts, like most other forms of informal criticism, have had a moderate impact on media policies.

Formal Criticism

Formal criticism comprises protests about media performance lodged with the appropriate government agency that has corrective powers. Earlier we mentioned the FCC's Broadcast Bureau in Washington as a formal center for citizen complaints. We have also mentioned FCC hearings prior to granting broadcast licenses or when license renewal has been challenged. In such hearings, interested parties have a chance to present their perspectives on media policy, in hopes of countering media industry pressures and the pro-industry biases that public regulatory bodies usually develop.

Despite widespread recognition that it is desirable to provide the public with such formal avenues for criticism and policy suggestions, there are a number of unsolved problems. Most fundamental and least soluble is the problem of making sure that the complaints and suggestions thus aired are representative of community beliefs. The laudable desire to listen to the voices of dissent may lead to inadequate concern about the merits of dissenters' claims and the damage to more general public interests.

A few examples of questionable protests will illustrate the problem. Some of these protests were ignored; others were heeded. The 1978 miniseries "Holocaust," which dramatized Nazi atrocities, was loudly opposed by a variety of groups claiming that it generated anti-German feelings and hatred between Jews and gentiles. Yet it was widely acclaimed by many critics and attracted between 38 and 48 million viewers nightly. Similarly, in 1977, between 30 and 40 million people watched each episode of the "Godfather" I and II series, which dealt with Mafia ventures, and considered the program a worthwhile performance. Yet thousands of Italian-Americans denounced the show as a slander against Italians and complained through various political channels. Stories about abortion, drug addiction, the activities of religious cults, or the exploits of discredited politicians have often been suppressed or toned down because they brought about a flood of protests.

Lack of money can be a major barrier to using formal protest channels — to challenge industry representatives effectively in an FCC hearing or before a court of law. In the past, protest groups have had to rely on their own limited resources, except when the broadcast industry has voluntarily shouldered their legal fees. Because payments in such cases were restricted to legal costs, protest groups have been encouraged to undertake litigation, rather than negotiating settlements. It has been suggested in recent years that the FCC should pay the expenses of protest groups. But, unless Congress allocates special funds for this purpose, the resources of the agency are too slim to do so.

In general, lawsuits involving claims about harmful television programming have been unsuccessful. A widely publicized example is the trial of Ronny Zamora, a teen-ager who was convicted by a Florida court for murdering an 83-year-old woman. His parents sued the three networks for negligent programming, claiming that television shows had incited and taught their son how to murder. The suit was dismissed by a federal judge who ruled that the media had not been negligent. In 1978, a California court likewise dismissed a negligence suit against NBC brought by the parents of a young rape victim. The rape had mimicked a scene from the movie "Born Innocent," which had been shown on television four days earlier.

To enhance public influence on communications policy, there have been proposals to place ombudsmen — formal spokesmen for the public's interests — in various public agencies. Alternatively, a central ombudsman office has been proposed to assist public interest groups and individuals in preparing and presenting their complaints and suggestions. Thus far, these proposals remain in the drawing board stage.

Media Councils

Another avenue for channeling criticism to bring about changes in media performance is the "Media Council." Media councils are elected or appointed bodies that hear complaints by individuals or groups about mass media output. They have been widely used in Great Britain, some American states, like Minnesota, and some cities, like Seattle. Media councils examine the validity of complaints brought to their attention and publicize their findings. The investigation may produce accommodation of clashing interests. It may also embarrass some of the parties so that they mend their ways. Generally, media councils lack power to enforce their recommendations.

Controversy over the usefulness of media councils came to a head in the United States in 1973 when a private research organization, the Twentieth Century Fund, created a task force to look into the establishment of an independent, private national press council to monitor the major national news sources: wire services, the weekly news magazines, and the national newspaper syndicates. The council, as proposed by the task force, was "to receive, to examine, and to report on complaints concerning the accuracy and fairness of news reporting in the United States, as well as to initiate studies and report on issues involving the freedom of the press."[7] The council would provide independent appraisals of media performance whenever fairness and representativeness of news were questioned.

The proposed council was to consist of 15 members drawn from the public and the journalism profession, but no member could come from the institutions that were being monitored. It would meet regularly as well as in special meetings, and its findings would be released to the public in reports and press releases. Aside from the power of publicity, there would be no means to enforce the council's recommendations.

Like British and Minnesota press councils, it would act on complaints only after attempts had failed to settle the matter directly with the media organization involved. Complaints could come from individuals, organizations, or the council itself. For instance, the council might on its own investigate whether presidential debates which excluded third-party candidates met the spirit of the fairness rules for television. Or it might consider an appeal against the dominance of sports programs on Saturday afternoons, if the media had refused to consider the complaint.

Though media councils have been fairly successful, they have failed to gain wide acceptance in the United States largely because of opposition by the press.[8] The Twentieth Century Fund proposals, for instance, were rejected, two to one, by media organizations. Newspeople feared that the council would impair editorial independence and force them to change news policies. They claimed that such a watchdog organization was unnecessary because they were serving the public well. However, they were willing to give space to the activities and reports of the council.

Alternative Media

Information needs that have been neglected or poorly served by the regular media have also been met by literally hundreds of specialized media. These include a plethora of publications concentrating in whole or in part on political commentary. The *New Republic, Mother Jones,* the *National Review,* and, at times, the *New Yorker* are examples. They also include professional and trade journals, company publications in large organizations, journals devoted to a multitude of human interests such as religion, sports, fine and popular arts, automobiles, stamp collecting, and bird watching. If an audience numbering into thousands and even millions of people constitutes a "mass," these are, by definition, mass media.[9] Modern means of information distribution bridge the distances that physically separate people interested in the less common pursuits so that they can be brought together as a "mass" audience for specialized publications. The demand for targeted information has increased in recent years; witness the mushrooming of specialized magazines such as the popular *People Magazine, Psychology Today,* or *Sports Illustrated,* or the even more focused *Ski, Photography,* or *Car and Driver.* Their popularity brought about a major change in advertising strategy that led to the demise of broadly oriented magazines like *Look, Life,* and *The Saturday Evening Post.*

Alternative media also have developed in the newspaper field. There is a large foreign language press in the United States serving various nationality groups. Examples are the Arabic and German and Polish language presses, and publications serving the needs of the Hispanic and black communities.[10] There are also local community newspapers, appearing daily, every other day, or once a week.[11] They present community news for which the metropolitan press does not have space and which would have little interest for its readers. There are even special news supplements in the regular daily press that are targeted for and distributed to various neighborhoods within the city.

Radio stations in many American cities serve specialized groups, and a few cities even have specialized television outlets. The lush growth of such media serves as a partial antidote to the concentration of ownership in the more general mass media that we described in Chapter 2. The potential role of cable television as yet another means for serving special community interests will be discussed more fully later in this chapter.

For many people, the term "alternative media" conjures up visions of the politically radical, iconoclastic, counterculture newspapers that were plentiful in the late 1960s and early 1970s. This was the time when dissatisfaction over the Vietnam War was at a peak and large numbers of people, particularly among the young and minority groups, opposed the positions taken by the regular media. They therefore created the "underground" press. The name was applied because these media carried on the flagrant opposition to government policy that is often forbidden in other countries, driving such media into locations hidden from the police. "Underground" actually was a misnomer for the American media of protest, because they were allowed to operate quite openly. But it gave them an aura of fighting the establishment at great personal risk.

The mushrooming of such media in the sixties and seventies — at one time there were nearly 1,000 underground newspapers and 400 radio stations — shows the vitality and flexibility of the mass media system.[12] The abrupt decline of underground media with the end of the Vietnam War — there are only a handful left, and most of them have either turned middle-class or have become predominantly pornographic — also shows that when the need ends, the system is able to prune its unneeded branches.[13]

Underground media like the *Seed*, the *East Village Other*, the *Berkeley Barb*, the *Rat*, or *The Great Speckled Bird* went beyond rejecting the current government and political establishment. They also rejected the values and culture of American mainstream society. In this they differed from the more usual social responsibility journalism which supports basic American values and attacks only their perversions. Politically, the underground media were generally left-wing in orientation: communist or socialist or anarchist. They used a style that attracted attention by being totally subjective and visually and verbally shocking. Profanity, explicit sexual pictures, and arousing cartoons and drawings abounded because the staffs of these media felt that their attacks on American society must be shocking and exciting to succeed.

The rise of the underground press shows that mass media can still be started and operated with modest means. They were financed mostly through advertising for such things as counterculture records, music productions, X-rated movies, and classified advertisements for sex partners, nude models, drugs, and similar attractions. Staffs were paid meager salaries or no salaries at all.[14] The papers concentrated on features, rather than regular news stories, assigning their limited personnel only to stories that they planned to use, rather than covering a full series of regular beats. For daily news and some features, they relied on cooperative news services such as the Underground Press Service (UPS) and Liberation News Service (LNS).

To beat the high cost of printing, the underground media used offset processes that permitted them to duplicate their pages at a fraction of the cost of regular printing. Most of the papers were peddled on street corners near university campuses whenever they were ready. There were no set numbers of issues per year, no regular publication schedules, no business staffs or circulation departments. At their height, readership was estimated at 10 million, with most issues used by several people.

Underground media were not limited to the comparatively unregulated print realm. They also flourished in the regulated broadcast field. Underground radio stations featured mostly rock music and disc jockeys who commented on society, sexual matters, the drug culture, and other counterculture interests. The FCC rarely interfered with their unconventional activities, except when they flouted the law too brazenly. For instance, when a Texas rock station tipped off the local drug community about a drug raid planned by police, there was an investigation into the sources from which the station had received advance information.

The tolerance of the government to such broadcasts demonstrates that governmental control over media content, however offensive, has a light touch. Few countries equal and none exceeds the freedom to express radical viewpoints presently enjoyed by American media. In fact, some of the causes pressed by underground news sources ultimately became part of the mainstream of politics. In the end, loss of public support, rather than official censorship, led to the steep decline in this genre of journalism.

THE IMPACT OF NEW TECHNOLOGIES

Many of the complaints about the mass media focus on insufficient diversity in mass media offerings. Technology can solve this problem now. Simultaneously, it has sharply reduced the dangers of monopoly control over information. Cable television can vastly multiply the number of television channels available in any community. Systems now in operation or in the planning stage project from 20 to 80 separate channels in a given locality.

Satellites can beam an almost limitless number of radio and television signals to all parts of the world, which can be received through ordinary and cable channels. In the late 1970s, an RCA communications satellite, Satcom I, stationed in a fixed orbit some 22,300 miles above the equator, carried enough programs in its leased channels to fill the needs of even the largest multiple channel cable systems many times over. Plans were in the offing for adding even larger satellites and for distributing receiving equipment to all commercial television stations to permit them to receive satellite programs directly. This would free them of dependence on the current network programming system because satellites can carry an extensive array of programs generated by local stations and other sources, in addition to network offerings. This system vastly expands programming options.

Cassettes and video discs can store electronic fare so that users can play what they want when they want it. Pay cable and over-the-air television give access to channels carrying special entertainment or special interest programs at moderate costs. Warner Cable in Columbus, Ohio, has developed Qube, an audience-participation cable system that permits limited access to individual programs. People pay solely for those programs they choose to watch. Students can enroll in television courses viewable only by people formally enrolled in the course.

Newspapers can now be printed and transmitted electronically. Laser beam and optical fiber technology are adding to the arsenal of communication tools. Though a number of technical puzzles still require solution, and though costs for some technologies need to be brought down, we have moved from the age of channel scarcity to the age of plenty.

The opportunity to talk back to our electronic servants through two-way communication has also moved from the realm of science fiction to the realm of reality. Two-way channels on cable television permit viewers to be seen and heard and to interact with others watching the same programs. Two-way communication through older technologies, such as two-way radio and the telephone, has also been perfected to integrate outlying areas with the social service systems available in more populated centers. In Alaska and Northern Canada, for example, these technologies are used to deliver various educational and health services and to give the people a greater voice in government policies that affect them.[15]

Barriers to Development

Usually, technology tells us what is possible, rather than what is likely to happen, particularly in the short run. A number of political barriers stand in the way of using these new technologies more fully. Above all, there are the usual bureaucratic barriers to change. Many new developments never get off the ground because bureaucracies impose so many regulations to guard against possible abuses. Standards are frequently unrealistically high, raising costs beyond economically feasible levels. State and local rules, piled on top of federal regulations, complicate the picture even further. Not only do they add more requirements, but their rules often are mutually conflicting.

Every major technological revolution — and the information transmission revolution is major — has brought about economic and political dislocations. Such massive changes have been fought by those whose knowledge and equipment will be made obsolete by them. Communications technologies involve large investments so that their sudden obsolescence becomes a major financial blow.

Current owners also develop a squatter's mentality about rights they have acquired, such as the right to use certain frequencies. To justify retaining what they already have, they point to the market needs that they are filling. Newcomers, on the other hand, want to reallocate facilities afresh on an equal basis, even before they have established a market for their services or can guarantee that such a market will develop. This raises the specter of allocating facilities to operators who do not currently need them, while denying them to established operators.

New types of programs made possible by new technologies may threaten the jobs of current providers of similar services. For instance, cable round-the-clock educational programs, structured like regular classrooms, are operating successfully in several localities. Medical programs teach people better medical self-care methods. Such programs, especially if expanded, pose a threat to the teaching and health professions. At the same time, standards may be set up for professional performance that may force practitioners to alter their methods of operation. They may even be obligated to participate in telecast programs that expose their performance to public scrutiny. All these considerations lead to resistance from professionals whose support is essential.

Obstacles have also arisen because any new technology benefits various groups unevenly. Each group fights to win acceptance for whatever technology and regulations seem most beneficial to the interests it favors. Such battles may be prolonged and final decisions delayed. Because bureaucratic inertia sets in once the initial decisions have been made, power struggles are fiercest before the initial status quo is determined. While these power struggles are going on, technology advances, raising new problems requiring solutions, further delaying the green light for implementation of new systems.

The Emergence of Cable Television

A brief account of the rocky history of cable television development in the United States will illustrate the problems faced by technical innovations. It will also illustrate the many political decisions that must be made to fit a new information technology into the existing legislative and administrative structure.

When cable television (CATV) — the transmission of television signals through a coaxial cable — first became available in 1949, it was viewed as a serious threat by established broadcasters.[16] They feared that the availability of numerous television channels capable of transmitting original and relayed programs would lead to a large menu of programs like the variety offered by current radio shows. This would splinter television audiences. Smaller audiences would mean smaller advertising revenues and smaller profits for the existing stations. It might also mean poorer programming because smaller incomes would require curtailment of programming expenditures.

Ultimately, cable television coupled with satellite technology might destroy the networks entirely. Superstations could pick up programs directly from satellites and broadcast them nationwide. This network nightmare has actually come to pass in Atlanta, Chicago, and San Francisco, where such superstations are now in operation.[17] Television networks were also concerned that cable operators would be able to pirate, rather than buy, their signals and broadcast the programs they had produced at high cost.

The initial response of the FCC was typical of what regulatory agencies ordinarily do in these types of situations. It protected the status quo with regulations that prevented the newcomers from destroying established interests. These regulations limited the types of programs that cable television could broadcast. In the process, the growth of the industry was stunted.

Gradually, combinations of interest groups were able to persuade public officials that cable technology was in the public interest because it could reach people in locations inaccessible to regular television signals. The idea of breaking the near-monopoly enjoyed by the networks over broadcasting was also attractive. So was the possibility of opening up many new channels for broadcasting for groups hitherto shut out of a limited spectrum.

By 1972, these pressures were sufficiently strong to produce an easing of FCC regulations on the types of signals that cable television could import from distant areas. This gave the system a new lease on life. However, in what is also a typical move when new technologies arise, the FCC imposed a number of very costly regulations to force cable television to serve public needs that had never been met in the past. These included the requirement for a minimum of 20 channels, including channels for broadcasting by the general public, educational institutions, and local governments. There were also requirements for two-way facilities and for carrying signals of local broadcasters.

When these rules turned out to be still too burdensome to allow rapid development of CATV, they were eased again in 1976. Further loosening of service requirements imposed on the new industry is likely; it may even be totally freed from federal regulations. Meanwhile, the resistance of the established industries to this new competition has gradually eased. In fact, a number of them, heeding the old adage, "if you can't lick 'em, join 'em" have invested heavily in cable facilities.

FCC rules and the opposition of the established industries are not the only hurdles faced by the cable industry. There are numerous local political hurdles as well. Laying of cables requires permission from local authorities. To avoid undue duplication of facilities, franchises have to be granted. Some thought must be given to the time allowed to franchisees to develop their facilities, and the requirements to be imposed about serving outlying areas where service may not be profitable initially, if ever. Service to rural areas may pose insurmountable economic problems, particularly in the western plains and the Rocky Mountain states. Alternatives to cable, such as microwave relays or satellite broadcasts, transmitting regular over-the-air television signals, might have to be considered. The political ramifications of these technical problems raised questions about standards and terms for awarding the franchises, and the choice of governmental agencies to control CATV and reap the tax and regulation income. State utility commissions have fought hard to take on this role. Local authorities have resisted.

Governments have several policy options for dealing with cable systems. They can play a hands-off role, allowing the system to develop as its private owners please.[18] This is the policy advocated in the 1978 proposals for revisions of the Federal Communication Act. The precedent for this policy is the traditional stance of government toward the print media. If we believe that government should regulate information supply only when transmission channels are scarce, as happened with early radio and television, then it makes sense to leave cable television unregulated like print media. When media outlets are as plentiful as is true now, market forces presumably come into play. Necessary services will then be supplied in a far more flexible and responsive way than is possible when government regulations intervene.

The only restraints that may be needed are safeguards to protect national security and social norms. Hence the usual restraints applied to print media — limits on publication of security information, limits on obscenity, some protection of the interests of children — might be applied to cable television. Regulations to assure that the availability of two-way circuitry would not pose a hazard to privacy might also be necessary. People must be protected from unauthorized prying into their viewing habits and disclosure of their identity when two-way circuitry is used for public opinion polls or voting.

A second policy option is to treat cable television as a common carrier, like the telephone or rail and bus lines. This would make transmission facilities available to everyone on a first-come-first-served basis. The rationale for designating CATV as a common carrier would be similar to that used for the telephone. It is a widely needed vital resource for the transmission of information which should be available to everyone on demand. The FCC and various local governments like the common carrier concept. But the Supreme Court held in a 1977 decision that cable could not be considered a common carrier. An Arkansas operator, Midwest Video Company, therefore could not be required by *federal* regulations to provide public access channels.[19] The ruling pleased the cable industry because it preserves its control over policymaking. However, the ruling does not bar state and local authorities from imposing common carrier status on the industry.

The third policy option is to confer public trustee status on the cable industry. This is a status akin to that of the television and radio industry at the present time. It entails several service obligations for the industry, including adherence to the fair and equal time provisions, the right of rebuttal, and limitations on materials unsuitable for children or offensive to community morality. A series of rules about access to cable would most likely include requirements for public and government access channels, and channels set aside for public education, public safety, and medical and social service information.

The rationale for trustee status has been twofold. The scarcity argument has been powerful in the past in television and radio regulation. It obviously makes no sense for cable television, which can provide virtually unlimited channel capacity. The other argument for trustee status is that television is a highly influential medium that should be regulated to make certain that valuable programs are broadcast and harmful ones avoided. This is a powerful argument with strong support in much of the world. It is the argument which Third World nations have made so persuasively, as discussed in the last chapter. But it is not the argument on which the American system was built, and it is incompatible with First Amendment philosophy.

The American system rests on the notion that free interplay in the marketplace of ideas, rather than government, should determine what the public good is. Government control over communication is deemed undesirable precisely because it permits government to enforce its own standards and call them good, while labeling opposing views as bad. Government should limit itself to protecting the free flow of information and the right to receive and dispatch all kinds of news. These American traditions point to the hands-off policy approach as the answer for cable television development.

Whether cable television is treated like any private enterprise, like a common carrier, or like a trustee, its costs have to be paid. There are three financing possibilities, each with different policy consequences.

Like television at present, CATV can be sustained through advertiser support. This will mean that programming must have mass appeal and that it will therefore share the strengths and weaknesses of current programming. Sponsor influence may be greater in the cable age because competition for sponsors will be keener when channels multiply. Many stations, particularly those with small audiences, may even find it difficult to attract enough sponsors to pay for their operations.

Because of the drawbacks of advertising-supported programming and the difficulty of securing enough advertising, current cable television relies largely on audience payments. These generally take the form of a monthly service charge for the facilities, to which an installation charge may be added. Special programming may be available for a flat rate of $7 to $10 monthly, in 1980 dollars, or on a per program basis. This method of financing is quite popular in many foreign countries but it has been resisted in the United States. People do not like to pay for services in locations where good services are available free of charge. Aside from mountainous areas, this is normally the case in the United States. The quality differential between the free service and the pay service must generally be substantial before large numbers of people are willing to subscribe. And unless large numbers are willing to subscribe — about 20 families per mile of cable are needed — CATV presently is uneconomical.

There could be some major changes in this financial picture, however, if the worst fears of the current networks are realized. If their financial base is sufficiently undermined by cable television competition, they, too, may have to charge fees. Such a development might strengthen cable television immeasurably, provided it could offer programs which could successfully compete against the network programs.

A major social drawback of service charges is that poor families, which most need many of cable's benefits, are least able to pay. Instead, middle-income families, who already enjoy many social advantages, benefit most. Education and information made available to them through cable programs enhance their status, leaving lower-class people even farther behind. The knowledge gap between the information-rich and the information-poor grows, rather than diminishes. When important social problems are widely discussed before heterogeneous television audiences, on the other hand, the gap narrows.[20]

If advertising revenues and privately paid fees are ruled out, the only remaining alternative is government subsidy. This could be a subsidy paid to the poor only, or a subsidy paid to the industry on a basis similar to financing of public television. As we have stressed throughout this book, when information enterprises are dependent on government for their financial support, their independence is endangered. Since it is an axiom of American politics that the press must be free from government control, major financial links, other than a subsidy to the poor, should be ruled out.

THE SHAPE OF THE FUTURE

Several major concerns stand out for the future. In the first place, the new technologies require a complete rethinking of the scope and purposes of federal regulation of broadcast media. The 1934 Communications Act was premised on the notion of scarcity of transmission facilities. This made it essential to parcel them out equitably and to make certain that the limited number of franchisees served broad public interests.

Forty-five years later, the regulatory mechanism remains unchanged, although its basic rationale has disappeared. Despite mushrooming broadcast outlets, forces moving towards deregulation and greater stress on traditional First Amendment values are weak. Dissatisfaction with the services supplied by private entrepreneurs has created pressures for increased, rather than less, regulation, and for greater controls over program content. This is the major challenge facing broadcast policymakers now. They can yield to domestic and international pressures and make government the arbiter of what is good and safe for the public; or they can leave that role in private hands, at the mercy of nonelected media tycoons. Given these alternatives, this author casts her choice with the latter option, believing with Thomas Jefferson that "Error of opinion may be tolerated where reason is left free to combat it."[21]

Another important area of public concern about the impact of the communications revolution relates to two-way communication. It has been hailed as the gateway to genuine direct democracy. In the future, the public business can presumably be conducted in front of the television set. Citizens can watch the proceedings of legislative bodies and cast votes of approval or disapproval.

Pilot projects have already been conducted. In San José, California, school board meetings were televised. All sides of controversial school issues were aired, and the televised discussion was supplemented by newspaper articles. The public was then given a chance to vote on policy suggestions through two-way cable or through ballots printed in the local newspapers. The bulk of votes came from the same types of interests whose influence on school policies had been dominant in the past. Middle-class people voted, but most lower-class people did not participate as had been hoped.

The possibility for electronic voting raises some important constitutional issues. The United States now is a representative democracy, with elections at regular intervals. Between elections, officials make decisions they consider to be in the public interest. The Constitution did not provide for direct democracy governed by a series of plebiscites. It would lead us too far from the topic of this chapter to discuss the merits of direct democracy versus representative democracy at various governmental levels in the United States. Suffice it to say that any major changes in form of governance should be seriously debated, rather than accepted as part of technological change.

The possibility of using the two-way circuitry for educational programs of various types, particularly those which would improve the status of disadvantaged groups, raises fewer controversies. The major obstacle here, beyond making the technology available, is motivating people to use it. Both successes and failures have been recorded in initial experimental programs.

Spartanburg, South Carolina, experimented with cablecasts of high school subjects to permit adults to earn high school diplomas without leaving home. Sixty-two percent of the adults in the area lacked a high school diploma. The 15-week program made use of interactive technology; students used an eight-button terminal to answer the teacher's questions and ask for help with problems. For people who took the course, results were as good as those obtained from actual classroom attendance. But the program had to be discontinued because too few people were enrolled to keep the per-pupil cost within defensible limits.[22]

By contrast, a program geared to senior citizens in Reading, Pennsylvania, became very popular. This program linked three senior citizen centers and connected them to various public places such as the public schools or the city council. On a given day, the seniors might hook up with a city council session and ask questions. Questions and answers could then be heard and viewed in all the centers. Participants in the three centers could also interact with each other. All programs were produced and conducted by senior citizens. Potentially shut-in and shut-out adults were thus reintegrated into the community. They became more aware of mutual problems of the aged and problems of the community. The community benefited from hearing their views about public policies.[23]

A major concern brought into focus by the availability of large numbers of channels on cable television is the question of national consensus. Fears have been expressed that specialized television fare in news and entertainment will diminish attention to politics and will fragment the national consensus that is now sustained by national media. Would people watch news and public service programs if they had to turn the dial to a different channel? A music fan might watch music programs only, a black or Hispanic person might only tune to stations concerned with black and Hispanic affairs. They would thus miss out on happenings in the broader culture.

Messages from national officials might reach a vastly diminished audience unless a large number of cable television producers agreed to have their programs pre-empted at any particular time. Specialization of media would increase the difficulty of getting government messages through to all the publics that government is trying to reach. Officials might need to issue several versions of public messages, each tailored to a different audience. This might mean more political manipulation, along with the possibility of a better fit between audience needs and public messages. The electoral chances of minority candidates and parties might grow with increased ability to concentrate on selected audiences. Government programs might operate more successfully, given ampler opportunities for one- and two-way communication with selected audiences. The possibilities for change are staggering, but too ill-defined as yet to hazard predictions.

Fears about adverse consequences of political fragmentation are not shared by everyone, of course. Many people point out that fragmentation, produced when alternative media were used in the past, has not ruptured the national consensus. They argue that fragmented interests create the demand for fragmented media, rather than the reverse. If there is political and social consensus, people will seek out information pertaining to the larger community. Even if the new media system will lead to increased fragmentation, many people do not find this objectionable, believing that pluralism is preferable to the melting pot ideals of prior generations.

A media-induced push toward pluralism may also herald a push toward more local control over information programs. We have already mentioned the common requirement that cable systems must reserve channels for local government affairs. This gives local governments a better chance than ever to have their affairs aired before local audiences. Channels reserved for local school systems or for police and fire departments likewise serve to publicize local institutions. If publicity means power, the new communications media are apt to enhance the power of local institutions, possibly at the expense of national ones. The two-way capacity, which makes programming attractive to local people even if it lacks the polish of national shows, may give local organizations large enough audiences to enable them to remain solvent.

While the possibilities for strengthening local communities through increased publicity are good, CATV, when combined with satellite technology, also has the ability to deflect interest away from the local scene and produce global villages of like-minded people. Programs can be created for specialized audiences and targeted to these audiences all over the nation. For instance, medical information can be relayed through cable to doctors throughout the country; so can programs on crime fighting for police personnel, or volleyball programs for volleyball buffs. This is akin to the services presently rendered by specialized journals and magazines and may enhance professional competence in many fields. The birth of national cable television networks, like the Cable News Network owned by Atlanta-based Turner Communications, already heralds future movements in this direction.

Yet another problem brought about by the coming age of broadcast plenty is the fate of public television. As we discussed in Chapter 2, public television was organized to provide an alternative to the typical programming available on the commercial networks. It also was to be an outlet for programs geared to minorities. These are the very services that cable television presumably will perform on a commercial basis. Since public television has always depended on public subsidies, and since its audiences have been quite limited, aside from its children's programs, there will be strong pressures to abandon it.

The problems we have outlined thus far are undoubtedly not the only ones ahead. Many others will require decisions that go far beyond solving technical issues. The direction of communications policy is at stake, and with it the tone, and possibly the direction, of American politics generally. John M. Eger, a former director of the White House Office of Telecommunications Policy, has remarked that this is indeed "a time of decision." "For as we are moving into a future rich in innovation and in social change, we are also moving into a storm center of new world problems." The new technologies are "a force for change throughout the world that simply will not be stopped, no matter how it is resisted." And then he asks, "Are we ready for the consequences of this change? Are we prepared to consider the profound social, legal, economic, and political effects of technology around the world?"[24]

Currently, the answer is "no." The structure for communication policymaking at all governmental levels is fragmented and ill-suited to deal with the existing problems, to say nothing of those many more that must be anticipated.[25] Policies are improvised when pressures become strong, yielding in a crazy quilt pattern to various industry concerns, to public interest groups, to domestic or foreign policy considerations, to the pleas of engineers and lawyers, and to the suggestions of political scientists and economists. Narrow issues are addressed, but the full scope of the situation is ignored.[26] Neither Congress nor the executive branch is willing to enter this thicket of controversy at a time when so many other battles must be fought. It is not likely that policy leadership will emerge. "Muddling through" was the watchword for the 1970s and muddling through is likely to be the watchword for the 1980s as well.

SUMMARY

In this chapter we have examined the dissatisfactions that many people feel about the performance of the mass media, especially television. We described the various channels through which such discontents may be aired and noted the limited effects that criticism has generally had in changing media content. We also surveyed briefly the many alternative media created to fill in the gaps left by mass media. Such media serve a vast variety of special purposes that cannot and need not be served by the more general mass media.

Among alternative media, the underground press is particularly interesting. It demonstrated that government will tolerate a journalism that attacks major public domestic and foreign policies, even in war-time. The tolerance of the general public for published radical dissent is much less, though, making it difficult to keep such publications financially afloat over long periods of time. The mushrooming of underground print and broadcast media during the Vietnam War era also demonstrates that, in a business dominated by giants, it is still possible for small enterprises to operate successfully on a variety of shoestrings.

The second major aspect of our inquiry in this chapter involves the consequences of mass media changes brought about by new technologies. We briefly described some of the new electronic tools and sketched their capabilities in bringing about the age of broadcast plenty and the age of two-way mass communication. Their impact on life and politics in the United States could be enormous, but is impossible to predict at this early stage of development.

We also examined various aspects of regulatory policy that will be called upon to integrate the new media into the existing mass media regulatory structure. Most importantly, we pointed to major political changes that could arrive, almost unannounced, if the political impact of the new technologies is not considered and guided carefully enough. The forces pushing in the direction of direct, rather than representative, democracy are strong, and so are the forces for greater government control of media content. Whichever way the die is cast, deliberate choice, rather than drift, should be the basis for the decisions.

NOTES

1. *Julius Caesar,* act 4, sc. 3, line 218.
2. *Chicago Tribune,* August 24, 1979.
3. Joseph R. Dominick and Millard C. Pearce, "Trends in Network Prime-Time Programming, 1953-74," *Journal of Communication* 26 (Winter 1976): 70-80; Eric Barnouw, *The Sponsor: Notes on a Modern Potentate* (New York: Oxford University Press, 1978); Bernard Rubin, *Media, Politics, and Democracy* (New York: Oxford University Press, 1977). Edward Jay Epstein, *Between Fact and Fiction: The Problem of Journalism* (New York: Vintage, 1975).
4. John Hohenberg, *A Crisis for the American Press* (New York: Columbia University Press, 1978); Lee B. Becker, Robin E. Cobbey, and Idowu A. Sobowale, "Public Support for the Press," *Journalism Quarterly* 55 (Autumn 1978): 421-430.
5. David Altheide, *Creating Reality: How TV News Distorts Events* (Beverly Hills, Calif.: Sage, 1976); Hohenberg, *A Crisis for the American Press;* Edwin Diamond, *The Tin Kazoo: Television, Politics, and the News* (Boston: MIT Press, 1975); Herbert Schiller, *Mass Communication and American Empire* (New York: Augustus M. Kelley, 1969).
6. "The A. J. Liebling Counter-Convention," *Chicago Journalism Review* (May 1972): 16-24.
7. *Chicago Journalism Review* (April 1973): 20.
8. John E. Polich, "Newspaper Support of Press Councils," *Journalism Quarterly* 51 (Summer 1974): 199-206.

9. W. Phillips Davison, "Functions of Mass Communication for the Collectivity," in W. Phillips Davison and Frederick T. C. Yu, *Mass Communication Research: Major Issues and Future Directions* (New York: Praeger, 1974), pp. 66-82.
10. Roland E. Worseley, *The Black Press, U.S.A.* (Ames, Iowa: Iowa State University Press, 1971); Henry La Brie III, ed., *Perspectives of the Black Press: 1974* (Kennebunkport, Maine: Mercer House Press, 1974).
11. Morris Janowitz, *The Community Press in an Urban Setting: The Social Elements of Urbanism,* 2nd ed. (Chicago: University of Chicago Press, 1967).
12. They are described more fully in John W. Johnstone, Edward J. Slawski and William W. Bowman, *The Newspeople* (Urbana, Ill.: University of Illinois Press, 1976), pp. 157-181; Laurence Leamer, *The Paper Revolutionaries: The Rise of the Underground Press* (New York: Simon and Schuster, 1972); Jack A. Nelson, "The Underground Press," in Michael C. Emery and Ted Curtis Smythe, *Readings in Mass Communication* (Dubuque, Iowa; W. C. Brown Co., 1972), pp. 212-226.
13. *New York Times Magazine,* February 15, 1976, "Up From the Underground."
14. Johnstone, et. al., *The Newspeople,* pp. 157-179.
15. Heather E. Hudson, "Implications for Development Communications," *Journal of Communication* 29 (Winter 1979): 179-186.
16. CATV stands for "Community Antenna Television."
17. WTG in Atlanta, WGN-TV in Chicago, and KTVU in San Francisco.
18. Benno C. Schmidt Jr., "Pluralistic Programming and Regulation of Mass Communication Media," in Glen O. Robinson, ed., *Communication for Tomorrow: Policy Perspectives for the 1980s* (New York: Praeger, 1978), p. 214.
19. No. 77-1575.
20. George A. Donohue, Phillip J. Tichenor, and Clarice N. Olien, "Mass Media and the Knowledge Gap: A Hypothesis Reconsidered," *Communication Research* 2 (1975): 3-23.
21. First Inaugural Address.
22. William A. Lucas, "Telecommunications Technologies and Services," in Robinson, *Communication for Tomorrow,* p. 248.
23. Red Burns and Lynne Elton, "Reading Pa.: Programming for the Future"; Eileen Connell, "Reading, Pa.: Training Local People"; Mitchell L. Moss, "Reading Pa.: "Research on Community Uses," all in *Journal of Communication* 28 (Spring 1978): 148-167.
24. John M. Eger, "A Time of Decision," *Journal of Communication* 29 (Winter 1979): 204-207.
25. Lucas, "Telecommunications Technologies and Services," p. 248.
26. Ithiel de Sola Pool, "The Problems of WARC," *Journal of Communication* 29 (Winter 1979): 187-196.

READINGS

Diamond, Edwin. *The Tin Kazoo: Television, Politics, and the News.* Boston: MIT Press, 1975.

Epstein, Edward Jay. *Between Fact and Fiction: The Problem of Journalism.* New York: Vintage, 1975.

Hohenberg, John. *A Crisis for the American Press.* New York: Columbia University Press, 1978.

Leamer, Laurence. *The Paper Revolutionaries: The Rise of the Underground Press.* New York: Simon and Schuster, 1972.

Robinson, Glen O., ed. *Communication for Tomorrow: Policy Perspectives for the 1980s.* New York: Praeger, 1978.

Worseley, Roland E. *The Black Press, U.S.A.* Ames, Iowa: Iowa State University Press, 1971.

Index